second edition

person perception

second edition

person perception

DAVID J. SCHNEIDER
University of Texas at San Antonio

ALBERT H. HASTORF
Stanford University

PHOEBE C. ELLSWORTH
Yale University

ADDISON-WESLEY PUBLISHING COMPANY

Reading, Massachusetts
Menlo Park, California
London • Amsterdam • Don Mills, Ontario • Sydney

TOPICS IN SOCIAL PSYCHOLOGY

Charles A. Kiesler
Series Editor

ACKNOWLEDGMENTS

The author wishes to thank the copyright holders for permission to reprint in this text the following figures and tables:

Fig. 4.1. From E. E. Jones, S. Worchel, G. R. Goethals, and J. F. Grumet, Prior expectancy and behavioral extremity as determinants of attitude attribution, *Journal of Experimental Social Psychology* 7 (1971): 70.

Table 4.1. Data from E. E. Jones and V. A. Harris, The attribution of attitudes, *Journal of Experimental Social Psychology* 3 (1967): 6.

(*continued on page vi*)

```
    Library of Congress Cataloging in Publication Data

    Schneider, David J      1940-
       Person perception.

       (Topics in social psychology)
       First ed. by A. H. Hastorf, D. J. Schneider, and
    J. Polefka.
       Bibliography:  p.
       Includes index.
       1.  Social perception.  I.  Hastorf, Albert H.,
    1920-     joint author. II.  Ellsworth, Phoebe, joint
    author.  III.  Title.
    HM132.H35  1979        301.1        78-67455
    ISBN 0-201-06768-4
```

ISBN 0-201-06768-4
DEFGHIJKL-AL-898765432

For Doris, Barbara, and Roger

ACKNOWLEDGMENTS (*continued*)

Table 4.2. Data from L. Ross, G. Bierbrauer, and S. Polly, Attribution of educational outcomes by professional and nonprofessional instructors, *Journal of Personality and Social Psychology* 29 (1974): 615. Copyright 1974 by the American Psychological Association. Reprinted by permission.

Table 5.1. Data from D. Bem, Self-perception: An alternative interpretation of cognitive dissonance phenomena, *Psychological Review* 74 (1967): 189; and from L. Festinger and J. M. Carlsmith, Cognitive consequences of forced compliance, *Journal of Abnormal and Social Psychology* 58 (1959): 207. Copyright 1959 and 1967 by the American Psychological Association. Reprinted by permission.

Table 5.2. Data from S. Schachter and J. E. Singer, Cognitive, social, and physiological determinants of emotional state, *Psychological Review* 69 (1962): 390, 392. Copyright 1962 by the American Psychological Association. Reprinted by permission.

Table 5.3. Data from R. E. Nisbett and S. Schachter, Cognitive manipulation of pain, *Journal of Experimental Social Psychology* 2 (1966): 235.

Table 5.4. Data from R. E. Kraut, Effects of social labeling on giving charity, *Journal of Experimental Social Psychology* 9 (1973): 556.

Table 5.5. Adapted from M. D. Storms, Videotape and the attribution process: Reversing actors' and observers' points of view, *Journal of Personality and Social Psychology* 27 (1973): 169. Copyright 1973 by the American Psychological Association. Reprinted by permission.

Fig. 7.1. From S. Rosenberg, C. Nelson, and B. S. Vivekananthan, A multidimensional approach to the structure of personality impressions, *Journal of Personality and Social Psychology* 9 (1968): 290. Copyright 1968 by the American Psychological Association. Reprinted by permission.

Fig. 7.2. Data from N. H. Anderson, Averaging versus adding as a stimulus-combination rule in impression formation, *Journal of Experimental Psychology* 70 (1965): 396. Copyright 1965 by the American Psychological Association. Reprinted by permission.

Fig. 10.1. R. E. Nisbett and N. Bellows, Verbal reports about causal influences on social judgments: Private access versus public theories, *Journal of Personality and Social Psychology* 35 (1977): 619. Copyright 1977 by the American Psychological Association. Reprinted by permission.

foreword

This series *Topics in Social Psychology* is directed toward the student with no prior background in social psychology. Taken as a whole, the series covers the ever-expanding field of social psychology reasonably well, but a major advantage of the series is that each individual book was written by well-known scholars in the area. The instructor can select a subset of the books to make up the course in social psychology, the particular subset depending on the instructor's own definition of our field. The original purpose of this series was to provide such freedom for the instructor while maintaining a thoughtful and expert treatment of each topic. In addition, the first editions of the series have been widely used in a variety of other ways: such as supplementary reading in nonpsychology courses; to introduce more advanced courses in psychology, or for the sheer fun of peeking at recent developments in social psychology.

We have developed second editions that serve much the same purpose. Each book is somewhat longer and more open in design, uses updated materials, and in general takes advantage of constructive feedback from colleagues and students across the country. So many people found the first editions of the individual books useful that we have tried to make the second editions even more thorough and complete, and therefore more easily separated from the rest of the series.

This volume tackles the problems of social perception—the factors affecting the way we see others. It includes discussion of age old concerns, such as when we like others and when we don't. It also presents and critically discusses recent evidence on such questions about the attribution of motivational states to others as: do the others *intend* to cause harm to a third person? Undergraduates have always found the topic of social perception interesting, and I think this volume is the best writing I have seen at this level.

Charles A. Kiesler

We began talking about a revision of the earlier edition **preface**
of this book four years ago. The first edition appeared
at a time when person perception as an area of research
had reached a stage of adolescence; the appearance of the adult form was
already apparent but the rapidly increasing enthusiasm for the area was
matched neither by theoretical sophistication nor by a strong basis in empirical
data. What we could only dimly see then, namely that person perception
would become a mature focus of research concern for social psychology, has
come to pass.

In the past decade the attribution literature has grown by leaps and has
divided itself into questions about perception of self and perception of others.
Research on information processing approaches to person perception has
become much more salient, and research areas such as nonverbal and expressive
behavior have increasingly been seen as relevant to person perception processes.

Although when we began the revision in 1976 it was already clear that the
relevant research literature had grown enormously, we initially thought in
terms of a general updating with some increase in length to take account of
some new areas that we wanted to introduce. Schneider and Hastorf agreed
that the former should take the major responsibility for the revision. Polefka
was committed to other things and withdrew, so Ellsworth was invited to help
out in general and to provide expertise in the nonverbal and expressive areas.
Naturally enough these things never work out quite the way they are planned.
What we hoped would be a summer's hard work turned out to be two years of
concentrated activity as we exchanged drafts of chapters, argued with one
another about the interpretations of this or that new material, and tried to
bring all the old and new material into a focus and a mutually supportive
relationship. Our file of correspondence is larger than many book manuscripts,
and we have met for week-long periods several times. We have enjoyed the
collaboration and have all benefited from our intense and invigorating
discussions.

This edition is much longer than the first. This reflects not only the
updating of the traditional attribution and impression formation areas, but the
addition of much new material. In the first edition we stayed with what might

be called the fashionable, mainstream areas of research. In this edition we have included material from areas that are not so familiar to traditional person perception researchers, and it is our hope that such researchers will come to see that the field has been occupied with a relatively small set of the interesting questions that might be asked.

This then is a major revision. Although we began by changing the earlier edition, through successive revisions we dropped more and more of the old in favor of the new. The reader who is familiar with the first edition will recognize some sections and sentences, but we estimate that less than 10 percent of the present edition comes from the first. We probably would have finished sooner if we had ignored the earlier edition, but that is another story.

A number of people have helped in numerous ways. Families and friends have been patient. Mark Snyder and Chuck Kiesler read the entire manuscript and helped with suggestions for trimming it and focusing it on the most relevant issues. One or more chapters have been read by Norman Anderson, Nancy Cantor, Reid Hastie, Nancy Hirschberg, Sam Kingsley, Robert Kleck, Leslie McArthur, Tom Ostrom, and Roger Tourangeau. The authors especially want to express their thanks to Joyce Sanders, Hazel Saldana, Sharon McMillan, and Linda Delgado for typing, editorial help, and forbearance. Either the National Science Foundation or the National Institutes of Health have provided research support to all of us at various times. A portion of that research is reported herein. The Boys Town Center for the Study of Youth Development at Stanford University provided support for Hastorf. It also provided a locus for meetings.

San Antonio   D. J. S.
April 1979   A. H. H.
                                                                               P. C. E.

contents

attribution research 64

self-attribution 86

*person perception and
nonverbal cues:* snap
judgments and reactive
attributions   *117*

*impression
formation* 151

Some Issues in Perception   **introduction**

PERCEPTION OF PEOPLE AND OBJECTS

There is nothing more important to us, with the exception of ourselves, than the world of other people. Other people are easily able to influence our joys and satisfactions and can cause us sadness and pain. Consequently, we are all interested in learning about other people, and we all have very strong convictions about how we come to know and to understand other people. When you get to know another person you are engaged in a process of perceiving that person. You not only see the other person as a physical stimulus, but you observe behavior; furthermore, you draw conclusions about what you have seen.

Imagine, for example, that you have just entered the classroom for your first meeting of a social psychology course. Your attention is naturally drawn toward the professor; not only is she standing in a rather dominant position in the room, but you are particularly interested in her. She is new to the faculty this year, and you have not been able to find out whether she is hard or easy, stimulating or dull, nice or arrogant, helpful or aloof. You observe her physical appearance: the color of her hair, the color and style of her clothing, her shape and height. You notice how she walks and her mannerisms; perhaps you pay attention to the way she talks. Of course, you will be especially concerned with the content of her comments. From all this you will draw conclusions. You will decide that her hair is brown, her suit is light green, she has a nice figure, and she appears to be about 5'6" tall. She paces and makes frequent gestures with her hands; she has trouble looking away from her notes and her voice is hesitant. You may even draw further conclusions that she is nervous and that she seems likely to make you work hard in the course. You may go further still and decide that she is insecure because she is new, but that she seems to be a basically nice, helpful, and intelligent person.

You do all this and more. You perceive your professor, and obviously this perception involves several complex processes that operate at different levels. But how you perceive people is from a psychological perspective one aspect of general perception and cognitive processes. You perceive both objects and people. The process by which we gain knowledge of others is clearly a complex one, and people are much more complicated than are most other stimuli. It is not surprising, therefore, that psychologists have concentrated their efforts on exploring less complex phenomena, such as the perception of size, shape, and distance. Social psychologists have begun to explore how we know others, however, and our goal in this book is to define some current ways of thinking about person perception, to describe some of the research, and to point to some problems that demand exploration.

Both philosophers and psychologists have long been intrigued with the nature of the human perceptual process. One explanation for their interest is that people are naturally curious about their contact with the outside world and wonder how their experiences are caused and to what degree they reflect the world accurately. Beyond general curiosity, the reason for the interest stems from an apparent paradox, the basis of which lies in the difference between the nature of our experiences and our knowledge of how those experiences are caused.

Anyone who takes the trouble to think about and to describe his own experiences usually finds himself overwhelmed with both their immediacy and their structure. One's experience of the world is dominated by objects that stand out in space and that have such attributes as shape, color, and size. The immediacy of such experiences becomes obvious if you close your eyes, turn your head in a new direction, and then open your eyes again. A structured world of objects is immediately present in awareness, without delay and without any consciousness of interpretative or inferential activity. The world appears to be given to us in experience. Yet a causal analysis of these events indicates a very different state of affairs.

You have opened your eyes and you experience a blue vase about six inches high situated on a table. The vase appears to be at a certain distance, and its shape and color are equally clear. Let us now remind ourselves of the causal events that are involved. Light waves of a certain wavelength are reflected off the vase. Some of them impinge on the retina of your eye, and if enough retinal cells are irritated, some visual nerves will fire and a series of electrical impulses will be carried through the sensory apparatus, including the subcortical centers, and will finally arrive at the cortex. This description paints a picture of a very indirect contact with the world: light waves to retinal events to sensory nerve events to subcortical events and, finally, to cortical events, from which visual experiences result. What is especially important is that this causal description reveals a very different picture than does our naive description of experience. (This causal description led a famous German physiologist to remark that "we are aware of our nerves, not of objects.") Thus, we have a conflict between our everyday-life experiences of objects and an analysis of how these experiences come to exist. How *does* the human being create a coherent perceptual world out of a maze of physical impingements?

THE ACCOMPLISHMENTS OF PERCEPTUAL ACTIVITY

Our world of experience has structure   Let us begin with this fact of experience and explore how the structure may be achieved. First of all, we know that our experiences are ultimately dependent on our sensory apparatus, which for visual experiences would include both the retina of the eye and the sensory neurons connecting the retina to the visual areas of the cortex. This apparatus plays, in a manner of speaking, the role of translator. Light waves impinge on the eyes and we experience color. Sound waves impinge on the ear, and we experience pitch. Without the sensory apparatus we would have no contact with the external world. There remains, however, the question of the nature of this translation.

A number of philosophers and psychologists have conceived of the translation process as an essentially passive one, completely determined by the physical properties of the stimulus and by the structure of the receptors and sensory nervous system. They conceive of our sensory apparatus as working somewhat like a high-speed translation device. Physical impingements are looked up in an impingement-experience dictionary, and the proper experience is created in the perceiver.

This conception has led to arguments as to how much of this dictionary is present at birth and how much is the product of our learning history. One reason for the popularity of the passive recording view of perception is the immediacy and "givenness" of our experience. Our experiences are immediate and they feel direct. These feelings led to the belief that the translation process must be automatic and built in.

One argument against that position stems from the fact that our experience of the world is highly selective. If we passively translated and recorded all stimuli, our world would be a jumble of experiences; while you were reading a book, you would also be aware of the pressure of your clothes on your body and of all the sounds around you. But from a myriad of impinging stimuli, we are actually aware of only certain objects and certain attributes of those objects. Anyone who has asked two different persons to describe the same scene has been struck by the fact that they often describe it very differently: each selects different events and different attributes of the events. Given this phenomenon, we must be more than passive translators. In fact, we must be active processors of information. The world is not merely revealed to us; rather, we play an active role in the creation of our experiences.

In one demonstration Leeper (1935) used an ambiguous picture that can be seen as either an old hag or as an attractive young woman (Fig. 1.1). Most who inspect the picture closely and continuously for a time see first one and then the other. Leeper had the original picture redrawn so that one version emphasized the young woman (Fig. 1.1b) and another emphasized the old hag (Fig. 1.1c). Subjects who were initially shown one of these redrawings found themselves "locked in" on that view later on when the original ambiguous picture was presented. One hundred percent of the subjects who had had prior experience with the version emphasizing the hag saw only the hag in their first look at the ambiguous picture; 95 percent of the subjects who had had prior experience with the version emphasizing the young woman saw only the young woman when first looking at the same ambiguous picture. The subjects had been given a set to process the input stimuli in a certain way, and they

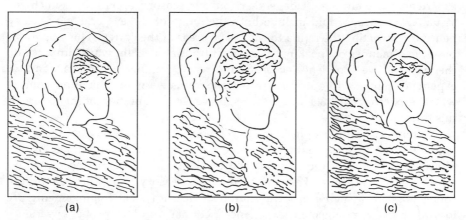

(a)   (b)   (c)

Fig. 1.1 The young woman and the old hag. (From Leeper 1935.)

created a structure consistent with that set. Although our experiences are both immediate and structured, extremely complex participation by the organism, including the active selection and processing of stimulus impingements, is involved in their creation.

This active role played by the perceiver has been described in terms of the influence of set or expectation in the achievement of structure. The Leeper research demonstrates that our perception of an ambiguous figure can be strongly influenced by an expectation created by our first viewing of an apparently similar picture. Anyone who has observed the spectators at athletic events can't help noticing that two apparently reasonable people can experience a play in football or basketball in very different ways as a function of having been "tuned" by different expectations and purposes. This fact of experience was illustrated by a case study of a football game (Hastorf and Cantril 1954). It so happened that Dartmouth and Princeton played each other in football one November afternoon. The game turned out to be very rough, and tempers flared both during and after the game. Immediately following the game, partisans for both schools made accusations that the other school had played rough and dirty football. The school papers, the school alumni magazines, and a number of the metropolitan newspapers highly publicized the whole affair. There was clearly a very real disagreement as to what had actually happened during the game. What is of special interest to us in our attempt to understand the achievement of structured experiences were the results of showing a movie of the game to a group of Dartmouth students and a group of Princeton students. Keeping in mind that an identical movie was shown to both groups of students, it is interesting to refer to the number of infractions perceived in the same film by two groups of people with different loyalties and different expectations (see Table 1.1). Students (particularly those from Princeton) tended to see the team from the other university as having committed the most infractions.

TABLE 1.1
Data from Questionnaire Checked While Seeing Film
(From Hastorf and Cantril 1954.)

	Mean number of infractions checked against	
	Dartmouth team	Princeton team
By Dartmouth students	4.3	4.4
By Princeton students	9.8	4.2

Not only do people pay attention to different things, but they differ in how they categorize events. It is very difficult to stay at the level of raw experience in the perceptual process, although historically a number of psychologists have felt that with proper training people could see events and objects without categorizing them. However, most of us give verbal labels to what we see, and this helps to structure our world. For example, the subjects in Leeper's experiment did not see a complex pattern of light and dark nor even "a person" (a possible category); they saw an old hag or a young woman. The categories we use are derived from our past history and are largely dependent on our language and our cultural background. Some of these categories are apparently ubiquitous and well-agreed on by perceivers. Classification of objects according to the attributes of size and shape seems obvious, but we can also perceive in terms of color and texture. We may even see things in terms of functions instead of size, color, or shape: the large blue pen and the small red pencil are suddenly similar when we want to jot down a telephone number. Moreover, people differ in their use of categories as a function of their experiences or purposes. For example, Dittman, Parloff, and Boomer (1965) have nicely demonstrated that dancers, unlike most people, are more responsive to bodily cues than to facial cues. Whatever the nature of the categories we use, they play a crucial role in our processing of information.

Our world of experience has stability   When we open our eyes and look at a scene, we are not overwhelmed with constant shifts in the picture as our eyes and our attention wander. There is a certain enduring aspect to our experience. We select certain facets of the situation and stick with them. Check this statement against your own experience with the ambiguous picture in Fig. 1.1. If it was like the experience of most people, your first interpretation (or perceptual organization) of the picture, whether it was the old hag or the young woman, continued to demand your attention. It was hard to "find" the other one. You may make various attempts to shift the focus of attention by blinking your eyes or by concentrating on a certain part of the picture, but those stratagems do not always work.

The most obvious example of stability in our experience is *the constancies* in perception. Constancy phenomena have been most carefully described in regard to the perception of size, color, shape, and brightness. Let us consider size constancy as an example. You are sitting in a chair in your living room. Another person walks into the room, moves over to a table by the window, picks up a magazine, and then goes across the room to sit down and read it. What are the successive visual-stimulus events impinging on your retina and your successive experiences? Every time the person moves closer to you, the image on your retina, or *proximal stimulus*, gets larger; in fact, if she moves from 20 feet away to 10 feet away, the height of the image on your eye doubles in size. The opposite occurs as she moves away from you, because the size of the retinal image is inversely proportional to the distance of the object from you. Furthermore, when the person moves near the window, more light is available and more light is reflected to the retina. Yet your experience does not fit this description of the stimulus events. While the person is moving about the room, you experience her as staying the same size and the same color. In spite of dramatic alterations in the proximal stimulus (that is, the image on the retina), you experience a stable world. Given this discrepancy between proximal-stimulus events and experience, the person must actively process information to produce stability of experience.

Let us think of the perceptual act as a complex form of problem-solving, the goal of which is to create a stability in which our perceptions bear some relationship to external events. We can then draw an analogy between perceptual problem-solving and scientific problem-solving. Just as the scientist attempts to reduce a complex jumble of events to a small set of variables that serves as a set of determining conditions for a particular phenomenon, so we search out the invariant aspects of a situation to produce stable perceptions. The scientist searches for invariance in order to understand and to predict the world; we as perceivers also seek to understand and to predict our immediate world so that we may behave in that world to our advantage. In other words, the perceptual act can be said to generate understanding that we can use as a basis for action.

Our world of experience is meaningful   The connotation of *meaningful* here is that structured and stable events are not isolated from one another but appear to be related in some orderly fashion over time. Both structure and stability are probably necessary for meaning to exist. Because it is so common for the world of experience to make sense to us, the most powerful way to point out the importance of the phenomenon is to try to conceive of a world that does not make sense. Events would follow each other with no apparent causal relationships. Almost every event would entail surprise. Nothing would seem familiar. The general experience would be one of chaos. Such a state of affairs is so alien to our everyday-life experience that it is extremely difficult to imagine. Our experiences usually *are* meaningful because they are structured and they are stable; they are related because they seem familiar, but particularly because the events have implications for one another.

The person actively processes stimuli, categorizes stimulus events, and relates those stimulus events to both past and present events. Each of us has a linguistic coding system that involves a set of implicative relationships. The impinging stimuli provide the raw material; the person, with the aid of language, produces the meaning.

Past experience, language, present motivational state, and goals for the future influence our perceptions of the present. Our past learning has a significant influence on perception, but it always operates within a framework of purposive activity. We have all learned many rules, and the ones we apply are selected to achieve particular purposes. The perceptual process is an achievement by the person, and perception would not exist without active problem-solving. Our perceptions do have meaning, they do make sense; and meaning and sense derive from both our own past experiences and our present purposes. Without the presence of meaning and sense as active, organizing agents, perception as we know it would not exist.

All behavior and all perception include the influences of both our past experiences and purposes. Unfortunately these two powerful determinants of our perceptions have often been termed *distorting influences*. Perception was thought to be stimulus-determined unless past experience or motivational state entered the picture and caused us to deviate from "what we ought to see." The notion of the existence of an "objective observer" who sees the world accurately because he has had no past experience or because he is disinterested is patently false. If such a person did exist, we would have to predict that he would not see a structured, stable, and meaningful world.

In summary, our past experiences and purposes play an absolutely necessary role in providing us with knowledge of the world that has structure, stability, and meaning. Without them, events would not make sense; with them, our perceptions define a predictable world, an orderly stage for us to act on.

The Perception of People

Let us now turn our attention more explicitly to the perception of other people. The characteristics of the world of experience in general should be the same for our experiences of people, but are there special facets to our experience when we perceive other human beings? Is there not more to our experience of other people than their size, color, and shape? The answer is certainly yes.

As an aid in our discussion of person perception, consider an example of one person describing another. In *Eminent Victorians*, Lytton Strachey describes Dr. Thomas Arnold, headmaster of Rugby School:

> Such was the man who, at the age of thirty-three, became headmaster of Rugby. His outward appearance was the index of his inward character: everything about him denoted energy, earnestness, and the best intentions. His legs, perhaps, were shorter than they should have been; but the sturdy athletic frame, especially when it was swathed (as it usually was) in the flowing robes of a Doctor of Divinity, was full of an imposing vigour;

and his head, set decisively upon the collar, stock, and bands of ecclesiastical tradition, clearly belonged to a person of eminence. The thick, dark clusters of his hair, his bushy eyebrows and curling whiskers, his straight nose and bulky chin, his firm and upward-curving lower lip—all these revealed a temperament of ardour and determination. His eyes were bright and large; they were also obviously honest. And yet—why was it?—Was it in the lines of the mouth or the frown on the forehead?—It was hard to say, but it was unmistakable—there was a slightly puzzled look upon the face of Dr. Arnold (Strachey 1933, pp. 193-94).

First of all, this description is a special example of person perception because it is more organized than many of our experiences in everyday life—partly, no doubt, because the author is attempting to communicate his perceptions to others. The author also goes well beyond just providing us with a description of Doctor Arnold's physical characteristics and behavior. Many of the characteristics listed are the result of inferences by the author, and yet they are cast as if they were just as clear and as given in experience as is Doctor Arnold's physical height. The leap from describing such characteristics as hair color and eyebrows to inferences about "energy" and "ardour and determination" is made with considerable agility. The author also includes statements about Doctor Arnold's intentions; he appeared, at least to Strachey, as having "the best intentions." This tendency, not only to perceive others as having intentions but also to make a value judgment, is, as we shall see, often apparent in our perception of others. The description also includes inferences (stated as perceptual facts) about enduring personality characteristics, such as "honesty" and "earnestness." Finally, although the author cannot specify the cues, he infers that Doctor Arnold felt puzzled; he perceives the other's feelings.

SPECIAL FEATURES OF PERSON PERCEPTION

As this example indicates, there are special features of our perception of other people and important ways in which the perception of people differs from the perception of objects. In many ways object and person perception are similar, but they also differ in several crucial ways.

People are causal agents   While both people and objects move, normally we think of the "behavior" of objects as caused by some external force, while we think of the behavior of people as caused by the actor. We often perceive people as causal agents. People may intend to do certain things, such as cause certain effects; and because we see people as one source of their actions, we consider them capable of varying their behavior to achieve their intended effects. Our perception of others' intentionality often leads us to organize the behavior of other people into intent-act-effect segments that form perceptual units. We infer the intentions of another, but we go further. If we perceive a particular intent on several occasions, we are prone to perceive the other as having an enduring personality characteristic. For example, a person who seems to intend to hurt others much of the time will be quickly labeled as hostile. As we will see when we get to the chapters on attribution theory, intention plays a major role in the perception of people and their behavior. A number of contemporary philosophers have concerned themselves with the distinction between intentional or purposive behavior and behavior not guided by intention. Purposive behavior must be explained with regard to some intention or other mental reason, while nonpurposive behavior requires a different sort of explanation. For example, it makes sense to ask why a person pushes you deliberately in a movie line (was he trying to get ahead of you, show his displeasure at your conversation, act nasty?), but it makes little sense to ask why a person who has tripped and is falling down pushes you. In the former case, the person does something; in the latter case, something (say, an icy spot on the sidewalk) does something to him. Note that our evaluations of other people depend heavily on our perception of their intentionality—did they mean to do it?

Our perception of nonpurposive behavior is often much like our perception of physical events. The person slipped because of an icy spot, just like the ball went to right field because it was hit in a particular way. The laws of physics work, whether the object is a person or a baseball. However, not all unintentional behavior is neatly summarized by physical principles. For example, suppose your social psychology professor frowns when a student asks how many exams there will be in the course; although you will probably not feel that the professor intended to frown, it would not occur to you that the response is due to the professor's state as a physical object. You will see the frown as having been caused by the professor's personal qualities as well as the question. The professor seems peeved or hostile.

Expressive, affective, and emotional behaviors are generally not intended, but are seen as reactions to stimuli. Because these reactive behaviors are seen as involving psychological characteristics in addition to causal stimuli, they are of considerable interest to the student of person perception.

Other people are similar to us Because we assume others are like us in important ways, we infer that they possess attributes which, unlike size and behavior, we cannot observe directly but which we are aware of in ourselves. In particular, we perceive others to possess emotional states; we see them as feeling angry, happy, or sad. Except in unusual circumstances, we are not inclined to see physical objects as possessing the psychological characteristics we feel we possess.

Not only do we use knowledge about how our own goals and intentions produce behavior to infer something about the inner workings of other people, but we may even project our characteristics onto others (see Chapter 10). Moreover, as we will see in Chapter 5, we may use knowledge and rules for understanding the behavior of others to understand ourselves. The basic point is that insights about self and about others mutually reinforce one another, and we do have some "natural" insights about why people do what they do.

Social interactions are dynamic We may cause an object to move, but most of us do not see the object as having special reasons for moving. It just moves. However, when we interact with people, we may be aware that they are adjusting their behavior in response to ours. We may be trying to change the behavior of the other person, but the other person may have purposes and goals also. Thus, in trying to understand the behavior of the other person we must determine how that other person understands our own behavior. In an interaction each person must understand not only what the other is doing but also what he or she sees as the relevant stimuli in the environment. Our prototypic social psychology professor may have responded to the student's question about exams by frowning because the professor thought the student was being hostile or was not seriously interested in the course material. As a perceiver you must understand that the other person is also a perceiver.

SIMILARITIES BETWEEN OBJECT AND PERSON PERCEPTION

We have been emphasizing differences between the perception of people and objects. However, there are certain similarities, particularly at the most general level. Perceptions of people and their behavior are also structured, stable, and meaningful.

Our experiences of other people are structured   Just as we create structure in the inanimate world by categorizing stimuli into objects and their attributes, so we create order in the world of people by categorizing them and their behavior. The number of ways that we can categorize people is overwhelmingly large; we can go well beyond any of the possible schemata for inanimate objects. The dictionary, for example, contains thousands of trait names describing ways in which we can perceive people as different. Often we use categories that have been functional in the past. The football coach will employ very different categories for perceiving members of the freshman class than will the Dean of Students or a professor of physics. You may remember that the description of Doctor Arnold by Strachey was heavily couched in "good Victorian" words like "vigour," "eminence," and "determination," rather than those we might be more likely to use today, such as "warm," "happy," or even (given Doctor Arnold's position) "intellectual."

It is worth emphasizing that when we describe, and probably when we think about, the behavior or characteristics of a person we use words representing fairly abstract qualities to do so. We give structure to our perceptions of others by placing separate instances of their behavior in common categories. So, for example, hitting someone, yelling at a friend, and gossiping about an enemy might all be classified as instances of hostility or aggressiveness. It is of some interest to know what kinds of categories people use, because the researchers assume that how perceivers categorize behavior or people influences how they interpret the behavior of others and, consequently, how they react to the other. As we will argue in the next chapter, the same behavior can be labeled differently: aggressive, irresponsible, or exuberant. Presumably, the category chosen will affect the perceiver's reactions to the behavior. I am scared of aggressive behavior, irritated by irresponsible behavior, and amused by exuberant behavior. Presumably, people differ in the categories they employ. We are all familiar with the aggressive, "bratty" kid whose mother sees him as simply "too full of energy." The hospital patient may be "poor Harry" to his wife but "the broken leg in Room 103A" to the hospital staff.

Several researchers have argued that the categories people use show developmental trends. Peevers and Secord (1973) have shown that whereas younger children rely on appearance, roles ("He's a daddy"), and generalized evaluations ("He's nice")—in short, on relatively external and nonpsychological features of others—older children and adults rely more on abstract, internal, motivational, trait-like categories. Livesley and Bromley (1973) have also shown major developmental trends towards the use of more psychological constructs with increasing age. This suggests that whereas small children have rather primitive ways of structuring their perceptions of people, adults are able to organize their perceptions around categories that involve assumptions about how people cause their behavior. However, even among people at a similar developmental level, different perceivers may use different categories to structure their perceptions (Brown 1976).

Dornbusch *et al.* (1965) demonstrated that our past experiences and our present motives affect the categories we use when they explored the categorizing activities of ten- and eleven-year-old children at a summer camp. Children who had lived together in the same tent for two or three weeks were requested in an interview situation to describe their tent mates. The interviewer carefully avoided stipulating any categories; he asked the children to "tell me about ————." The interviews were then coded in order to classify the categories the children had employed in describing one another. An example of a category is "neatness." A statement was classified in this category if it described the other person as being either neat or sloppy. The authors were primarily interested in

Drawing by C.E.M.; © 1961 The New Yorker Magazine, Inc.

what categories were used, not in where the person was placed within the category.

Especially pertinent to our thesis is a comparison of the categorization employed by a common perceiver of different stimuli with the categorization by two different perceivers of a common-stimulus person. The category overlap was greatest when the same perceiver described two different children (57 percent); the overlap for two different perceivers describing the same stimulus person was smaller (45 percent) and not very different from the overlap obtained when the descriptions of two different perceivers, each describing a different person, were compared (38 percent). The last figure was interpreted as the amount of overlap created by a common culture. These data imply that the perceiver plays a dominant role in selecting which characteristics of other people to observe (and describe). We do not passively record the attributes of the other person, but select and organize perceptions in terms of categories that are particularly useful.

However, we should be very cautious in designating an individual described by two perceivers as "a common-stimulus person." It is highly likely that when one person interacts with different people on different occasions, he or she is really not the same stimulus person. His or her behavior will vary as a function of the situation, which includes the nature of the other participants. This fact is an example of the complexity of both social interaction and person perception. How you categorize and perceive me will influence how you behave toward me; your behavior, in turn, will influence how I behave. Our point, for the moment, is to stress the role the selecting and categorizing activities of the perceiver play in creating his perceptions of the other and in producing structure in his world of other people.

Our experiences of other people have stability The behaviors engaged in by another person vary widely over even brief periods of time; thus, the interpersonal acts of another provide the mind with as continually varying a stimulus as the size of her body provides the retina when she walks across the room. Were we to perceive as discrete all the acts of another person, our experiential world would be as rapidly changing and unstable as our experience of her size if that were dependent merely on the size of the retinal image. The stability in our experience of other people seems to be produced by processes analogous to those involved in the constancies in object perception. We search to perceive the invariant properties of other people as well as the invariant properties of objects.

In perceiving attributes of another person, we focus not on her behavior, which is ever-changing, but on more invariant characteristics such as her intents and purposes. Since these invariant properties cannot be perceived directly, our search for invariance is centered on discovering functional relationships between behavior-effect sequences, which are observable, and intentions, which are not. For example, suppose that another person shoves you in the hall, verbally abuses you in a class, and criticizes your friends in private. The behaviors and the contexts in which they are expressed differ, but the same end is achieved: the other person hurts you. Yet the effect is an invariant function of the behavior and the context, just as proximal size is an invariant function of object size and distance. In the attribution to her of the intent to hurt you, an invariance will have been achieved. Whenever we can assume that the person had the ability to produce the behaviors and hence the effects, when we can assume that she was the cause of what occurred, we tend to attribute to her the intent of producing the effect. This attribution of intent provides us with knowledge that will make our future interactions with the person more predictable.

Should we observe the same person behaving in a similar manner toward others, we go further and attribute to her the dispositional property of desiring to hurt other people; we consider her hostile or aggressive. This attribution of a dispositional property to another results again from the search for invariance. If we can classify a person according to certain traits or concepts, we can increase the predictability of our interpersonal world. An aggressive person will act to hurt not only us but others as well. We can predict her behavior in a wide variety of situations. It is also possible that such inferences about enduring dispositions will lead us into misperception (see Chapter 10).

Our experiences of other people are meaningful We see other people as organized entities, and their action nearly always makes sense. Nonetheless, the behavior of others does confuse and puzzle us on occasion. These may well be the occasions that set off our interpretative machinery, and we become conscious of our hunches about the intent of the other. It is probably a good guess that if a person is consistently puzzling to us, our inability to make sense of him leads us to avoid further interactions with him. No wonder the behavior most of the people we "know" makes sense!

What are the processes by which we develop these organized perceptions of others as meaningful entities?

First, as already pointed out, we often organize their behavior into intent-act-effect units, and that procedure not only enables us to develop some behavioral organization but also permits and even pushes us to develop some hypotheses covering their enduring intents and dispositions or personality traits.

Second, meaning derives from the fact that other people are similar to one another and to us. We all share a certain number of important characteristics: we all behave, think, and feel, and some of the structured meanings we experience derive from the assumption that other people are like us. The assumption of similarity—"That's the way I would feel"—can lead to assumed relationships between both behaviors and intents, and also leads to some errors (see Chapter 10). Even though the process may not be conscious, we often operate as follows: "I engage in behavior *A* and also in behavior *B*," therefore, "If he engages in behavior *A*, then he must also engage in behavior *B*." The same operation would apply to intents and feelings.

Third, the similarity assumption, our past experiences, and cultural-linguistic factors give rise to theories of personality. As George Kelly (1955) has emphasized, scientists are not the only people who build theories about how and why people behave. Perceivers also develop theories about "what makes people tick." These theories have been called *implicit personality theories*. Such theories allow perceivers to go beyond behavioral and trait information to infer that the stimulus person is more or less likely to have other qualities that have not been manifested. Thus, most of us would be likely to assume that a person who behaves in a warm manner would also be likely to behave in a kind manner, even though we had never seen that person behave in a kind manner.

Finally, meaning derives from familiarity. When we have coded a person's behavior in a similar way a number of times and have made the same inferences about the causes of the behavior, then meaning and the feeling of understanding may result. This is especially true when we perceive that certain traits are correlated. A behavior is familiar not only because we have seen it before but also because it implies other behaviors. Implicit personality theories, the assumed correlations between traits that we carry around in our heads, are generalizations from behavior we may have observed in ourselves and one or two other persons. Once we have acquired these theories, we can then apply them as a general rule. The process is identical to the one that produces a phenomenon usually called *group stereotypes*.

One way in which we simplify the complex world of other people is to organize them into groups. We talk of Germans, Jews, and Italians; of college students, policemen; even of little old ladies in tennis shoes; and we attribute certain characteristics to all members of each group. On reflection, we are all perfectly willing to grant that college students come in all different shapes and sizes and that they have very different orientations toward the world; yet we still find ourselves classifying people into groups and then imputing certain characteristics to the members of the groups. We neglect both situational pressures and disconfirming evidence in our push to categorize a person according to group membership.

Fink and Cantril (1937), using college students as subjects, demonstrated this tendency in a study that was concerned with analyzing certain stereotypes students have of one another. A group of undergraduates at Harvard, Yale, Princeton, and Dartmouth were presented with a list of 50 adjectives such as athletic, brilliant, conceited, juvenile, sophisticated, and studious. Each student was asked to select the five adjectives that best described a Harvard man, a Yale man, a Princeton man, and a Dartmouth man. The first findings of interest were that students made their selections with very little hesitation and that there seemed to be considerable agreement among them as to the nature of the stereotypes they held concerning students both at other institutions and at their own. For example, when 100 students at Dartmouth were asked to describe a Harvard man, the majority of the 500 selected adjectives came from only 10 to 15 words out of the 50 available. When students described themselves, they chose adjectives that were somewhat more complimentary than those they chose to describe others. For example, in describing themselves, Harvard men were most likely to select the following five adjectives: blase, intellectual, cultured, sophisticated, and broad-minded. Students at Dartmouth, Princeton, and Yale agreed with parts of the Harvard man's self-stereotype: they, too, saw him as blase, sophisticated, and intellectual, but added snobbish and conceited, somewhat less complimentary adjectives, to complete the list. Although the study was conducted some years ago, similar findings would probably be obtained today. (See Friendly and Glucksberg 1970 for a relevent example.) The adjectives included in such a study today would be different, and the specific content of the stereotypes might have changed in the intervening years, but the tendency to classify people into groups and to attribute certain personality traits or dispositions to the members of those groups is still present.

Korten (1974) has recently studied the formation of stereotypes in Ethiopia and the United States. She found that the two cultures differed in what was salient to the stereotypes held by its members. Americans, for example, place much greater emphasis on "abilities and knowledge," while the Ethiopians stress "interpersonal interactions."

Our impressions of another person are also a form of stereotype; we abstract certain aspects of his or her behavior, organize them around certain dispositions, and develop a picture of the person. This process permits the development of meaning in our experience of other persons. It can also restrict our awareness of some of another's behavior. Group and individual stereotypes do create stability and meaning, but they may well do it at the risk of inaccuracy.

Summary and Prospects

We have now set our task. We have identified certain characteristics of our world of experience, which includes the world of other people. It has structure, it has stability, and it has meaning. Furthermore, perception is not the passive translation of physical energies into experience, but is a process demanding active participation by the perceiver, who selects and categorizes, interprets and infers to achieve a meaningful world in which action is possible. We have also described some special features of our perception of other people. Behavior is one of the main sources of stimulation, and it is both complex and ever-changing. One of the ways we make sense out of this complexity is to make inferences that go beyond the behavioral data. We perceive other people as causal agents, we infer intentions, we infer emotional states, and we go further to infer enduring dispositions or personality traits. The social psychologist is interested in this process because it is one of the most salient outcomes of social interaction and, by the same token, one of the major determinants of the nature of interactions. One of the major variables that influences our behavior vis-a-vis another person is the sort of impression we have formed of that person and the dispositions we have attributed to that person.

The rest of this book will be largely concerned with the set of psychological processes that underlie our perceptions of others. We present these

TABLE 1.2
Person Perception Processes

	I	II	III		IV	V	VI
	Attention	*Snap judgment*	*Reactive Attribution*	*Purposive Attribution*	*Trait implications*	*Impression formation*	*The prediction of future behavior*
Stimulus:	Appearance, context, behavior stream.	Categorized appearance and behavior.	Behavior units where the perceiver is dominated by the hypothesis that the actor has responded to a powerful internal or external stimulus.	Behavior units where the experience is dominated by intentionality on the part of the actor.	The attribution of a trait.	Perceiver's hypothesis that a group of traits are attributed to the actor.	Behavior units, snap judgments, traits, general impressions.
Output:	Selecting and categorizing.	Immediate affective reactions (attraction or withdrawal) and stereotyped judgments.	A causal hypothesis as to why the behavior occurred, pointing to the effects of particular stimuli and inferences about why the person responded to the stimuli.	The attribution of a trait, intention, attitude, or ability.	The hypothesis that certain other traits also exist.	The formation of a general judgment, often likeability. Organization of the stimuli.	Prediction as to how a person will behave in certain classes of situations.

processes as a sequence, but that is not meant to suggest that there is anything necessarily linear or inevitable about the sequence. In other words, perceivers need not go through all the sequences—they may stop at any point, and they may backtrack or skip steps. What we propose is not inevitable, but we think it is rather common.

Note in Table 1.2 that we are proposing that there are six stages or subprocesses. Each of these processes begins with certain characteristic stimuli and results in certain characteristic kinds of outputs or responses. Let us review the major characteristics of these processes.

We begin with an account of how perceivers deal with the main stimuli of person perception: the person, behavior, and a context. People as visual stimuli have certain characteristics; their physical appearance includes things such as hair color, height, weight, skin color, style of dress, type of shoes, and so on. It is important to recognize that perceivers can and do draw direct inferences from these static, nonbehavioral cues. These kinds of direct inferences, such as "blond women are fun-loving," involve little or no complex cognitive effort and will be called snap or stereotypic judgments. However, the perceiver does more than simply respond to the person as a snapshot; usually the perceiver also sees the stimulus person enacting some behavior. Before the perceiver can draw any inferences from this behavior, though, the perceiver must structure the behavior itself, find the relevant units or divide it into its component parts, and label or categorize the behavior. The perceiver must in some sense define what the actor is doing. Furthermore, the perceiver will undoubtedly notice that the behavior is enacted in some physical, social, and psychological context. The behavior occurs in a particular setting, in a certain kind of room, in the presence of certain kinds of people (or none at all), and with certain general psychological background variables. The perceiver also has the job of defining the context, of deciding what kind of situation the actor is in, and what sorts of stimuli the actor is responding to. Chapter 2 will consider the problems involved in responding to people as physical stimuli, and in coding and organizing their behavior. It will also address the question of snap judgments and stereotyping.

At this point, our perceiver has perhaps made some direct inferences about the actor based on appearance, has decided what kinds of behavior have been exhibited, and has decided in what context the behavior was exhibited. The perceiver may wish to know why the actor behaved in a certain way, and may move on to inferences typically called attributions. Exactly how this attribution analysis is performed depends heavily on what kind of behavior is involved. For this purpose, we distinguish two kinds of behaving.

In the first the behavior is perceived to be purposive; we might call such behavior action. Attribution theorists are inclined to suggest that action is caused by some combination of environmental and personal forces and that the perceiver's job is to determine which forces the actor responded to in order to determine what the actor was trying to accomplish. Thus perception of intent plays a major role. Perception of purposive behavior will be considered in Chapters 3 and 4. Chapter 5 will then explore whether attribution ideas can help explain perception of self as well as others.

In the second kind of attributional process the person perceives the behavior as reactive. Behaviors that are usually perceived as reactive include nonverbal or expressive behaviors as well as some more habitual, nonconscious behaviors; as a class, these behaviors are seen as nonpurposive. Put another way, these behaviors are seen as caused but not as intended. When the behavior is sudden and typically coded as a short sequence, the perceiver commonly looks for a simple cause—the stimulus responsible for the behavior. When the behavior is of longer duration and looks habitual or nonconscious, the perceiver is not prone to seek a cause, but to the extent a cause is sought, to assign it internally to the person. The person is seen as having a habit. These behaviors are also often seen as symptoms. Reactive attributions are discussed in Chapter 6.

Either kind of attribution may lead to further inference work in an attempt to figure out what kind of person exhibits these behaviors. One common inference is that certain traits exist in the person. Of course, not all perceptions lead to trait attributions. If you see a person squint in the sunlight (an unintentional behavior) or pick up a pencil she just dropped (an intentional behavior), you won't have to look very far for an explanation, and the explanation probably won't be very interesting or involve important psychological characteristics.

However, the perceiver may for some reason be firmly convinced that the actor possesses a certain trait. This may well set off a process that we will call the *trait implication process*. The perceiver may simply infer that the actor has certain other characteristics as a kind of stereotypic judgment. Our friends and acquaintances as well as the mass media can teach us certain "rules" about which traits go together. Beyond this, the perceiver may make a composite judgment—if a person is warm, stupid, and happy, how likable would he be? Chapter 7 will deal with these complex cognitive acts.

Chapter 8 deals with the prediction of future behavior. We assume that one of the primary functions performed by this combination of person perception processes can be to provide the perceiver with a prediction of how the actor would behave in some future situation. We do not imply that all person perception processes end up with a predictive judgment, but making a guess as to how the other will behave can be a very salient issue.

In Chapters 9 and 10 we take up questions about the adequacy of our judgments about others and the processes underlying these judgments. Can judgments be accurate? Are there characteristic ways in which we go astray when we try to understand others?

Finally, in Chapter 11 we will once again go through the entire set of person perception processes trying to highlight particularly salient or troublesome issues. The tone of the last chapter will be somewhat critical. Although we feel that person perception models have been valuable, they are also limited and in some cases wrong. In the final chapter we hope to point out some of these problems to give future directions for research.

perception of people, behavior, and contexts

In the last chapter we emphasized the complexity of perceiving people and their behavior. We also emphasized the active role of the perceiver in this process. Perceivers do not merely react passively to the stimuli provided by others; they select and categorize information and go on to infer more general characteristics of people. Indeed in some cases the processing of person information gets quite elaborate, and the conclusions go well beyond the immediate physical stimuli to include psychological states and enduring dispositions of the stimulus person.

Although we can get information about others by reading or hearing about them (Warr and Knapper 1968; Brandt and Brandt 1972), person perception normally begins when we actually see or hear another person, and it generally involves more than just the perception of the person. Usually we perceive that person doing something—behaving—and we are also aware of a context for that behavior. The behavior can be relatively minute and simple, such as a cough or the raising of an eyebrow, or it can be extended and complex, such as fixing a flat tire on a car. The range of behaviors people perform is immense. So is the range of contexts in which they behave. The context may include the physical setting for the behavior, the behavior of others, the weather, the heat of the room, and even future events or physical settings if the perceiver thinks these are relevant to the perceived person's current behavior. Often we speak of contexts in terms of situational forces, external forces, or merely situations.

These, then, are the beginning elements of the person perception process: (1) a person (2) who is usually performing some behavior or behaviors (3) in a context or situation. In the remainder of this chapter we will examine these basic elements. Subsequent chapters will concentrate on further inferences drawn from the perceptions of these elements.

Snap Judgments about People

The perceptual process begins with a concrete person, whom we will call the stimulus person or actor. Of course, we normally see the stimulus person doing something, but suppose we could freeze the person in midstream or catch the person relatively motionless. Could you draw conclusions about a figure in a wax museum or a person in a photograph? The answer is an obvious yes. For centuries portrait painters and photographers have been trying to convey the essence of personality and character through pictures. Of course, great artists often rely on deliberate ambiguity, where no sure inferences can be drawn. The Mona Lisa is a prime example.

When you look at a photograph or portrait you may notice both dynamic and static aspects of the person. Static cues refer to the relatively unchanging aspects of the person such as physical features (height, weight, hair color, skin color, length of nose) and artifacts (clothing, cosmetics, and other props or accessories to appearance). Dynamic cues refer to "stop-action" slices of behavior such as facial expressions (smiles, frowns) and bodily posture. In this chapter we will concentrate on static cues. There are a variety of complex questions surrounding the perception of dynamic cues that are best postponed until we have considered other aspects of the person perception process.

To get some idea of what can be expressed by static cues look at the famous portrait of Annie Mae Gudger by Walker Evans (Fig. 2.1). What can you tell about this woman? Is she rich or poor? Happy or unhappy? Intelligent? Hardworking? Some of your conclusions may of course come from the woman's expression, what we have called dynamic features, but other important characteristics such as dress, hairstyle, and general shape of the body also convey information. It is important to note that your inference about the woman may be incorrect or incomplete, but the issue is not one of the adequacy of the perceptual process but of the nature of that process itself. You may wish to read James Agee's *Let Us Now Praise Famous Men* for a description of Annie Mae Gudger.

Physical features and artifacts (static features) are aspects of every person we see, whether that person is live or in a photograph or in a painting, and most of them are immediately accessible and obvious. Everyone has height, weight, and (usually) clothing, and ordinarily we see these things immediately. People do draw inferences from static features. These inferences are usually rather immediate and do not involve complex cognitive processes; to emphasize that immediacy we will call them *snap judgments*. Snap judgments do not involve complex hypotheses about the intentions and motives of the stimulus person or the cause of behavior. People with long noses and high foreheads may be seen as intelligent, but ordinarily we do not assume that they have acquired a long nose to try to appear intelligent. Similarly, fat people may be perceived as impulsive and insecure, but they are hardly fat because they want to be insecure. We do recognize, of course, that certain appearance variables,

Walker Evans, Courtesy of the Walker Evans Estate.

Fig. 2.1 Portrait of Annie Mae Gudger.

particularly clothing, are intentionally controlled. People do diet, keep a stiff upper lip, and try to look stunning. Sometimes we may use static cues as the basis of a more considered, more reflective judgment involving intentionality, particularly when something about the stimulus person's appearance is strange or unexpected. Most of the time, however, when we draw inferences from static appearance cues, they are of the immediate, snap judgment variety rather than the more complex and reflective judgments about intent.

Why do people make these snap judgments? After all, they sometimes are wrong or incomplete. Such judgments do have some utility. It is often useful to know what qualities another person has before we meet that person. For one thing, we can avoid people who are likely to be threatening or boring. If you want to find out more about a person you can strike up a conversation, but that will leave you at the mercy of norms about conversational decency; it is sometimes harder to end a conversation, particularly a boring one, than to start one. If you think about it for a moment, it may be more useful to know negative than positive things about someone you have never met, particularly if you are motivated to avoid anxiety or boredom. Perhaps this explains why so many snap judgments seem to be about negative qualities. We may have worked harder to develop cues for avoidance than cues for approach.

Another useful function of snap judgments is that they can form the basis of conversational openers. If I can assume that a bearded person has liberal (well-groomed beard) or radical (scraggly beard) political views, I have some basis for opening conversation with him. Depending on my own political views, I can either steer the conversation away from or toward certain topics.

Snap judgments can be useful, and people may actively make such judgments in an effort to get a quick hold on what another person is like. However, we suspect that most of the time snap judgments are not conscious efforts; they simply happen. A perceiver *may* have learned through experience that muscular men are dimwits, that blond women are "loose," or that people with glasses are intelligent. However, while some people may actually have had such experiences, it is unlikely that most people have personally experienced very strong relationships among properties such as these—assuming, of course, that such relationships are very weak or nonexistent in the real world. It is more likely that most of our snap judgments are based on culturally provided stereotypes. This is perhaps most obvious when we consider the snap judgments made on the basis of skin color or race, but in fact our culture teaches us a variety of things about people of particular hair color, hair length, and clothing styles. These stereotypes are often reinforced by the mass media. While the television industry has made some effort to reduce gender and racial stereotypes, it still emphasizes correlations among some physical features and psychological characteristics. On television, happy-go-lucky women are more than likely blonds and career women are usually brunettes. Blond men are heroes, and almost all villains are dark-haired: try to visualize a typical television crook.

PHYSICAL FEATURES

People do not ordinarily intend to convey specific impressions through their physical features, but perceivers are prone to draw inferences anyway. In this section we will review research findings on inferences from a variety of physical characteristics, including facial features, body type, race, and physical handicaps. Keep in mind that the specific results are given mainly for illustrative purposes; many of the inferences drawn from physical features are culture-bound, and apply only for some sorts of perceivers. Many of them, especially those involving the definition of beauty, may change rapidly as fashion changes. We are merely trying to show that physical characteristics do influence perceptions, but the specific perceptions are often highly variable from culture to culture and from time to time.

A variety of facial characteristics lead to inferences about the stimulus person. For example, people with low foreheads and short noses are seen as happy, trustworthy, and generous, whereas people with long noses are perceived as unhappy (Bradshaw 1969). Thin lips connote conscientiousness, protruding eyes connote excitability, and various combinations of features lead to definite inferences about personality characteristics (Secord, Dukes, and Bevan 1954).

A large number of studies have examined inferences based on body type. Most often researchers have contrasted three distinct body types suggested by Sheldon (1940). *Endomorphs* are heavy and fleshy, *ectomorphs* are skinny, and *mesomorphs* are muscular. As you might expect, people have distinct impressions of the personalities of the three types (Wells and Siegel 1961; Sleet

1969; Dibiase and Hjelle 1968). The muscular mesomorphs are attributed most of the positive traits such as energetic, well-adjusted, self-reliant; the more obese endomorphs are assigned traits such as unpopular, lazy, talkative. Ectomorphs are perceived as ambitious, tense, and suspicious. Moreover, both men (Wiggins, Wiggins, and Conger 1968) and women (Beck *et al.* 1976) have distinct preferences for the particular body builds of members of the opposite sex, although there are also major individual differences in these preferences.

Color and style of hair also produce definite stereotypes. In the minds of perceivers, "blonds do have more fun" because blond women are seen as more beautiful and social, while brunettes are perceived as more intelligent and dependable (Lawson 1971). Blond males are perceived as kind, but dark-haired men are perceived as strong (Roll and Verinis 1971) and intelligent (Lawson 1971). Bearded men are perceived as psychologically strong (Roll and Verinis 1971), and secondary sex characteristics such as hairy arms and chests lead to perceptions of virility and power (Verinis and Roll 1970).

The list of physical characteristics is as endless as the list of personality traits, so perhaps nothing more is to be gained by building up a dictionary of relationships. However, we would like to emphasize four general classes of physical characteristics because of their social significance: skin color, physical handicap, gender, and physical attractiveness.

Skin color   As everyone knows, the color of one's skin leads to inferences about other characteristics. Several studies on racial stereotyping confirm the view that in this society people with black and brown skin, and probably those with yellow skin to a lesser extent, are assigned more negative characteristics than those with light skin color (Brigham 1971). Older studies (which may be outdated) suggest that when white subjects judge members of the Negro race, darkness of color does not affect perceptions—the perceptions are uniformly rather negative (Secord, Bevan, and Katz 1956). However, in judging Caucasians, darker skin is associated with traits such as hostility, shyness, and dishonesty (Second, Dukes, and Bevan 1954). It appears that both skin color *per se* and racial group can contribute to inference processes.

Handicap   Physically handicapped persons are also assigned different traits than nonhandicapped persons. In one of the earliest studies (Mussen and Barker 1944), college students were asked to rate physically handicapped people on 24 personality traits. Handicapped people were perceived as being more conscientious than average, quite persistent, and more religious. They were also seen as tending to be reserved, creative, unselfish, and gentle. Mussen and Barker also reported that the physically handicapped were rated as feeling more inferior and as being more unhappy.

Richardson *et al.* (1961) demonstrated remarkable uniformity in people's preferences for different types of handicapped people. They presented individual subjects with six pictures of a young child who varied in the type of physical handicap. The consistent preference ordering among these six pictures were: first, able-bodied; second, a leg brace; third, in a wheelchair; fourth, the left hand missing; fifth, a facial disfigurement; and, interestingly enough, the obese child was the least preferred. This rank ordering was similar for people of different socioeconomic classes, different geographical areas, and different ages.

Gender   It is probably no surprise that males and females in our society are assigned somewhat different traits. Men have been perceived—by both men and women—as being more informal, calm, logical, and ambitious. Women have been perceived as being more tactful, shy, and frivolous (McKee and Sherriffs 1957). Generally, the traits assigned to men have been more positive, and men are perceived as being more normal and psychologically healthy than women (Broverman *et al.* 1970; Deaux 1976b).

Physical beauty   Finally, not only are physically attractive males and females evaluated more positively than less attractive people (see Berscheid and Walster 1978), but they are perceived as having more positive traits (Dion, Berscheid, and Walster 1972; Miller 1970; Snyder, Tanke, and Berscheid 1977). Some of the traits assigned to attractive people (both male and female) are modesty, sociability, kindness, strength, sexual responsiveness, and outgoing-ness. We hasten to point out that whereas skin color, handicap, and gender are relatively objective cues, physical attractiveness is partially in the eye of the beholder, since people do differ somewhat in what they perceive as attractive.

When we consider skin color, handicap, gender, and physical attractive-ness as variables affecting the perception of others, it becomes obvious that we are dealing with what are usually called stereotypes. People do have culturally derived stereotypes about stimulus persons with particular physical charac-teristics. Stereotypes are reinforced not only by parents and peers but also by the mass media.

However, even with a benign and unprejudiced culture, it is likely that our cognitive needs to categorize would still lead to some stereotyping, although not necessarily along present lines. In fact, the very success of our cognitive system depends on drawing inferences with minimal data. As we will see in the chapter on impression formation, stereotyping is one feature of cognitive information processing.

ARTIFACTS

Whereas physical features are, within limits of diet and surgery, unmodifiable, people can and do vary their dress to create a more presentable impression of themselves. Of course, dress and other artifacts may convey information about the stimulus person inadvertently as well. Such things as wearing lipstick (McKeachie 1952) or glasses (Thornton 1944; Hamid 1968) affect what traits the person is seen as having, and in an extensive study Gibbins (1969) found that perceivers tended to agree on the characteristics possessed by women wearing particular clothing styles. We all recognize this to at least some degree because we take the time to dress carefully and to buy our clothes with an eye for fashion and situational appropriateness. The very existence of fashion

"I knew it! You had humanist
written all over you!"

Drawing by Wm. Hamilton; © 1974 The New Yorker Magazine, Inc.

suggests that people think they will be judged on the basis of their clothes or
their appearance, and the available research evidence suggests that this is true.
There are even books that tell men and women how to dress for success in the
business world.

Behavior

Although we can and do draw conclusions from the mere appearance of a
stimulus person, further steps in the person perception process usually require
the observation of behavior. So let's assume that I observe your behavior.
What do I see? What I see is a figure which, because of past learning, I take to
be a person who is moving various body parts and making sounds that (if I am
lucky) I can understand as words. I observe that you bend your body down,
move your arms and hands so that you can grasp an object—a pencil—and
that you further move your body and arms to put the object close to a third
person, who immediately moves body and arms to grasp the object. I hear you
say, "Did you drop this?" and I hear the other person say, "Yes, thanks."

To put a fine point on this matter, I observe far more: smiles, dress, leg
movements, and so forth. I also observe more detail in the sequence of your
behavior than I have described. I may have noticed how many fingers you
used to grasp the pencil, and I could, if need be, describe several of the minor
atomistic details of your behavior. I may note that you point your toes in a
particular way when you reach down, and I may describe your bending down
as fluid or jerky. Let us agree for the moment that bending down is a complex
bit of behavior, and that we may carry the matter quite far if we try to get into

these complexities. In fact, it may be argued that the description has already been carried too far. I saw you pick up a pencil that was dropped by another person, and I saw you hand the pencil to the other person. What's all this stuff about bending, grasping, reorienting the body? Are we not being a bit technical and, well, academic? Perhaps. And yet there is an important point here. What we perceive and what we say (or think) we have perceived about another's behavior are different. Just as we create a coherent perception of a blue vase from many sensory stimuli, we create perception of behavior from a large number of movements and sounds. I think I saw you pick up an object and hand it to another person. Quite obviously, that's an interpretation on my part. In the example given the interpretation is not profound, and it is hard to see how it could lead to problems.

However, consider another example. He says, "I think you're mistaken." She says "I think you're an ass." He says, "I don't wish to continue this conversation." His face gets red and he walks away with considerable speed and arm-waving. My description: she made him angry. Obviously, my description again involves interpretation. This time, however, the interpretation may produce some problems. Was he angry? Perhaps, but then conceivably he may only have been acting angry to make her feel guilty or, for that matter, to prove what a great actor he is. I have also asserted that his anger (assuming that it was genuinely anger that I "saw") was a response to her insult. Was calling him an ass an insult? It would be to me, but it might not have been to him; perhaps it is a term of endearment between the two. Technically I also have no right to assert that his anger was a response to her behavior. Perhaps he meant to discontinue the conversation all along, and she just managed to get her sentence in before his final statement and exit.

Fortunately, such objections are often specious. If I were to observe the actual behavior there would be several additional nonverbal cues that would help in the interpretation process. I would have observed whether his anger appeared suddenly after the insult or whether he seemed angry all along. Perhaps he may have looked surprised or hurt at being called an ass. Still the essential point remains—I have interpreted what I have seen. You may get some feeling for how much interpretative activity goes on in behavior description by trying to describe the behavior of a friend without interpretation. Or even better—try to describe one inning of a baseball game without using baseball terms. Just "facts," please. What do you really see? Imagine if you will what kind of description of a baseball game might be provided by someone who had never before seen a game.

We often become aware of interpretation when people disagree about what has happened. Where there is interpretation there is room for error and bias. It is trivially easy to demonstrate that two perceivers do not always interpret the same action in the same way, and legal scholars have long recognized the unreliability of eyewitness accounts of crimes (see Levine and Tapp 1973; Buckhout 1976).

This, then, is a major problem in analyzing person perception. How do perceivers code and describe behavior? Why is the same behavior sometimes described differently? Unfortunately, this is also a place where we have to admit that we do not know much. Most of what we know about how behavior is described and coded comes from impressionistic accounts and philosophical analysis rather than from empirical research. On the basis of these accounts and perhaps a bit of common sense, we are able, however, to say some things with assurance.

DIVIDING THE BEHAVIOR STREAM

The first, and often least recognized, problem is that behavior does not occur as a set of unrelated episodes. Behavior is continuous; in the instructive phase of Barker and Wright (1955), there is a behavior stream. Behavior, like streams, can be divided, but the divisions will be somewhat artificial. You are always behaving and to say that you stop, stoop, pick up an object, and hand it to another person is to favor discrete description over actual continuity. You may have done all these things, but they were performed as a continuous action. It is worth pointing out in this context that behavior can be subjected to more or less fine-grained analysis. As Dickman (1963) and Newtson (1973) have shown, subjects who observe behavior can see relatively large (and few) or small (and many) units of behavior.

Although people can be either microscopic or macroscopic in their division of the behavior stream, an important question about the naturalness of such division remains. Are there natural units to behavior—natural in the sense that nearly everyone would agree that there are "breaks" in the action where one kind of behavior stops and another begins? Newtson and Engquist (1976) found that there was consensus among observers on such "breakpoints" in action sequences. Furthermore, the behavior that occurred at the break-points was more informative than the behavior in the rest of the action sequence. For example, subjects who saw slides from the breakpoints could describe what had happened more accurately than subjects who saw slides of nonbreakpoint behavior. Subjects who had previously seen a film of the entire sequence also recognized slides of breakpoints more accurately than slides of nonbreakpoints.

There seem to be natural breakpoints in most behavior sequences, points at which behavior changes markedly (Newtson, Engquist, and Bois 1977). However, the perceiver also has some control over how finely the behavior stream is divided. Often we are prone to see action or behavior sequences as governed by particular intentions or stimuli (From 1971), and we suspect that the level of analysis often reflects what intentions or stimuli are salient. For example, when I tie my shoe all my movements are governed by that particular intention, and ordinarily there is little information to be gained from trying to break down the sequence into the component parts, precisely because there are no separate conscious intentions governing the various finger movements. On the other hand, when a five-year-old child tries to tie a shoe, the child seems to have separate intentions for many of the component finger movements; here it makes more sense to break the sequence down into the various components. Similarly when a person sees a snake, jumps, says, "Oh my God," and backs up three steps, it generally is not useful to code each of the separate movements because they were all reactions to the sight of the snake.

Another factor that affects level of coding is immediately perceptible changes in the behavior or in the environment. For example, perceivers tend to code predictable behavior more broadly than unpredictable behavior, and sudden shifts in what the person is doing lead to more fine-grained coding (Newtson 1973; Wilder 1978). Newtson *et al.* (1978) found that when the behavior results in readily observable changes in the environment, behavior coding tends to be organized around these changes. However, when environmental changes provide no such organizational framework, perceivers resort to a more microscopic coding strategy.

Perceiver purposes also control the level of unitization. I may wish to know how you tune your car and I will likely code your behavior rather broadly in terms of categories such as adjusting the carburetor and gapping the spark plugs. On the other hand, if I wish to know how you gap the spark plugs, I will code the action sequence more finely. What we wish to know about behavior often dictates how microscopically we code it. For example, Ebbesen, Cohen, and Lane (1975) have found that when perceivers wish to remember what the actor has done they use a rather fine unitization, whereas the coding is more macroscopic when a more general impression is desired.

DESCRIBING BEHAVIOR

The first problem in observing behavior, then, is dividing the behavior stream. The second is describing the behavior. At whatever level of analysis you are working, the behavior can be described in several ways. I can say that you have handed another person an object she has dropped, I can say that you have helped another person, or I can say that you were detoured from getting to the store to shop for your shoes. Whatever my reasons for using one description over another, I have described the same physical behavior. The fact that behavior can be described in several ways creates a fair amount of philosophical mischief and also creates practical problems. If he is in a particularly bad mood, a husband may yell at his wife. He says, "I was just telling you how I felt"; his daughter says, "You yelled,"; his wife says, "You hurt my feelings"; and a pseudo-Freudian neighbor says, "You were expressing your repressed anger toward your mother." While each describes the same behavior, the descriptions vary so much that four different behaviors seem to have occurred. You may wish to reflect on differences between "He pulled the trigger" and "He killed Sam" as descriptions of the same behavior.

There are, of course, many ways that the same behavior can be described, but in this chapter we want to emphasize four distinct types of description: (1) neutral, (2) consequence, (3) reactive, and (4) stylistic. We do not claim that these are the only classes of behavior description, but they are especially important for the study of person perception.

Neutral descriptions Neutral descriptions are those that describe the behavior without any particular reference to the psychological state of the stimulus person. "He shouted," "He talked loudly," "He moved his mouth and certain words were emitted," "She laughed," "She glanced at the car": these descriptions do not tell us very much about what the actor wanted to accomplish, whether or not the behavior was intended, what emotions the actor had, or what kind of person the actor is. They are really descriptions only of behavior. Note also that neutral descriptions can be more or less microscopic. We could, if we wished, describe each of the behaviors as a series of muscular movements.

We hope you will recognize that although these descriptions are neutral in the sense of implying very little about the actor, we have refrained from calling the descriptions objective. In each case the perceiver has provided some interpretation of what has gone on; however, generally the interpretations do not involve inferences about psychological states. But what is considered neutral is partially a matter of how terms are normally used and whether there is consensus. "Lee shouted in the presence of Dick" is neutral only to the extent that others would agree with the description. One of our children is prone to claim that her parents shout at her when they criticize, even though less involved observers would have trouble detecting a raised voice. Clearly her description is not neutral, but indicates her assumptions about intentions and correlations of voice tone and content of utterances.

Neutral descriptions can be given for almost any behavior, but ordinarily such descriptions are not particularly informative. They tell us what happened, but they do not orient us toward any particular explanations of why the behavior was enacted; the other three classes of descriptions each carry with them the suggestion that there are particular kinds of causes at work in producing the behavior.

Consequence descriptions Earlier we distinguished intentional behavior — *action*—from behavior not guided by intentions. It is assumed that *actions* must be explained with some regard to intentions or other mental reasons, while nonintentional behaviors require a different sort of explanation. For example, it makes sense to ask why a person coughed *deliberately* at a concert (was she trying to attract someone's attention, act bored, show her displeasure at the musical piece or the performance, show that she is not bound by the conventions of good concert behavior?), but it makes little sense to ask why a person with a bad cold coughs. In the former case the person does something, while in the latter case something (say, a tickle in the throat) does something to her.

For the moment let us concentrate on descriptions of intentional behavior. While such behavior *can* be described in various ways, usually action descriptions make explicit or implicit reference to the intentional nature of the behavior. When we say that behavior is intentional we may mean one of two things. First, we may mean that the person consciously wanted to do the behavior that was performed. The behavior was not accidental, habitual, or a spontaneous reaction to some stimulus. People can cough deliberately—that is, intentionally—such as when they are trying to draw attention to some behavior discreetly or when they are trying to show displeasure; or they can cough as a reaction to an infection or to a tickle in the throat.

Second, intentionality of behavior may also refer to the actor's wanting particular consequences of the behavior to happen. Even deliberate behavior has unintended consequences in addition to the intended ones. This point becomes important because action is often *labeled* by reference to the consequences of the behavior. When we say that Alice opened the door, fed the cat, drove to work, or did not solve the equation, we are not literally describing what she did in terms of her physical behavior, but rather we are describing what happened as a result of that behavior. What Alice did when she opened the door was to get out of her chair, walk to the door, grasp it in a particular way, and pull on it. The door's opening was the consequence of all that activity.

When we describe a behavior in terms of its consequences, we divide the behavior stream in a particular way. To say that Alice opened the door is generally not merely to make reference to Alice's touching and pulling on the door. Rather the perceiver is drawing attention to Alice's having stopped one activity, say sitting in her chair, and to her walking over and opening the door. Ordinarily the whole sequence of getting up, walking over to the door, pulling on it, and returning to her seat is included. From the perceiver's point of view all of these acts were oriented to the same consequence, namely an open door. The perceiver feels that the whole 15-second episode was controlled by Alice's intention to have an open door.

However, there are often several consequences of a given behavior sequence. As Alice walked over to open the door she also vacated a seat, walked between a friend and the television, and made a noise as the door opened; we could, of course, describe the behavior in terms of each of these consequences. Why do we organize our behavior descriptions around some consequences and not around others? Part of the answer is in terms of the perceiver's own purposes and values. The friend whose view of the television program was momentarily interrupted would be more likely to use that consequence as a description than would the person who asked Alice to open the door. Even so, in a given case some consequences are more likely to receive attention than others. We are probably likely to attend more closely to immediate than to remote consequences; we talk about Alice's opening the door but not about wear and tear on the door's hinges. Perceivers are also more likely to pay attention to consequences that the actor seemed to intend. However, Alice's intentions are unlikely to be public knowledge; how does the perceiver know which consequences (if any) Alice intended? Our cultural expectations play a role here. It is simply more likely in our culture that people open doors because they want them open than because they want to make noise. Generally we assume, for example, that people desire positive and not negative consequences of their behavior (Jones and Davis 1965). But quite apart from such general assumptions we make about behavior, there are cues in the behavior itself that tend to point to intended consequences. Alice takes the most direct route she can to the door, she does not stop between the friend and the television as she might if she truly wanted to be disruptive, and she does not open the door as roughly as she might if she wanted to make noise. With more complex and extended behaviors, the perceiver might have more difficulties figuring out what the actor intended, but usually the perceiver would be able to rule out several possibilities by observing the behavior itself.

Finally, the perceiver may be oriented toward consequences that are unusual or particularly salient. If Alice stumbled on her way to the door and knocked over a Ming vase, this consequence would probably be salient enough to take precedence in the description. Unintended consequences of deliberate behavior can form the basis of descriptions when they are dramatic enough; however, action is mostly described in terms of what seems to be its intended consequences.

Reactive descriptions   We have made a major distinction between behavior guided by intention and behavior not guided by intention. Psychologists who have studied person perception have generally been most concerned with the former—with action. However, unintended behaviors also present interesting interpretational problems. We can distinguish such acts into two rough classes: *reactive behavior* and *habitual behavior*. Reactive behaviors include many expressive and nonverbal behaviors, and as a group they are distinguished by being caused by a strong or sudden internal or external stimulus. For example, your scream of terror and contorted face in response to an intruder climbing through your bedroom window are generally not intended behaviors; rather they are seen as behaviors caused by an external stimulus. Similarly, a cough as a response to a tickle is caused but not intended, and your shout of "Damn it" and snapping of your fingers halfway to the concert will be seen as caused by your sudden realization that you forgot the tickets.

Such reactive behaviors are ordinarily described in ways that make explicit or implicit reference to psychic states, particularly emotions. The husband was angry, John was scared, Jane just remembered that she forgot the tickets. Note again that whereas such descriptions do not describe the actual behaviors, they are frequently used as summary statements about what went on precisely because they provide more information than does a neutral description of the behavior. It is probably less important to know what John did when he was scared than it is to know that his behavior was a response to the emotion of fear.

Reactive descriptions tend to be used when there is a sudden or dramatic change in behavior or when behavior is extreme in some way. However, behavior need not be dramatic to be described in reactive terms; many rather subtle behaviors—such as a quick glance or a quiet sigh—are also perceived as involuntary responses to stimuli and are used as evidence about some internal state (such as suspicion or relief). Reactive descriptions draw attention to the fact that certain behaviors are caused but not intended; we try to understand what caused the behavior rather than what the behavior was intended to cause.

Stylistic descriptions   Another common form of description draws attention to the stylistic elements of behavior. "Joan solved the equation with ease." "John reached for the cigarette without thinking." "Sam fought bravely." Such stylistic descriptions have several common features. For instance, they generally do not assert anything about intentionality, and in fact they frequently explicitly deny intentions. In the first description above, Joan certainly intended to solve the equation, but she did not intend to solve it easily. In the second description John had no relevant intention at all. However, stylistic accounts do imply something about personal qualities. Joan is smart, John is distracted or addicted, and Sam is brave. It is just that the personal qualities implied are not the sorts of qualities that normally lead to specific intentions. Often stylistic accounts are used to refer to habitual behavior.

Habitual behaviors are a curious hybrid class. Usually you do not exactly intend to reach for your tenth cigarette of the morning (indeed you may have recently intended not to have another cigarette), but then you do not usually reach for a cigarette as a reaction to anything, either. Habitual behavior often looks somewhat goal-directed, but typically it has a repetitive or automatic quality to it; in using stylistic descriptions for habitual behavior we draw attention to the fact that the goal-directedness is an appearance. However, it is important to recognize that while habitual behavior is often described stylistically, not all stylistic descriptions refer to habitual behavior. Sometimes we merely want to call attention to the way (e.g., bravely) a particular behavior is performed.

Thus far we have emphasized the importance of stylistic labels for habitual or nonconsciously performed, repetitive behavior. However, such labels are also commonly applied to purposive behavior when the perceiver wants to call attention to the way something was done. There is a major difference between facing a final examination calmly and anxiously, but because there are so many different ways of being calm or anxious, we are usually not concerned with the specific behavioral referants of these labels. To be brave is not to perform a particular behavior; rather it is to perform any number of behaviors in a particular way in a particular context. Person perception theorists have largely ignored the stylistic elements of behavior, but such features are generally quite important. Novelists, journalists, and others who wish to communicate the essence of character quickly often resort to stylistic description. In Chapters 6 and 11 we will return to stylistic description and the importance of behavioral style in making inferences about others.

Alternative labels   It is worth noting that all behaviors have many alternative descriptions, not only in the sense of how microscopic the description is but also in the sense of which of the many features of the behavior are emphasized. We have suggested that whereas neutral descriptions are always possible, the other descriptions seem to vary depending on the perceiver's purposes and on the "look" of the behavior. Intentional behavior looks deliberate and planned, reactive behavior often starts suddenly and ends quickly, and habitual behavior has a repetitive and unplanned appearance. We do not mean to suggest that the differences are always as clear as we have made them seem, and we have tried to point out that different people often do not use the same descriptions for the same behavior. All we mean to say is that frequently behavior has a quality to it that may orient the perceiver to one kind of description or another.

Finally we want to suggest that how behavior is labeled may influence how it is interpreted. When Jim yells at his wife, he can be seen as exhibiting immature or hostile behavior. The perceiver who codes the behavior as hostile will likely come to different conclusions about the kind of person Jim is than the person who sees his behavior as immature.

The type of label may also affect subsequent inferences. Behavior that is labeled in terms of consequences may push the perceiver toward perceptions of intention. Behavior coded in terms of psychic state will more likely lead to reactive attributions to internal or external causes but not to intentions. Stylistic descriptions usually carry their own inferences in the descriptions.

The Context

Just as behavior cannot occur without an actor, it cannot occur without a context. Occasionally mimes and dancers try to eliminate contextual distractions by performing in featureless environments, but in real life behavior always unfolds in a physical, cultural, and social setting.

PERCEPTION OF CONTEXTS

The context, or what we will often call *situational* or *external* forces, also provides important information for the person perception process. Recent theorists have made much of the proposition that behavior is perceived as jointly determined by situational and personal factors. However, they have tended to assume that the situational forces are clear to the perceiver, and that the major problem is inferring personal factors given the situational forces.

In reality, a fair amount of cognitive work goes into interpreting what the relevant situational forces are. In order for the person perception process to make sense, perceivers have to have a taxonomy of situations as well as of persons. This may require a bit of explanation. Consider first that one way we have of making sense of other people and their behavior is to categorize. We begin the process of understanding behavior by seeing it as an example of some more general category, such as aggression. And, as the next chapter will make clear, we also try to understand people by attributing characteristics to them;

these attributes (say, dominance or need for approval) are dimensions along which people vary. In short, we see people as having personal characteristics, personalities, that dispose them to behave in certain ways.

But for a perceiver to be able to understand and think about situations, the perceiver must also have some ideas about features common to situations. If people have dispositional properties, so do situations. Perceivers seem to understand that certain types of situations tend to produce certain kinds of behavior. So, for example, students tend to behave differently in a classroom than they do at a dormitory or fraternity party. Not only people, but also situations, have personalities (Moos 1976).

As yet we know very little about how perceivers understand and classify situational forces. Several studies (e.g., Frederiksen 1972; Price 1974; Schneider, Hastorf, and Mesibov 1978; Forgas 1978; Magnusson 1971; Magnusson and Ekehammar 1973) have examined perceived dimensions of situations, but as yet there is not enough research to assess how general these dimensions are.

We might wish to think of situations or contexts as having both physical and cultural features. Each type of feature facilitates and inhibits certain forms of behavior and determines what we consider to be appropriate behavior. It is obvious that both physical and cultural factors set limits on what we can do. For example, people cannot carry on a decent conversation in front of a loud stereo, nor are they likely to yell at their bosses or professors. Physical and cultural factors can also facilitate certain forms of behavior. The physical layout of a building affects work patterns as well as the likelihood of people meeting (Moos 1976), and cultural factors affect how closely people stand while engaged in a conversation (Hall 1966). Furthermore, our perceptions of context affect how we perceive the appropriateness of behavior. A person who wore a heavy sweater to a Texas picnic in July would be thought strange, as would a person who talked to herself all through a class meeting.

THE IMPORTANCE OF CONTEXT

It may seem somewhat paradoxical to emphasize the perception of context in a book devoted to perceiving persons. In fact, although the perception of context has been almost ignored by person perception researchers, there are several reasons why we should concentrate some attention on this topic.

Social context factors   One of the important features of any environment is the presence of other people. We assume that when Joe is in the presence of Susan, at least some of Joe's behavior will be directed to Susan. Joe may merely be trying to avoid Susan, or he may be trying to create a good impression through his appearance and demeanor. Of course, Joe and Susan may be interacting, in which case it is easy to see how Susan forms a relevant context for Joe's behavior. Susan is also a perceiver, and Susan is simultaneously affecting the behavior of Joe and trying to interpret Joe's behavior. Thus, in many situations perceivers themselves form an important part of the context for the stimulus person's behavior.

Perceivers often fail to recognize the role their own behavior may have on the stimulus person. However, Susan would do well to remember not only that her behavior affects Joe's behavior, but that her behavior is affected by her perceptions of Joe. (See Kelley 1950 and Bond 1972 for relevant research examples.) Further, if Susan perceives Joe as hostile, she may behave in a way that makes Joe hostile. These self-fulfilling prophecies have been studied by several psychologists. For example, Rosenthal and Jacobson (1968) demonstrated that teachers who expect their pupils to do well do tend to get higher achievement. Despite many criticisms of the particular research methods in this study, several other psychologists have also found self-fulfilling prophecies in classroom situations (Zanna *et al.* 1975). Word, Zanna, and Cooper (1974) also demonstrated self-fulfilling prophecies in interracial social behavior. The nonverbal behavior of white interviewers was more positive to white than to black interviewees, and subjects treated like the black interviewees displayed less positive nonverbal behavior themselves.

A particularly careful study of self-fulfilling prophecies by Snyder, Tanke, and Berscheid (1977) illustrates some of the processes that may go on. As we have noted earlier, people in our society have generally positive stereotypes about physically attractive people. In the experiment a male and female subject had a get-acquainted conversation over an audio hookup. Although they could not see each other, the male was given a picture of the female that was either attractive or unattractive. (The pictures were not of the actual female subjects, and the females did not know that the males had "their" pictures.) The men who interacted with women they thought were attractive conversed in a more positive way than men who interacted with the "unattractive" females. Thus the men's behavior was affected by snap judgments or stereotypes they had of their conversation partners. Of even greater interest was the behavior of the women. Women who were conversing with men who thought they were attractive responded to the men's positive behavior by behaving more positively themselves. Thus the women provided behavioral confirmation of the stereotype the men had of them. The men were nicer to the women they thought were attractive, and the women were nicer in return. Perhaps this is why attractive people are perceived as having so many positive characteristics; other people are more likely to draw positive behavior out of them.

These studies on behavioral confirmation or self-fulfilling prophecies indicate that the appearance and behavior of perceivers can constitute an important context for the stimulus person's behavior. The trouble is that perceivers are probably usually not aware of this.

Inferences from contexts   Often contexts serve as cues for snap judgments about the stimulus persons in them. It is usually safe to assume that a person in a record store owns a stereo, that people at certain resorts are Jewish, and that people at the student union are students or faculty. We may have stereotypes about people who attend particular colleges, frequent certain bars, or hang around with certain people. It may even be reasonable to assume that people who go to discos are extroverted, that people who attend obscure foreign movies are introverted, and that people who work in certain occupations are ambitious.

Whether or not particular snap judgments based on context are true, socialization agents such as parents seem to feel that contexts are cues for judgments. Most of us receive some training in knowing what kinds of situations are "safe" to be seen in, and most people have knowledge about how to use contextual cues to project a particular image. Particularly important in this regard is the social context. People are judged by the company they keep; knowing the "right people" or being associated with an attractive person of the opposite sex is usually taken (or is thought to be taken) as a cue for certain kinds of social status. Gurwitz and Dodge (1977), for example, have shown that people are willing to infer characteristics about a person just by knowing typical behaviors of her friends.

Contexts and labeling Contexts also help us understand behavior. The same behavior in different contexts may lead to different labels. Imagine one person striking another on the rump. This behavior could be called aggressive if the context were a public street, applying discipline if the context were a home with a parent striking a child, playful if the context were a basketball locker room, or encouraging if the context were the sideline at a football game. Humming loudly to oneself might be called rude, crazy, or absent-minded, depending on the situation, and the so-called labeling theory of deviance suggests that terms such as *criminal* or *insane* are nothing more than ways one group in society judges the inappropriateness of behavior in certain contexts (Goffman 1961; Becker 1963; Scheff 1966). Whether or not we wish to go this far, it is clear that the same behavior can lead to different labels, depending on the situation.

Context and appropriateness We have emphasized that the physical and social contexts as well as cultural norms affect people's definitions of appropriate behavior. Price and Bouffard (1974) have shown that people have well-developed notions about what behaviors "go with" what contexts. Kissing is seen as appropriate on a date, but not in the classroom or on a job interview. Fighting is thought to be more appropriate in one's own room than in a classroom, and writing is more appropriate in a classroom than at a family dinner.

Perception of the appropriateness of behavior is an important element in the person perception process. Inappropriate behavior is generally thought to be undesirable, and because we assume that people normally want to produce desirable behavior, we are often at particular pains to explain undesirable behavior. So inappropriate behavior often leads the perceiver to ask why the behavior occurred; it pushes the perceiver to continue the interpretation process. At the same time such behavior probably pushes the perceiver toward certain sorts of inference processes. As we will see in the next chapter, appropriate behavior can often be explained in terms of contextual or situational forces; appropriateness is a cue that the person is responding to the situation. Inappropriate behavior, on the other hand, seems to demand an explanation in terms of the actor's characteristics; clearly the person has either inadequate knowledge of situational forces or a peculiar set of intentions.

Contexts and attribution   In the next chapter we will explicitly consider attribution theories. The attribution framework assumes that perceivers make some decision as to whether behavior is caused by dispositional (personality) characteristics of the stimulus person or by situational forces. It stands to reason that before such a decision can be made, the perceiver must have been aware of situational forces and must have categorized them in some way. For example, consider a perceiver observing a mother helping her child with math homework, and assume that the perceiver has decided to call this behavior helpful. Is the mother a helpful person? The perceiver might be inclined to believe so if the mother were missing her favorite television program to help with the homework. In this case the perceiver would have to know that the television program was a salient element of the context for the mother. The perceiver would also have to know that the mother regarded the television as a positive part of her environment and not as a distraction or nuisance. Furthermore, the perceiver might try to understand several other features of the context: norms about helping children with homework and cultural values for achievement. If the perceiver were to take these aspects of the context into account, the attribution might not be that the mother was helpful but that she wanted her child to get good grades.

The point is simple, really. Before the perceiver can weigh dispositions and situational forces, the perceiver must know something about the context of the behavior and the forces from the context that might influence the stimulus person's behavior. The perceiver must notice the relevant aspects of the context and code them appropriately.

The Role of the Perceiver

Up to this point we have discussed general factors that affect perceptions of people, behavior, and contexts. However, it is obvious that there are often major individual differences in how these stimuli are perceived and interpreted. We propose that there are three major points at which individuals may differ in how they process these stimuli. Perceivers may differ in (1) what they pay attention to, (2) how they label or categorize what they have observed, and (3) what inferences they draw from the categorized person, behavior, or situation.

As we noted in the previous chapter, the perceptual world is far too complex to be perceived in its entirety. The perceiver must select what to pay attention to. Sometimes the stimuli themselves virtually seem to dictate what will receive attention. It is probably the case that moving, brightly colored, large and unusual objects capture the attention of the visual senses, whereas loud and changing stimuli seem to capture and hold the attention of the auditory senses. Much of the time the perceiver's purposes, values, and expectations play a significant role in attention. A doctor presumably pays attention to different aspects of physical appearance during a medical examination than at a party, a policeman notices different aspects of behavior while on duty than you or I would, and you will pay attention to different aspects of your house or apartment depending on whether you want to hang a new picture, install a new stereo, or plan a large party. We consciously direct our attention to different things depending on what we want to do.

John Goldin (1975) conducted a study that shows the effects of goals on attention. In this study college men looked at folders describing college women who varied in physical attractiveness, academic competence, and attitude similarity. These factors had very different effects on the men's rank ordering of the women, depending on the type of future interaction the men anticipated. The men who anticipated a possible romantic interaction paid most attention to attractiveness, while those who anticipated an academic counseling session tended to pay more attention to competence. The effect of attitude similarity was greatest when the men did not think they would interact with the women at all.

Perceivers differ markedly in how they label and code the appearance and behavior of other people. In the last chapter we discussed the work of Dornbusch et al. (1965), which showed that children use different categories to describe the same person, but that the same perceiver tends to use the same categories to describe many others. It appears that our purposes, values, and expectations lead us to code and label events in our own way. A psychologist who is concerned with nonverbal behavior or the mechanics of behavior sequences may code an action sequence in terms of relatively microscopic movements, while "normally" a more molar approach might be taken. An insurance salesman may be inclined to make judgments about whether the client's behavior is enthusiastic or whether the client's polite behavior seems feigned. At a party the salesman may be more likely to code behavior in terms of how interesting, humorous, or entertaining the person is. Codings of what a person is doing can also affect what we pay attention to. Zadney and Gerard (1974) found that perceptions of an actor's intention affected what perceivers reported the actor had done.

An experiment by Duncan (1976) illustrates the role of certain values on behavior coding. He asked perceivers to watch a videotape of two other supposed subjects discussing a problem. The discussion became quite heated and finally one of the participants shoved the other. Duncan varied the race of the two participants, and asked his perceivers to rate their behavior at various points in the discussion. When a black shoved a white, 75 percent of the perceivers (who were whites) labeled it as violent behavior, and when a black shoved a black, 69 percent saw it as violent; however, only 17 percent saw a white's shoving a black as violent, and only 13 percent saw a white shoving a white as violent. In short, when a person shoves another, the behavior is much more likely to be seen as violent when a black does the shoving. When whites shoved, the dominant behavior codings were dramatizing, playing around, and aggressive behavior. Fewer than 10 percent of the subjects saw a black as playing around or dramatizing, whereas 62 percent of the subjects used these designations for the white shover. One cannot tell from this experiment precisely what caused this differential behavior coding, but there is a strong suspicion that the subjects' values as well as their expectations must have affected the ways they perceived the behavior.

Finally, we must remember that our purposes, values, and expectations can determine the interpretation we make of coded experience. Consider an example of a student yelling at his professor after the professor has just returned an exam. A friend who had already pegged the student as a man with a temper might later report, "Joe was impulsive again. I wish he'd learn to control his temper." On the other hand, a friend who knows Joe to be even-tempered and mature might say, "Joe was really angry," and might even add an interpretative statement such as, "The professor must have really made a serious error because Joe almost never gets angry." The friend has seen Joe as acting angrily rather than immaturely, a judgment based on previous information about Joe.

Snyder and Uranowitz (1978) had subjects read a detailed case history of a woman. Subsequently subjects discovered that the woman was living either a lesbian or a heterosexual lifestyle. This knowledge affected what the subjects remembered. For example, subjects who knew she was a lesbian remembered more of her behavior that was consistent with a lesbian lifestyle, and when they made errors they were in the direction of remembering (incorrectly) behavior consistent with the knowledge about lifestyle. Providing different sets led to differing interpretations of the same information.

Summary

Often when we see people even for the first time we make some judgment about them based on their physical appearance, style of dress, and the like. We have termed such judgments *snap judgments* to emphasize that they are generally nonreflective inferences based mostly on culturally derived stereotypes.

We also observe other people behaving. Behavior is continuous, and perceivers must divide it into separate episodes that are then coded and described. However, even the same episodes of behavior may be described in several different ways. Some descriptions are neutral because they imply nothing particular about the psychology of the actor. A more common form of description utilizes the consequences of the behavior, and such consequence descriptions orient the perceiver toward explanations of behavior based on the actor's intentions. Some behaviors, however, are clearly not governed by intentions. When the behavior seems to be caused by a strong stimulus, we are prone to use reactive descriptions that imply something about the actor's psychological state as a reaction to the stimulus. Finally, we employ stylistic descriptions when we wish to draw attention to the ways in which behavior is performed.

Perceivers also must understand something about the physical, cultural, and social context of behavior. Often contexts help the perceiver interpret behavior, and they may lead to inferences about the actor. Perceivers often fail to recognize the role that they play as a part of the actor's context.

Perceivers vary in what aspects of people, situations, and behavior they pay attention to, and their own needs, values, purposes, and past experiences also affect how they code or describe these things. Finally, perceivers may also differ in what kinds of inferences they draw from the information they have.

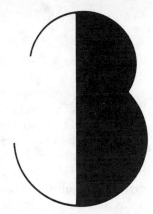

In the previous chapter we discussed how the **attribution**
perceiver processes basic information about
the stimulus person, the behavior, and the
context. We noted that the perceiver may have made a snap judgment about
the stimulus person based on physical appearance or even the context. The
perceiver has made at least an implicit judgment about what kind of behavior
(e.g., purposive, reactive, habitual) the stimulus person has performed, and the
perceiver has a sense of what the context of the behavior is. Probably more
often than not the person perception process stops right here, because there is
nothing particularly interesting or questionable about the stimulus person.
However, there are times when the perceiver wants to know more about the
stimulus person, and the perceiver may try to determine why the other person
acted in a particular way. This part of the person perception process is called
attribution.

   Imagine that you have just seen a particular person, Joe, shouting and
waving his arms in front of another person. Based on appearance (Joe is about
20 and the other person is about 40), clothing, and physical context (the front
of a classroom after a class), you make a snap judgment that this is a student
exercising his vocal cords before a professor. You further hear Joe shout: "The
damned test was unfair." After observing an exchange of comments between
the professor and Joe, you are fairly clear that Joe's behavior is angry, and that
his angry comments are a reaction to the professor. Thus, you might make a
reactive attribution. If Joe were simply shouting and cursing, you might stop
there; or you might go on to ask what kind of a person Joe is to get so angry.
You might, however, go through a somewhat different process. You might
note that although Joe seems angry, his behavior is not simply a reaction to the
professor. You note that Joe's arguments, though impassioned, are well reasoned. His behavior seems to have a purposive quality to it. In trying to
explain his behavior you feel you must take his intentions as well as his
reactions into account. You may wonder why Joe is being so argumentative.
Joe has caught your attention and you are interested in explaining his
behavior. In attempting such an explanation, you will take account of various
contextual features, norms about appropriate student behavior, norms about
students' performing well on exams, the behavior of the professor, the exam

itself; and you will use this information in helping to decide why Joe is acting this way.

Person perception researchers study how perceivers infer the causes of behavior. The general process of determining the causes of behavior is called *attribution.* There are two basic kinds of attribution processes. The first was illustrated when you decided that Joe's behavior was an angry reaction to his professor. Reactive attributions occur when we see the person's behavior as being a relatively nonconscious, often involuntary, response to some internal or external stimulus. Joe's angry behavior was caused by the professor, and later upon reflection Joe might become angry at himself when he suddenly remembers his immature outburst. The essence of reactive attribution is the identification of the internal (such as a thought) or external stimulus that provoked a particular reaction. That stimulus is not always obvious, but even if it is, the perceiver may take the reactive attribution process further by asking what sort of a person is provoked by that kind of stimulus or why the person reacted in that way. Not everyone is made angry by the behavior of professors, and not everyone who is made angry responds by assaulting the person in the ivory tower. Reactive attributions will be further considered in Chapter 6.

The other form of attribution occurs when the perceiver decides that behavior is intended or purposive. Joe's initial shouting may have been an impulsive reaction to anger, but you have decided that Joe's continued arguing has a purpose. If Joe was merely angry you would say he was shouting or angry. But you have decided that his behavior looks purposive enough to be termed arguing. Why is Joe "arguing" as opposed to "shouting"? A reasonable judgment might be that Joe wanted to get his grade changed, but Joe could have other intentions. He may have wanted to make the professor angry, to fail the course, to provoke the professor to hit Joe so he would be fired, to show a friend how tough he is, to try out some new technique in assertiveness training. Why *is* Joe arguing?

Attribution processes come into play when we want to understand the behavior of others, to determine why it occurred, to figure out what caused it. This chapter deals with how we understand purposive behavior. Action, intended or purposive behavior, is not only complex, but it is also intimately related to the inner workings of the actor. The fact that action is related to actor purposes is a double-edged sword from the perceiver's standpoint. The good news is that meaningful, organized, and stable understandings of the action can be achieved by seeing the behavior as caused by these purposes, goals, and intentions. The bad news is that purposes, goals, and intentions are not the sort of things that can be perceived directly even by the actor. They must be inferred, and the perceiver must be willing to go beyond—well beyond—the information given by the behavior. The perceiver must infer psychic causes to understand something of the actor's personality. A presumptious business, this. But we perform such activities every day—many times. We seek to simplify our understanding of the behavior of others (and self) by inferring general causes for the behavior, and this causal ascription or attribution is perhaps the most important or at least the most daring of all the cognitive activities involved in person perception.

The Phenomenology of Social Behavior

PERSON AND OBJECT PERCEPTION

The major impetus to research on attribution was the theoretical analysis of Fritz Heider as presented initially in his paper on phenomenal causality (1944) and as elaborated in *The Psychology of Interpersonal Relations* (1958). Heider begins with three fundamental assumptions. The first is that adequate understanding of people's social behavior rests on a description of how they perceive and report their social worlds. Heider calls his psychology naive because it is based on the phenomenology of the average person and it relies heavily on common-sense language for describing person perception. Second, he assumes that people would like to predict and control their environments. He says that people want to be able to anticipate the effects their behavior will have on the environment and on themselves, and that they also would like to be able to structure their worlds so as to produce favorable outcomes. Their success rests, of course, on their ability to predict, particularly to predict the behavior of others. Third, Heider believes that there are basic similarities between object perception and person perception, and that the process of predicting the physical environment does not differ fundamentally from the process of predicting the behavior of others. The social world may be less predictable than the physical, but what predictability there is in the social world is achieved by the same processes that are involved in perception of the physical world.

Heider relies on a model of perception developed by Egon Brunswik (1956), usually called *probabilistic functionalism*. Brunswik sees the fundamental problem of perception as the coordination of perceptions with objects. Conscious experiences are always mediated both by the environment and by the physiology of the perceiver. As we pointed out in Chapter 1, what we "see" is not a passive reflection of the objects in the world, but an active interpretation of these objects. The retinal size of an object varies widely as it or we move about, yet we perceive the size as constant because we take account of the distance from object to retina; our perception is determined by our application of the invariance between retinal size and actual object size and distance. Brunswik was concerned with the processes by which we are able to perceive the characteristics of an object despite wide variability in the environmental conditions under which it is perceived. How are we able to know the "true" object and its characteristics?

Normally when we perceive objects we try to go beyond their mere surface characteristics, and often we are particularly interested in how objects fit into a causal texture. When objects "behave," we become aware that objects have certain properties that dispose them to react to environmental forces in particular ways. The fact that a ball is round means that the ball is disposed to roll when some environmental force pushes it. Heider argues that people also have dispositional properties that pre*dispose* them to behave in certain ways. For example, friendly people seem inclined to behave in a friendly way with only a slight push from norms and other aspects of the context.

However, there is unfortunately no perfect correspondence between dispositional properties and behavior. If the enduring or dispositional properties —such as friendliness—that we attempt to attribute to others were perfectly coordinated with a particular kind of behavior, and if there were a finite number of friendly behaviors that could be manifestations only of friendliness and of nothing else, the attribution would be completely determined, and the understanding of the process would be easy. But just as retinal size is only probabilistically related to object size, so a given behavior is only probabilistically related to a given personality trait. The example shown in Fig. 3.1 serves to illustrate the problem.

Helpful behavior may be an indication of either friendliness or of a desire to control, and the attribution you choose will probably make a difference in your reaction to the helper. You will feel quite differently about interacting with a person who wants to control you than you will about interacting with another who is friendly. The point of this discussion, however, is that behaviors are rarely if ever a perfect indication of one and only one dispositional property. Nevertheless, we do perceive stability in this complex, indeterminate environment of other people by making inferences about the other person's motives and dispositions. Heider's analysis represents an attempt to deal systematically with the conditions that affect the inference process.

ASPECTS OF PERSON PERCEPTION

The perception of causality   Central to Heider's entire theoretical position is the proposition that people perceive behavior as being caused, and that the causal locus can be either in the stimulus person (actor) or in the environment. Most of us feel we control and determine at least part of our actions, and we perceive others as having similar powers. In this most general of attribution processes, we act as scientists in attempting to find sufficient and necessary reasons for the occurrence of a particular behavior.

In Chapter 1 we emphasized that our perceptions of both the physical and social world are structured, stable, and meaningful. One of the fundamental ways we organize our experiences is in terms of causality. We feel uncomfortable with the notion that events just happen, that they are random or accidental; this leads us to feel that most or all events have understandable causes. Both Piaget (1930) and deCharms (1968) have suggested that our perceptions that events are caused are rooted in our own feelings of efficacy

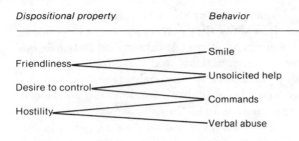

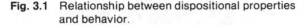

Fig. 3.1 Relationship between dispositional properties and behavior.

when our actions produce changes in the environment. Whatever their roots, our perceptions of causality are often immediate and compelling.

The Belgian psychologist Michotte (1963) reports a number of simple experiments which show that people immediately perceive causality. A small object, *A*, glides along and touches a stationary object, *B*. *A* stops, and *B* immediately begins moving in the direction *A* would have taken. In this situation subjects say that *A* pushed *B* or caused *B* to move. If, on the other hand, the movement of *B* is delayed for a brief time (more than 0.2 seconds) after *A* strikes it, the perception of causality is destroyed. From this demonstration we can at least say that subjects have a bias toward using causal language; moreover, there is every evidence that the perception of causality in this situation is direct and immediate. Heider and Simmel (1944) demonstrated similar effects when subjects viewed a short movie of one large and two small geometric figures moving around a boxlike structure with a "door" in it. In one sequence subjects perceived the larger shape to be "chasing" the smaller ones, thus causing them to flee, and they often attributed dispositional characteristics to the shapes. For example, the large figure was seen as a bully.

As we will see in the next few chapters, there is a wealth of additional observation and experimental demonstration that prove people organize their conceptions of the world at least partially around assumptions about causality. It seems to be a basic way of providing structure to experience. In fact, the tendency is so pervasive that people may even find causal reasons for random or chance events, and the propensity to perceive cause constitutes an important bias in our processing of information (see Chapter 10).

Heider not only emphasized our propensities to see the behavior of others as caused, but he also suggested that actions are caused by some combination of personal characteristics and environmental forces. The person may have done something because he had to do it, the environmental forces being unusually strong; or he may have done something because he wanted to do it, internal dispositional properties being strong enough to cause the behavior within the existing environment. In Heider's analysis an action outcome or effect is perceived to be an additive function of the effective environmental force and the effective person force. The person force is in turn a multiplicative function of the other's power or ability and the effort he exerts (referred to as trying). Experimental evidence does show that perceivers treat performance as a multiplicative function of ability and effort (Anderson and Butzin 1974). The additive relationship between environmental and personal force implies one of three things: (1) environmental force or personal force could produce the action outcome if the other were absent (either a woman with a rake or a strong wind could remove leaves from a lawn); (2) the environmental force could work toward the same end as the personal force and thus supplement it; or (3) the environmental force could work to oppose the personal force and thus reduce its effectiveness. The multiplicative relationship between ability and trying, on the other hand, implies that if either component were absent, the strength of the personal force would be zero. A person could try very hard to produce an event, but if with no power, the exertion would come to naught. Likewise, power becomes a force only when effort is exerted. In order to make an attribution of internal or external causality, the perceiver must estimate the relative strengths of the environmental and personal forces. One of the most important decisions the perceiver makes is an estimate of the extent to which the internal rather than the environmental force (including other people) was responsible for the effects of a person's actions.

The perception of can   *Can* is a dispositional property that refers to a relationship between ability and environment. A person may have high ability (be strong), but because the environmental forces are also strong (a house weighs many tons), that person may not be able to perform certain tasks (lifting the house). So the *can* factor has an internal component—ability, and an external component—environmental difficulty. Before attributions of *can* are made, we must know something about the environment, such as how difficult a particular task is. If a task is extremely easy, then virtually no ability is required to perform it; on the other hand, if a task is extremely difficult, so much ability is required that we say no one can do it. Therefore, if the environment is extremely easy or hard to cope with, we cannot infer much about an actor's abilities.

The perception of trying   In the naive analysis of action, perception of trying has two components, both internal: intention and exertion. The first refers to *what* a person wants to do (not *why* he or she wants to do it), and the second refers to how hard he or she tries to do it. When a professor says a student is trying hard in a course, the professor usually means both that the student wants to do well (that is, the student wants to learn the material and/or get a good grade) and that the student is working hard by doing the reading carefully and by attending class regularly. Perceived exertion is affected by perception of the person's abilities and environmental difficulty. A person of low ability must work harder on a given task than a person of high ability; difficult tasks require greater trying than easier ones. Heider does not discuss perceptions of exertion in great detail, probably because how hard a person works is often obvious; sweat and hours are good metrics for exertion.

Perceptions of what a person wants to do are not so immediately apparent because of the existence of *equifinality*, which in Heider's system refers to the existence of a number of paths to the same goal. What the person wants to do may be fixed, but there are a number of means to achieve aims. People who wish to demonstrate their friendliness may greet you warmly and engage you in conversation, invite you to dinner, and send you a card on your birthday. If things go as planned, you may infer that such a person is friendly toward you or is a friendly person. At the same time, a given action usually accomplishes several things. By talking with you on the street, a person may make you late for class, anger some other person who wants his or your attention, block traffic, and so on. Presumably, at least some of these consequences were unintended. In order to make dispositional inferences about the other person, the perceiver must determine which of the effects of an action were intended. Some of the cues we use in estimating whether or not the person is trying to produce a given effect are verbal statement of goals, the extent to which exertion is displayed, and behavior when actions are thwarted. In the latter instance, if a person attempts to avoid the encountered obstacle or engages in several behaviors that lead to the same apparent goal, we infer that the person is trying to reach that goal.

In his discussion of how people analyze action, Heider points to variables that are important determinants of our attributions of dispositional properties to others. We take into account information regarding the strength of environmental forces, and we then infer both ability and trying. Heider focuses attention on the distinctions between internal and external causality, personal and impersonal causality, and on the fact that our perceptions regarding *can* and *try* determine to a great extent the attribution of both intent and dispositional properties to others. Heider's discussion, however, cannot be considered a systematic theory that makes concrete, unequivocal predictions for actual situations. There have been three major attempts to rectify this lack of specificity: the first was presented by Jones and Davis (1965) in their paper, "From Acts to Dispositions"; the second by Kelley (1967) in "Attribution Theory in Social Psychology"; and the third in a paper by Kelley (1972a), "Causal Schemata and the Attribution Process," in a volume containing other influential analyses of various issues in attribution theory (Jones *et al.* 1972).

Attribution Models

CORRESPONDENT INFERENCES

The Jones and Davis (1965) attribution analysis makes some simplifying assumptions in the basic Heider model. Like Heider's model, it assumes that behavior has effects and that the perceiver attempts to infer the cause of behavior from the effects. Behavior is accounted for to the extent that it can be related to the personal disposition of the person perceived or to the environment; Jones and Davis concern themselves only with one's attributions to the other person. Thus, they are concerned primarily with inferences about internal causality. They also simplify Heider's discussion by assuming that actors are aware of what effects would result from their action and that they had the ability to create those effects. The perceiver then tries to infer what effects the actor intended to create, and under certain conditions those intentions are used to infer dispositional properties of the person.

The authors introduce the term *correspondence* to describe the extent to which (1) a given intention could cause the action, (2) a given dispositional property could produce the intention, and (3) by implication, a given dispositional property is responsible for the action. In general, an inference is correspondent to the extent that the same or similar words describe the behavior and its underlying cause. If a host serves a terrible dinner and one of the guests tells him the meal would have made Julia Child proud, you might call the guest's behavior kind and infer that (1) her intentions were kind, (2) her kind intention stemmed from a general disposition to be kind, and (3) therefore, she behaved in a kind way (complimented the host) *because* she is a kind person. Thus you would have inferred a personality trait *corresponding* to the behavior. You could, of course, infer noncorresponding reasons for the behavior. If, for example, the guest was an employee of the host and the dinner took place just before promotions were to be decided, you would have less confidence in your inference that the guest was kind because there are other salient reasons for the guest's behavior. In general, correspondent inferences are both extreme and certain. "She is very kind" is more correspondent than "She is fairly kind." Correspondence is assumed to be affected by several factors, but the most important ones are social desirability and number of noncommon effects.

Social desirability The variable of social desirability has two functions for Jones and Davis. In the first place, it is assumed that people intend desirable effects from their actions. A night on the town may have the effects of providing me with a good time, reducing my bank account, and giving me a hangover. Presumably I intended the first effect and not the other two.

Second, socially desirably effects provide little information about the distinctiveness of people. By social desirability of effects in this context, Jones and Davis really mean how usual or "normal" the effects are. If a woman performs a socially desirable, expected act, we have little evidence about her except that she is similar to most other people. For example, if a person asked a friend for a loan of a dollar and it was granted, we would not be prepared to say that the lender is particularly kind or helpful. Since most people would have done the same thing, the friend could simply have been responding to a norm about granting small loans to friends. We cannot tell whether her behavior was caused by her generosity or by her adherence to social norms. If, on the other hand, the friend had the money (that is, the ability to make the loan) and she refused to do so, we would be more likely to say that she is unkind, stingy, or something of the sort because her behavior was not normative. So the simple rule: *As the effects of behavior deviate more markedly from what the average person would do or norms say should be done, we can infer more about the person relative to other people and our attributions become more correspondent.* All other things being equal, we would feel more confident saying a woman is generous if she has given $500 to someone in need than if she has loaned 50 cents to a friend. Experiments by Ajzen (1971), Kane *et al.* (1976), and Lay *et al.* (1973) confirm that unpopular, non-normative, and statistically infrequent behavior lead to stronger inferences than more popular, normative, or common behavior. These findings support the Jones-Davis Model that suggests that "correspondence increases as the judged value of an attribute departs from the judge's conception of the average person's standing on that attribute" (Jones and Davis 1965, p. 224).

In a more recent theoretical paper, Jones and McGillis (1976) have made some additions to correspondent inference theory. They stress that correspondence will be increased to the extent that behavior departs from what the perceiver expects the stimulus person to do. Furthermore, they make quite explicit the idea that correspondent inferences reflect *information gain* about the stimulus person. For example, you might expect a career woman to support equal pay for males and females. If she does support that position you will know that she is like most career women, but you will know relatively little else about her. If, on the other hand, she supports males receiving greater pay, you will feel you have gained information about how she differs from other similar women, and you will be inclined to form a correspondent inference: she really believes what she says.

According to Jones and McGillis there are two general sources of expectations about others. *Category-based* expectancies are those we have on the basis of knowledge about what particular kinds of people are like. Thus, if you were to be surprised if a wealthy businessman started preaching socialism, your surprise would rest on the expectation that the category "businessman" is usually associated with more conservative political views. Category-based expectancies are like stereotypes (Chapter 2). *Target-based* expectancies are gained from knowledge about a particular actor. Thus, most of us would assume that a person who favors a larger welfare program would also favor tougher antiracism laws. To know that a person is a supporter of George Wallace, Ronald Reagan, or Edward Kennedy sets up expectations about other beliefs. According to the Jones-McGillis Model, there should be higher correspondence when behavior departs from target and category expectancies (or both). Evidence supports that view (Jones *et al.* 1971; Miller 1976).

However, the matter of inferences involves more than departures from expectancies. A person could perform an unexpected act for several reasons. For example, in the case of giving $500 to another person, reasons other than generosity—such as a high need for approval—could have produced the same behavior. For example, since generosity is socially approved, the person who gives $500 to another may simply have a higher need for approval than the person who lends 50 cents. Jones and Davis discuss this problem of interpretation under the rubric of noncommon effects.

Noncommon effects It is assumed that the actor is observed performing several actions or that action is a conscious decision in the light of known alternative courses of action. The idea behind noncommon effects is to find the effects that are unique to the chosen course. Suppose you have a friend who has recently had the opportunity of going through the agony of choosing a college. You observe that she chooses to go to Dartmouth over Smith or the University of Chicago. Table 3.1 shows some of the possible effects of attending each of the three. We can be relatively certain that the academic reputation was not a factor, because it is common to all three colleges, but there remain several noncommon effects. In picking Dartmouth over Chicago, your friend may have desired to be in a rural environment or to be away from home. The choice of Dartmouth over Smith could have reflected a preference for coeducation or for a rural over a smalltown environment. So although in this example you think you know something about your friend, there is still some ambiguity. However, if the choice had been Dartmouth over Stanford or Harvard, we could be reasonably certain that the noncommon effect of rural location was the determining factor. So the effect unique to the choice, namely getting a college in a rural environment, is seen as the intended effect.

In effect, Jones and Davis have postulated that correspondence of attribution will increase as the perceiver is able to eliminate possible causes of behavior. Newtson (1974) has studied this hypothesis experimentally, and he did find that there is greater correspondence as more effects are eliminated by an actor's choice. However, a choice to behave in a certain way could eliminate possible effects while it leaves several remaining. To observe that a student has chosen to babysit for a professor rather than drink with friends provides some information about him, but there could still be several effects of choosing to babysit (ingratiation, having a quiet place to study). Newtson also found that

TABLE 3.1
Common and Noncommon Effects of College Choice

Dartmouth	*Smith*	*University of Chicago*
In wilds	Small town	Large city
Coeducational	All-female	Coeducational
High academic reputation	High academic reputation	High academic reputation
Far away	Far away	Close to home

Dartmouth	*Harvard*	*Stanford*
In wilds	Large city	Small city
Coeducational	Coeducational	Coeducational
High academic reputation	High academic reputation	High academic reputation
Far away	Far away	Far away

there was greater correspondence when there were few rather than several effects remaining for a chosen behavior.

The attribution of intentions and personality characteristics or dispositions to others results, then, from a complex processing of information regarding qualities of the environment and of the person. The actual process of such attribution is probably not so conscious and rationalistic as Jones and Davis imply, but their model will serve as one working description of the processes of perceiving others.

PERSON AND SITUATION ATTRIBUTION

In a series of influential papers, Harold Kelley (1967, 1972a, 1972b) has explored some general questions about the perceived causes of behavior. While his analysis owes an obvious debt to Heider, he has moved well beyond the Heider Model to explore the general role of causality for social behavior.

There are in reality two distinct Kelley models. The first (Kelley 1967) initially concentrated on environmental attribution, but is readily applicable to internal attributions as well. This model assumes that the perceiver has available several observations of the actor's behavior and that the perceiver also has information on the behavior of other people in a similar situation. Kelley suggests that "An effect is attributed to the one of its possible causes with which, over time, it varies" (Kelley 1967, p. 108), and we will call this first model the *Covariation Model*. Whereas the *Correspondent Inference Theory* emphasizes the differential informativeness of behaviors in different settings and concentrates on attributions to specific dispositions, the *Covariation Model* assumes that perceivers make a general decision about whether the behavior was internally or externally caused without necessarily worrying about specific dispositions. Thus, the typical perceptual outcome from a study based on the Jones and Davis Model is an attribution to a particular disposition or attitude for the stimulus person; a more typical dependent measure in a study based on the Kelley reasoning would be whether the behavior was caused by general internal or external forces.

The second Kelley model, like the Correspondent Inference Theory, assumes that the perceiver has information only about a single instance of an actor's behavior. In this model (Kelley 1972a) the perceiver assumes that the behavior could have been produced by various combinations or configurations of causal factors. Thus, the perceiver must employ a particular causal schema to decide which particular combination of causes could have produced the behavior. We will term this model the *Causal Schemata Model*. Note that this model, like the Jones and Davis Model, also assumes that perceivers are interested in making attributions to specific dispositions.

It should be pointed out that these two models are not completely distinct from one another nor are they totally different from the Jones-Davis Model. However, it will simplify exposition to keep them separate for the time being. In a later section we will briefly explore their relationships. For now, let us turn to the Covariation Model.

Covariation Model   Each day we encounter a variety of behaviors performed by different people under different circumstances. We are all aware that people differ, and we are perhaps only slightly less aware that behavior differs as a function of the situation. Surely, we would expect most people to behave differently in the presence of the president of the United States than in the presence of their favorite dog. It is also true that behavior may change with time or with more particular characteristics of the situation.

Kelley (1967) took explicit account of the fact that behavior of people seems to vary as a function of who is behaving, what the objects or entities in the situation are, and how the entities are encountered. We may note that some people like a particular movie while others do not, that some movies are liked more than others, and that a movie may be liked more in a theater than on television. In examining reactions to dogs we note that some people are dog lovers while others are not, that some dogs elicit love while others are ignored and hated, and that reactions to the dog vary according to whether it is barking or playing. In formal terms, Kelley notes that behavior varies with *persons* (or actors), with *entities*, and with *modality* or *time*. The terms *modality* and *time* may cause some initial confusion. Kelley is simply suggesting that even a dog-lover facing a perfectly lovable dog will not produce perfectly consistent reactions. For example, the dog-lover may like to pet a dog but not like to take it for walks; the dog-lover may pet the dog when it is clean but not when it is wet; the dog-lover may act more friendly to a nonbarking than to a barking dog, and may like the dog more at 5 p.m. than at 5 a.m. Thus, reactions to dogs vary not only according to the actor's attitudes toward dogs and according to the dog's qualities, but according to the *context* in which the reaction to the dog takes place. Kelley calls these contextual features *modality* and *time*.

In the Covariation Model, it is assumed that the perceiver has information about how a single actor has reacted to a single entity. The perceiver will first want to know whether the actor's behavior is the same to the entity over several different times and ways of interacting with the entity. Are movies and dogs consistently liked better in some situations than others? Thus, *consistency* information refers to generality of the behavior across modality/time or context. Second, the perceiver will want to know whether the actor behaves in a particular way to only a particular stimulus or entity or whether the actor behaves the same way to all similar entities. Does Jane like all dogs or only this one? *Distinctiveness* information, then, refers to the generality of the behavior across entities. Third, the perceiver will seek information about how other people have reacted to the entity. *Consensus* information refers to generality of reaction across actors.

Suppose you wanted to know whether Joe (actor) is really in love with Helen (entity). Ideally, you would like to know whether Joe's behavior toward Helen is consistent. Is he loving and attentive both at parties and in more private circumstances? If Joe's behavior is more attentive in party situations than in private (low consistency), you might be inclined to feel that Joe values

Helen more for her ability to cast a good light on him at parties than for her more private qualities. Joe's reactions might be perfectly natural, but they are hardly the stuff of which love is made. Suppose, however, that Joe passes the *consistency* test: he seems to like Helen in a wide variety of situations (high consistency). However, we still cannot say for sure that Joe is in love with Helen. Perhaps Joe is quite nice to everyone in a wide variety of circumstances (low *distinctiveness*), surely commendable behavior but hardly love for all that. So we will want to know if Joe is discriminating. We would be more inclined to say that Joe loves Helen if we were to find out that he is much nicer to Helen than to his other friends; in that case, the *distinctiveness* of his behavior would be high. However, we are still not home free. Suppose we were to find out that everyone seems to like Helen (high *consensus*). That speaks well for Helen but leaves us unsure about whether Joe is in love with her. Only if Joe is also nicer to Helen than most other people are (low *consensus*) would we feel confident that Joe loves Helen.

To make a confident attribution we would need information on all three things. If Joe's behavior to Helen is similar in many different contexts (high consistency), addressed to her alone (high distinctiveness), and more positive than most people's (low consensus), we would be inclined to say that Joe loves Helen. If the evidence of consistency, distinctiveness, and consensus had taken a different pattern, we would not have been so likely to conclude that Joe loves Helen, but we might have felt confident in drawing other conclusions. For example, if Joe's behavior were consistent, nondiscriminatory (he seems to love everyone), and few other people seem to love Helen (low consensus), we might be inclined to see Joe as a loving person. According to Kelley, the combination of high consistency, low distinctiveness, and low consensus pushes us toward a person (or actor) attribution. On the other hand, high consistency (Joe always shows affection to Helen), high distinctiveness (he likes Helen more than others), and high consensus (everyone likes Helen), focuses the attribution onto external factors—in this case, Helen. In the example given in the last paragraph, the combination of high consistency (Joe is always nice to Helen), high distinctiveness (he is nicer to Helen than he is to most people), and low consensus (no one else is nice to Helen) would push the perceiver to yet another type of attribution. There must be something unique about the Joe-Helen relationship—say Joe loves Helen—which we might call entity-actor interaction or combination.

The validity of this model was tested by Leslie McArthur (1972). She gave her subjects several brief statements containing combinations of consistency, distinctiveness, and consensus information. For example, consider the behavior "John laughed at the comedian." Consistency information was varied by telling subjects that John has almost always (high consistency) or has almost never (low consistency) laughed at the same comedian. Distinctiveness information took the form of whether John also laughed at other comedians (high) or at no other comedians (low). Consensus information was varied by stating that other people also laughed at the comedian (high) or others did not laugh at the comedian (low). These three types of information were combined in descriptions of situations involving information about emotions (Sue is afraid of the dog), accomplishments (George translates the sentence incorrectly), opinions (Bill thinks his teacher is unfair), and actions (Barbara contributes a large sum of money to an auto safety fund). Subjects were asked to say whether the emotions, actions, accomplishments, or opinions were due to (1) something about the actor (e.g., John likes comedians or perhaps has a sense of humor), or (2) something about the stimulus or entity (e.g., the comedian was funny). Although our previous discussion has concentrated on actor and entity attributions, McArthur allowed her subjects to make other kinds of attributions as well: something about the circumstances (e.g., John was drunk), some combination or interaction of the person and stimulus (e.g., John likes the particular comedian), or other combinations (e.g., John likes this comedian when John is drunk).

McArthur found that for all combinations of information actor attributions were the most common followed by circumstance attributions. Entity or stimulus attributions were relatively infrequent. There are two important points to make about this. First, subjects seem more inclined to see behavior as due to internal (actor) dispositions than to external (or stimulus) factors, a point we will return to in Chapters 5 and 10. Second, although attribution theorists have stressed the importance of internal (actor) and external (stimulus) attributions, in McArthur's data other attributions (particularly circumstance) were relatively common; in fact, well over half the attributions were to neither person nor situation.

What patterns of information give rise to these various attributions? McArthur's data generally support Kelley's reasoning, although her results are fairly complex. Actor attributions were most common with high consistency (John always laughs at this particular comedian), low consensus (no one else laughs at the comedian), and low distinctiveness (John laughs at most other comedians). Given that combination of information, subjects are prone to decide that John has a great sense of humor. Attributions to the comedian (stimulus attribution) were high when John always laughs at the comedian (high consistency), everyone else laughs at the comedian (high consensus), and John laughs only at this comedian (high distinctiveness). A funny person, this comedian. Note that while both stimulus and actor or person attributions require high consistency, the two attributions are opposite in the consensus and distinctiveness information.

What about the other six patterns of information? Generally, high consistency with either low consensus-high distinctiveness or high consensus-low distinctiveness result in perceptions of a particular unique interaction between John and the comedian. The patterns that have John behaving inconsistently to the comedian (John likes the comedian tonight in person, but not tomorrow on television) push perceivers to circumstance attributions. If John is an unreliable fellow, people feel that John's laughter tonight must be due to his good mood or perhaps to his being drunk.

McArthur did not find these sources of information equally important. Consistently information was mainly important in controlling whether the attributions were to circumstance on the one hand or to the actor or stimulus on the other hand. Distinctiveness was the main determinant of whether the attribution was to the actor (John laughs at everyone) or to the stimulus (the comedian is funny). Interestingly, consensus information was quite unimportant in general. However, Ruble and Feldman (1976) pointed out that in McArthur's study consensus information was always presented first so that subjects may have forgotten about it when they made their attributional judgments. They found that consensus information was more powerful when it was presented last.

However, Ross (1977) and Nisbett, *et al.* (1976) have argued that consensus information is generally underutilized by perceivers. Since both Kelley and Jones-Davis emphasize the importance of consensus information, this constitutes an important disconfirmation of attribution models if true. We will postpone a fuller discussion of this problem to Chapter 10. Despite this problem, results of McArthur's study and the studies of others (Karaz and Perlman 1975; Zuckerman 1978a; Ruble and Feldman 1976) generally confirm the Kelley Covariation Model. Behavior is attributed to the cause with which it varies.

One important limitation on Kelley's original model is that perceivers are assumed to have complete information on a variety of possible causes. But commonly if we observe an actor in only one situation we may not have information about consistency or distinctiveness. Do people still make attributions with incomplete information, and, if so, how? Orvis, Cunningham, and Kelley (1975) argued that the perceiver tries to find the most appropriate pattern to match in the case of missing information. For example, stimulus attributions are pronounced with a high-consensus, high-distinctiveness, high-consistency pattern (HHH); person attributions follow a low-consensus, low-distinctiveness, high-consistency pattern (LLH); and circumstance follows a LHL pattern. If these are three primary patterns, what does a perceiver do if he knows only that the consensus is high (that is, a H— condition)? Of the three primary patterns presented, the H— set is most compatible with the HHH. If all we know is that everyone laughed at the comedian, we are likely to infer that John laughs only at this comedian (high distinctiveness) and that he always laughs at him (high consistency), and this pattern would suggest an entity attribution. Similarly, if the perceiver knew only that John laughs at the comedian only some of the time, signaling low consistency (—L), the perceiver should match the information with the nearest complete paradigm (LHL) and infer that no one else laughed and that John laughs only at this comedian (LHL)—leading to a circumstance attribution. In general, Orvis *et al.* did find that subjects filled in incomplete information according to the closest complete paradigm and made their attributions accordingly.

Causal Schemata Model More recently, Kelley (1972a) elaborated a model to account for perceptions of single observations of behavior. Kelley assumes that the perceiver tries to make sense of a configuration of causal factors. Several causes could have produced the behavior; which was the effective cause? He assumes that people have causal schemata to interpret the world and that these causal schemata:

> reflect the individual's basic notions of reality and his assumptions about the existence of a stable external world—a world comprised of permanent, though moving and apparently variant, objects; a world separate from and independent of himself; and a world seen by other persons in the same way as by himself (p. 153).

Causal schemata allow us to make causal sense of the world, and they provide stability and organization to the perceived world.

Perhaps an example will make the logic clear. High school teachers have some sense that a student may work hard in a course for any of several reasons. The student may wish to please parents, may have a crush on the teacher, may wish to go to Harvard, or may simply enjoy the material of the course (and it should go without saying that these reasons are not mutually exclusive). Either wanting to please parents or enjoying the task may be a *sufficient* cause for hard study. This, then, is a situation that Kelley terms *Multiple Sufficient Causes*, a situation where any of a number of factors are sufficient to cause the behavior.

Attribution theorists have, however, not been concerned to predict how people infer effects from causes, but rather the reverse. According to the Kelley notion (which he adapts from Piaget), the schema just described is reversible because we can infer cause from effect, as well as the reverse; more generally, if we know that the effect (hard work) has occurred and if we know something about one of the other causes (concern for parental approval), we can infer something about the other cause. If we know that the student has no concern for parental approval and that she worked hard, the schema in Fig. 3.2 indicates that the other cause, enjoying the material, must have been at work. Conversely, if we know that the student hated the material but worked hard, we could infer concern for parental approval. If, on the other hand, we were to discover that a person who worked hard also had concern for parental approval, we could infer nothing about enjoyment as a cause since the presence of one sufficient cause (parental approval) is enough to explain the behavior.

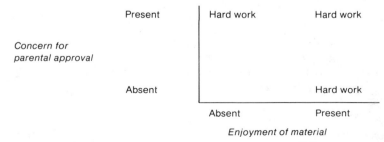

Fig. 3.2 An example of multiple sufficient cause.

Thus, given that the effect has occurred, perceivers should make stronger inferences that *A* was the effective cause when *B* is absent than when *B* is present. When *B* is present, *A could be* the effective cause; when *B* is absent, though, *A must* be the cause. When an effect has occurred and one cause is known to be present, the second cause will be *discounted* as an effective element in the causal picture. This is known as the *discounting principle*.

While most relevant research had measured perceptions of internal causes when external causes were present or absent, the Kelley Model does not require that one cause be internal and the other external; both could be either internal or external. For example, helping behaviors should be attributed more strongly to altruism if desire for approval is not also present; note that both causes are internal.

In the examples given, both causes *facilitate* the behavior, but Kelley's Model can also handle situations where one or both causes *inhibit* behavior. For example, suppose we know that the student's hard work is facilitated by enjoyment of the material and that it is inhibited by his athletic pursuits. If we know he has studied hard and that the inhibitory cause was also present (that is, it is football season), we should be willing to make a strong inference that he enjoys the work since he "overcame" the inhibitory cause. Conversely, when the inhibitory cause is absent we should infer weaker enjoyment, since there was nothing to overcome. Kelley calls this tendency to increase the perceived power of a facilitative cause when behavior overcomes an inhibitory force *augmentation*. In one research example, competitive behavior was seen as due to competitive motivation more when a game encouraged cooperative rather than competitive behavior (Enzle, Hansen, and Lowe 1975). Thus the perception of the competitive motivation force was augmented.

Another type of causal schema is *Multiple Necessary Cause*. The logic now suggests that if the effect were present, then both causes must also be present, but if the effect does not occur, either or both of the causes may be absent. For example, many forms of achievement require both effort and ability. Similarly, you may assume that a professor will help you with something you do not understand if the professor is both a helpful sort and has time. You may feel that your roommate will agree to your request for some quiet study time only if she is both in a good mood and has work of her own to do (see Fig. 3.3).

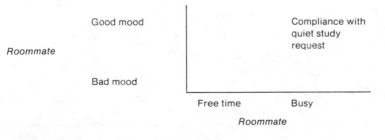

Fig. 3.3 An example of multiple necessary cause.

The logic of the Multiple Necessary Cause Schema is fairly simple. If the effect is present, then *both* causes must also be present. Note that with this schema there may be considerable uncertainty about some causes when the effect has not been produced. If the effect is not present, the perceiver would know that at least one cause was absent, but the perceiver would not know which one (or both) was the culprit. When a student fails an exam, the lack of success (effect) could be produced by inadequate trying, low ability, or both.

Kelley discusses several other kinds of causal schemata, which we will not discuss in detail. For example, the causes and the effects can be graded in strength. In this case if the perceiver knows how strong the effect is and knows how strong one cause is, the perceiver can infer the strength of the other cause. As shown in Table 3.2, it is reasonable to believe that as enjoyment of the material and parental pressure both increase, the number of hours spent studying should go up. If the perceiver knows that each increment in parental pressure produces five hours additional study time and that each enjoyment increment produces two additional study hours, it will be easy to determine that with only a moderate amount of pressure resulting in nine hours of studying, enjoyment of the material must be great. Of course, perceivers rarely have such exact knowledge, but may, nonetheless, be able to relate the strength of effects to the strength of causes, even if only crudely.

COMPARISON OF MODELS

We have now examined several attribution models; clearly the models, at least in broad outline, have some validity. In the next chapter we will explore research generated by these models. But before we do this, it will be useful to summarize the general features of attribution models, to point out their basic similarities and differences. Table 3.3 summarizes the major differences.

According to Kelley (1973), if the perceiver has information on several actor behaviors over time as well as the behavior of others in the situation, the Covariation Model applies. If the perceiver has information on only a single actor's single behavior, then the perceiver will use the Causal Schema Model. Although Kelley (1973) has considered the Covariation Model as one kind of causal schema, in point of fact, the logic of the two models is different. Further-

TABLE 3.2
An Example of Graded Causes and Effects

Enjoyment of material	Number of hours spent studying		
Like	4	9	14
Neutral	2	7	12
Dislike	0	5	10
	Weak	Moderate	Strong
		Parental Pressure	

TABLE 3.3
Comparison of Various Attribution Models

	Initial information	Cognitive process	Attributional outcome
Correspondent Inference (Jones-Davis)	1. Behavior of single actor 2. Knowledge of: (a) effects chosen and foregone (b) desirability or expectedness of effects often calculated from consensus (1) category-based (2) individual-based	Correspondence increases as: (1) noncommon effects for many decision alternatives decrease (2) social desirability or expectedness of behavior decreases	Personal disposition corresponding to behavior
Covariation (Kelley)	1. Behavior of actor 2. Other behavior of actor (a) over similar entities (distinctiveness) (b) over contexts (consistency) 3. Behavior of others (consensus)	Quasi-statistical reasoning with consistency acting as error and high distinctiveness and consensus leading to entity and low distinctiveness and consensus to person attributions	External (entity, circumstance) or internal (person) attribution
Causal Schema (Kelley)	1. Behavior of single actor 2. Knowledge of probable causes 3. Knowledge of strength of one cause	1. Decision about which causal schema applies 2. Application of causal schema (a) discounting (b) augmentation (c) division (graded effects)	Specific dispositional or external cause depending on causes considered

more, although Jones and McGillis (1976) have attempted to relate the Jones and Davis Correspondent Inference Model to the Kelley Covariation Model, it is actually much closer in spirit to the Causal Schema Model.

First consider the case of observation of a single bit of behavior. Both the Causal Schema Model and Correspondence Model allow the perceiver to make an attributional choice between person and entity-situation. If one has information that an effect has occurred and has information on the presence or absence of one possible cause, inferences about another cause are possible. The discounting principle suggests that if an environmental force is strong and if it facilitates the same behavior as an internal disposition, nothing can be concluded about the internal disposition. If, on the other hand, the environmental facilitative force is weak and the effect occurs anyway, it must be because of the personal disposition. The augmentation principle suggests that if external forces "fight" the internal disposition, attribution to the internal disposition is stronger in the presence of the external force.

The Jones-Davis Correspondent Inference Theory would generally make the same sorts of predictions. However, while Kelley seems to feel that people learn general cognitive schemata, Jones and Davis have the perceiver weighing forces in terms of noncommon effects and social desirability. Behavior that violates expectations leads to internal correspondent attributions. Presumably expectations about the actor's behavior are based on the perception of strong external (category-based expectations) or internal (person-based expectations) forces. So the greater correspondence after expectations are disconfirmed is very much like Kelley's augmentation principle. Similarly, behavior that confirms expectation can be thought of in terms of discounting; when there are group membership or consistency forces that would lead a person to do something, we are less certain that the behavior was performed because of some unique intention.

Kelley's discounting principle and the Jones-Davis notion of noncommon effects are also quite similar. Jones and Davis have suggested that if there are many common effects between a chosen and an unchosen action, you will be unsure which of the effects was intended. This is similar to a discounting of a single cause if there are several other potential causes. One way in which the Jones-Davis Model is more powerful is that it is not limited to considering only two possible causes, so that many potential causes can be discounted with few noncommon effects.

Whatever the differences in hypothesized cognitive processes between the two models, they generally make the same predictions. It is important to note, however, that the major attribution in both models is a specific person or dispositional force. Thus, both models suggest that when one observes single behaviors in the presence of specific environmental or personal forces, something can (under some circumstances) be inferred about the specific internal force. We remind the reader that although the Correspondent Inference Theory allows only for internal attributions, the Causal Schema Model can easily be extended to include attribution to external forces.

There are other differences between the models. For example, nothing in the Jones-Davis Model corresponds to the Multiple Necessary Cause Schema. Also, the Jones-Davis Model assumes that the actors make a choice among alternatives, and nothing in the Causal Schema Model allows for easy incorporation of these choice data.

What happens when we move from the single-behavior to the multiple-behavior case? Kelley's Covariation Model assumes that people have information on the extent to which the actor's behavior is generalized over other actors (consensus), other entities (distinctiveness), and contexts (consistency). These kinds of information have parallels in the other attribution models.

Jones and McGillis (1976) have examined the relationships among these covariation factors and various perceiver expectations. For example, consensus information is similar to category-based expectations because both involve knowledge about the actual or probable behavior of other people. For both the Correspondent Inference Model and the Covariation Model, high consensus (or meeting category-based expectations) pushes the attribution toward external factors.

Consistency and distinctiveness are superficially similar to target-based expectations because both involve knowledge about the actor's other behavior. However, there are major differences: for Jones-Davis, departures from expectations (inconsistencies) are most informative about the person, while for Kelley, consistency with past behavior leads to the strongest person attributions. There are ways of resolving this apparent contradiction (see Jones and McGillis 1976), but the two theories are really pointing to different variables and processes. Kelley's theory points to one obvious fact—if we see a person behaving consistently over many contexts and entities, we will certainly feel that we know something about the person. Clearly, however, we will also feel we have gained interesting information about a person to the extent that the person violated our expectancies based on his or her past behavior. But the two kinds of information are different. Kelley wants the perceiver to decide whether the behavior was caused by a general internal characteristic, such as being a movie-lover. However, situations in which violation of expectancies leads to correspondent attributions are those in which a *specific* attitude is inferred. For example, if we knew a person never liked movies but found that she really enjoyed *Star Wars*, we would indeed feel that we have learned something about this person—perhaps that she likes science fiction movies. We would not have gained any information about her general dispositions, but we would know more about her attitudes toward a given movie or perhaps toward a class of movies. This kind of inference counts as a person-stimulus attribution for Covariation Models.

It is possible to formulate even more elaborate comparisons of the various attribution models. Although the models often use different terminologies, they also often make equivalent predictions given equivalent data. Nonetheless, the theories do differ because they point to the importance of different kinds of information, processes of reasoning, and outcomes of the attribution process.

We would also like to emphasize that there is no reason to prefer the blandness of consistency to the spice of diversity. Let's relish the differences among the models.

We think it is also appropriate to reemphasize a point we make often throughout this book. It is unlikely that there is a single model of human cognition or motivation that describes all behavior or all thinking in all situations. We suspect that sometimes people act as if they believed in the Correspondent Inference Theory, while at other times they perform the naive statistical reasoning of the Covariation Model. There is no reason to believe that people cannot do both — a great deal depends on what kinds of information the person has and what she or he wants to find out. Faced with information about choice and wanting to infer something about a specific disposition, people may use a form of Correspondent Inference Theory. However, if the person is more interested in a generalized attribution to the environment or to the person, a form of Covariation Model analysis might be useful. We doubt that perceivers try on every model or care much about finding the most correct attribution using the most adequate form of reasoning. It is more likely that they think about the question that interests them and that they stop when they get an answer that satisfies them (Jones 1976).

The kinds of attribution models we have been considering have had a remarkable impact not only on the study of person perception but on psychology in general. In this chapter we have dealt with the theories in some detail and have described some research that supports the theories in broad outline. In the next chapter we will consider research that has been stimulated by attribution models. Some of this research was designed to test a single model, but our concern in the next chapter will be less on the adequacy of the individual models than on the power of attribution theorizing to generate new research and to explain important issues in person perception. In Chapter 5 we will further apply attribution ideas to perception of self.

Summary

While attribution ideas have a long history, the seminal work of Fritz Heider (1958) formalized these ideas and brought them to the attention of social psychologists. Central to Heider's thinking was the idea that we perceive the behavior of people as purposive and intentional, and that behavior can be seen as caused by a combination of internal (person) and environmental factors. In more recent years several psychologists have tried to formulate attribution theories based on the Heider insights, models that employed simplifications but that were better able to generate empirical research.

Correspondent Inference Theory as developed by Jones and Davis concentrates on attributions to specific personal dispositions. Jones and Davis hypothesize that attributions become more correspondent as behavior departs more from the usual (or consensus), and to the extent that the behavior chosen is different from nonchosen behavior in relatively few ways.

Kelley's Covariance Theory suggests that behavior is caused by the factors with which it covaries. Behavior can be seen to vary (or be generalized) over actors, entities, and contexts. Generally, behavior that is consistent over contexts, in which many people engage (high consensus), and that is performed only in the presence of a particular entity (highly distinctive) is seen as being caused by that entity. On the other hand, behavior that is consistent, that few people perform, and that is nondistinctive in the sense that the same behavior is performed to several similar entities is seen as being due to personal characteristics of the actor. Finally, Kelley's Causal Schema Model suggests that when people know that two causes could have produced an effect, under some circumstances knowledge that the effect has occurred and whether the other cause is present allows inferences about the other cause.

While these models have basic similarities, they also differ in important ways. In particular they emphasize different processes, information available to perceivers, and outcomes of the attribution process. Each of the models has something important to offer in our understanding about perceptions of human behavior.

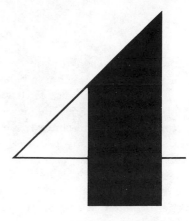

In the last chapter we discussed a number of attribution models. These models have appealed to psychologists partially because they give people credit for reasoning about their social world. They have also been influential because the attributions we make about others are likely to be important intervening variables between the raw stimuli presented by other people and our behavior toward them. Some of the research we discuss in this chapter was motivated by the desire to test one or another implication of one or another attribution model. However, most of the research was stimulated by a concern to explain certain salient problems in person perception: attributions of attitude, perception of behavior change, attributions following success and failure, and attributions of responsibility.

Representative Research Problems

ATTRIBUTION OF ATTITUDE

Role playing and normative demands   It is obvious that in social life people may on occasion make statements they do not believe. People may publicly conform to the group's attitudes for a variety of reasons (Kiesler and Kiesler 1969), and there is always the possibility that a person may lie in order to ingratiate (Jones 1964). Needless to say, there are also more benign forms of distortion. Gouldner (1960), Goffman (1955), and others have pointed to powerful norms in our society which tend to guarantee that in specified circumstances certain kinds of information will be communicated. A friend who has failed an exam is usually comforted; the "faces," or self-presentations, of others are usually accepted in public. Furthermore, we tend to tailor our public pronouncements to fit the existing attitudes of our audiences, at least in "polite company"; too much disagreement is in bad taste. Under these circumstances, we may find inferring the real attitudes and beliefs of another problematical. Given that there are occasions when there is no correspondence between another's true attitudes and public behavior, we have an attribution problem.

The public expression of attitudes could be a function of internal factors (real attitudes) or external factors (normative demands).

Let's examine for a moment our perceptions of a politician's "true" attitudes. In running for office, a politician must balance off several competing pressures. Politicians may want to state their own opinions on various issues, but they must also make sure that these public expressions are popular enough with the electorate and sufficiently congruent with their party's policy to enable them to be elected. The extent to which a politician's stated opinion on an issue is popular with the public (or congruent with his party's policy) affects the perception of that opinion as an expression of true beliefs. For example, one somehow feels confident that Sen. Edward Kennedy believes in busing when he makes a probusing speech in Boston during a period of great animosity toward busing. We would not be so certain about the beliefs of a politician who makes a similar speech before the NCAA National Convention or before a suburban group advocating school integration. In terms of the Jones and Davis Model, we make a more correspondent inference in the case of the Boston speech, because the behavior is low in social desirability and because speaking his own mind truthfully is the only effect that Senator Kennedy could have intended. According to Kelley's augmentation principle, one will feel that a particular cause (in this case Kennedy's attitudes) produces the behavior when the other causes (desire for public approval) is not also a likely cause.

Supporting this reasoning, Mills and Jellison (1967) found that a speech given to a "hostile" audience was perceived as a more sincere speech than the same speech given to a "friendly" audience. Furthermore, subjects in the hostile audience were more persuaded.

Eisinger and Mills (1968) extended this thinking in an experiment concerned with the effects of extremity on perceived sincerity. They found that subjects perceived a communicator who argued an extreme position on either side of an issue as being more sincere than a communicator who argued a moderate position. If the communicator argues the subject's own position, it is plausible that the sincerity may be merely a function of agreement with the subject. On the other hand, if the communicator takes an extreme position counter to that of the subject, perceived sincerity may be due to the perception that he has taken an unpopular position. Thus, the perception of sincerity seems to be a function of the person's capacity to counteract normative, external forces.

This sort of effect can be observed in other sorts of situations as well. For example, each of us has to play certain roles on occasion. Since the role exists as a kind of external force, attribution theories predict that real attitudes can be inferred with more certainty when the person behaves out of—rather than in—role.

In an experiment by Jones, Davis, and Gergen (1961), subjects listened to a tape recording of a supposed job interview. Half the interviews were for the job of a submariner and half were for the job of an astronaut. Subjects (and supposedly the interviewee) were told that the submariner job required other-directed qualities, such as the ability to get along with others, while the astronaut job required more inner-directed qualities. Within each of these conditions half of the interviewees described themselves as other-directed, and half described themselves as inner-directed.

The result was that some subjects heard an interviewee describe himself as "in-role"—as having the characteristics called for by the job (that is, astronaut-inner, or submariner-other)—while other subjects heard one of the "out-of-role" descriptions (that is, astronaut-other or submariner-inner). Since the in-role descriptions could have been produced either by the interviewee's real characteristics or by the interviewee's attempts to appear qualified for the job, subjects should feel somewhat doubtful about the interviewee's real characteristics. On the other hand, out-of-role behavior could, in this simplified analysis, have been caused only by the interviewee's real disposition. As expected, out-of-role interviewees were perceived as revealing their true characteristics more than were in-role interviewees.

However, the results given above make sense only if the interviewee wants to get the job—that is, if the interviewee is responsive to the external job forces. An experiment by Messick and Reeder (1972) showed that out-of-role behavior leads to strong attributions only when the interviewee wanted the job. Also, not all personal dispositions are subject to the role-playing effect. It is probably easier to role-play some dispositions than others. Reeder, Messick, and Van Avermaet (1977) argued that people with certain skills can role-play both the skilled and the unskilled roles, while unskilled people presumably are less able to role-play skilled roles. So, for example, a person who behaves in an intellectual manner has to have intellectual skills whether or not she is responding to external role demands, whereas a person who acts nonintellectual could be either intellectual or not. When a person acts nonintellectual, attributions are more subject to the presence or nonpresence of external demands.

Jones-Harris   Another kind of experiment to test the same basic idea in a different context was performed by Jones and Harris (1967). They performed several experiments in which perceivers read essays defending either the popular side (Castro is bad) or the unpopular side (Castro is good) of a controversial issue. The perceivers were further told that the essay writer could have chosen the side of the essay to defend or that the essay writer was assigned a particular position. Theoretically, according to Correspondent Inference Theory and Causal Schemata Models, behavior performed under the strong external constraint of experimenter demands to write a particular essay should be uninformative about the writer's true attitudes. One's best guess about the writer's attitudes under those circumstances would be that the writer conforms with the moderately popular side. On the other hand, when the speaker has chosen which side to defend, the speaker's attitudes can be inferred with some confidence.

The theoretical predictions and actual results are shown in Table 4.1. As expected, perceivers inferred true attitudes in line with those expressed when

TABLE 4.1
Predictions and Results from a Study of Attitude Attribution
(After Jones and Harris 1967)

	Choice*	No choice*
Anti-Castro (popular position)		
Prediction	Highly anti-Castro	Moderately anti-Castro
Result	17	23
Pro-Castro (unpopular position)		
Prediction	Highly pro-Castro	Moderately anti-Castro
Result	60	44

* Higher numbers indicate more pro-Castro.

the writer had a choice—that is, when there was no other cause present. However, contrary to predictions, they also inferred attitudes from behavior (although less strongly) even in the presence of the strong external, no-choice force. It has been suggested that "behavior engulfs the field" (Heider 1958), and perhaps we really do judge people on their behavior even when we should "discount" internal causes of behavior because strong external causes (in the form of social pressure or money) are present.

However, before suggesting that attribution models are incorrect in their predictions, we should examine some other possible explanations for this tendency to infer attitudes from behavior under external constraint. One possibility is that the subjects in the Jones and Harris experiment who argued unpopular positions did a good job of arguing. Perhaps the cogency of their arguments was "held against" them. They were required only to argue the position; their eloquence may have been taken as evidence of conviction. People who are forced to argue against their own positions ought to do so with minimal persuasiveness.

In one of the Jones and Harris experiments there is some evidence that bears on the interpretation of using minimal persuasion when arguing against your convictions. In that experiment subjects were instructed to give a speech either in favor of or against a popular position, and each gave an ambiguous speech. The very ambivalence of the speech may have indicated that the subject's heart was not in the essay, and it would be relatively easy to infer that the subject did not believe what he was instructed to say. The data support this conjecture. When the speech itself was ambivalent, subjects instructed to give the pro-speech were seen as more anti than subjects who were instructed to give the anti-speech.

A number of studies have also investigated the style or quality of role-playing as a factor in attitude attributions. For example, Jones, Worchel, Goethals, and Grumet (1971) varied the number of arguments that were given for and against the advocated position. As expected, when the writer wrote a strong essay (four essays for and none against the argued position) the basic Jones-Harris pattern of results was reproduced: subjects perceived the essay writers as being in favor of the position they argued, with some (but not complete) reduction in this tendency when the essay writers supposedly had no choice in which side to defend. When, however, the essay was weak (two essays for and two against the argued position) subjects perceived the essay writers who had a choice as believing the positions they argued, but subjects saw the no-choice writers as holding the *opposite* position from the one they argued. Schneider and Miller (1975) also found that quality of arguments affects the tendency of behavior to engulf the field. When the essay writer used stupid and irrational arguments, there was a lessened tendency to attribute true attitudes in line with the defended position under no-choice conditions. However, these same authors found that the enthusiasm of a videotaped speaker did not affect the basic Jones-Harris effect.

Another variable that might affect the relationship of choice and attribution is an expectancy about what the stimulus person's true attitudes are. Jones and McGillis (1976) have argued that target-based expectancies—those based on prior information about the stimulus person—ought to play a role in attribution. One assumes that a liberal woman would make liberal statements even if she had not been asked to make such statements. However, when a liberal publically makes a conservative statement, matters are more complex. If she did not have a choice, one assumes that coercion was responsible for the speech. If she did have a choice, however, then she must really have believed what she said. Our liberal friend must really be quite conservative on this issue because she overcame her own constraining consistency needs. The general prediction, then, is that choice will not affect attributions if the public statement is expected. If it is unexpected, then inferences to real attitudes should be much stronger under choice than under nonchoice. Jones et al. (1971) manipulated expectancy through knowledge of other attitudes; Miller (1976) manipulated expectancy through physical appearance. These studies confirmed the predictions (see Fig. 4.1).

There is also some evidence that choice is not particularly salient for the perceiver in this situation. Miller et al. (1977) got a reduction in the Jones-Harris effect by asking the subjects how much choice the stimulus person had. However, other attempts to make the external constraint salient by having the perceiver write essays beforehand under constraint show minimal effects on the basic Jones-Harris finding (Snyder and Jones 1974).

Remember: the basic attribution prediction of more correspondent attributions with weak rather than strong external forces has been confirmed. The problem is that perceivers seem to be making too much of the behavior in the no-choice or high external force conditions. In truth, the Jones-Harris effect is hard to destroy. Perceivers have a perverse lack of sensitivity to the attribution prediction and are seemingly irrational in their failure to consider strongly the role of external forces in affecting behavior. This important result is actually part of a much larger set of biases in the attribution process and will be considered in a different context in Chapters 5 and 10.

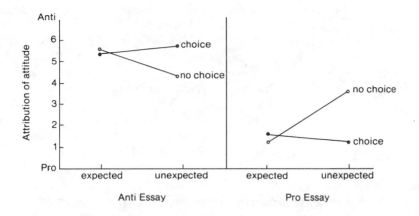

Fig. 4.1 Attribution of attitude as a function of expectancy, choice and essay direction (strong essays only). (From E. E. Jones *et al.* 1971.)

BEHAVIOR CHANGE AND ATTRIBUTION

Quite obviously, our behavior changes from situation to situation and from moment to moment. However, there are situations where behavior change is quite dramatic. Our feelings about the predictability, stability, and dependability of others may be affected by how we perceive these changes.

Status and power When a person changes behavior dramatically, a perceiver might be interested in whether the change was caused by some dispositional property not manifested earlier or because some external force produced the change. One key determinant of the attribution would certainly be the salience of any external forces. Hastorf *et al.* (1965) reasoned that the person who changes behavior in the presence of strong external pressures will be seen as less responsible for the changes than someone who changes in the presence of weak external pressures; hence, the evaluation of the former will change less. Previous research (Bavelas *et al.* 1965) had shown that in small discussion groups, the group structure could be changed by the systematic application of reinforcement techniques. Specifically, subjects who talked little in an initial discussion were given nonpublic reinforcements for talking more in a second discussion. Not only did they talk considerably more in the second discussion session, but the ratings of their leadership and quality of ideas given them by the other group members also increased. If the other group members perceived those subjects' increased verbal output as due to internal causality (e.g., "He really is a good talker; he just needed the first discussion to get warmed up"), the higher leadership and ideas ratings make sense. The Hastorf *et al.* (1965) study was designed to test this interpretation. Subjects listened to tape recordings of two discussion sessions in which the lowest talker in the first discussion became the highest talker in the second. The control subjects merely listened to the tapes, whereas the experimental subjects were informed each time a participant had received a reinforcement for talking. As predicted, when asked to rate the participants, the experimental subjects saw the increased talker as acting under the influence of external forces, and they were less likely to see his leadership capacity as changing upward. When one cause is strong, the other is discounted.

In everyday life, there are a variety of people (such as teachers, supervisors, policemen) who have the legal right, the moral obligation, and the desire to pressure people to change. You may note that when professional change agents try to change behavior, a situation exists where a more powerful or higher-status person tries to change a less powerful or lower-status person.

Is change by nonpowerful people perceived differently than change by the more powerful? This was investigated in one of the earliest attribution experiments. Thibaut and Riecken (1955) ran two experiments in which the subject asked both a high- and a low-status confederate to comply with a reasonable request; both complied. In general, the locus of causality was seen as internal for the high-status confederates and as external for the low-status compliers. There was more correspondence between behavior and attributed intent for the high-status confederates; they were perceived as acting primarily from feelings of good will rather than from external pressures.

Thibaut and Riecken showed that low-status people were seen as particularly subject to environmental forces. This has great implications for the social psychology of supervisor-subordinate relations since, among other things, the supervisor may try to get conformity to standards through the application of reward and punishment, forces that are external to the subordinate person.

Strickland (1958) tested the proposition that monitoring of subordinates would bias the attribution process. Each subject acted as a supervisor of two workers who performed a boring task for ten trials. The subject was asked to monitor the performance of Worker A on nine trials and of Worker B on only two trials, and the subject was given authority to fine each worker for failing to perform up to a standard. In reality, the persons being supervised were not workers, but the subject was not aware of that fact, since he was provided with realistic-looking records of performance. Despite the fact that A and B had nearly identical, good performances, the subject-supervisor indicated on a questionnaire that he trusted B more than A and that he saw A's performance as more externally controlled than B's. Since the subject-supervisors saw their monitoring pressure as high, the behavior of A, who was monitored more often, was seen as externally caused. This effect has been replicated under a variety of conditions by Kruglanski (1970).

An experiment by Johnson, Feigenbaum, and Weibey (1964) examined a familiar situation that involves powerful people attempting to initiate change. Teachers were asked to teach two children: Child A, who always performed well, and Child B, who performed consistently poorly for some teachers and who improved dramatically for others. The teachers attributed the consistently

poor performance of *B* to factors internal to the child (poor ability and motivation) and attributed the improvement of *B* to their own (the teachers') efforts,
although they also saw the improving *B* as having higher skills and motivation
than the nonimproving *B*. Teachers of the improving student seemed to see
their own teaching as better than did teachers of the consistently poor student
(certainly a realistic perception). It may be argued that, at least from the
teacher's perspective, effective teaching operates as a more dramatic influence
than does ineffective teaching. If good teaching is perceived as a stronger
environmental force than bad teaching, then the fact that the improvement of a
student is perceived as due to forces external to the student suggests that strong
external forces bias the attribution process toward an inference of external
causality. Kite (1964) also found that when workers performed a task successfully, supervisors attributed behavior to the supervisory techniques of reward
or punishment (that is, the behavior was externally caused) more than when
the workers failed. In a poor performance situation when the supervisor had
used punishment (which was perceived as a stronger external force than reward), the subject's behavior was perceived as less internally caused than when
the supervisor had used reward. Again, the perception of a strong environmental force biases attribution toward external causality.

Bias in change agents   However, the perceptive reader will immediately note a
compelling alternative explanation for these data. In these studies, the external
force was provided by the perceiver-subjects; therefore, it is unclear whether
the subjects' conclusions that the external force caused the subordinate's performance was a purely rational attributional judgment or whether they were
motivated to take credit for the subordinates' success. I could take credit for
my students' successes either because of a rational judgment or because I
wanted to bolster my self-esteem.

It is certainly clear that one can bolster one's self-esteem by taking credit
for success and by denying blame for failure. Do such tendencies operate in the
confounded situation where the perceiver has a vested outcome in explaining
the behavior of another? Are perceivers rational (at least in the sense of using
attribution analysis), or are their perceptions affected by their motives to look
good?

Beckman (1970) asked subjects who had had some teaching experience to
try to teach mathematical concepts to two students whom they could not see
(the students were actually fictitious). One of the two students always maintained high performance while the other was either consistently low, improved, or got worse. Not only were the teachers asked about their perceptions
of the students' performances, but observers also made these judgments based
on a written description of the study. Since the actual information in this
situation was meager—and, it could be argued, was equally available to the
actual teachers and to the observers—the teachers and observers should have
come to the same conclusions if only rational information processing was
involved. Indeed, the teachers and observers did not differ in most conditions.
However, when the student improved the teachers took more credit for this

good outcome than the observers allowed them; thus there is a strong possibility that there were ego-enhancement motives present. It is, however, worth noting that when the teachers had in some sense failed—that is, when one student got worse over time—the teachers were not less likely than observers to see poor teaching as a cause. Other experiments (Polefka 1965; Schopler and Layton 1972) also show that subjects take an unusual amount of credit for successfully influencing another, but that they do not necessarily deny responsibility for unsuccessful influence.

However, several other experiments (Beckman 1973; Ross, Bierbrauer, and Polly 1974) have found little evidence for ego-enhancement motivation. In the Ross *et al.* study the teachers (some of whom were actually professional teachers) engaged in a realistic teaching situation, and—perhaps more importantly—the observers could see the entire teaching situation. *Professional teachers* were inclined to see their teaching as *more* responsible for failure than for success, a result opposite to results in the previous studies. The nonprofessional teachers did display a slight tendency to see their own teaching as more responsible for student success than for student failure, and this tendency was stronger than that for the observer (see Table 4.2). However, while one can find minimal evidence for the operation of ego-enhancement factors in this experiment, the clear thrust of the results is toward the idea that teachers, particularly experienced ones, are not prone to use ego-enhancement over "rational" attributions strategies. It is worth considering that when the teaching situations contain more of the clues present in real life (such as interaction between student and teacher, experienced teachers) as in the Ross experiment, ego-enhancement motives disappear. However, it is also important to note that self-esteem biases may have been camouflaged by the teachers' desires to appear unbiased and modest. The professional teachers may have been particularly prone to such tendencies.

These results are in some ways comforting. Quite obviously, if teachers never took the blame for poor student performance, they would never have any reason to try to improve. It is therefore important to be clear that almost no studies find evidence for denial of blame for failure. Surely less harm is done by taking too much credit for success, but the results from Ross *et al.* suggest that even that tendency may not exist (or at least may not be admitted) for experienced teachers who have future performances to worry about.

Obviously, the data on the existence of ego-enhancement bias in attributional judgments is somewhat mixed. We will be considering this whole question again in Chapters 5 and 10; for now we can simply say that while ego-defensive biases are sometimes present in judgments we make about others, they do not appear to be inevitable.

SUCCESS-FAILURE

In the previous section, we have considered how behavior change is perceived, especially by people who are responsible for effecting the change. In the present

TABLE 4.2
**Mean Ratings for Causes of Student Success and Failure by
Professional Teaachers, Nonprofessional Teachers, and Observers**
(Adapted from Ross *et al.* 1974)

	Success*			Failure*		
	Profes-sional	Non-profes-sional	Ob-servers	Profes-sional	Non-profes-sional	Ob-servers
Instructor factors	6.30	8.81	8.12	8.53	8.25	8.25
Student factors	9.09	9.22	8.93	7.20	8.09	7.58

* Higher numbers indicate stronger attributions to the indicated factor.

section we consider attributions for general performance outcomes. We are less concerned with whether success or failure is perceived as due to *general* internal (e.g., student) or external (e.g., teacher) characteristics than with attributions to *specific* internal and external characteristics. As you will recall, Heider suggested that either environmental (luck, task difficulty) or internal (ability, trying) variables could cause success or failure.

Even when a person's performance is attributed to internal causes, we may still ask whether the performance is due relatively more to ability or to trying, and intuitively one would react differently to a person who failed because of lack of ability rather than due to lack of effort. Several experiments show that people are held more responsible for motivational than ability-caused failures. For example, Jones and deCharms (1957) found that when failure had consequences for others, a person who failed for motivational reasons was seen as undependable and was evaluated quite poorly. Lanzetta and Hannah (1969) showed that supervisors gave stronger punishments to high-ability than to low-ability subjects who fail. That result was particularly marked when the task was difficult. One interpretation of the result is that when failure is less attributable to lack of ability and more attributable to lack of trying, supervisors will be more likely to hold the learner responsible for his failure and to punish him out of frustration.

Different types of attributions There seem to be two important questions involved in attributions for success and failure: (1) was the outcome determined by internal or external factors, and (2) if the outcomes were partially under internal control, were they determined by ability or trying (or both)? Weiner *et al.* (1972) have suggested there are the four logical possibilities shown in Table 4.3 derived from using both an internal-external and a stable-unstable distinction. For example, luck is external and unstable, while ability is both internal and stable. Luck comes and goes (as does effort), while ability (and task difficulty) are rather stable attributes of persons and situations.

TABLE 4.3
Four Kinds of Attribution after Success and Failure
(Adapted from Weiner *et al.* 1972)

	Stable	*Unstable*
Internal	Ability	Effort
External	Task difficulty	Luck

Frieze and Weiner (1971) examined the kinds of information that determine attributions to these four attributes. They gave subjects information that a person had succeeded or failed. In addition, they were told that others had suceeded or failed on this task 100 percent, 50 percent, or none of the time; Kelley called this kind of information consensus information. Consistency information was given in the form of how often the actor succeeded or failed on this task, while distinctiveness information concerned the success or failure of the actor on similar tasks.

The results from this study are complex, but general trends emerge. First, the internal attributes of ability and effort were generally higher when the person's performance was markedly different from that of others (that is, when consensus is low), while the external factors, particularly task difficulty, were highest with high consensus. The internal factors are also seen as more responsible for success than failure, while the external factor of task difficulty is assumed to account for failure more than success. Just to be clear, we note that these results do not mean that perceivers see someone who succeeds as having higher ability or effort than one who fails (a rather trivial result), but that high ability or effort is more responsible for success than is low ability or effort for failure.

The stability of attributions is affected by consistency information. As you might expect, when the person's performance is consistent (stable) over time, both ability and task difficulty are assigned major causal roles. To a lesser extent, success or failure on similar tasks also affected the stable attributions.

The result that success leads to internal attributions and that failure leads to external attributions has been found often. The other attribution results are more dependent on the type of experimental task, manipulation of information factors, and dependent measures, but generally the results from other studies are mostly consistent with those of Frieze and Weiner (Karaz and Perlman 1975; Fontaine 1975; Cordray and Shaw 1978).

One problem with these research studies is that they are conducted by exposing subjects to verbal material, and in everyday life people may have access to other cues for making attributions. For example, although effort can be an important inference from performance (such as when a teacher tries to explain the poor homework of a student), often in performance situations we can observe effort directly. Condray and Shaw (1978) found that when perceivers could see how hard an actor worked, effort became the major explanation for performance. Ability and task difficulty were important primarily when there was less evidence that effort affects performance. The nature of the task itself may also influence attributions to ability and effort. Kun and Weiner (1973) found that as the task became more difficult, perceivers increasingly used the multiple necessary cause schema — that is, they assumed that both effort and ability were important for success. On easier tasks subjects assumed that either effort or ability would do the trick. There were also important interactions with success and failure. Almost independently of task difficulty, subjects assumed that both ability and effort must be present for success (multiple-necessary causes), but that either can be responsible for failure (multiple-sufficient causes).

There are two lessons to be learned from this research. First, the internal-external distinction is too crude by itself; the stable-unstable dimension is a useful addition. Second, the Kelley models do a reasonably good job of predicting attributions after success and failure. However, problems of attributions after success or failure are not exhausted by this analysis.

Attribution and gender   Attributions to ability and effort may also be affected by variables having to do more with perceiver beliefs than with information-processing tendencies. Among the several possibilities, we will examine gender partially because it has received a great deal of experimental attention lately. Men and women often are perceived as having different traits, and the "feminine" traits (such as being fearful) are generally less valued by the society than are typically "masculine" traits. A series of studies by McKee and Sherriffs (1957) show this clearly. Men were perceived (by both men and women) as being more informal, calm, logical, ambitious, boastful, and reckless, whereas women were perceived as being more sophisticated, tactful, lovable, religious, fearful, shy, and frivolous. More important, there was also agreement that the masculine traits were more socially desirable, and, in fact, women were somewhat more inclined than men to see the feminine traits as less desirable.

Women also receive lower job evaluations. Women are concentrated in the less prestigious professions, and within a given profession women have the less prestigious specialties. For example, in medicine women are more highly represented in pediatrics than in the higher-prestige specialty of surgery (Gross 1967). Feather (1975) has found a high correlation between occupational prestige and male domination of that occupation. It may be that high-prestige professions discriminate more against women, but it is also possible that "female" professions are perceived as less prestigious *because* they have a higher percentage of women (Touhey 1974).

Even when doing the same things, men and women may be perceived differently. For example, Pheterson, Kiesler, and Goldberg (1971) showed that prize-winning paintings were rated equally highly when ascribed to male and female painters, but nonprize paintings were rated more favorably when ascribed to males. In other words, at high levels of success women seem to receive credit for their success, but for less than complete success, men receive more credit than women do. Some wag has commented that we will know we have eliminated sexism in job performance evaluations not when we have a female Einstein but when a stupid female has as good a chance of getting a good job as a stupid male.

Attributions for successful performance are also made differentially to men and women. When men and women perform equally well, the women are seen as trying harder (Taynor and Deaux 1973; Feldman-Summers and Kiesler 1974); on a male-oriented task, women are seen as succeeding not because of ability, but more because of luck or task ease (Deaux and Emswiller 1974; Feather and Simon 1975). These attribution results indicate that success for women is not attributed to stable-internal abilities, but to more external or unstable attributes.

Kay Deaux (1976a) notes that both men and women think males are more competent and therefore expect women to perform worse than men, particularly on male-oriented tasks. When males succeed, expectancies are confirmed and the perceivers explain the success through an internal, stable attribution: ability. Unexpected female success, on the other hand, leads the perceiver to search for an unstable attribution to explain the "momentary" departure from expected performance. There are two choices—luck and effort—and Deaux argues that the choice is dictated by the structure of the task. On tasks (such as multiple-choice tests) where luck could play a role in performance, luck may be especially favored as an attribution. On other types of tasks (such as becoming a successful businessperson) where luck is presumably a more minor factor, effort will be the attribution of choice.

The Deaux analysis has the additional feature of applying more generally to male and female failure. The analysis suggests that failure is unexpected for males and expected for females. We should predict therefore that female failure will be seen as resulting from stable, internal factors of ability, whereas male failure should be seen more often as due to lack of trying. Feather and Simon (1975) have found that lack of ability is seen as a more important cause of female than male failure, but did not find the expected motivational difference.

Needless to say, the general differences in attributions for male and female success and failure not only constitute an interesting attribution problem, but have significant real life consequences. You may wish to speculate about how a history of having others over-attribute success to effort or underattribute it to ability might affect subsequent performance of male and female achievers as a form of self-fulfilling prophecy. The next chapter will more fully consider self-attribution and its relationship to performance.

Primacy-recency A study by E. E. Jones et al. (1968) raises a number of important issues about ability attribution. In five related experiments, subjects observed a stimulus person perform a series of 30 intelligence-test-type items of considerable difficulty. In each case, the stimulus person answered 15 of the 30 items correctly. Although there was a variety of conditions, in the three of interest to us, the stimulus person (1) started out well and then declined in performance (descend); (2) started out poorly and improved (ascend); or (3) performed consistently throughout (random). On a second series of 30 items, the stimulus person gave her answers and the subject tried to predict whether or not they were correct. The subject also rated the stimulus person's intelligence and estimated how many correct answers she had given on the first set of 30 trials (in effect, a measure of recall). The data are relatively consistent. Subjects attribute more ability to the performer who gets worse over trials than to the ascending or consistent performer, whether the attributions involve predictions of future performance, recall of past performance, or the dispositional property of intelligence.

One explanation for the Jones *et al.* results has been articulated by Jones and Goethals (1972), who hypothesized that when information coming first is seen as being relatively stable, later information will be assimilated to this stable information (see Chapter 7). Thus, subjects tend to view later information as being consistent, or congruent, with the information they already have. In the Jones *et al.* experiment, the descending stimulus person performed much better in the beginning than did the ascending stimulus person. After the first ten trials, when the descending stimulus person had solved seven problems correctly and the ascending stimulus person had solved only three correctly, the subject had probably already formed the hypothesis that the descending stimulus person was bright and the ascending stimulus person was not very bright. Since abilities such as intelligence are considered to be very stable and unchanging under a wide variety of circumstances, subjects having made the initial attribution to the ability would be loathe to change that attribution and would instead be inclined to assimilate the new information to the stable attribution they had already made. Thus processing of information in the later states of the experiment was probably biased, and because of that bias they remembered the descending stimulus person as having solved more items than was actually the case. Subsequent research by Jones, Goethals, Kennington, and Severance (1972) supports this interpretation.

ATTRIBUTION OF RESPONSIBILITY

Heider argued that the distinction between internal and external causality was important, particularly because people are held responsible only for behavior they are perceived to have intended. In other words, attributions of internal causality are necessary before responsibility can be assigned. However, there are some problems with that view. In the first place, the term *responsibility* has many meanings (Fishbein and Ajzen 1973; Mesibov 1974; Hamilton 1978). When we say someone is *responsible* for effects, we can mean any or all of the following: (1) the person caused the effects to happen, (2) the person intended the effects to happen, (3) the person is morally responsible for the effects, (4) the person has legal liability for the effects. Social psychologists have not always been clear which meaning they intend.

There are other problems with responsibility attributions. For one thing, it is quite clear that responsibility ascription is not limited to cases where the person intended to create certain effects. I can be held responsible for acts of negligence or in some cases for merely being associated with dangerous materials. Thus, most people would likely hold me somewhat responsible for a child's death if I left a loaded gun lying about in open view, even though I never intended for the child to die.

An even more important problem with responsibility attributions is that the causal texture of the world is such that causes have causes, and this raises the issue of where we place the major responsibility. For example, it makes perfectly good sense to say that a person robbed a bank because he or she wanted money, but wanting money is caused in part by being out of work, which in turn is caused by the person's socialization experiences or the general economic situation, which in turn are caused by—well, let's stop here. The perception of such a causal sequence makes sense, and an experiment by Brickman, Ryan, and Wortman (1975) indicates that people do pay attention to remote causes; but noting the causal sequence does not tell us where to assign responsibility. Needless to say, political beliefs may affect this decision. In our society, liberals tend to take the long causal view and conservatives the short view in assigning responsibility.

Despite the many problems in defining what is meant by responsibility, it is extremely important that we study this topic. For one thing, attributions of responsibility affect how we evaluate and react to others. Recall our discussion on pp. 72-73 of how attributions for success and failure affect reactions to the person. We seem to hold another person responsible for action that she or he has intentionally caused, that has been affected by trying. This can even affect perceptions of physical conditions. As you will recall from Chapter 2, there are strong stereotypes associated with various physical "types," particularly with being obese. De Jong (1977) has shown that adolescent females are strongly influenced by their perceptions of responsibility in their evaluations of obese peers. He assumed that if an obese person offers an "excuse" for the excessive weight by reporting a glandular disorder, the severity of negative evaluation made by others should be ameliorated. As predicted, obese teenagers with no glandular "excuses" were judged to be lazier, less self-disciplined, and less likable than equally obese girls who reported the existence of a thyroid condition as a cause for their weight problem.

Severity effects   There is an extensive philosophical literature on the analysis of intentions, motives, causes, and responsibility. Although many problems in this area are amenable to empirical testing, person perception researchers have limited themselves to a very small number of these problems. In part this is because they have become involved in trying to explain a particular phenomenon most clearly demonstrated by Elaine Walster (1966). She presented subjects with a description of an accident: Lennie B. parks his car on a hill, sets the handbrakes, and leaves. Later, the brake cable snaps and the car rolls down a hill. The consequences of the accident are either trivial (the car hits a stump and stops) or great (the car is badly damaged).

The subjects were asked: "Do you feel that any responsibility should be assigned to Lennie for the automobile accident?" Interestingly enough, subjects attributed more responsibility when the consequences were severe than when they were mild. Although Lennie was not seen as more careless when the consequences of the accident were severe, subjects held him to a stricter moral code (for example, saying that he should have had his brakes checked more often).

Walster assumed that the idea that chance events could cause a major calamity is very threatening, since this implies that a calamity could happen to anyone. Therefore, in the severe accident condition, subjects tended to blame a person rather than chance. Their reasoning might be: Since the possibility that such a thing could happen by chance is too threatening to think about, Lennie must have been at fault; he must have done something I wouldn't do.

Another similar explanation of the severity effect is the *just-world* hypothesis of Lerner (1965). He has proposed that people like to believe that the world is just and that people deserve what they get (and vice versa). Presumably, if Lennie had bad things happen to him, he must have deserved them.

Kelley Shaver (1970b) has proposed a different kind of model called *defensive attribution*. He has suggested that people are motivated to avoid blame (not to avoid harm, as Walster and Lerner suggest). Therefore, people should be loath to blame the perpetrator of a bad act to the extent the perpetrator is similar to them in some way. Presumably, perceivers should also assign *less* responsibility for severe rather than mild consequences, since the former should be more threatening. Shaver (1970b) has found that less responsibility is attributed to similar than to dissimilar others, but he did not show that severity affects responsibility attributions (Shaver 1970a, 1970b). However, McKillip and Posavac (1975) have found the predicted effect—that there is greater responsibility assignment to a dissimilar actor for severe rather than mild consequences, but that for a similar actor there is greater responsibility for the less severe outcome. It should also be pointed out that other researchers including Walster herself have failed to replicate the severity results (Walster 1967; Shaw and Skolnick 1971).

An experiment by Chaiken and Darley (1973) tends to support the defensive-attribution rather than the just-world explanation. Subjects who thought that they were going to be either supervisors or workers in an experiment observed a videotape of a supervisor accidentally disrupting the worker's work, which caused the worker to lose either a small or large amount of money. The two hypotheses come into conflict most clearly for future workers. Just-world predicts devaluation of the victim (the worker) by all subjects because people deserve their bad consequences; defensive attribution, by contrast, predicts that subjects will not devalue someone similar to themselves.

Results showed that the suffering worker was not particularly disliked by future workers, a result more consistent with defensive attribution. Also supporting the defensive attribution model was the finding that future supervisors perceived chance as more responsible and the supervisor as less responsible for the consequences of the supervisor's bungle than did future workers. This was particularly true when the consequences were severe.

Although the dominant tendency has been to look for motivational reasons for the tendency to attribute greater responsibility for severe rather than mild accidents, cognitive factors also play a role. Fischhoff (1975) has shown that subjects have a general tendency to see past events as more likely to occur than they in fact are; retrospectively, past events seem predictable. This would lead one to expect that subjects would feel that poor Lennie B. should have foreseen the accident. This by itself does not explain the tendency to attribute more responsibility for the severe accident. However, if Lennie should have known what would happen it makes a certain amount of sense to hold him responsible for the more severe consequences. Mesibov (1974) further showed that severe accidents were seen as more likely to occur than mild ones, giving additional reason to hold people responsible for severe accidents. In other words, from the perceiver's point of view, Lennie's accident (particularly the one with severe consequences) is not really an accident, but something Lennie should have foreseen. Given the subjects' erroneous assumptions about the predictability of past events, their tendency to hold a person responsible for consequences of foreseeable events in proportion to the severity of the consequences makes perfect sense. Indeed observers do hold people more responsible for severe rather than mild foreseeable consequences of action (Harvey, Harris, and Barnes 1975). Brewer (1977) has presented a somewhat more complex analysis of attribution of responsibility in terms of logical information processing, and her model also notes that many past studies have confounded severity and probability of outcome (see also Younger, Earn, and Arrowood 1978).

Other questions There are actually many other questions of some interest for the student of responsibility attribution. For example, to what extent is intention a major factor in such judgments? Research we have just reviewed shows that responsibility is attributed even with no intentions to produce bad consequences, although attribution of responsibility is higher for intended rather than accidental actions (Mesibov 1974). We must also keep in mind that events are never due to single causes. Brickman *et al.* (1975) have found that subjects take account of several causes in assigning responsibility, and Kelley's notions of multiple causes should also alert us to the possibility that several factors may have to be considered before responsibility is assigned. The mere fact that in many cases responsibility can be attenuated by invocation of extenuating circumstances (see Austin 1956, Feinberg 1965, and Hart 1949 for some philosophical discussion of the role of cause in excuses) points to further complexities. Finally, we note that even if a person is held responsible for intended acts, we still have the problem of explaining intentions. For example, I may criticize a student knowing full well that I will cause the student some anxiety. Although I would accept responsibility for that anxiety, hopefully you do feel differently about that attribution depending on whether I was *only* intending to hurt the student by being malicious or whether I wished to use the anxiety to spur the student on to greater glories. Attributions of responsibility are complex, and these complexities have only begun to be studied experimentally.

Quite obviously research on attribution of responsibility ought to have some important implications for legal responsibility. However, whereas most of the research we have reviewed has dealt with responsibility for the consequences of accidents, cases where people have to decide guilt and innocence, degree of culpability, and kind and amount of punishment are mostly those where the consequences were directly caused (although not necessarily intentionally) by the perpetrator. For example, Landy and Aronson (1969) used a drunk-driving situation and varied the status of the driver and the man he killed. Subjects gave the defendant a longer jail term if the victim was a pillar of the community rather than a gangster. In simulated legal situations, at any rate, people are held more responsible for crimes that hurt "good" people. Another result was that a high-status defendant was given a lighter sentence than was a low-status-defendant.

Other characteristics of the victim and the wrong-doer also affect the severity of judgment. For example, attractiveness of the offender (Sigall and Ostrove 1975) and marital status of a rape victim (Jones and Aronson 1973) affect the sentences assigned for simulated crimes. Characteristics of the judges can also play a role. Selby, Calhoun, and Brock (1977) find that men are more likely than women to feel that the victim of a rape had some causal responsibility for her plight. Rapists are also more likely to emphasize the causal role of the victim than are rape counselors (Feild 1978).

These studies constitute a sample of recent research on judgments of legal responsibility. It is a safe prediction that not only will such studies become more numerous in the future, but that they will increasingly draw on the rich literature about attribution processes.

Another intriguing set of questions has developed around the attribution of freedom or autonomy to the other person. We are particularly prone to hold people responsible for actions they have freely chosen. Ivan Steiner (1970) has proposed a general model of psychological freedom that has implications for the research on attribution. For example, Davidson and Steiner (1971) argued that a person who performs in a consistent manner will be perceived as less free than one whose behavior is more variable. In this study, teachers rewarded students on every trial (consistent) or only in half the trials (variable). As predicted, the students saw the teacher as having greater freedom when he used a variable rather than a consistent schedule. According to attribution models, perceivers should feel more confident about making dispositional inferences and, therefore, also be more extreme in these inferences when the stimulus person is perceived as free. As predicted, students were more extreme in describing the teacher after variable than after continuous reinforcement, presumably because the former teachers were perceived as being more free.

Freedom is also an important attribution in choice situations. Steiner, Rotermund, and Talaber (1974); Harvey and Johnston (1973); and Jellison and Harvey (1973) have all shown that there is greater perceived freedom of choice when the alternatives are close together in attractiveness. There is also greater perceived choice when the person has to choose between attractive rather than unattractive alternatives (Harvey and Jellison, 1974).

Another interesting question is how the actor's personality affects perceived freedom. The available research (Kruglanski and Cohen 1973; Trope and Burnstein 1977) suggests that people are seen as less constrained when their behavior is in line with their personal dispositions. However, it is easy to think of examples where strong personal characteristics create perceptions of constraint. Novels and plays are filled with characters whose tragedy lies in their inability to overcome their passions, needs, or values. And, of course, there are a variety of interesting legal issues surrounding questions of whether actions performed in the heat of passion or by people judged to be mentally ill are fully free and responsible actions.

Developmental issues   Heider (1958) and Piaget (1930) have both argued that there are clear developmental trends in assignment of responsibility. Generally young children (below the age of five or six) were thought to assign responsibility more in terms of whether the consequences were good or bad than in terms of what the intentions were. Piaget argued that although a preschool child may be able to perceive intentions, the child's level of cognitive development causes a reliance more on objective facts than on the consequences. Younger children also have trouble putting themselves in the position of other people and seeing things from another's perspective.

In various tests of Piaget's theory, subjects of various ages have generally been asked to judge which of two children who cause accidents is "naughtier." One child has "bad" intentions, and the consequences of his actions are relatively benign (for instance, he tries to get at some forbidden cookies and breaks a dish). The other child has "good" intentions but the effects of his action are relatively severe (for instance, he tries to help set the dinner table and breaks several dishes). Using this paradigm, the research evidence (Karniol 1978) generally agrees that older children are more inclined to judge the child on the basis of intentions, and younger children are more inclined to judge the child on the basis of consequences. These results have led to the claim that younger children do not pay attention to intentions in judging action; some researchers say that preschool children are incapable of taking intentions into account.

However, much of the past research has been badly flawed, so these conclusions are not necessarily accurate. One problem has been that most of the research dealt only with action that resulted in accidental consequences (and indeed this is also true of most of the research on adults reviewed in this chapter). Even preschool children can tell the difference between accidental and intentional consequences (King 1971). Furthermore, even younger children can take account of intentions in evaluating intentional action (Armsby 1971; Buchanan and Thompson 1973).

Another problem with past research has been that only bad consequences were considered. Baldwin and Baldwin (1970) showed that most preschoolers were able to judge kindness on the basis of intentions. Yet another problem is that past research has employed verbal stories; research using videotaped materials show that younger children are more inclined to utilize intention if they can actually see what is going on (Chandler, Greenspan, and Barenboim 1973).

Costanzo, Coie, Grumet, and Farnell (1973) varied age, positiveness of intention, and actual consequences. Thus research shows that when the consequences of an action are negative, preschool children do not rely on intentions in judging the act. However, when the consequences are good, even younger children judge the well-intentioned act as better. Thus the general evidence suggests that whereas younger children are not inclined to use intention information for judging accidents with bad consequences, they do use intention to judge how good an act is.

Heider's theory postulated several levels of responsibility. In the first level the person is held responsible for any act connected with him. In the second level he is held responsible for any action he caused, whether or not the

"And just how do you find out who's been naughty and who's been nice?"

Drawing by Levin; © 1975 The New Yorker Magazine, Inc.

consequences were intended. In the third level he is held responsible only for effects he should have foreseen. In the fourth level he is held responsible for acts whose consequences he intended. Finally, Heider argued that the person is not held entirely responsible even for his own intentions. Generally, studies designed to test this progression of stages has found that adults assign increasing responsibility as the action moves from Level 1 to Level 4 (Level 5 is probably misplaced because it implies a kind of external causality, whereas Level 4 implies fully internal causality). Children, on the other hand, are inclined to assign more responsibility than adults at the lower levels and generally to discriminate less than the adults among the levels (Shaw and Sulzer 1964; Harris 1977).

Most of the developmental research has provided perceivers with information about intentions, but obviously, attributions of responsibility must often rest on prior attributions of intentionality and causality. Are children capable of inferring causes and of assigning internal or external reasons for action? Several studies suggest that while they are far from perfect causal reasoners, children as young as three or four can use covariation information to assign causality (Shultz and Mendelson 1975; Siegler and Liebert 1974); Divitto and McArthur (1978) tested the sensitivity of children to the Kelley information factors. Even first-graders used consistency and distinctiveness information. However, consensus information was used less by the younger children than by the older children to make judgments.

Generally, then, even young children *can* infer actor and situation causes in line with Kelley's Covariation Model. However, the logic of the Causal Schema Model, particularly discounting, is more complex. As one might expect, younger children have trouble taking two or more causes into account in explaining action. Several studies have found that young children have trouble discounting one cause if another is present (Smith 1975; Karniol and Ross 1976; DiVitto and McArthur 1978). Thus, although young children seem able to utilize information about covariation of variables to infer that one causes the other, they are not capable of utilizing information about several possible causes.

Generally the developmental literature suggests that children do have somewhat more primitive views of causation and responsibility than do adults. They have trouble seeing that strong external forces diminish the possibility of internal causality, and they are inclined to judge action on the basis of external consequences rather than on intentions. However, children are capable of sophisticated reasoning about responsiblity, and under some circumstances show an ability to consider intentions in their judgements.

Summary

The research literature generally confirms models. When there are strong external forces that could have produced behavior, perceivers tend to discount the possibility of actor forces. Behavior should be uninformative when environmental forces are strong, although perceivers sometimes draw inferences about the actor from such behavior. Another line of research has shown that high-power people tend to see their own behavior as responsible for changes in others. There is some possibility that this attribution is biased by the need to feel that one has been successful, but such biases do not appear to be pervasive. There is a large literature on attributions for success and failure. Generally, most researchers have found it useful to look not only at how internal or external attributions are, but also at their stability. Attributions to ability are generally made for consistent behaviors, particularly successes, whereas effort attributions are more likely for inconsistent performances. Finally, we noted that people are held responsible for consequences of intended behavior, but that, surprisingly, they are also held responsible for consequences of accidents.

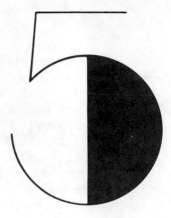

Quite understandably, person perception research has concentrated on the perception of other

self-attribution

people. On the assumption that attribution inferences guide our behavior toward people, attribution models were developed. In recent years, these models have also been used to explain our perceptions of ourselves. Philosophers and psychologists have long been interested, of course, in the sources of our feelings about ourselves, but they have not generally considered the possibility that our self-perceptions are manifestations of the same underlying psychological proceses that generate our perceptions of other people. Nor, we suspect, is that possibility likely to occur to most other people.

The reasons for that are not hard to understand. After all, when we think about other people, our purpose is usually to discover their intentions, abilities, traits—more generally, the causes of, or reasons for, their behavior; but presumably we have immediate access to our own inner states in a way that no other person does. Surely, under ordinary circumstances, I know what I want to do, and the only mystery for me is whether external circumstances (in relationship to my own abilities) will allow me to pull it off. My perspective is of being "inside" and looking out. I know what is "inside," and I wonder about what *will* happen. However, in approaching other people I know what *has* happened, and I want to learn why. In this case, my perspective is that of an outsider looking in. Often, then, we seem to take different perspectives, to have available different information, and to ask different questions when we try to explain our own and others' behavior.

However, these phenomenological differences should not blind us to the possibility that we may use the same sorts of information about self and others and that we may analyze the causes of behavior similarly in the two cases. Certainly in explaining the past behaviors of self and others, we are, in both cases, weighing internal and external determinants of behavior, and, so, both self and other perceptions ought to be amenable to the same sorts of attributional analysis. For the first part of this chapter we will explore the ability of the general attribution analysis to explain self-perception. In the latter part of the chapter we will examine the differences between self- and other-perception.

It is possible that person-perception researchers would never have seen the parallels between self- and other-perception without a strong push from two rather extraordinary lines of research from other traditions in social psychology. It is instructive to note that these two lines of research reached full flower at the same time as the dramatic renewed interest in attribution problems during the middle and late 1960s. One of these lines of research was Daryl Bem's attempts to give a self-perception explanation for the effects of social pressure on beliefs. The other was the work of Stanley Schachter and his students on perception of emotions.

Models of Self-Perception

BEM'S THEORY OF SELF-PERCEPTION

Bem's theory tried to explain how we know which attitudes we hold. In trying to explain some classic research on the effects of social pressure on attitude change, Bem suggested the radical idea that our own attitudes are inferences from information about our own behavior and about various external forces. In fact, he suggested explicitly that we infer our own attitudes in exactly the same way and using exactly the same sorts of information as when we infer the attitudes of others. Initially, Bem was not concerned with general person perception processes, but it soon became obvious that if he were correct, general attribution models could be used to explain self-perception.

Forced compliance   The Bem analysis was originally presented as an alternative to the theory of cognitive dissonance (Festinger 1957). Before outlining Bem's theory, we will review a key dissonance experiment in order to provide a context for the following discussion. In the initial statement of the theory, Festinger defined cognitive dissonance as a function of the number, the relevance, and the importance of contradictory cognitions. Dissonance is assumed to be uncomfortable, and the individual is therefore motivated to reduce it, usually by altering his cognitions about either the world or himself. When a person says one thing and believes another, dissonance is created. Since the cognition about what one has said cannot easily be changed, dissonance in this case will most likely be reduced by bringing one's belief more in line with the statement. However, to the extent that the person had justification for engaging in the behavior, the dissonance is lessened; another cognition, consonant with the cognition that one has made the statement, has been added. The "lie" is justified.

The classic experiment in this area was conducted by Festinger and Carlsmith (1959). Subjects worked on a boring task and were then recruited to tell another subject that the task had been interesting. They were offered either $1 or $20 for giving the false information. The prediction was that subjects would experience more dissonance and would change their attitudes about the task more in the $1 condition, since the payment was less sufficient to justify the lie. The prediction was confirmed. Subjects saw the task as more interesting when they had been paid the smaller amount of money for telling another person it was interesting. When subjects engage in counterattitudinal behavior, they change their attitudes toward their public behavior to the extent that there is inadequate justification for the behavior (see Zimbardo, Ebbesen, and Maslach 1977).

Bem's explanation for these results begins with the question of what naive observers would say about the subject's private opinion if they knew only (1) what the subject had said and (2) how much the subject had been paid for making the statement. The observer could attribute the publicly stated attitude to internal causes ("That's his real attitude") or to external causes ("He's only saying that for the money"). To the extent that perceivers operate in an either/or fashion—choosing one or the other cause—they will be led to conclude that the highly paid subject probably said what he did for the money, and the poorly paid subject said what he did because he really believed it. The reasoning might be something like the following: If the subject made the speech for as little as $1, he must surely believe what he said, since $1 is not a very powerful incentive for him to lie about his beliefs. If he made the speech for $20, then he may well have been lying, since most people would probably tell a small lie for such a large amount of money. Thus, the perceiver might be inclined to attribute the subject's speech to his real attitudes when external forces are not very strong ($1), and might be inclined to attribute the subject's speech to external forces when they are ($20). This would be an example of the discounting strategy suggested by Kelley (pp. 56-57).

Bem did show (1965, 1967) that subjects exposed to the instructions of the Festinger and Carlsmith experiment and to information about the subject's speech and payment inferred that the $20 subject enjoyed the task less than the $1 subject did. In other words, perceivers do not seem to see subjects' behavior as a reflection of their true attitudes when external forces are strong, a standard attribution finding (see Chapter 4).

Bem argues that the Festinger-Carlsmith subjects acted like these outside observers in assessing their own attitudes. Perhaps the subjects in the original Festinger and Carlsmith experiment changed their attitudes through some similar attribution process. We might assume that initially the subjects did not have particularly clear attitudes about how interesting the task had been, but

TABLE 5.1
Ratings of Enjoyment for a Dull Task by Subjects in the Original Festinger-Carlsmith Experiment and by Bem's Observers

	Festinger-Carlsmith subjects*	Bem observers*
Control	−0.45	−1.56
$20	−0.05	−1.96
$1	1.35	0.52

* Higher numbers indicate more enjoyment.

that when asked by the experimenter to indicate their attitudes, they relied on perceptions of their own behavior. The $1 subjects may have said, "I guess the task was interesting, since I said it was interesting for such a small amount of money. The only real justification I could have had for saying so is that it's true." The $20 subjects may have said to themselves, "I have no particular reason to think the task was *really* interesting. I know I *said* it was, but clearly I said so to get the $20." So the $1 subjects may simply have attributed greater internal causality to themselves than the $20 subjects did.

Actually, the dissonance and self-perception explanations for results in such forced compliance situations are similar. While the theories differ (Kiesler and Pallak 1976), it has proved difficult to find a definitive test of which theory is better, and there is even suspicion that no such test is possible (see Greenwald 1975). For our purposes, it is relatively unimportant which theory works best for forced compliance. Whether or not self-perception theory accounts for results in forced compliance experiments, it has stimulated other interesting research.

Intrinsic motivation   The controversy over forced compliance is not completely irrelevant to self-perception theory, however. Among other things, it has pointed the way to an analysis of an important problem with many real-life implications. One can rephrase the forced compliance situation as an analysis of how reward affects feelings of enjoyment. As you will recall, subjects who were promised a little money to say they liked a dull task, seem to have increased their liking for the task. Is it also possible that too much reward can lower people's enjoyment even for activities they initially like? People generally do tasks either because they enjoy them for their own sake (intrinsic motivation) or because they expect some external reward (extrinsic motivation) for doing them. Many educational and industrial theorists have long felt that rewards in the form of pay, gold stars, or grades may actually interfere with intrinsic motivation. If you begin to feel that you are studying for an exam only to get a good grade, you may lower your enjoyment of the course. Put in attribution terms, salient external forces may lower the perceived power of internal forces through the operation of the discounting principle.

In a classic demonstration, Lepper, Greene, and Nisbett (1973) worked with three- to five-year-old children. One group of subjects was promised an award for drawing some pictures; a second group was not promised an award, but later received one unexpectedly; and a third group neither expected nor received an award. One to two weeks later, the children were observed to see how much they played with the drawing materials. Results showed that the children who had previously *expected* a prize (and received one) for previous playing with the materials now played with them less than those who had not expected an award, whether or not they had actually received an award. Overjustification by external forces clearly reduced the perceived force of internal wants and desires. Another common external force for achievement situations is a deadline, and working against a deadline also lowers subsequent work

(Amabile, De Jong, and Lepper 1976). A study by Kruglanski, Friedman, and Zeevi (1971) showed that the same kinds of effects obtain for ratings of task enjoyment. People who are given rewards for doing tasks report less enjoyment of them than people who are not given such external rewards.

Despite criticisms on both methodological and theoretical grounds of these experiments (Calder and Staw 1975; Reiss and Sushinsky 1975; Kruglanski 1975; see also replies by Deci, Cascio, and Krusell 1975; Lepper and Greene 1976; and Reiss and Sushinsky 1976), the overjustification effects seem well established (Condry 1977). Greene, Sternberg, and Lepper (1976) have shown that the effect has considerable generalizability to academic situations. Children who were rewarded each day for 12 days for working on certain kinds of math problems did, indeed, spend time working on them. However, when rewards were withdrawn, subjects spent even less time at the activities than they had before the rewards had been introduced. The fact that the experiment took place in a typical classroom setting and that it extended for several weeks provides additional confidence that the phenomenon is a real one and that it has practical significance.

However, there are some major qualifications on the generality of the phenomenon. Not every reward for every task decreases subsequent intrinsic motivation. For example, while money often acts to reduce intrinsic motivation, verbal praise does not (Deci 1971, 1972; Anderson, Manoogian, and Reznick 1976). It is possible to argue that while money is almost always used as an external incentive force, verbal praise also has information properties by telling the person that he has been successful. Thus, verbal praise may actually increase intrinsic motivation by increasing the person's feelings of competence and self-confidence (Deci 1975).

Even money can increase intrinsic motivation under some circumstances. When winning money is an essential part of the task (such as playing a stock market game or playing Monopoly), subjects who win money report liking the task more than those who do not (Kruglanski et al. 1975). One interpretation is that when the external reward suggests that the task is dull, reward lowers extrinsic motivation; but when the reward is inherent in the task and when it functions solely to provide information about performance, it will increase intrinsic motivation (see also Kruglanski 1975).

It is important to note that it is not the reward itself that affects intrinsic motivation. Before external rewards can reduce intrinsic motivation, the rewards must be expected (Lepper et al. 1973) and salient (Ross 1975). These results further suggest that it is the meaning of the reward rather than the actual reward itself that affects intrinsic motivation. It is clear that when strong external reasons for behavior become salient, the individual may come to feel that these—rather than the more internal forces—control behavior. These findings certainly fit well within Bem's self-perception model, and illustrate that we discount internal forces in the face of strong external forces when we attribute causes of our own as well as others' behavior.

SCHACHTER'S THEORY OF EMOTIONAL SELF-LABELING

Bem's basic statement of his theory of self-perception is that when internal cues about our feelings are "weak, ambiguous, or uninterpretable" (1972, p. 5), we infer our feelings on the basis of our observations of our own behavior and the situational forces that constrain it, just like an outside observer who has no access to our internal state. We have many possible sources of information about our feelings including internal cues, behavior, and the situational context. If the internal cues are vague or uninformative, we have to rely more heavily on behavior and the situational context. Most people probably feel that as a general rule the internal cues must be the most important of these sources of information, but Bem argues that in fact internal cues are *usually* rather "weak, ambiguous, and uninterpretable," and so we very often rely on observations of our behavior in its context. The work on forced compliance and intrinsic motivation indicates that internal cues can be quite unimportant in informing us of our global attitudes toward a variety of activities.

Still, one could argue that the internal feelings associated with occupations such as performing a dull task, or working on a set of novel puzzles, or drawing pictures are probably rather global and bland, that these are just the sort of situations where one would expect internal cues to be weak and ambiguous. They are trifles: they do not engage our passions. Most people would argue that the internal cues associated with powerful emotions are unmistakable—for example, that the difference between grief and fury is instantly recognizable to us. Schachter's (1964) theory boldly claims that this is not so. Like Bem, he argues that internal cues are not sufficient to tell us what emotions we are feeling, even in the case of emotions that are usually regarded as fundamentally different, such as happiness and anger.

Schachter's claim that there are few noticeable differences in the internal cues associated with the various emotions is consistent with the findings of many researchers who have tried to study the physiology of the emotions. Very often these researchers have failed to find physiological differences that correspond to differences in experienced emotion. With a few notable exceptions (Ax 1953; Funkenstein 1955; Tourangeau and Ellsworth 1978), it is hard to find studies in which the autonomic response of fear was clearly different from the autonomic response of anger, or even from the "unemotional" autonomic arousal produced by running around the block. There are tremendous individual differences in physiological responses to emotional stimuli (Lacey 1950). For at least a decade before Schachter proposed his theory, most theories of emotion had come to postulate some sort of *general* state of physiological arousal, not differentiated into distinct emotions (Lindsley 1951; Duffy 1962).

In a theory that postulates an undifferentiated state of physiological arousal some other nonphysiological mechanism must be added to explain why we *feel* so different and behave so differently when we are happy than when we are angry. Like Bem, Schachter added a cognitive component to the general arousal postulate, arguing that we *infer* our emotions on the basis of other cues. However, Schachter did not emphasize exactly the same cues as did Bem. While Bem emphasized observations of one's own behavior and the situational context and while he deemphasized internal cues, Schachter emphasized observations of one's own internal state and the situational context, and did not really address himself to behavioral cues. Schachter proposed that the experience of emotion requires two things: (1) a state of undifferentiated physiological arousal, which tells the person that she is agitated, and (2) a cognitive inference, based on situational cues, which tells the person what the agitation means.

In a famous experiment designed to test this model Schachter and Singer (1962) aroused subjects by giving them injections of epinephrine (adrenalin). Some subjects were told correctly that the injection would produce an elevated heart rate and other symptoms of arousal; others were told that it would produce numbness and other symptoms that have nothing to do with arousal; a third group was told nothing. Then the subjects were exposed to a confederate who behaved euphorically or in an angry-aggressive manner. The injection provided the undifferentiated arousal, and the confederate provided a situational definition. In general, those subjects who were unaware of the true reason for their arousal (that is, the ones who had been given false information or no information at all about the injection) reported emotions more congruent with the confederate's behavior, and they also behaved more emotionally than the subjects who knew that their arousal was due to the injection. The results indicate that people will seek (and find) an emotional definition when they are physiologically excited and do not know why; when they know that their arousal comes from an "unemotional source" (the injection), they will not seek or find an emotional definition.

The claim that the situational context provides the information that differentiates among the emotions, however, is considerably weaker, since the subjects with unexplained arousal who were exposed to the happy confederate were not much happier than the subjects who were exposed to the angry confederate. According to the hypothesis, subjects who were ignorant of the effects of the injection should be particularly prone to take on the emotional coloration of the confederate's behavior, but, as Table 5.2 indicates, this was not strongly the case. Thus, there is as yet no strong evidence that an arousal-

TABLE 5.2
Self-reports of Emotion on the Schachter and Singer (1962) Experiment

	*Euphoria**	*Anger**
Informed	0.98	1.91
Ignorant	1.78	1.39
Misinformed	1.90	—

* High number indicates relative happiness, and low number indicates relative anger.

plus-cognition model can account for *qualitative distinctions* in the subjective experience of emotion.

There is, however, evidence that unexplained arousal can intensify an emotion triggered by other environmental cues (Zillmann, Johnson, and Day 1974; Cantor, Zillmann, and Bryant 1975). In the latter experiment, subjects were asked to exercise for a brief time. Physiological arousal from the exercise decays over time, and there is a point where subjects no longer feel that they are physiologically aroused, although objectively (in terms of blood pressure) they are. If subjects are shown erotic stimuli during this phase, they say they are more sexually aroused than when (a) they have fully recovered from the exercise (and, therefore, have no physiological arousal) or (b) are still aroused by the exercise but know that the exercise has aroused them. In other words, unexplained arousal is defined in terms of salient environmental stimuli (erotic pictures). Subjects felt more aroused by the pictures with unexplained arousal than with no extraneous arousal or than with explained extraneous arousal.

Misattribution   These experiments suggest that unexplained arousal tends to exaggerate the impact of environmental cues. But what if the arousal is actually created by an emotional stimulus? Can environmental cues be used to redirect this arousal so that the subject infers a different emotion? Kelley's Causal Schema Model would suggest that if there are two possible situational factors that could have produced a behavior, the perceiver should be less certain that either is the true cause than if only one factor were present. Does this work for attribution of emotion? Theoretically, if a person's attention can be directed (or misdirected) to salient alternative explanations for feelings, the usual expected emotional attribution can be avoided or lessened.

Ordinarily, for example, when a painful stimulus causes physiological arousal we have no trouble defining that arousal as pain, simply because the stimulus is immediately present and constitutes a good explanation of internal feelings. But what if there were also an additional explanation possible? Then the reaction to the stimulus may be "misattributed" to the second cause. In particular, when pain can be attributed to something other than a painful stimulus, feelings of pain should be lowered. Nisbett and Schachter (1966), for example, showed that experienced pain could be manipulated. Before being shocked, half of the subjects were told that it would not be painful (low fear), and others (high fear) were told it would be painful. Then subjects were given a placebo drug that was described as having some minor side effects. Half of the subjects were told that these side effects were those actually produced by shock (palpitation, heart rate increase, and so on), and the others were told that the pill would cause effects irrelevant to the shock (itching, headache). The subjects were then given a series of shocks and were asked to indicate when the shocks became too strong. Presumably, subjects who expected the pill to have shock-like effects should attribute their pain symptoms to the pill and should be willing to take more shocks. As Table 5.3 shows, this, in fact, happened, but only under low-fear conditions. When subjects expected the shocks to be painful, the

TABLE 5.3
Threshold of Shock in Subjects as a Function of Fear and Attribution
(From Nisbett and Schachter 1966)

	Pill attribution*	Shock attribution*
Low fear	25.75	15.75
High fear	26.31	28.19

* Higher numbers indicate subjects tolerated more shock.

number of shocks they took was not affected by whether or not they thought the pills had caused the symptoms. The fear instructions had provided strong internal cues or cognitions that the shock caused the pain. However, the low-fear subjects, who had no such strong internal cues, took stronger shocks when they thought that their symptoms were due to the pill. Having weak internal cues and a strong external explanation for the feelings, they were able to tolerate more pain.

Nisbett and Schachter used a supposed drug to manipulate external cues, but another kind of external cue is the subject's own behavior. In an experiment by Bandler, Madaras, and Bem (1968) subjects were given a series of trials in which they were induced either to escape or to "take" shocks. An observer would infer that subjects were more pained by shocks they chose to avoid, and in this study, subjects acted like observers of their own behavior. When they escaped shock, they rated shocks as more painful than when they chose to take the shock. The influence of the external event (in this case, the subject's own behavior) influenced self-attributions. Corah and Boffa (1970) have replicated the general finding, using white noise rather than shock as the aversive stimulus.

Other emotional states have also been manipulated through misattribution techniques. For example, people who suffer insomnia report that they fall asleep earlier if they can attribute their arousal to a pill that supposedly arouses them (Storms and Nisbett 1970). Under conditions of high test anxiety, women who are experiencing severe menstruation symptoms do better on a test presumably because they have a natural misattribution for their anxiety arousal (Rodin 1976). In a forced compliance situation, subjects who can attribute the arousal of cognitive dissonance to other sources have reduced tendencies to change their attitudes to match their behaviors (Zanna and Cooper 1974; Kiesler and Pallak 1976).

There are obvious applications of misattribution techniques to psychotherapy (Valins and Nisbett 1972). Since psychotherapy often involves attempts to reduce or redirect anxiety and fear, several research studies have tried to show the power of such techniques in reducing fear. For example, avoidance of expected shock can be reduced if the fear arousal is attributed to other sources (Ross, Rodin, and Zimbardo 1972), and conditioned fear responses extinguish more rapidly when the fear arousal is attributed to extraneous sources (Loftis and Ross 1974).

Davison and Valins (1969) raised the further question about whether misattribution in such situations can play a role in the maintenance of behavior change. Subjects whose behavior changes in conjunction with drug therapy (such as tranquilizers) can easily attribute such changes to the drug as an external force and may not interpret them as changes in their own personalities. If behavior change is to be maintained after drugs are withdrawn, it is necessary to convince the subject that a "real" (that is, self-induced) change has occurred. In their experiment, Davison and Valins gave subjects a series of painful shocks. They then gave the subjects a "drug" called paratoxin (actually a placebo), and the subjects were told that paratoxin would make shocks less painful to them. After the paratoxin had "taken effect," the subjects were given a second series of shocks. Unknown to the subjects, the second shocks were lower in intensity so that the subjects believed they had tolerated more shock in the second than in the first series. Then half the subjects were told that paratoxin was actually a placebo, and the other half were told that the effects of the paratoxin had "worn off." When a third series of shocks was administered, the researchers found that the group that had been told that paratoxin was a placebo withstood more shock than did the group that believed in the paratoxin's effectiveness. Both groups of subjects thought they had tolerated greater shock in the second than in the first series (remember that the experimenters had cleverly reduced the actual shock intensity without the subjects' knowing it). Although half the subjects could attribute their greater "pain tolerance" to external factors (the "paratoxin"), the other half realized that their greater tolerance could not be due to such external factors (since "paratoxin" had been revealed as a placebo). The latter could attribute their greater tolerance only to internal factors, since there were no strong external factors perceived to be at work. It is, therefore, understandable that they tolerated more shock in the third series because they attributed their tolerance to a dispositional state. Their increased tolerance for pain was attributed to themselves.

Physiological cues and emotion attribution We have discussed the strong possibility that emotions have less to do with a specific kind of physiological arousal than with environmental cues. This is not to suggest, however, that "internal" physiological cues are never utilized. Valins (1966) conducted an experiment investigating the extent to which internal stimuli are used to label feelings. He reasoned that emotional experiences of subjects should be influenced by the perception of internal stimuli. He provided subjects with amplified feedback of "your heartbeat" (the feedback was actually preprogrammed) while they looked at *Playboy* centerfolds. During exposure to half the pictures, the heartrate remained constant for all subjects; during exposure to the other half of the pictures, the heartrate increased for some subjects and decreased for the others. As Valins had hypothesized, the subjects rated the pictures as more attractive when their heartrate changed (either increased or decreased), presumably because they had had evidence of greater emotional arousal in those conditions. The pictures that had been accompanied by an alleged changed heartrate were also preferred as payment for the experiment. However, Barefoot and Straub (1971) showed that the Valins results did not obtain when subjects could spend only a short time viewing the pictures. In this case, subjects presumably did not have the opportunity to make salient favorable attributes of the "liked" pictures. In fact, unexplained arousal does seem to initiate an information search process (Girodo 1973).

Later, Valins extended his research to include the perception of fear. Valins and Ray (1967) chose subjects who were afraid of snakes. Snakes were the feared stimulus; shock was used as a control stimulus. Some subjects heard their "heartrate" increase in response to the shock stimulus, but not in response to pictures of snakes. A control group that also received shock and saw snake pictures were given no information about internal reactions. As predicted, the control subjects had a greater fear of snakes in a behavioral test than the experimental subjects did. The experimental subjects had evidence that they were aroused by shock but not by snakes, and their behavior indicated less fear of snakes.

It should be pointed out, however, that physiological arousal is itself affected by the feedback. Subjects who are told that appropriate sounds represented heartrate increases while they were exposed to pictures of violent deaths had their *actual* physiological arousal increase more than those who thought the sounds were unrelated noise (Hirschman 1975). At the moment it is clear that there are mutual influences between actual arousal, cognition of arousal, and felt emotion, but the exact relationships are unknown (see Harris and Katkin 1975 for further discussion).

It should also be pointed out that there are alternative explanations for some of these results (Calvert-Boyanowksy and Leventhal 1975) and that under some circumstances the results are not replicated by other researchers (Rogers and Deckner 1975; Kellogg and Baron 1975). Although self-attribution of emotion results are not always robust, there is good evidence that internal states such as emotions can be influenced by plausible alternative explanations for arousal (as in misattribution paradigms) and by perceptions of one's own physiological arousal.

Qualifications on self-perception models   There are some major problems with the self-perception hypotheses, problems that lead to a major qualification of their generality. For example, although Nisbett and Schachter (1966) found that subjects who attributed mild shock symptoms to a pill *tolerated* more subsequent shock than subjects without this misattribution, there were no differences between groups on how much pain subjects *reported* feeling. Valins and Ray (1967) were able to manipulate subjects' approach to previously feared snakes, but not their reported fear of snakes. These studies suggest that behavior, but not attitudes, are affected by misattribution processes.

Studies which *have* found strong effects for self-attribution of *attitudes* have typically found a strengthening of previous attitudes. For example, in the experiment of Bandler *et al.* (1968), subjects who escaped shocks rated them as more unpleasant than control subjects, but (and here is the catch) subjects who chose to take the shocks did not rate the shocks as less unpleasant than control subjects. Thus, Bandler *et al.* were able to manipulate attitudes in a direction consistent with the subjects' previous beliefs that the shocks were unpleasant, but not in a direction inconsistent with previous beliefs. Brown, Klemp, and Leventhal (1975) manipulated the strength of the actual shock using the Bandler *et al.* procedure. They also found that generally the subjects who chose to take shock did not have lowered reports of shock unpleasantness. The subjects who chose to escape did rate the shocks as more unpleasant than the subjects who chose to take them and control subjects, but only with high levels of shock. That is, as the escape behavior became more congruent with the actual stimulus intensity, escape behavior did strengthen beliefs that the shocks were unpleasant. However, the behavior of taking the shocks that was incongruent with initial attitudes did *not* affect attitudes.

Taylor (1975) has argued that as knowledge of attitudes becomes more important, subjects will be less inclined to infer attitudes from behavior. She did a conceptual replication of the Valins (1966) study. In Taylor's study females inferred their attitudes toward male pictures on the basis of physiological arousal. She found that when there were no consequences for the picture judgments, the results supported the self-perception hypothesis—final attitudes reflected the physiological feedback. On the other hand, when the subjects had to meet the person in the picture (and attitudes are presumably more important), the physiological feedback had little effect on attitudes toward the pictures.

Clearly, our own behavior is not always used as information from which we infer our attitudes and emotions. We can have two broad classes of information about our own inner states. The first and most obvious is our direct, conscious feelings. But we may also have information from our own behaviors, from our own emotional reactions, and from the behavior of others toward us (although this latter has not been investigated by attribution researchers). When the person has to make an explicit judgment about his or her own inner states, these sources of information may be differentially weighted and averaged together (Brown *et al.* 1975).

Several factors affect the weights. Salience or attention may increase the importance of certain information, while ambiguity and unclarity of information may reduce its importance. In particular, internal states are often unclear, thus reducing the importance of such information and giving behavior and other external cues relatively more weight. As Bem has stated, "To the extent that internal cues are weak, ambiguous, or uninterpretable, the individual is functionally in the same position as an outside observer, an observer who must necessarily rely on those same external (behavioral) cues to infer the individual's inner states" (Bem 1972, p. 5). We might add that when situational cues are ambiguous, people may attend more to internal cues. Finally, the importance of the decision may affect the weighting of information. Taylor's (1975) study suggests that subjects may discount physiological information when their judgments about attitudes have future consequences.

Past literature suggests that behavioral information affects judgments about attitudes and feelings most strongly when the behavioral information supports the initial attitudes and feelings. When the two conflict, attitudes are not changed to reflect behavioral or physiological information, although behavior may be affected. That is, although subjects who are exposed to information which says that a painful stimulus is not painful do not change their reports of pain, they may act as if the stimuli are not painful. One possible reason for this discrepancy is that a nonconscious reevaluation of the stimulus takes place that affects subsequent behavior but that does not show up immediately in reported feelings. Another possibility suggested by Nisbett and Valins (1972) is that when subjects are exposed to information discrepant from their initial feeling or attitude states, they develop a hypothesis that their feelings or attitudes may be different than they thought. They wish to test the hypothesis by behaving differently toward the stimulus before reporting a change. Thus, Valins and Ray's (1967) snake phobic subjects who were presented with physiological data that they were not afraid of snakes may have wanted to approach a snake (which they did) to test the hypothesis of no fear before reporting an actual change in fear.

All of this is not to suggest that the self-perception hypothesis is fundamentally wrong, but it does suggest that people do not inevitably use behavioral or other external information to judge their own inner states. Judgments about one's inner states seem to involve complex cognitive processes using a variety of different kinds of data.

Facial expression and emotion labeling   In discussing the tendency to use one's own behavior as a clue for inferring one's emotions, we have so far avoided mentioning one of the most widely recognized of all emotional behaviors—the expressive behavior of the face. Does this kind of behavior also influence our experience of emotion? The usual assumption is that we feel the emotion first, and then we express it on our faces. The very term *expression* implies that a force which already exists inside pushes itself out by wrenching the facial muscles. But some psychologists have argued that the reverse process operates: that the facial muscles may be an important *source* of the different emotions, so that the experience of our own emotions is dependent on the proprioceptive feedback from the face. Facial "expressions," according to this view, are not merely passive reflections of our inner states; instead, they may actively influence or help to create our emotional feelings.

The idea that expressions affect the emotions they signal is not new. Charles Darwin (1872, 1896) suggested that bodily symptoms of emotion influenced subjective feelings of emotion, and William James (1884, 1890) took the even stronger position that bodily changes *caused* subjective feelings of emotion. Unfortunately, the James theory concentrated attention on the perception of visceral changes, and, as we have seen, the search for physiological distinctions corresponding to the basic emotions has not met with much success. However, patterns of facial muscles *are* reliably associated with these basic categories of emotion (Ekman, Sorenson, and Friesen 1969; Ekman and Friesen 1971); this suggests that facial expression is more promising than visceral expression as a basis for subjective emotion.

This "facial feedback" theory leads to the hypothesis that if the face is prevented from assuming an emotional expression, the person will experience little or no emotion. Similarly, some theorists have argued that if a person "puts on a happy face," the person will actually feel happier. If we assume that facial expression serves as a behavioral cue—like escaping shock or approaching a snake—similar predictions can be derived from Bem's self-perception theory.

In an attempt to test this hypothesis, Laird (1974) used slides of Ku Klux Klan members or of children playing to induce emotions that would contrast with those provided by facial instructions. Subjects held their faces in either a frown or a smile while looking at both kinds of pictures. While the type of picture had a big effect on subjects' moods, the facial expression also had a small but significant effect. Subjects who frowned felt more aggressive than subjects who smiled, whether or not the slide was consistent with aggression. A smile also tended to produce a feeling of "elation," but this effect did not reach significance.

In an application of the hypothesis to feelings of pain, Lanzetta, Cartwright-Smith, and Kleck (1976) gave subjects a series of shocks and asked them to try to either suppress or exaggerate their expression of pain. They found that subjects who were told to hide their feelings actually reported feeling less pain from the shocks.

However, some negative evidence comes from a study by Tourangeau and Ellsworth (1978), who used a design that effectively ruled out the possibility that subjects were making a conscious inference of what they were supposed to feel based on what they were told to do. They found that the face did *not* have a significant effect on feelings of fear or sadness, indicating, perhaps, that the positive findings of previous studies were a result of such conscious attributions. They found that emotional stimuli affected subjective experience, facial expression, and physiological responses, but that the effect of the stimuli was not modified significantly by facial expression, as the facial feedback hypothesis predicts.

Thus the evidence that we can affect our emotions by consciously changing our facial expression is weak. The Lanzetta *et al.* study indicates that pain may be controlled by will power in this way, but "real emotions" such as fear and sadness are apparently more difficult to influence.

Some theorists have argued that attempts to control one's emotions will actually have the opposite effect, that "bottling up" our feelings only serves to intensify them. Most commonly, this point of view has been expressed in terms of a personality variable: some people wear their hearts on their sleeves, make mountains out of molehills, and generally lead histrionic lives—but really are rather shallow and do not suffer deeply; other people put on a brave front, keep a stiff upper lip, and lead lives of quiet reserve—but really may be torn up by raging invisible emotions. Most of the data supporting this point of view come from anecdotal reports by clinical psychologists and psychiatrists, but there are also some empirical studies of the correlation between expressive behaviors and physiological responses, especially the Galvanic Skin Response (GSR).

Buck and his colleagues (1972, 1974) have found weak but consistent results indicating that males show more automatic responsiveness with less readable facial expressions and less "personal" self reports. Studying males only, Lanzetta and Kleck (1970) found a very strong correlation (over .60) between GSR responsiveness and inscrutability. But Lanzetta, Cartwright-Smith, and Kleck (1976) found that when they instructed their subjects to disguise their facial expression of pain, GSR showed fewer arousal responses and subjects reported the pain as being less intense.

How can we account for the fact that in some studies the people whose facial expressions are undecipherable show the greatest arousal? One possibility, similar to that suggested by Buck and by Lanzetta and Kleck, is that some people have a strong desire to hide—perhaps even to deny—their feelings, while other people don't mind openly showing their emotions. If one of those who try to hide their emotions (usually male) feels emotionally aroused, he may also feel anxious about letting it show. This anxiety could have two effects. First, it could produce extra arousal, in addition to that already produced by the emotional stimulus, which would increase his physiological response—thus, his GSR and heartrate should be higher than those of a person who did not feel this additional anxiety. Second, it could lead the person to try to inhibit facial expression of his emotion—thus, his expression should be less easy for a stranger to read. Presumably, if very careful and sophisticated measures of the face were taken, both the original emotion and the attempts to mask it should be evident (Ekman and Friesen 1969a). We know that the more strongly a person feels the emotion (both autonomically and in terms of self-report), the less successful he will be at hiding it.

This hypothesis about the anxiety behind the poker face, though similar to those advanced by several other researchers, is still quite tentative. It is also possible that the effort and concentration required to conceal the outward display of emotion are sufficient to increase physiological arousal (Tourangeau and Ellsworth 1978). An adequate explanation of these findings requires a much more complex experimental design and much more detailed measures of the face than any researcher has yet attempted.

Self-Attribution and Behavior

It is always at least interesting and sometimes important to know why people have the attitudes and feelings they do. Research discussed in this chapter suggests that our feelings and beliefs are often inferred from our own behavior and from various external stimuli. It is also important, however, to try to understand the implications for the person. In particular, one important question is whether these self-attributions affect behavior.

A variety of research studies suggest that self-attributions may affect subsequent behavior. We will briefly consider two kinds of studies which support that conclusion. In one type subjects are led to believe that their past behavior resulted from a particular motive or from their being a particular kind of person. In a second, emotional arousal is misattributed to a particular source, and the subsequent attributions may affect behavior.

The effects of labels   As an example of the first type, people who gave to a charity were either explicitly labeled or were not labeled as "givers"; likewise, nongivers were explicitly labeled or not. As expected, those who were given the label of "givers" subsequently gave more to another charity appeal than those who had not been labeled, and there was a slight tendency for the reverse to occur for those who were labeled as nongivers (Kraut 1973), as is shown in Table 5.4. In another study, a group of children who were told they were neat did, in fact, become neater than a nonattribution control group or than a group that was lectured about the virtues of neatness. The same type of effect occurred for telling children they had the ability or motivation to do well on school work (Miller, Brickman, and Bolen 1975). In fact, as these authors point out, lecturing someone to be tidy or to work hard is often ineffective, precisely because such appeals imply an attribution that the person is not neat or is not trying hard.

However, present evidence suggests that positive labels are more likely to affect subsequent behavior than are negative labels. As Table 5.4 shows, Kraut (1973) found a very weak tendency for the people labeled as nongivers to give less money in the future. Furthermore, studies (Steele 1975; Gurwitz and Topol 1978) that have attempted to get people to act consistently with negative labels

TABLE 5.4
Mean Contribution as a Function of Previous Behavior and External Labels
(From Kraut 1973)

	Label	No label
Donor	$.70	$.41
Nondonor	.23	.33

have found that people behave in ways that disconfirm the negative labels. Thus in the Steele study women who were told they were uncooperative were *more*, rather than *less*, likely to volunteer for help when asked. This suggests that people may often be motivated to show that a negative label does not fit. Of course, many parents, teachers, and coaches seem to believe that telling a person her or his performance has been terrible will spur better performance. There are surely situations in which negative labels do generate self-confirming behavior, but the conditions under which this occurs are not well understood.

There are potentially important implications of this research on the effects of self-attribution on subsequent behavior. A number of social scientists (Becker 1963; Scheff 1966) have suggested that much deviant behavior—including crime and mental illness—can be explained in terms of labeling. The argument is that when people exhibit some forms of behavior, observers are not only inclined to provide a negative label for that behavior, but to make a dispositional attribution to the actor as well. Thus a person who talks to himself and is sometimes seemingly incoherent will be called mentally ill or crazy. Labeling theory goes further to suggest that once the label has stuck, the person accepts it and tries to behave in ways consistent with the label; others may also enforce the consistent behavior by rewarding behavior consistent with the label.

The data reviewed in this section suggest that self-attribution following labeling can occur, but that there is no clear evidence yet that negative labels lead to confirming behavior. However, we note that whereas the experiments we have reviewed have used limited labeling (typically only once), negative labels may be applied consistently and constantly over much longer periods of time in real life. We need more research to determine what conditions lead to the acceptance of negative labels and when such acceptance leads to confirmatory behavior.

Self-generated attributions   A second class of studies concerns the effects of attributions people draw from their own behavior on their subsequent behavior. A study by Freedman and Fraser (1966), while not designed as a demonstration of self-perception, is clearly applicable. Housewives were induced to place a small sign in their window or to sign a petition supporting a particular social issue. Virtually all complied with this small request. Later, a different experimenter asked permission to place a large, ugly sign in each woman's front yard. There was a substantial amount of compliance to this second request, more than for a group of housewives who were simply asked to place the sign in the yard without first having complied with the smaller request of posting a window sign or of signing a petition. One explanation for this foot-in-the-door phenomenon is that once the women had complied with the first request, they adopted a view of themselves as compliance-prone or helpful. A study by Snyder and Cunningham (1975) provided a direct test of the self-perception explanations of the foot-in-the-door phenomenon and found it to be an adequate explanation. Future behavior may then be affected by self-perceptions based on past behavior.

Lepper (1973) and Uranowitz (1975), among others, have extended this line of thinking to studies of morality and helping. Lepper replicated and extended a well-known experiment by Aronson and Carlsmith (1963) on resistance to temptations in children. In the original experiment it was shown that children who are given a mild threat for not playing with a toy devalue that toy more than children who are given a strong threat for not playing with it. Children under strong threat could reason that their not playing with the toy was due to a powerful external force, while children in the weak threat condition may be more inclined to see internal reasons ("I didn't like it") as responsible for their not playing with the toy, since the external threat was relatively weak and nonsalient. In the Lepper study, second-grade children were induced by either strong or mild threats not to play with a toy. As predicted, the mild-threat children reported that they liked the toy less than did the strong-threat children.

Lepper also got a measure of cheating in an entirely different kind of situation. He found that the children who had not played after mild threat cheated in the new situation less than children who had not played with the toy after strong threat. The best explanation of these results is that when the children had not played after strong threat they felt their behavior was externally controlled, and their self-perceptions were unaffected. On the other hand, the children who resisted after mild threat must have come to feel that they were honest, and this self-perception of honesty kept them honest in a new situation that allowed cheating.

Earlier we discussed a class of studies in which attribution of diffuse physiological arousal was affected by external cues and behavior. One interesting possibility is that attribution of arousal may affect moral behavior (Schachter and Latane 1969). If one is about to cheat, arousal in the form of guilt may act as an important inhibition. Normally, the arousal is correctly labeled as guilt because of strong internal and external labeling cues. Dienstbier and Munter (1971) showed that if arousal is attributed to other sources, cheating by male subjects was increased presumably because guilt-induced inhibitions were lowered. Dienstbier *et al.* (1975) induced children to do something wrong. Half the children were told that their feelings were due to guilt over being bad while the others had their feelings attributed to fear of getting caught. In a new situation where it was impossible to get caught, the guilt-attribution subjects have internal attributions of emotion that should apply to this new moral situation, while the other subjects should feel free to cheat when they cannot be detected by the external force they think is responsible for their arousal. As predicted, these subjects cheated more than guilt-attribution subjects. Dienstbier *et al.* (1975) offer interesting speculations on the role of such attributions on socialization of moral behavior.

Success–Failure

One of the most obvious and important areas of research on self-attribution deals with attributions after success and failure. In the last chapter we reviewed some literature on attributions for others' successes and failures. There we argued that it is important to know why others have succeeded or failed, because we need to make predictions about their future behavior and often because we have to decide whether to reward or punish others for their successes and failures. Self-attributions are important for the same reason. Each of us has to decide what kinds of career goals to pursue and what kinds of tasks to undertake; in effect, we must make predictions about our future performance. We also tend to reward ourselves after successes by feeling proud or occasionally by celebrating, and we sometimes feel self-anger, shame, guilt, or embarrassment after failure. However, there are more general effects of self-attributions. Our feelings about our own abilities and efforts affect our general self-esteem (see Schneider 1976) and may affect our motivation and behavior in a wide variety of situations. Given the powerful theoretical thrust that self- and other-perception can be explained by general attribution models, an obvious question is whether self-attributions following success and failure follow the same pattern as other-attribution. Do you and I view the causes of my successes and failures the same way?

Several studies have examined the effects of success and failure on people's judgments about ability, effort, luck, and task difficulty. In general, as one would predict, people see ability as more causally active for their successes than for their failures (Frieze and Weiner 1971; Fitch 1970; Weiner and Kukla 1970; Kukla 1972; Lefcourt *et al.* 1975; Gilmor and Minton 1974; Fontaine 1975). There are also, however, reports of ability attributions being less important for success than for failure (Feather and Simon 1971a; Luginbuhl, Crowe, and Kahan 1975; Nicholls 1975). The results for effort attributions are clearer; effort attributions are stronger following success than failure (Frieze and Weiner 1971; Fitch 1970; Wortman *et al.* 1973; Luginbuhl *et al.* 1975; Weiner and Kukla 1970; Fontaine 1975; Nicholls 1975; Feather and Simon 1971b). These results support the idea that internal factors are seen as important causes of success.

How can we explain the tendency to see successes as more internal than failures in purely attributional terms? It is fairly clear (see p. 74) that consistency with past performance is a prime cue for ability attributions, and that both ability and effort attribution are increased with low consensus (the person doing much better or worse than average). If, in the typical experiment, perceivers assume that they have been generally successful in the past, the consistent success would tend to be attributed to ability more than would the inconsistent failure. If the success seems markedly different from the average, the lack of consensus would provide additional impetus for internal attributions.

This kind of attribution model would lead one to expect people who have a particularly high self-confidence or self-esteem to perceive more personal responsibility for success than their low counterparts and to take less responsibility for failure. Success is consistent with confidence, and failure is inconsistent with confidence. Several studies have compared attributions to ability versus luck after success or failure by subjects who differ in their confidence, expectations for success, depression, or self-esteem. Highly confident subjects attribute success more to ability than do less confident subjects, while the reverse is true for failure (Feather 1969; Feather and Simon 1971a; Lefcourt *et al.* 1975; Gilmor and Minton 1974; Kuiper 1978). Furthermore, people who tend to feel that internal control is important tend to see both successes and failures as internally caused (Krovetz 1974; Lefcourt *et al.* 1975).

If one is willing to assume that most people—or at least people with certain personality characteristics—have a history of past successes, then these results are readily explainable in attributional terms. However, while many of these findings do have a reasonable attribution interpretation (see Miller and Ross 1975), we should not be blinded to the obvious alternative—that people want to take more credit for their successes than for their failures. As we saw in the last chapter, many psychologists seem to feel there is a conflict between ego-biased attribution (that is, attribution based on personal motives to look good) and "rational" attribution (that is, based on attribution models). There has been considerable research attempting to show that attributions are partially controlled by the ego-needs of the perceiver.

EGO-DEFENSIVE BIASES

Several studies support the notion that ego-enhancement or ego-defensiveness needs are involved in self-attribution after success or failure. One strategy for showing this is to vary factors that should increase or decrease ego-bias and to observe the effects on attributions. For example, Miller (1976) varied not only how successful subjects were but also how ego-involved they were in the task. If the ego-bias hypothesis were correct, one would expect that subjects' tendencies to take more credit for success than for failure would be stronger when the task was important or ego-involving. Miller did find that tendencies to ascribe success to ability and failure to task difficulty were stronger when the task was ego-involving.

Another strategy for demonstrating ego-bias is to compare the attributions of ego-involved participants for their successes with those of presumably non-ego-involved observers. While this strategy seems sound, in reality one can never be sure that actors and observers have equivalent information. Furthermore, although observers may not be particularly ego-involved in the outcome of an actor's performance, they may have biases of their own. Therefore, differences between actor and observer attributions need not support the notion of ego-bias.

The data from such comparisons do show that generally actors take more credit for success and less for failure than observers give them, particularly when the actors and observers are competitors. This would mean that an actor who wins says that success is due to her own skills, while the losing observer is unwilling to give the winning actor so much credit (Streufert and Streufert 1969; Snyder, Stephan, and Rosenfield 1975; Stephan, Rosenfield, and Stephan 1976). Of course, while there is some evidence of bias here, it is unclear whether it is the actors, the observers, or both who are biased.

A final strategy is to make explicit comparisons between the predictions of attribution theories and actors' actual attributions for themselves. Disagreements do not support the idea of ego-bias *per se* because people may not be smart enough to use the models properly, or the models themselves may be wrong. But if the departures from the model appear to be systematically controlled by ego-bias, we would be willing to entertain the idea that ego-bias played a role. Stevens and Jones (1976) did find that after success and failure subjects' attributions did depart substantially from the predictions of Kelley's Covariation Model, and that these departures were generally in the direction of being ego-defensive.

Attributions following success and failure seem to be a complex mixture of rational (insofar as attribution models are rational) and motivational tendencies. Whereas it is clear that there are major similarities between the ways we perceive others and ourselves, there are also suggestions that people are a bit too ready to seize on self-serving attributions for their own performance. These issues will be further discussed in Chapter 10.

CONSEQUENCES OF SELF-ATTRIBUTION AFTER SUCCESS-FAILURE

What are the consequences of attributions to self or situations? As one might expect, people feel more pride after success when they have tried than when they have not tried. Both ability and motivation affect shame after failure; subjects with high ability and little effort feel particularly ashamed (Weiner and Kukla 1970). Effort attributions also mediate self-rewards (Weiner, Heckhausen *et al.* 1972). Implications of the Weiner *et al.* (1972) and Kukla (1972) models of achievement motivation for the relationships between attributions and performance are discussed by Weiner and Sierad (1975) and Latta (1976).

Attribution findings also have implications for changing the behavior of people in achievement situations. The evidence suggests that people who consistently fail or who have low self-confidence will often attribute their failure to a lack of ability. Of course, that is often a veridical judgment, but in many achievement situations poor ability can presumably be compensated for by increased effort. However, consider Heider's suggestion that behavior is perceived to be a multiplicative function of ability and trying. If a person feels that she or he has no ability to control outcomes of behavior, then all the effort in the world will make no difference, and the person may cease trying. Martin

Seligman (1965) has called this phenomenon *learned helplessness*. The evidence suggests that exposure to unavoidable, aversive stimuli sometimes (Hiroto and Seligman 1975; Klein, Fencil-Morse, and Seligman 1976; Sherrod and Downs 1974), but not always (Hanusa and Schulz 1977; Roth and Bootzin 1974; Wortman *et al.* 1976; Wortman and Brehm 1975) results in deterioration of subsequent performance.

The experience of repeated failure has many components. Typically after several failures one feels unhappy, frustrated, and ashamed. In addition to the extent that the person has tried to solve the problems, he or she is likely to feel that there is no contingency between performance and outcomes, and the evidence does suggest that learned helplessness effects are most likely with perceived noncontingencies between performance and outcome (Cohen, Rothbart, and Phillips 1976; Koller and Kaplan 1978).

As you will recall, outcomes can be attributed to ability, effort, luck, or task difficulty. With relatively few failures task difficulty or luck are frequent attributions. Failure which is attributed to luck or the task should not necessarily affect subsequent performance; one could reason that with a different task or if one's luck "turned," effort might be rewarded in the future. However, repeated failure would suggest that performance does not vary with effort (assuming that the person tried at least some of the time) or with luck or task difficulty; therefore the failures must be due to lack of ability. An attributional analysis suggests that the perception of low ability would inhibit subsequent effort. Actually the research done with college students suggests that repeated failure that is attributed to lack of ability often results in *increased* rather than decreased trying and effort (Wortman *et al.* 1976; Hanusa and Schulz 1977). Obviously, this may be another instance of people reacting to negative labels by increased efforts to disconfirm the label (see p. 102).

Of course, most college students have a long history of relative success behind them. It is possible that they find it hard to accept the attribution of no ability. Perhaps people with a more consistent history of failure might be more willing to believe that failure results from lack of ability, and they might cease trying. People might stop working too soon, and one way to break this cycle of failure would be to get people to work harder after failure.

Carol Dweck (1975) suggested that children who seem helpless in the face of failure could learn to work harder and perform better by attributing their failures to lack of trying rather than to lack of ability. She worked with a group of students who generally expected to fail and who seemed to give up after failure. Some of these students were given success experiences, but this treatment did not reduce subsequent poor performance. However, another group of subjects was told after failure that they had not worked hard enough. These subjects, who were essentially given a reattribution for failure, did make marked improvements in performance.

Recently Jones and Berglas (1978) have suggested that people who have experienced noncontingencies between effort and ability and task outcomes may try to protect a fragile self-image of competence by arranging to fail because of some obvious external factor such as alcohol, lack of sleep, or press of family concerns. These self-handicapping strategies were demonstrated experimentally by Berglas and Jones (1978). Their subjects worked on problems and all were told that they had succeeded. Noncontingent subjects actually worked on insoluble problems, so presumably they perceived no correlation between their effort and performance. Contingent subjects worked on soluble problems. Subjects were then asked to take a drug that they were told would facilitate or retard their future performance. Male subjects who had noncontingent success chose the drug that would handicap future performance; contingent male subjects chose the drug that was likely to help performance. Drug choice by female subjects was unaffected by success contingency. These results suggest that at least males who are unsure why they succeeded in the past and who are unconfident of success in the future may try to arrange attributions for possible future failures to factors outside their control.

These studies suggest that the feeling of ability to control the environment seems to increase a person's trying. This not only confirms one implication of attribution models, but has important implications for enhancing the behavioral outcomes of people who are resigned to chronic failure and inactivity. It is important to note that at present we do not have enough evidence to say that attributions of lack of ability inevitably or even usually result in learned helplessness. However, it is an intriguing possibility, and more research will surely be addressed to this question.

Self- Versus Other-Perception

As noted at the beginning of this chapter, much self-attribution research has resulted from the wedding of traditional Heiderian-based attribution models with independent research on emotional labeling and perceptions of own attitudes. Not only can most self-attribution results be explained within general attribution paradigms, but Bem explicitly assumed that self-perception was only a particular variant of general person perception. Thus far, this chapter has accepted that assumption.

However beautiful the idea of subsuming self-perception under general person perception models is, we must be careful. The question of interest to most person perception researchers has been how we make attributions to others (usually strangers) based on minimal information. Everyday experience suggests that we know more about the causes of our own behavior than about behavior causes of any other person, particularly a stranger. On those grounds alone, we might expect self- and other-attributions to differ from time to time.

THE JONES-NISBETT MODEL

In looking over some of the early attribution research, Jones and Nisbett (1972) found what they believed to be a salient difference between self- and other-perception. For example, in the Jones and Harris (1967) study of perceptions of true attitudes described on page 66, perceivers thought essay writers held the attitudes they espoused even when the essay writers had no choice about which side to defend. In the study (Jones *et al.* 1968) of ability attribution after increasing or decreasing performance described on page 76, perceivers thought that subjects who got worse over time were smarter than those who got better. However, in a variant of that study, when subjects were asked about their own behavior in a similar situation, they did not perceive ability differences but rather felt that the difficulty of the items changed over time.

Jones and Nisbett suggest that these results can be explained by assuming that observers tend to favor internal, dispositional explanations of an actor's behavior, while actors tend to favor situational, external explanations of their own behavior. For example, I see my vote in the last election as determined by qualities of the candidates, while an observer might be more inclined to see my political ideology as playing a determining role. I feel I am nice to people because they are nice people, or perhaps because I feel under normative pressure to be nice; others will see my nice behavior as due to my being a nice person. A nine-year-old child we know well has a nice way of explaining her tired, grumpy behavior when she gets home from school by claiming everyone is picking on her or by claiming that everyone else is grumpy. For her, the situation is the effective cause, while her family is more inclined to dispositional attribution.

There is now a considerable body of research support for this phenomenon (Harvey, Harris, and Barnes 1975; Harvey, Arkin, Gleason, and Johnston 1975; Gurwitz and Panciera 1975; Goldberg 1978), although not all studies (Wolosin, Sherman, and Mynatt 1972; Miller *et al.* 1974) do find the effect. As one research example that tested the Jones-Nisbett hypothesis directly, we describe an experiment by Nisbett, Caputo, Legant, and Marecek (1973). Subjects were asked to explain their reasons for choosing their college major and for liking a girlfriend. When subjects explained their own reason for choosing a major, they tended to see their own qualities and those of the subject areas as being equally important in the choice. However, when explaining their friends' behavior, they gave greater weight to personal characteristics of the friends than to the qualities of the major in determining the choice of a major. When asked why they liked their girlfriends, subjects referred much more often to the women's personal qualities than they did to their own. When explaining their friends' behavior, however, they referred equally often to the qualities of the girlfriend and to those of the friend. The results, therefore, tended to support the Jones and Nisbett hypothesis.

Informational differences   Why would observers be consistently predisposed to perceive internal causes of the actors' behavior, while the actors would be predisposed to perceive more situational control? Jones and Nisbett argued that actors and observers differ in both the information available to them and in the ways they process that information (still others have argued for the role of motivational factors). Consider first informational differences. Normally, actors have more information about their past behavior than the observers, and they may realize that the present behavior is not typical of usual behavior. Also, the actor may have better information than the observer about his or her own intentions and goals in the situation. The observer, lacking evidence to the contrary, is usually forced to assume that present behavior is indicative of past behavior, and that the actor intended to cause the given effects in the situation.

Monson and Snyder (1977) have recently emphasized that normally actors can be expected to know more about the causes of their behavior than can observers. If the behavior is really under the control of the situation, actors will tend to be more accurate in perceiving that; if, on the other hand, the behavior is controlled by dispositional characteristics of the actor, the actor should also be more likely to perceive that correctly. The implication of this model is that actors are not inevitably more likely to perceive situational control than observers. However, the predominant tendency in the research literature for actors to perceive more situational control may result from a veridical perception, because researchers have generally created experiments with strong situational forces.

Interestingly enough, it now seems likely that there are individual differences among people on how subject to situational forces they are. Bem and Allen (1974) have shown that some people are quite consistent from situation to situation, while others are more variable. Mark Snyder has suggested a fundamental personality variable, called *self-monitoring*, which is related to both behavioral consistency and perceptual style. People who score high on the Self-Monitoring Scale (Snyder 1974), "out of a concern for the situational and interpersonal appropriateness of their social behavior, are particularly sensitive to the expression and self-presentation of others in social situations and use these cues as guidelines for managing their own social behavior" (Snyder 1976, p. 57). Because they are concerned with social expectations, they vary their behavior more according to situational forces (Snyder and Monson 1975), and their behavior is less predictable from knowledge of their internal attitudes (Snyder and Swann 1976; Snyder and Tanke 1976). High self-monitors are also somewhat better at controlling their own expressive behavior and at making it situationally appropriate (Lippa 1977). However, even more relevant to the present chapter, high self-monitors differ from low self-monitors in their attribution styles. High self-monitors see themselves as more situationally contolled than do others, whereas low self-monitors make more dispositional attributions about themselves than do others (Snyder 1976). This suggests, of course, that people whose behavior is situationally controlled perceive that fact, while those whose behavior is fairly consistent and presumably dispositionally controlled are also accurate in their perceptions.

Information processing bias We should also consider the possibility that even if self and others have equivalent information, they may process the information differently. That is, the difference in attributions can possibly be explained in terms of different assumptions or perspectives taken by actors and observers. One possibility is that actors and observers make different assumptions about how consistent, distinctive, and common the actor's behavior is. As we have seen in Chapter 3, a pattern of high distinctiveness and high consensus pushes attributions toward entities or situational forces, whereas low distinctiveness and low consensus lead to person attributions. Perhaps actors are more likely than observers to assume that their behavior is common (high consensus) and distinctive, which could account for their tendency to greater situational attributions. Lee Ross (1977) has argued that people tend to judge their own behavior as being relatively common; they assume that other people would likely respond to situational demands the same way as they have done. This False Consensus Bias has been demonstrated in an experiment by Ross, Greene, and House (1977). Subjects' estimates of how likely others were to have particular preferences, expectations, daily activities, and habits were clearly biased toward their ratings for self. In a behavioral demonstration, subjects were asked to walk around campus wearing a large sandwich board sign. Those who agreed to do this estimated that 62 percent of their peers would also do it, whereas those who refused estimated that 67 percent of their peers would also refuse.

Not only are perceivers inclined to see their own behavior as more common than it is, but an experiment by Eisen (1977) suggests that they may also see their own behavior as more distinctive than observers do. In her experiment, Eisen gave subjects information about their emotions, beliefs, actions, and achievements and asked them to estimate their standing on similar kinds of items. She found that subjects were less willing to generalize to other items than were observers. However, it is important to note that these results held only for socially undesirable items; it is possible that ego-bias entered in, because seeing failure as nondistinctive is one way of shifting blame to external force.

There is some evidence that actors infer more consensus than observers, and there is evidence that at least for negative behaviors actors also infer greater distinctiveness. The combination of low consensus and high distinctiveness would push attributions toward the situations.

Observers may also make systematic errors in the ways they process information. Jones and Nisbett (1972) argued that different kinds of information may be salient for actors and observers. Actors do not ordinarily watch themselves behave; the very position of their eyes forces attention to the situation. Also from the actor's point of view, behavior changes as the situation changes. The observer, on the other hand, is likely to pay particular attention to the actor, and the relevant comparison for the observer is likely to be other actors rather than other situations, particularly since the observer is often more likely to see several actors in the same situation than the same actor in different situations. Hence, the observer is more likely to perceive differences of behavior as being coordinated with the different actors. Thus, actor-observer differences may be due to attention or salience of information.

An experiment by Michael Storms (1973) illustrates the point. In Storms's experiment, two subjects participated in a conversation while two observers watched. Each observer watched only one of the participants. This conversation was videotaped and was later played back. For half of the actors and observers, the videotape was played back in such a way that they saw it very much as they had experienced it; that is, the actors saw a videotape of the other person, and the observers saw the person they had been asked to monitor. In other conditions, however, subjects had their orientations reversed; the actors saw themselves in the conversation rather than the other person, and the observers saw the videotape of the subject they had not monitored. Subjects were then asked to rate to what extent their friendliness, talkativeness, nervousness, and dominance were due to either personal characteristics or due to those of the situation.

In the control conditions, in which there was no video playback, the subjects tended to attribute their own behavior more to situational forces than did the observers (see Table 5.5). This was also true when the subjects and actors saw the videotape from the same perspective as they had originally participated in it. However, when the perspectives were reversed, the attributions also tended to reverse. When the observers now observed the other person in the situation, they tended to see more situational attribution. When the actors now observed themselves, much as an observer would, they tended to perceive less situational attribution.

Another experiment that varied perspective was performed by Regan and Totten (1975). They asked observers to empathize with the actor on the reasonable assumption that this would make situational forces more salient. As predicted, empathizing observers did show increased situational and lessened dispositional attributions.

TABLE 5.5
Dispositional and Situational Attributions for Actors and Observers in Different Conditions
(After Storms 1973)

	No videotape*	Videotape*	
		Same orientation	New orientation
Actor			
Dispositional	27.35	26.10	27.50
Situational	25.10	25.95	20.70
Observer			
Dispositional	27.30	27.10	25.75
Situational	22.50	22.20	24.15

* Larger numbers indicate greater attributions.

A number of other experiments (Wegner and Finstuen 1977) have also tried to change the perspective of actors and observers. For example, Sherrod and Farber (1975) used a variant of the Storms procedure. Actors worked on a difficult intellectual task and were told they had failed. As expected, the actors were less inclined to attribute the failure to their own abilities than were observers. In a second phase of the experiment, actors and observers switched roles. Former observers who now failed as actors were much less inclined to see ability as the cause of their failure than they had been as observers. Actors who became observers became somewhat more dispositional in their ratings. These results support the idea that changing roles does affect the salience of certain information. However, Sherrod and Farber also found that former observers were more likely to change when they took on the actor role than were the actors when they took on the observer role. Eisen (1977) found similar results when she gave subjects information characteristic of the other roles' perspective. Thus there is some suggestion that actors have more difficulty changing their perspective than do observers, perhaps because actor attributions are based on fuller information.

These experiments suggest that what actors and observers find salient in the situation also pushes them toward particular kinds of attributions. Actors find the situation more salient, whereas observers find the actor more salient; consequently, attribution is more situational and less dispositional by actors than observers. In Chapter 10 we will examine salience effects in somewhat greater detail.

Motivational differences   As we have already seen (pp. 104-106), actors may be too inclined to see their successes as due to internal factors and their failures as due to external factors. Indeed, several experiments point to the conclusion that actors relative to observers see negative outcomes as situational, whereas this difference between actors and observers is either reversed or not present for positive outcomes (Harvey, Arkin, Gleason, and Johnston 1975; Harvey, Harris, and Barnes 1975; Stephan 1975; Eisen 1977; Taylor and Koivumaki 1976; Snyder, Stephan, and Rosenfield 1976; Wells et al. 1977). However, the fact that actors are sometimes self-enhancing in their attributions cannot completely account for actor-observer differences, because many studies already reviewed find that observers are sometimes more dispositional than actors for neutral and positive behaviors. Furthermore, in such studies it is not always clear whether actors or observers are the most biased. For example, observers might be motivated to see negative behavior in dispositional terms. As we argued in the discussion of attribution responsibility (pp. 77-80), observers may have a particular need to see negative behavior as resulting from "bad character." To see bad behavior as caused by situational forces means that anyone (including the observer) would do the same thing when situational forces are strong. The point is that observers may be just as biased (although for different reasons) as actors.

In this regard, Miller and Norman (1975) have suggested that, in fact, observers might be inclined to overperceive dispositional causes for the behavior of others. Feeling that one knows why another person behaves the way she does gives one the feeling of living in a predictable world, one that can be controlled. Miller, Norman, and Wright (1978) showed that when perceivers expect to interact with someone (and therefore have especially high needs to predict her behavior), they are more inclined to dispositional attributions than when they do not expect interaction. In Chapter 10 we will have more to say about the biases produced by our needs to perceive causality, but for now the research of Miller *et al.* suggests that observers as well as actors can be biased by motivational factors.

IMPLICATIONS

The Jones-Nisbett hypothesis, if true, has the most far-reaching effects, both theoretical and practical. Here we examine two major implications. In the first place, the hypothesis suggests that just as observers tend to see dispositional causes of behavior, so might traditional personality theorists have tended to oversubscribe to a trait or dispositional point of view. In recent years, the idea that people have internal, highly general traits and other dispositions has come under attack. Walter Mischel (1968, 1973) has argued that one of the reasons that traditional personality tests predict behavior less well than situational forces is that people do not have traits that control their behavior over a wide range of situations. And, indeed, many studies (see Sarason, Smith, and Diener 1975) have typically found that situations predict behavior better than do personality traits. And if you will examine your own behavior, you will note that whatever salient traits you feel you have do not "work" in every situation. If you consider yourself to be kind, you will surely allow that you are not kind in every situation. The point is that while each of us generally has some understanding of situational control over our behavior, most personality theorists have concentrated on personal dispositions rather than on situational analysis. Interestingly enough, when we perceive the behavior of others, we do tend to perceive the way the personality theories say we should—by paying too much attention to stable, internal characteristics.

Another implication of the Jones-Nisbett hypothesis is that observers should be inclined to overattribute responsibility for the behavior of others. We may tend to overperceive responsibility, particularly for the bad consequences of others' behavior. That, in turn, might reduce our tendencies to help.

West, Gunn, and Chernicky (1975) were interested in seeing what factors could induce everyday citizens to commit an illegal act, and they particularly wondered whether ordinary citizens could be made to commit a Watergate-type caper. When subjects were asked to rob an advertising company of microfilm, the way the caper was presented had a major role to play in how many people agreed to go along. For example, when subjects were promised $2000 for taking part, only 20 percent agreed to do so. When subjects were told that the Internal Revenue Service wanted the microfilms but that the government could offer no immunity for capture, only 5 percent agreed to participate. However, with IRS sponsorship and promised immunity (the conditions that came closest to matching what the Watergate burglars thought they had), 45 percent agreed to take part in the burglary. The point is that situational variables played a major role in whether subjects agreed to participate. When asked, the subjects agreed that the concern with situational conditions had been an important element in their decision either to take part or not. Observers, on the other hand, tended to see the causes of behavior, particularly the decision to accept, as being due to dispositional factors. Perhaps we judge the behavior of others harshly.

In a less politically cosmic study, Batson (1975) presented students with case histories of people in trouble. In each case, the main character in the case blamed the situation for his problems, but only 31 percent of the time did the case reader attribute the cause to the same situational source. Furthermore, the locus of causality was related to what the reader recommended for a "cure": person attributions more often leading to referral to mental hospitals that seek to change people and leave situational (societal) forces unchanged.

It would be inappropriate to become too moralistic about all this. Surely the tendency for observers to perceive more personal causation than actors is not overwhelming, and surely it can under some circumstances be reversed. Also, it is important to recognize that there is evidence only for actor-observer differences; it may be that actors are biased and observers are accurate. The results cited above in the discussion of West et al. indicate that this may not always be true, but we must not fall into the trap of assuming that observers are always more biased than actors. Furthermore, as we argued in the last chapter, attribution of responsibility is a highly complex business. So, although the Jones-Nisbett hypothesis does not of itself make a strong point about social and political judgments, it does suggest that we should continually ask whether the judgments we make about others' responsibilities for their behavior might not be biased by our tendencies to overperceive personal causation in the behavior of others.

Summary

Several theorists have argued that perception of one's own internal states is based on many of the same general rules used in perceiving the qualities of others. Daryl Bem has explicitly argued that people do not have privileged knowledge about their own motives, attitudes, and emotions, and that perception of internal states in both cases is based on inferences from behavior. Stanley Schachter has further suggested that emotions and feelings are based in part on inferences from environmental cues. The Bem and Schachter models have generated a large amount of research on the perception of internal states. The research evidence indicates that the two theories have some general validity, although they do not account for all details of the research literature. In particular, attitudes are often inferred from behavior as Bem's theory suggests, but only when the person cannot remember initial attitudes or only when the the initial attitudes are not salient. The perception of emotions has been shown to be strengthened by perception of environmental cues, and generally perception of emotions is affected by perceptions of one's own physiological reactions and possibly by feedback from the expressive behavior of the face. Perception of the strength of emotion can be altered by getting the person to misattribute the causes of the emotion to some external source, and such misattribution techniques have implications for psychotherapy.

A considerable amount of research has been addressed to perceptions of the causes of one's successes and failures. One reason for such interest has been to discover whether people are biased and ego-enhancing in their perceptions. The available evidence suggests that people are inclined to see success as more internally caused than failure. By itself, this result does not clearly support a bias position, because a similar tendency exists for perceptions of others. Furthermore, such a tendency has a rational basis if people expect to be successful, and the research evidence does suggest that people who expect success are especially likely to see the causes of success as internal ones. However, several tests of the bias position clearly support the existence of ego-enhancing bias, so it appears that attributions for our own success and failure are a mixture of rational and motivational processes.

Research addressed to the question of whether self- and other-perception are based on the same processes has indicated that perceivers are inclined to see situational forces as relatively unimportant as causes of others' behavior, and as relatively more important for self-perception. Jones and Nisbett have suggested that people may have different information in perceiving self and others, and that different kinds of information might be salient in the two cases. There is research support for both ideas, although attribution researchers have tended to concentrate on the salience hypothesis.

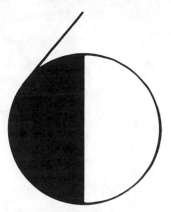

person perception and nonverbal cues
snap judgments and reactive attributions

Suppose I ask you to walk up to some woman on the street and ask her what time it is. You do it, the woman tells you that it's 3:15, you return, and then I ask you to tell me all you can about her. You will have learned almost nothing from the words spoken (that is, assuming that it really *is* 3:15), yet you will probably be able to generate a good deal of information about the woman. In addition to her appearance and dress (see Chapter 2), you will have seen quite a bit of behavior in a very short time. A wide sweep of the arm may suggest to you that the woman is an Italian (Efron 1941); a fixed stare may suggest that she is an Arab (Watson 1970). Her voice will also tell you something about where she comes from: many foreigners may stumble over the difficult word "three," and even if the woman is American, her accent may give evidence of her home. You may have an impression of the woman as more than usually feminine or masculine, depending on the bend of her knees or the tilt of her head (Goffman 1976). Her posture (Mehrabian 1969) and the duration of her gaze (Thayer 1969) may suggest a dominant or submissive attitude, and you may use this knowledge, in combination with other cues, to infer her social status. If she speaks to you in a monotone (Addington 1968) or shrinks slightly away from you, curling her arms in front of her chest (Spiegel and Machotka 1974), you may infer that she is a cold person. If she flinches when she first hears the sound of your voice, you may think she is nervous or shy. Whether the woman you describe actually resembles the woman you talked to is another matter, and a very difficult one. But right or wrong, people are able and willing to make a wide variety of attributions about the culture, status, and personality of others on the basis of nonverbal information.

This chapter will deal with the immediate snap judgments and more complicated reactive attributions we make on the basis of nonverbal behaviors such as the tone of the voice, the direction of the gaze, and the expression of the face. Those who have studied person perception and attribution have not generally studied "expressive behaviors" of this kind. In grappling with the processes by which people infer intentions from behavior and dispositions from intentions, traditional theorists have tended to ignore behaviors that are commonly seen as *unintentional*, such as nonverbal behaviors. By defining the inference of intention as a central mediating link in the process of attribution, these theorists have overlooked the possibility that people may also be able to arrive at a dispositional attribution without ever inferring an intention.

Many of the same psychological processes operate regardless of whether the behavior we observe is verbal or nonverbal, purposive or reactive; in this chapter we would like to explore the ways in which people's interpretation of nonverbal behavior resembles and differs from their perception of other behavior, and to fit the perception of nonverbal behavior into our overall schema of the person perception process.

What do we mean by *nonverbal behavior*? Although there is considerable scholarly controversy about the kinds of behavior that should be called nonverbal cues, most of the research in this area is concerned with the meaning of noninstrumental movements of the face, body, and vocal cords. This "meaning" may be what is revealed to the psychologist about the individual psyche or the social relationship or the culture, or it may be what is revealed to an ordinary observer who happens to perceive the person. Since this is a book about person perception, we will focus on the latter set of meanings.

In general, the domain of nonverbal cues is roughly equivalent to everything that the actors and the director bring to the performance of a play, everything that is *not* in the script or stage directions: facial expression, vocal expression, gesture, posture, timing, and to some extent the choice of where to stand and when to move.

In attempting a rapprochement between the study of person perception and the study of nonverbal communication, we are departing from the traditional framework of those investigators who have studied nonverbal cues. Most of these investigators divide up the field in terms of the separate nonverbal channels of communication, and many specialize in a particular channel. Thus, some people specialize in studies of interpersonal distance, some specialize in the gaze or the voice, and some study gestures, posture, or facial expression. It should be clear from the first paragraph of this chapter that particular kinds of inference are *not* restricted to particular channels. For example, I may infer that someone is Latin American on the basis of the distance he stands from me at a party, the lilt of his accent, the intensity of his gaze, or the fact that he greets another man with an embrace. But on another occasion I may use the same channels of communication—distance, voice, gaze, and touch—to infer that the person is a domineering oaf, a lonely person, or a would-be lover. There are no particular channels that "go with" personality or cultural or class background or mood states: any channel can provide information about any of these.

So far in this book we have discussed two major kinds of judgment: snap judgments and the more complicated judgments of motives and dispositions encompassed by the general term *attribution.* Nonverbal cues can be the basis for either kind of judgment. In Chapter 2 we argued that the signs that elicit snap judgments can be either static or dynamic, and we discussed the use of static, more or less permanent physical features like skin color and beauty as a basis for stereotyped inferences about a person's social and psychological characteristics. In this chapter we will discuss snap judgments based on more dynamic behavioral cues such as downcast eyes or a stammer.

But not all judgments made on the basis of nonverbal cues are snap judgments. Sometimes nonverbal cues, like other behaviors, require a little more thought before we can arrive at an interpretation, and sometimes they do not fit any of the well-worn rules of thumb that spring out automatically when we make a snap judgment. Many nonverbal cues, being variable, can also signal passing moods and reactions as well as more permanent dispositions, and, in fact, nonverbal cues are one of the primary stimuli for what we have called *reactive attributions.* We notice a nonverbal response, like the flinching of the woman in the opening paragraph, and we infer that it was a *reaction* to some stimulus, such as the sound of our voice. We may then go on to make other attributions about the kind of person who would be so startled by our gentle question, in this case the attribution that she is a particularly nervous person.

Thus nonverbal behavior, like other behavior, can stimulate either a snap judgment or a more complicated attribution. In each case, there are both similarities and differences to the kinds of judgments made on the basis of other cues.

Snap Judgments

STEREOTYPES ABOUT NONVERBAL BEHAVIOR

We have argued (in Chapter 2) that many of our initial impressions of another person are snap judgments—old and simple stereotypes, applied instantly and without thinking. Many of our beliefs about nonverbal cues are simple stereotypes of just this sort; here, too, we have little clichés about what behaviors mean, clichés that help to create as sense of predictability and meaning, sometimes at the expense of accurate perceptions. Novelists, directors of plays, and especially filmmakers draw on these stereotypes and reinforce them, so that very often we form impressions of the characters and their relationships before the dialogue even begins.

Much of the work of Albert Mehrabian (1972) is related to our stereotypes about nonverbal cues. He frequently uses the technique of having subjects pretend that they are interacting with a certain kind of person; while they are doing so he measures their nonverbal behavior. He has found, for example, that people tend to hold their bodies in a more tense position and to face the other person more directly when they are pretending to interact with a high-status person, and that they tend to close themselves off by crossing their arms in front of them and leaning away when they are supposed to dislike the person (Mehrabian 1967; Mehrabian and Friar 1969; Mehrabian 1968). These regularities indicate that there are stereotypes associated with nonverbal cues that people agree on when they are playing various kinds of roles, and there is some evidence that similar stereotypes operate when people are given the task of interpreting the behavior of others (LeCompte and Rosenfeld 1971; Reece and Whitman 1962; Mehrabian 1972).

Evaluative snap judgments As with other judgments in person perception, one of the first and strongest judgments made is a basic evaluative judgment. Clore, Wiggins, and Itkin (1975) found that subjects had no trouble rating a long list of nonverbal cues for positivity. Clore and his colleagues gave subjects a list of over 100 nonverbal behaviors and had them judge how positive or negative the behaviors were. They found that frowning, looking away or moving away, yawning, staring coldly, sneering, shaking one's head, and "rude" behaviors like cleaning teeth or fingernails were considered most unpleasant. The most positive nonverbal behaviors were looking, turning and moving towards the perceiver, smiling, nodding, opening the eyes and raising the eyebrows, and using expressive hand gestures. Very similar results were found by Horn (1977). In the Clore *et al.* study, subjects also judged videotapes of people engaging in these behaviors, and their ratings generally showed that the more positive behaviors the woman on the tape emitted, the more she was liked. As with snap judgments based on appearance cues, a simple positive or negative evaluative judgment appears to be especially common and important.

Specific stereotypes and their validity However, there is evidence that we have other, more specific stereotypes about tone of voice, gaze direction, and other nonverbal cues. Some of these stereotypes are so widely shared that they have become fully conscious, and serve as the basis for rules that are communicated as part of the socialization process. At a certain age, children in this culture are told that staring at other people is rude. Likewise, males and females at adolescence may receive explicit instructions about nonverbal cues that have undesirable sexual connotations. Males are taught the art of the firm handshake, and females are taught how to "sit like a lady." Little boys are allowed to let their hands rest like a jellyfish in the clasp of another male, and little girls can sit with their knees on a level with their shoulders, but at puberty these behaviors suddenly become impermissable.

Other stereotypes about nonverbal behavior are less likely to be consciously articulated or taught. Addington (1968), for example, found that people have a large number of stereotypes about voices, judging breathiness to be a sign of femininity and judging flatness to be a sign of masculinity, apathy, and coldness, and so on. Scherer (1974) has shown that even mechanically generated tone sequences have emotional meaning for people.

Whether these stereotypes are correct is a much more difficult question. It appears that sometimes the voice really is a good predictor of the speaker's internal dispositions, and people can use it with some accuracy; sometimes people use the voice as a predictor when there is no evidence that it is really correlated with the disposition they are trying to predict; and sometimes the voice seems to be a good predictor, but people may not use it. So far, the best evidence of accuracy has been found when people are making judgments of transient emotions and physical characteristics from the voice (Davitz and Davitz 1959; Kasl and Mahl 1965; Kramer 1963); they are less successful at making personality judgments (Kramer 1963; Hunt and Lin 1967).

People also use the direction of the gaze to make stereotyped attributions about others, and here too their accuracy varies. When the gaze occurs in combination with other situational cues there is some evidence that people's stereotypes about liking and hostility are reasonably accurate (Argyle and Cook 1976, Chapter 4). On the other hand, people may read too much significance into an averted gaze, assuming that the person is anxious or tense (Cook and Smith 1975; Kleck and Nuessle 1960), when in fact the evidence for the correlation is ambiguous (Argyle and Cook 1976). Similarly, people tend to assume that powerful people gaze more (Cook and Smith 1975; Argyle, Lefebvre, and Cook 1974; Kleck and Nuessle 1968), but the evidence indicates that in fact they often gaze *less* (Exline 1972). It may be, of course, that people try to outstare their potential rivals when they are struggling for domination, but withdraw their attention from their subordinates once they have achieved it.

SNAP JUDGMENTS ABOUT STATIC AND DYNAMIC CUES

There is good evidence that people use dynamic nonverbal cues to make snap judgments. The processes by which snap judgments are made are also probably much the same whether the cue is a physical feature or a nonverbal behavior. In both cases snap judgments are immediate, direct perceptions, requiring little in the way of conscious reasoning on the way to the conclusion. They are almost always responses to people we don't know very well, often people we are meeting for the first time. Snap judgments are very often evaluative in nature, although other kinds of judgments—such as judgments about power, cultural or class background, or specific personality traits—are also made on the basis of both appearance and nonverbal behavior. These stereotypes are elements of naive psychological theories used to predict and explain the behavior of others. There is a good deal of evidence that we use nonverbal cues in this way; there is less evidence that they provide accurate information.

Many nonverbal cues are different from physical features, however, because they can vary more quickly within the same individual. A person cannot decide to be six feet tall one day and five feet tall the next, but he *can* stand up perfectly straight one day and slouch lackadaisically the next. If we meet the person only on the first day, he may strike us as a rigid and stiff-necked person, but if we chance to meet the same person the next day, it will be hard for us to maintain this perception. Nonverbal cues tend to be dynamic; appearance cues tend to be more static.

On the other hand, this distinction is true only in a relative sense. All the cues we use in generating snap judgments change over time, even physical features. Hair color changes from brown to grey, muscles change from hard to soft, the silhouette changes from concave to convex. Dieting and exercise may change these physical cues at a faster rate; accidents and surgery may change them faster still. Nonetheless, meeting someone for the first time, we tend to assume these features are permanent, and we probably use them to infer relatively permanent traits. Hairstyles and facial hair are more quickly altered, and dress may change more than once a day. We may use these cues, especially dress, to infer more transient dispositions. That is, if we see a professor wearing tennis shoes, we may infer that he is an easygoing person, or we may infer that he is feeling particularly relaxed today.

Nonverbal cues probably differ in their implications about permanence. Certain voice qualities, for example, may be regarded as relatively stable, and may be used to make attributions about relatively stable characteristics. However, most nonverbal behaviors differ from most appearance cues because they can change during the same interaction. This volatility allows us to infer rapidly changing moods and reactions, inferences unlikely to be made on the basis of features that change more slowly. As a general rule, we can hypothesize that we make judgments of relatively permanent dispositions and traits on the basis of features that we know change slowly, and that we make judgments of relatively transient dispositions and psychological states on the basis of features that we know can change quickly. We are especially likely to make a transient dispositional attribution when we actually witness the change. It is to this class of attributions that we now turn.

Attribution: Special Properties of Nonverbal Cues

The process of making a snap judgment is much the same whether the stereotyped cue is a dynamic nonverbal behavior or a more static physical feature. There is a lot more to person perception than snap judgments, however; often we observe and try to interpret behaviors without a cut-and-dried stereotype to guide us. The study of the attribution process is an attempt to understand the more complicated inference rules people use in trying to interpret the behavior of others. Attribution theorists have not paid much attention to the processes by which people interpret the kinds of nonverbal behaviors we have mentioned. In dealing with attributions (unlike snap judgments), there are some important differences in the psychological processes and chains of inference that typically characterize the interpretation of verbal and nonverbal cues. In this section we will attempt to delineate some of these differences.

PURPOSIVE AND REACTIVE ATTRIBUTIONS

In a sense, there are a great many behaviors that are "nonverbal" besides the "expressive" behaviors we have been discussing. The chapters on attribution focused largely on descriptions of "nonverbal" behaviors, such as "Vern stepped on Leslie's foot," "Elaine's car rolled down the hill and hit a tree," and so on. It has been argued (Allport and Vernon 1933) that all behaviors have an expressive component not captured by an unqualified description of the action itself. Thus, one may say "Vern stepped on Leslie's foot," but someone who was actually on the scene would notice more than the simple fact that the behavior occurred. For example, one might notice that Vern's hands were shaking and that he was swallowing rather often, and conclude that Vern stepped on Leslie's foot *nervously*; or one might notice that Vern's jaw was clenched and his eye gleamed fiendishly, and conclude that Vern stepped on Leslie's foot *deliberately*; and so on. The behaviors usually discussed under the rubric *nonverbal behavior* are typically considered to be more purely expressive behaviors, or the "style" component of other behaviors.

Although the psychologists concerned with person perception and attribution have tended to ignore the stylistic elements of behavior, a good deal of what we know or think we know about others is based less on the fact that they performed certain actions than on their *manner* in doing so. If we ask someone a small favor, a grudging compliance is often more annoying to us than a friendly excuse. We all seem to have absorbed our parents' and teachers' maxim that "it's not what you say, but how you say it," and we all seem to have generalized it to the parallel belief that it's not what you do, but how you do it.

Nonverbal behaviors are seen as unintentional The kinds of judgments we make on the basis of nonverbal cues do not fit very well into traditional attribution models. These models deal mainly with *purposive attributions*. For example, Heider argues that in judging another person, our aim is to distinguish which of his behaviors are indicative of internal dispositions and which are a result of pressures from the environment. According to Heider (see Chapter 3), in order to decide that a behavior is indicative of an internal disposition, we must determine that the person is able to carry out the action (*Can*) and that he is (or was) trying to do so (*Try*). Neither of these judgments poses much of a problem for the observer of nonverbal expressive behavior, and neither is particularly useful in advancing the observer's understanding of the behavior. On the whole, we assume that just about everybody *can* laugh or cry, stare or look away, slouch or sit up straight. Similarly, we assume that hardly any of the ordinary people we meet laugh or cry, stare or look away, slouch or sit up straight *on purpose* in order to produce some effect. There is a strong assumption in this culture that many nonverbal "expressive" behaviors are *unintentional* (which means that they are not the result of trying) and *uncontrollable* (which means that trying would be useless anyway). Thus, the normal inference about nonverbal behaviors is that the person can do them and that he is not trying to.

Reactive attributions   Since nonverbal behaviors are typically seen as unintentional, we do not try to figure out what purposes they serve; instead we try to figure out what caused them. We make a *reactive attribution* because we infer that the behavior is a reaction to some stimulus, perhaps an idiosyncratic internal stimulus. Sometimes the stimulus may be obvious, as when a mother yells at a child and the child cries. At other times the stimulus may not be obvious, as when we see a child crying apparently for no reason at all.

One reason that Heider's model and much of the subsequent work on attribution theory fail to fit nonverbal cues is that the theories are talking about behaviors that produce visible effects, and the question the perceiver asks is whether or not the person intended to produce those effects. Heider argues that only intended effects are usually informative about dispositional properties, and Jones and Davis assume that the person knows what effects result from his behavior. Neither of these assumptions makes much sense in relation to nonverbal cues, because expressive acts simply do not have "effects" in the same sense that instrumental acts do. With a few exceptions, expressive acts have very little effect on the physical environment: that is almost part of the definition of *expressive*. An expressive act does, of course, have effects on the *social* environment, and, in a face-to-face conversation, most of all on the perceiver himself, but the perceiver usually assumes that those effects are unintended. He may even assume that the other person is *unaware* of his behavior and of the effects it caused.

Thus, in making a reactive attribution, we do not look at the various effects of the behavior and try to figure out which ones were intended; instead we look at the various possible *causes* of the behavior and try to figure out which ones were important in provoking the reaction. In some cases these inferences are obvious. If a person is relaxing quietly listening to a Mozart quartet, and suddenly the delicate music is overwhelmed by the racket of the neighbor's power lawn mower, we will have no trouble finding a plausible cause for the exasperated frown that appears on the music-lover's face. We make an easy reactive attribution. On the purposive side, if the person gets up and closes the windows, then goes back to peaceful listening, we will have no trouble inferring that shutting out the noise was the intended effect. We make an easy purposive attribution.

In other cases the inferences are not so easy. We have discussed the difficulties of untangling multiple effects and inferring intentions from actions in the chapters on attribution. Inferring the causes of a person's reactions can also be difficult. If we notice an expression of irritation on the face of our Mozart listener and there is no lawnmower, we won't know whether he is responding to something about the music, to something else in the immediate environment, or to some distant private thought. In this case, we may look further for the cause, or we may make a snap judgment: "What a sour, unpleasant person!" If we know the person well, we will be more likely to look for present causes and less likely to make a personality judgment.

Even with strangers, however, we may look for causes and try harder to interpret the behavior if we have a feeling that we ourselves may be the cause. When we catch a person looking at us, our first inference will probably be, "That person is attending to me" (Ellsworth in press; Argyle and Cook 1976). We guess that we must be the cause of the attention. In many situations, this first interpretation may be insufficient, and will provoke us to go on to make further attributions, all springing from the first one. In the case of the gaze, we may go on to ask, "Why is that person attending to me?", and possibly "What does that person want me to do?" We may not fully realize that the gaze is the stimulus for our perception that we are being attended to, and it may be that our degree of awareness of the immediate stimulus will affect the type of interpretation we reach.

Reactive behaviors are trusted The fact that many nonverbal behaviors are seen as unintentional spontaneous reactions has other implications for the attributions we make. We tend to assume the reaction is genuine; we tend not to consider ulterior motives. If someone tells us we have a good sense of humor, we may worry about the possibility that he is trying to weasel his way into our favor. If he is convulsed with uncontrollable laughter, we don't ordinarily entertain such suspicions. When the verbal and the nonverbal channels convey contradictory messages there is some evidence (Mehrabian 1972; Ekman and Friesen 1969a) that the nonverbal channels are trusted more. We assume that because these nonverbal reactions are unintentional, they cannot be intended to deceive; they must be "sincere." Mehrabian argues that the face is trusted most, the tone of voice is trusted next most, and the actual words spoken are trusted least of all (Mehrabian and Wiener 1967, Mehrabian and Ferris 1967).

Psychologists have long shared this common conception that the nonverbal channels are less easy to control and thus are more trustworthy sources of information about the communicator. Freud's famous statement that "no mortal can keep a secret. If the lips are silent, he chatters with his fingertips" (1905) has been echoed and reechoed by many other psychologists. Clearly, it is impossible, in an unrehearsed conversation, for the speaker to keep all of his behavior under perfect control. Ekman and Friesen (1969a) argue that for most people it is easiest to control the verbal channel. Thus, if you wish to flatter someone, it will be relatively easy to think up some ingratiating words. They also argue that the head and face can be controlled more easily than the rest of the body, so that the flatterer may nod and smile but betray her impatience through a clenched fist or a rapidly tapping foot. Actually, the face responds so quickly that a sudden emotional reaction may "leak out" on the face as well, but it will quickly be covered up with the mask of another expression, so that only a very astute observer who chances to be watching just at the crucial moment will be able to pick it up. Some facial expressions may come and go so quickly that they can only be detected in a frame-by-frame inspection of a film of the person's face (Haggard and Isaacs 1966). People vary a great deal in their "natural expressiveness" (Lanzetta and Kleck 1970; Buck *et al.* 1974), and also in the skill with which they can deceive others (Krauss, Geller, and Olson 1976; Kraut 1978), but psychologists believe that for most Americans the words-face-body ordering holds true. Certain special groups, such as dancers, however, may attend more to controlling their bodies than their faces or even their words, and their emotions may leak out in channels that most people can control. They may also attend to different channels in observing others (Dittman, Parloff, and Boomer 1965).

Since people believe that the nonverbal channels are more revealing of the true inner state and less likely to be consciously manipulated in the service of ulterior motives, they may often use these channels as especially trustworthy sources of information about *dispositional* qualities of the sender. Of course, many nonverbal cues may be seen as situationally controlled: if we see a person wince when he stubs his toe, we do not feel that we have gained any deep insight into his character, since his behavior is the normal response to a strong situational force. In Kelley's terms, the behavior is uninformative because of the high degree of consensus. If all people react to a stimulus in the same way, the reaction of any given person doesn't tell as much about her as an individual. But many situations are less constraining, in that they allow a wide variety of different responses: these are the situations in which we are likely to make an inference based on a person/situation interaction (see Chapter 4), and, in so doing, infer something about the person's internal dispositions. We ask, in effect, "What kind of person would react in this way to this situation?" Since the situation is not sufficient to explain the behavior, there must be a dispositional component as well, revealed by the person's spontaneous response to the situation. Thus, if we see a person wince when we mention the CIA, we will think we have learned something about the person's beliefs and perhaps about his character, and we will trust our new knowledge all the more because we believe that wincing is an unintentional behavior.

Of course, our *belief* that a piece of information is trustworthy does not necessarily mean that it *is* trustworthy. The evidence that our reactive attributions to nonverbal cues are accurate—like the evidence for accuracy of snap judgments—is fairly tenuous. There is pretty good evidence that we can make accurate judgments of people's emotions from their facial expressions—certainly not every time, but some of the time (Chapter 9), and there is also some evidence that the voice can provide accurate information about a person's feelings. But often when people form a strong impression or when they experience a swift sensation of insight on the basis of nonverbal cues, they may be biassed or just plain mistaken. Except for some types of facial and vocal patterns, we have very little evidence of reliable relationships between nonverbal behavior and specific moods, and even less about nonverbal behavior and more lasting personality traits.

Summary of the general rule   Thus a basic difference between our perceptions of nonverbal "expressive" behaviors and other behaviors is that we are likely to assume that expressive behaviors are unintentional (Mehrabian 1972; Wiener, Devoe, Rubinow, and Geller 1972; Ekman and Friesen 1969b). Both ordinary people and psychologists assume that many nonverbal cues are relatively uncontrolled expressions of the person's spontaneous reactions: we make a *reactive attribution. Since we assume the person did not intend or choose to* show us a behavior, we do not search for motives; we take it as a true reaction, and we search for causes that may be revealing of the person's character. With other behaviors, behaviors that achieve various *effects*, we look for the person's intentions: we make a *purposive attribution*. We may be more likely to doubt that the most obvious explanation of the behavior is the true one.

Qualifications to the general rule   Of course, none of these distinctions is absolute; the general rule is just a rough characterization of a tendency. First of all, neither kind of behavior is likely to occur alone, and the relationship between the instrumental and expressive aspects of a behavior sequence can often prove revealing. When a person is trying to accomplish some task, we typically make a purposive attribution, but nonverbal cues can provide additional information about the person's intentions and attitudes towards the task. For example, expressions of strain can give us clues as to how hard the person is trying, and can help us to make the appropriate Heiderian attributions of ability and effort. Expressions of unhappiness, or long distracted gazes at irrelevant things in the environment, may tell us that the person is not very interested in the task at hand, and then we may infer that she is not doing it because she loves it, but because it is a means to some other purpose.

Secondly, people may often have intentions about their own expressive behavior. In particular, we may often feel that someone is trying *not* to reveal true feelings. Cultural display rules (Ekman 1972) tell us that it is inappropriate to cry on a public street or to laugh in church, and so when people feel the impulse to do so, they try to mask the expression with a more appropriate one. In these cases, we assume that the basic expression is unintentional and spontaneous, and the "trying" goes with the attempts to conceal it.

Trying to hide an emotion is an example of a behavior that is both nonverbal and purposive. This is an important point, and an exception to the "general rule" that perceivers use in this culture. Nonverbal behaviors are not always seen as unintentional, and other behaviors are not always seen as purposive. Throwing a snowball or driving a car can be spontaneous reactions, though they involve intentional behaviors. Likewise, frowning or crying can sometimes be purposive acts designed to achieve some particular effect. Many behaviors have components of both, and the difference we have proposed is not meant to be an either/or distinction.

Nonetheless, as perceivers we tend to prefer the general rule, and to avoid thinking too much about the obvious exceptions. Of course we all know that *some* people can control their nonverbal expressive behavior—actors, for example—and we have heard of people who behave like actors in their everyday lives—con men, for example. But we prefer to regard this ability as something unusual and not quite respectable. In 1959 Goffman presented the thesis that much of human social behavior is an elaborately staged play, that all of us are fairly skilled actors, and that much of our supposedly spontaneous behavior is really under very careful control. This point of view proved rather upsetting to many people, not so much on scientific grounds as on aesthetic and moral ones. In effect, Goffman seemed to be suggesting that we should make purposive attributions where we have been accustomed to making reactive attributions or snap judgments, that behaviors we have assumed to be manifestations of a person's personality or his spontaneous reactions are really intentional strategies designed to create some effect. We have not assimilated this point of view into our psychological theories or our everyday world view, probably because it is so much at variance with our ingrained assumptions about the kinds of behaviors that are likely to be purposive and those that are not. Likewise, Argyle and Kendon's (1967) discussion of nonverbal behaviors as social skills has had little impact.

THE KIND OF INFORMATION COMMUNICATED BY NONVERBAL CUES

By this time, it should be clear that there is another major difference between the attributions we make on the basis of nonverbal cues and the attributions we make on the basis of other kinds of behavior and other kinds of communication. With some exceptions (such as finger-pointing), nonverbal behavior provides information about a much more limited range of events than does verbal behavior. Nonverbal behavior is taken as being indicative of people's attitudes, emotions, background, personality, and, perhaps most of all, their moment-to-moment reactions to their environment and to us. It tells us about people, and about their feelings about what they are saying or doing or seeing or hearing, and about their intentions, even though we see the cues themselves as unintentional. And nonverbal cues also tell us about the continuing progress of our companion's relationship to us in the course of an interaction, and across interactions. They can tell us very small, short-term things about our companion's reaction to us—such as the fact that she feels we have made our point and it is her turn to talk (Birdwhistell 1970, chap. 23; Duncan and Niederehe 1974), or much larger things about the relationship—such as the fact that she finds it uncomfortable to be in our presence. We do not often talk to others about the status of our relationships with them, but we do tend to maintain a serious interest in how others feel about us, and the fact that we can "discuss" our relationship nonverbally during the whole time that we are talking about something else is very useful to us.

Most students of nonverbal behavior agree that people use nonverbal cues primarily to make attributions about permanent or transient dispositions (Kleinke 1975), moment-to-moment reactions and changes in affect and attitude (Mehrabian 1972; Ekman and Friesen 1969b), and the state of the relationship and the other person's involvement in it (Argyle and Kendon 1967; Ellsworth and Ludwig 1972; Hall 1966). Mehrabian summarizes the general point of view by stating that the implicit messages of nonverbal cues are messages about positiveness, potency, and responsiveness (1972) as well as *immediacy*, which is a term roughly denoting interpersonal involvement.

This topical restriction on the meanings typically attributed to nonverbal cues requires that we qualify the statement we made earlier that nonverbal cues are more revealing than other behaviors. Popular writers have picked up on work by Mehrabian (Mehrabian and Wiener 1967; Mehrabian and Ferris 1967) and have made the spectacular claim that 55 percent of what is communicated is communicated by the face, 38 percent by the voice, and only 7 percent by the words spoken. The figures are the same as those put forth by Mehrabian, but the conclusions are overgeneralized. In Mehrabian's research, the same or different emotional messages were communicated in different channels, and he measured subjects' reactions to the communication as a whole. Mehrabian and Wiener (1967) found, not surprisingly, that there was no problem when the verbal and the vocal channels agreed in how much positive affect they implied: almost everyone made a strong rating in the expected direction. When the word and the tone of voice disagreed, however, they found that subjects relied almost entirely on the tone of voice. In a followup study, Mehrabian and Ferris (1967) found that when the communications were inconsistent, the subject's final judgments of liking depended more on the face than on the voice. Combining the results of these two studies, Mehrabian (1972) came up with the percentages given above. But of course he never claimed he was talking about anything other than *feeling*. Argyle has found a similar superiority of nonverbal over verbal cues in communicating liking (Argyle, Alkema, and Gilmour 1971) and dominance (Argyle, Salter, Nicholson, Williams, and Burgess 1970), another major dimension of *connotative* meaning (Osgood, Suci, and Tannenbaum 1957).

But if you pick up a book and read a sentence at random, you will immediately realize that it is ridiculous to claim that nonverbal cues account for all but 7 percent of the information that is conveyed. I pick up a book and I read: "Titian was a very old man when he achieved this masterpiece" (Forster 1939). It would take me an exceedingly long time to try to communicate this rather simple sentence nonverbally, and I would probably never succeed in conveying the message unless I resorted to various linguistic and charade-like tricks not commonly used in nonverbal communication in face-to-face interaction. For denotative communication and for referential communication about events and objects not immediately present, there is no substitute for language.

On the other hand, with the exception of a few great poems, novels, and plays, verbal communication—and especially spontaneous oral communication—may be as deficient for conveying feelings and swiftly changing reactions as nonverbal communication is in conveying that the square of the hypotenuse is equal to the sum of the squares of the two sides. For one thing, there isn't time. The face, the eyes, and the body can react quickly to ongoing events without having to plan how to express themselves, and they can do it while the person is talking about something else. Also, as Mehrabian and many others have pointed out, people may be "discouraged, generally, from an overt (linguistic) expression of their feelings, so they convey them in less consensual and less easily recognizable forms" (Mehrabian 1972, p. vii). Though the range of information communicated by nonverbal cues may be restricted, it is restricted to topics we care about a great deal: what other people are like, what they are attending to, what they think and feel about what they and we are considering or talking about, and, most of all, how they feel and what they intend to do about us.

THE AMBIGUITY OF NONVERBAL CUES

Private feelings are delicate, elusive, and often complicated. We are ambivalent about sharing them, and we lack the language to do so. For these and other reasons communication of these private feelings is often tentative and implicit rather than definite and explicit. Nonverbal cues, being the signals of these complicated secrets, are also often indefinite and inexplicit compared to spoken words. They also occur as part of a broader social context, and often cannot be understood without reference to that context. In this section we will provide evidence for the relative ambiguity of nonverbal cues, and then we will speculate about the reasons for this ambiguity.

In the abstract, of course, we do have some general ideas about the meaning of certain nonverbal cues, especially about whether they have positive or negative implications. We discussed these global evaluative responses in the section on snap judgments. In general, when people are asked to act out or to identify positive cues, they choose closer distances, more looking, leaning forward, and facing the other person directly. There are limits, of course: moderately close distances are generally preferred to "too close" distances, such as two or three feet (Lassen 1973; Patterson and Sechrest 1970). Basically, it seems as though custom permits an allowable range of affiliation or "intimacy." In the bland sort of interaction characteristic of laboratory experiments (and perhaps representative of dozens of day-to-day interactions with strangers), we prefer someone who is towards the "friendly" or "intimate" end of that range. But we do not like people who are so "friendly" that they move out of the permissible range.

Nonverbal behaviors have multiple meanings   When we move away from role-playing in the laboratory, and extend the range of social situations studied, the evidence for ambiguity increases. Although there are several popular books (Fast 1970; Morris 1977) that claim to provide "dictionaries" of the meaning of various nonverbal cues, most investigators now believe that such dictionaries are destined to be very limited in application. Aside from certain word-like gestures (such as nods and shrugs and various obscene gestures—Ekman 1976) and a few basic facial expressions of emotion, there is very little evidence that particular nonverbal cues have a definite "meaning." Most cues seem to take on much of their meaning in relation to the context in which they occur.

A direct gaze, for example, may indicate attraction (Rubin 1970; Mehrabian 1967) or dominance relationships (Strongman and Champness 1968; Thayer 1969). Sometimes a direct stare may be taken as a sign of dominance (Strongman and Champness 1968), but sometimes it may also be a sign of subordination (Exline 1972). For example, if you go into a professor's office, it is more likely that you will keep your eyes on him while he is talking than that he will pay such close attention to you while you are talking. Exline has carried out a variety of experiments illuminating the complicated interrelationships between direct gaze and perceived power (1972). A person may like or dislike another person who tries to establish eye contact, depending on whether the interaction is positive or negative (Ellsworth and Carlsmith 1968), threatening or comfortable (Ellsworth and Ross 1976). Kleinke, Staneski, and Pipp (1975) have shown that a woman's attractiveness and her decision to move closer to a male during the course of an interaction also affect his reactions to her direct gaze. Ellsworth and Langer (1976) and Bear, Cairns, and Goodman (in press) have shown that the same gaze will cause people to approach and offer assistance or to flee the gazer, depending on the circumstances. Thus a direct gaze can have unrelated or even opposite meanings, depending on its context.

Likewise, approaching and standing close to someone may indicate affection, and there is a good deal of research showing that people who like each other and who are comfortable in each other's presence tend to stay closer to each other (Mehrabian 1968; see Evans and Howard 1973 for a review). But being approached can also be a disturbing experience, especially when it is a stranger or someone we dislike who approaches us. Robert Sommer has conducted a considerable amount of research on situations in which people regard an approach as an invasion, and quickly depart (Sommer 1969). Distance, like gaze, can also be an indicator of power relationships (Evans and Howard 1973).

If someone approaches close enough to touch you, these feelings—whether positive or negative—will be intensified, and it should come as no surprise that those who study actual touching argue for a similar variety of effects. Most people have found that touching is regarded as a sign of friendliness and that it elicits helpful behavior (Kleinke 1974) and a willingness to share fairly personal feelings (Jourard and Friedman 1970). But these studies involved very slight touching by an innocuous young female, or by a "safe" experimenter. In the case of the female stranger, the "meaning" of the touch was immediately explained by her saying, "Excuse me. Did you happen to find a dime in the phone booth? I think I might have left one here a few minutes ago." Ellsworth and Langer (1976) and Bear, Cairns, and Goodman (in press) found that a gaze also elicited helpful behavior when its meaning was clear and the appropriate helpful response was obvious. It is probable that unexplained touching by a strange male would, like the unexplained gaze or Sommer's spatial invasions, provoke a speedy withdrawal. Finally, Henley (1974) has argued that touching, like the direction one looks or the distance one stands from someone, can be a sign of power, not of intimacy. High-status persons are free to touch low-status persons in public, but low-status persons cannot reciprocate.

Thus three of the most widely studied nonverbal behaviors—looking, approaching, and touching—each cover a broad range of meanings, varying with the situation, the relationship, and the personal histories of the inter-actants. The responses and interpretations elicited by a look, an approach, or a touch are neither invariant nor automatic. Instead, these cues provide flexible contributing factors in social interaction, combining with other factors to produce a behavioral response or an attribution. Unless the face is conveying an emotion, its meaning may also be unclear, differing in different contexts (Cline 1956); many gestures are similarly ambiguous. Spiegel and Machotka (1974) found that body positions were judged very differently, depending on whether the poser was naked or dressed. Thus most nonverbal cues are am-biguous because there is no direct sign-referent relationship between the cue and its inferred meaning.

While context goes some way towards resolving the ambiguity of non-verbal cues, some uncertainty usually remains. Even if we know where we are, whom we are speaking to, and what we are talking about, the meaning of a half-smile or a prolonged gaze may still be a matter of doubt. We may notice it, we may think "hm! odd reaction!", yet we will have a hard time explaining what it means in words. If a person says to us in words, "I'm not sure I believe you," we are surer of what he "means" than if he raises his eyebrows. From the raised eyebrows, we have another step of inference to make before we can conclude that the person means, "I'm not sure I believe you."

Nonverbal behavior and the expression of feelings   As we suggested above, the reason that nonverbal information is usually more ambiguous is probably that its domain is the domain of inner feelings about oneself and one's rela-tionships with others. The ambiguity is partly a function of our inability to discuss these matters and partly a function of our unwillingness.

In childhood, our ability to express ourselves nonverbally has a head start on our verbal abilities. For the first year or more of life nonverbal communi-cation is our only means of communication. Much of what we communicate at this time is emotional—much of it consists of the unspoken adjustment and coordination that makes a relationship run smoothly. A baby knows how to get its mother's attention, signal that it wants to be picked up, and adjust its movements comfortably to the mother while being carried. When the baby is tired of being carried, it can signal that, too, by changing from a comfortable accommodating extension of the mother into a resistant bundle of knobs and angles. By the time the baby learns to talk, it is already fairly adept at com-municating feelings and momentary reactions to social relationships nonverbally. When a child does learn to talk, the child does *not* start out by learning how to talk about these things: there is no need to, since he or she already knows how; second, the language is poor in verbal terms that capture the nuances and rapid changes involved; third, since parents have no direct access to the child's inner feelings, they are in a poor position to teach the child the appropriate words.[1]

Much of the "ambiguity" of nonverbal cues may be a function of the fact that we have not learned to speak about them, that for most of us the language is an unwieldy and unfamiliar tool, unsuited for matters of the heart. Something that is inexplicable in words is almost by definition "ambiguous." As the child grows older, and as more of his thought is controlled by his language, this wordlessness may have further ramifications. When someone is giving off nonverbal cues that make us uncomfortable, it may be hard for us to figure out what is wrong, since without verbal labels we have difficulty bringing our conscious attention to bear on a phenomenon. We will trust our discomfort and our belief that there is something odd or wrong about the other person, but we will have a hard time labeling that feeling. When we notice a nonverbal cue we often feel that it is more revealing than what the person is saying, but we are not sure *what* it reveals. With language we are relatively sure about what the person wants to say, but we are not always sure that we can trust him.

Besides being unable to define our feelings precisely, we may be unwilling to. That is, we may *prefer* to keep these communications somewhat ambiguous. Our culture discourages open discussion of intimate feelings, so we rarely feel free to reveal ourselves without having to worry about breaking a norm. In addition, we may have more private reasons for favoring ambiguity. We may sense that our inner motives reflect vulnerabilities or unworthinesses that we would hesitate to make explicit.

The assumption that nonverbal behaviors are unintentional contributes to their ambiguity because we do not feel that it is appropriate to come right out and ask "Why did you do that?" about a nonverbal cue, and we can usually count on our partner to share this reticence. For many nonverbal cues it may be hard to describe what it was that the person did, and even if we can describe it, we are timid about raising the issue, because the ambiguity of the cue means that we may be wrong about it, and the assumed unintentionality means that the other person may not realize what he did, and probably would not be able to tell us why he did it. We are much less likely to hold each other accountable for nonverbal behaviors than for behaviors that seem to be a part of purposive action sequences. The apparently nonpurposive nonverbal "code" differs from most human codes because others are not likely to make explicit comments on it; if they do, the signal can be denied. The existence of such a not-quite conscious, not-exactly systematic code which is perhaps assumed to be less

---

1. The authors are grateful to Robert Kleck for raising the issues in this paragraph.

conscious and less systematic than it really is may be very useful in human interaction. It allows people to express their feelings and to negotiate developing relationships with a measure of safety. A romance begins with gestures, and we wait to see that our gestures are welcome before we commit our feelings to irretrievable words. When we want to make ourselves perfectly clear we speak, or even write things down. But often, especially in love and war, we don't want to make ourselves perfectly clear; if we haven't named our sentiments or complaints, we are free to revise them without embarrassment.

THE PROBLEM OF AWARENESS

Related to the issues of ambiguity and intentionality is the issue of the perceiver's awareness of the attribution process. Because no one has really addressed the issue of awareness, it is hard to say whether the level of consciousness of the attributional process is or is not another factor that distinguishes attributions made on the basis of nonverbal behavior from those made on the basis of other behavior. Most attribution theorists, studying purposive attributions, describe the process as though the perceiver were consciously evaluating the evidence and arriving at a conclusion. These theorists do not actually claim that the process is fully conscious, and some of them explicitly state that the assumption of awareness is a convenient fiction (Bem 1972; Nisbett and Wilson 1977). But it strikes us that in considering the perception of nonverbal cues, the assumption of awareness is a little less convenient and a little more fictional.

What cues are noticed?   In the first place, the cue may not get even into the process, and so will have no effect at all. As Birdwhistell (1970) and other students of kinesics have pointed out, even in the course of very brief interactions each of us is constantly giving off a huge number of discriminable behaviors in all channels. When we meet another person, we cannot possibly assimilate all of these bits of nonverbal information, and so we still pay attention to what the other person is saying and to the management of our own behavior. Many of these potential stimuli may have no influence whatsoever, and one of the hardest tasks of the researcher is to figure out which ones are important.

The issue of selective attention is a fundamental problem in many studies of person perception, especially those that allow subjects to get involved in face-to-face conversations, but it is often more difficult for the student of nonverbal communication because there are a large number of potential cues, because they are constantly changing, and because they usually form a background for more discrete behaviors such as verbal utterances.

What cues are interpreted?   Even when we can be sure that a cue has an effect on the receiver (and thus in a sense we can be sure that the cue was "perceived"), the subject may not be consciously aware of this effect. The direct influence may precede an interpretation, or it may occur independently of one. Several investigators have found, for example, that standing very close to people or gazing directly at them can produce a physiological response — a faster heart-beat or a change in GSR (McBride, King, and James 1965; Nichols and Champness 1971; Kleinke and Pohlen 1971). Also, researchers have occasionally found that subjects appear to have no awareness of a nonverbal influence, even when their own behavior is responsive to it. While subjects can often recall gross levels of nonverbal behaviors (like whether the other person looked at them all the time or hardly ever), they often cannot verbalize subtler patterns that definitely influenced their behavior (Argyle and Cook 1976; Ellsworth and Ross 1976; Hess 1965). Much of the back and forth of conversation is controlled by very regular shifts in tone of voice (Duncan and Niederehe 1974), but few people are consciously aware of the signals that indicate when it is their turn to talk. Most investigators seem to assume that these adjustments take place outside of awareness and thus do not constitute "interpretation" in the usual sense.

Are the interpretations verbal? Sometimes, however, nonverbal cues do create a conscious impression in the perceiver. We do not know whether this impression is usually translated into a verbal proposition on the spot or whether our reactions are usually just "feelings" that are not verbally labeled — feelings that may influence our behavior but that we do not try to describe until someone asks us for an impression, at which point we fumble around and try to find the words that capture an experience. Regardless of the sequence of events, nonverbal behaviors often do create impressions that the subject can report. Because we are relatively inarticulate in verbal description of non-verbal behavior, our ability to identify the actual *evidence* for our inferences from nonverbal cues may be undeveloped. We may be left with a strong impression, but our explanations of where it came from are likely to be halting and indefinite.

We do not know how often people actually make trait or mood attributions on the basis of nonverbal cues in the course of everyday interaction. Numerous studies indicate that when people are asked to use nonverbal cues to make this sort of attribution they *can* do so (Mehrabian 1972; Addington 1968; Ekman 1972). But we do not have very much information about whether this is how people actually use nonverbal information in ordinary social interaction when no researcher is around to ask them questions. We know that a person's feelings and behavior are influenced by nonverbal cues from other people; we do not know whether this influence stems from an inference process resulting in verbal labels, or from some kind of nonverbal affective "inference" process. We do not know whether the inference is conscious, or unconscious, or partly conscious.

SUMMARY OF THE SPECIAL PROPERTIES OF NONVERBAL CUES

The main differences between our perceptions of nonverbal behavior and other behaviors, then, are that on the whole we perceive nonverbal behaviors to be (1) largely unintentional, (2) informative primarily about temperaments, feelings, and reactions, and therefore (3) relatively ambiguous. It is also possible that our analysis of nonverbal behavior is less conscious than our analysis of other behavior. We do not ordinarily make purposive attributions on the basis of nonverbal cues, since a purposive attribution involves an examination of purposes or intentions. In the case of nonverbal cues, we usually make stereotyped judgments about background or disposition, or reactive attributions about the cause of the behavior, depending in part on our acquaintance with the person. In making a reactive attribution, we assume that the behavior is a response to some internal or external cause, and we try to discover the cause in order to understand the meaning of the reaction. The association between nonverbal behaviors and reactive attributions is a rough and general one, and there are plenty of exceptions. Verbal statements and action sequences designed to achieve a goal may often be seen as highly reactive to some stimulus; for example, if a gun goes off in a room full of people, almost *every* behavior that in the next few minutes would probably be seen as "reactive" in some sense. Similarly, there are occasions when nonverbal behaviors may be seen as essentially purposive, as when a society hostess greets her guests. Nonetheless, the distinction is useful, and in general nonverbal cues are more likely to provoke reactive attributions than are purposive ones.

Attribution: Common Properties of Nonverbal Cues and Other Cues

Despite the special properties of nonverbal cues and the differences between reactive and purposive attributions, there is no reason that person perception based on such cues should be a field entirely divorced from the field of person perception in general. Many of the same basic questions—such as the questions about awareness that we discussed in the last section—are unanswered in both fields: What is noticed? How is it coded for memory? How is it retrieved from memory? When is the inference made? Equally important, many of the same basic processes that we have described for person perception and attribution in general apply to person perception on the basis of nonverbal cues as well. We discussed one of these, the process of making snap judgments, at the beginning of this chapter. We now turn to some other processes that the interpretation of nonverbal behavior has in common with the interpretation of all behavior.

DEPARTURES FROM NORMS ARE MEANINGFUL

As with other kinds of behavior, most nonverbal behavior is organized into very regular, predictable sequences. Goffman (1963) gives the example of the "civil inattention" of two strangers approaching and passing each other on the street. At a certain distance the two people will look at each other and, by brief and subtle shifts of eyes and body orientation, negotiate which of them will pass on the right and which of them will pass on the left. They will immediately look away from each other and will usually keep looking away while they pass each other. The mutual eye contact involved is part of a normative sequence that each participant has gone through hundreds of times. It is not "noticed" as anything special that provides information or requires interpretation. Departures from this normative sequence, on the other hand, may be noticed. That is, if one person *fails* to avert his gaze once the initial contact and negotiation have taken place, but instead keeps "staring," the other person may feel uncomfortable, may feel a need to interpret the other person's gaze and the reason for his continued attention, and may feel called upon to respond—but will probably be at a loss as to how to do so (Ellsworth, Carlsmith, and Henson 1972; Bear, Cairns, and Goodman in press).

These organized normative "background" sequences do not only occur in wordless interchanges between strangers. Duncan (Duncan and Niederehe 1974; Duncan and Fiske 1977) has conducted a program of careful systematic research on the nonverbal background norms governing the taking of turns in conversations. Speakers use a variety of cues—falling into Ekman and Friesen's (1969b) category of *regulators*—such as changes in tone of voice, syntax, intonation, body position, and gaze direction to signal when they are coming to the end of their utterances and when they are ready for their companion to take a turn.

Although these signals are sent, received, and used all the time in structuring and regulating the flow of conversation, this "communication" typically takes place at a level just below conscious awareness. If we start thinking about how our body is moving, where our eyes are looking, or where the pitch of our voice is going, most of us are quickly reduced to a state of muddled paralysis, unable to follow the gist of our companion's ideas and unable to formulate our own. Brown and Herrnstein (1975) argue that "a conversation with a psychologist whose research specialty is eye contact is . . . one of life's more disagreeable interactions," presumably because it brings into awareness behavior that normally flows smoothly and regularly just beneath the surface.

It is when the norm is broken that our attention is engaged. If we signal that we're ready for the other person to speak but the other person continues to gaze at us with the calm attention of a listener, or if we gesticulate to show that we're in the middle of a thought and want to continue but the other person begins on another topic, some of our attention may switch from the topic of the conversation to its mechanics, or even to the nature of our companion. If the conversation resumes an orderly course with no further disturbances, we may think no more of it. But if these tiny offenses are repeated, we may end up with the impression that the listener who fails to take an offerred turn is a cold, dull, or unresponsive person, or is contemptuous of what we are saying, while we may perceive the interrupter as being inconsiderate and overbearing. If the norms are broken consistently and regularly so that even the basic patterns of normal behavior are violated, we may begin to suspect that our companion is not quite right in the head.

As we have said before, we know very little about *how* these attributions are made. It may be that the clarity and awareness of the inference are related to the extremity and suddenness of the departure from baseline norms. Thus if a person makes a series of minor norm violations that extend over the course of a conversation, the receiver may not consciously notice them or make an attribution at the time, but may feel a vague sense of discomfort or annoyance. Later on, perhaps, if something causes the perceiver to reflect on the conversation or on the other person, the perceiver may organize these vague perceptions with a label. If, on the other hand, the norm violation is sudden and extreme—if, for example, you begin by saying, "I was just talking to Erving . . . " and the other person immediately leans forward, frowns, shakes her head, and interrupts—the event may be striking enough to capture your conscious attention right then, and you may make a more specific, concrete inference: that the other person doesn't like Erving. Of course, both processes may proceed simultaneously. The perception that "she doesn't like Erving" may focus the perceiver's attention differently during the rest of the interaction so that corroborative cues are more readily noticed and assimilated than they might otherwise have been. And it is also possible that the vague discomfort of an elusive impression brought about by numerous small departures from the norms may sensitize the perceiver so that a somewhat less salient event may precipitate an explicit conscious attribution during the course of an interaction.

We should also note that it is impossible to divide all nonverbal behaviors into categories of *normal* and *abnormal* and to argue that only the abnormal ones result in impressions. First of all, a history of interaction with someone who behaves quite normally may leave a general impression that "Sue is a good solid person" or "Joe is a nice guy, but a little dull." So normal behaviors can produce *some* attributions, at least the attribution of conventionality. Secondly, people undoubtedly differ somewhat in their perceptions of what constitutes normal behavior, overestimating the normality of their own behavior (Ross, Greene, and House 1977). Thirdly, nonverbal behavior is probably not so rigidly structured that all behaviors either uphold or violate the norms. Duncan and Fiske (1977) point out that even though turn-taking in conversations is regulated by quite definite norms, still there are often several more-or-less normative options available to interactants. Within the normal range," some people may provide many encouraging "listener noises" (such as "uh-huh" and "mm-hmm"), and other people may provide very few. Some people may use different combinations of legitimate signals for indicating that they want to take a turn than other people do. Not only the content but the form of a conversation is different when talking to a great-aunt than it is when talking to a classmate. Consistent individual differences in these "stylistic" choices may provide the same kind of vague cumulative impression that minor norm violations do.

Obviously turn-taking rules are not the only background against which nonverbal norm violations can be perceived. The example is a particularly clear one because the organizational structure of the normative baseline has been so carefully documented. But people who stand at a very unusual distance from us, or who gaze too steadily or not enough, or who move their faces in peculiar ways may all draw our attention and lead us to make dispositional attributions that we would not make in the case of more common behaviors.

Since slightly positive expressions are considered socially normative in many contexts in this culture, it may be that positive expressions such as smiles are considered somewhat less trustworthy than are negative expressions. A person may smile because she is really comfortable and happy, or because she wishes to convey an impression of comfort and happiness. There is evidence that people do try to cover negative emotions with positive masks (Ekman and Friesen 1969a), and also some evidence that when a person's nonverbal behavior contains both positive and negative elements, observers tend to interpret the sender's feelings as primarily negative (Bugental, Kaswan, and Love 1970; Frijda 1969).

There are also normative and non-normative reactive sequences. If we see a person cry at a funeral, or sit quietly and respectfully when a great sage is giving advice, or recoil in fear at the sudden appearance of a snake, we probably will not make any very complicated attributions. In all of those cases the stimulus is obvious and the person is making the "normal," expected response. We make an easy reactive attribution and think no more about it. But if we see a person laugh at a funeral, or sit quietly and respectfully when we are telling our best joke, or recoil in fear when a small child offers to shake hands, we are likely to think we have learned something about the person, and to think further about the meaning of the reaction. As with purposive attributions, unusual reactive attributions may lead to further inferences, such as trait attributions.

Thus, as with other kinds of behavior, we tend to notice and interpret departures from norms of social desirability and from common statistical norms as meaningful. We have a notion of what is appropriate, ordinary behavior for a given kind of social interaction, or for a given acquaintance, and as long as our companion's behavior runs "true to form" we probably don't think much about it. Whether we consider the behavior to be purposive or reactive, departures from our expectations wake us up and provoke us to make attributions.

All of this, of course, is quite consistent with what we know about attributions in general. Jones and Davis (1965) make the general point about the informational value of socially undesirable behavior. And Kelley's model is relevant in that consensus information is very often simply the information we have about what's normal, what most people do. When we are dealing with strangers, this kind of consensus information is typically all we have to tell us what is normal. But with people we know well, we have consistency and distinctiveness information as well. That is, we know what is normal for that person, and what we notice are departures from this somewhat idiosyncratic norm. Whether we infer a lasting trait or a more temporary mood on the basis of a nonverbal behavior probably depends on our familiarity with the person. If we catch sight of a person for the first time, and if the person is scowling without any noticeable provocation, we may infer that she has a hostile personality. We have seen the person on only one occasion, and if we have no reason to believe that one occasion is unusual or atypical, we infer a disposition on the basis of the scowl. If we know the person well, we are much more likely to infer that she is worried or that she is *reacting* to something annoying that just happened to her, and we may well ask, "What's wrong?" Having seen the person many times, we know that she does not consistently frown, so we are likely to infer a transient state rather than a permanent trait. Also, after a long acquaintance, we probably already have a stable image of the other person's personality, and new pieces of information would have to be very striking or powerful before it would occur to us to question our image. In short, the same nonverbal gesture may be taken as an indication of a permanent trait in a stranger and a passing state in a friend.

INCONSISTENCIES REQUIRE EXPLANATION

The fact that we regard departures from norms as meaningful and informative is one example of a more general tendency to notice and interpret *inconsistencies*. We have discussed not only behavior that is inconsistent with a norm, but verbal and nonverbal behaviors that are inconsistent with each other. Obviously there are many other possible kinds of inconsistency, and we would argue that they all pose problems for the perceiver. For the purposes of the present discussion we will focus on just three of the questions that have been studied: (1) What happens when the cue and the context imply different interpretations? (2) What happens when people habitually communicate conflicting messages? and (3) Can we use inconsistencies to tell when people are lying?

Nonverbal cues in context　The problem of cue and context has a long history of research. We have argued that many nonverbal cues allow for a variety of interpretations and that they are interpreted in context. Thus, up to a point, the problem of inconsistency doesn't arise unless the cue varies a great deal from the norms expected of the context. However, we have also argued that cues are not completely ambiguous; for example, the gaze does signal attention, an upright posture is taken as more tense and formal than a slouching position, and certain facial expressions have very clear meanings. Also, *within a particular situation*, a nonverbal cue may lead to very consistent interpretations (Ellsworth 1975; Ellsworth and Carlsmith 1973) that may be congruent or incongruent with what is expected. Thus it is possible to speak of cues as inconsistent with a social context.

　　Except in psychology experiments, people rarely see a cue alone, without a context. The situational context can also provide information about what the participants are likely to be feeling—sometimes information that agrees with what the nonverbal cues show, sometimes information that runs counter to those cues. In fact, most of the research on situational context has to do with facial expression—often a very clear source of information about emotion—and so it was relatively easy to construct experiments in which the facial expression would be consistent or inconsistent. Much of this research was carried out as part of an attempt to prove that facial expression had *no* intrinsic meaning, that the interpretation came entirely from the situation (Bruner and Tagiuri 1954). Most of the experiments were rather "loaded" because subjects were shown a picture of a facial expression chopped out of a larger photograph and were asked to make a judgment, and then they (or other subjects) were shown the whole photograph, including the face. The early researchers claimed that judgments were much more accurate when people had both the face *and* the context to judge from than when they had only the face, and these researchers concluded rather illogically that the face therefore provided very little information.

Ekman, Friesen, and Ellsworth (1972) have analyzed and criticized these studies in detail. They point out that the early researchers never seemed to consider that *either* source of information—face or context—could be relatively clear or relatively ambiguous. They simply assumed that faces were relatively ambiguous (as they often are) and that contexts were relatively clear. But situational contexts are often ambiguous, too, because you wouldn't know what emotion to expect. If you were shown a picture of someone sitting on a park bench, and if the person's face were covered up and you were asked to say what the person was feeling, you probably wouldn't have a very clear idea. The early researchers never thought to get judgments of *contexts* by themselves—only of faces by themselves. If I then uncovered the face of the person who was sitting on the park bench and you saw that the person was crying, you would certainly judge that particular combination of face and context in terms of the face.

Thus Ekman, Friesen, and Ellsworth argued that it was doubtless possible to get results showing that nonverbal cues are more important than the context or vice versa, depending on whether the experimenter combines an informative cue with an ambiguous context or an ambiguous cue with an informative context.

What is it about both sources that determines their relative influence on the judgment of the combination? One might examine the ambiguity of each source, the complexity of each source, or the intensity implied by each source. Some nonverbal cues (particularly facial expressions) and some contexts may be more closely associated with particular emotions than others. Thus, crying faces and funerals may have relatively clear implications, while a face showing mixed emotions or a placid neutrality may be more ambiguous, like the park bench. Ekman, Friesen, and Ellsworth suggest that a good experiment would examine various combinations of nonverbal cues and contexts that agreed and disagreed with each other. Thus, one might take a picture of a face that was judged with moderate agreement (moderate clarity) to be slightly happy, and see how it was interpreted in a context that was (1) also moderately clear and slightly happy; (2) very clear and very happy; (3) moderately clear and fear-arousing; (4) very clear and fear-arousing; and so on.

There is some evidence (Mehrabian 1972; Frijda 1968) that when face and context are both very clear but they contradict one another, the face is used as the basis for deciding what the person is feeling. Frijda also found that subjects felt a need to make up *explanations* for why the person was feeling an emotion so unusual in the context. He made a beginning at studying the kinds of cognitive mechanisms people use to resolve these inconsistencies, and this line of research seems promising for the future.

Mixed messages   Inferences based on nonverbal cues are primarily inferences about relationships and feelings, and thus are among the most important inferences we make. Incorrect decisions about what our companions think of us can lead to serious, perhaps even pathological, social problems. If we perceive hostile cues everywhere we look, we may end up finding ourselves labeled paranoid. And for the preverbal child, of course, almost all successful communication involves feelings and attitudes. It seems plausible that if a child is given confused or inconsistent nonverbal messages, these will have a very detrimental effect on his psychological development. In fact, there is a well-known theory that inconsistency between verbal and nonverbal channels in communication from the mother to the child may have a major influence in the etiology of schizophrenia (Bateson, Jackson, Haley, and Weakland, 1956). According to this *double bind* theory, the parents of emotionally disturbed children tend to send messages with built-in contradictions; for example, a mother may coo, "Do come over here and kiss Mummy" while she draws back apprehensively. The child is placed in a "double bind" because he receives two messages, and he doesn't know which one the mother really means. He may be paralyzed with indecision, feeling that there is no acceptable response: whatever he does he will be disobeying one of the mother's instructions.

There is not much empirical evidence for or against the double-bind hypothesis (Shuham 1967), although the idea has been quite popular. The most systematic research related to these ideas is that of Daphne Bugental. She found that mothers of emotionally disturbed children show more incongruity between the verbal and nonverbal channels than do mothers of normal children (Bugental, Love, Kaswan, and April 1971). One of the most frequent of the inconsistent cue combinations shown by the mothers of disturbed children was a combination of highly assertive and directive words with a very weak and hesitant tone of voice (Bugental and Love 1975). These mothers, not surprisingly, had children who were aggressive and difficult to control. Fathers of disturbed children, incidentally, did not show this inconsistency: they tended to be highly evaluative and directive in their communicative style (Bugental, Love, and Kaswan 1972). Thus what evidence there is tends to support the hypothesis that habitual exposure to inconsistent messages from mothers can have a negative effect on children. Of course, the direction of causality has yet to be demonstrated; it is possible that several years of life with a hellion can cause a demoralizing sense of powerlessness in the mother, which is reflected in the weakness of her voice as she tries to control the child. Bugental is conducting further research on these issues.

Lying   The mixed messages of the double-bind situation are not lies in the usual sense of the term. The mother may say one thing and mean another, but the usual assumption is that she does not know what she means, that her mixed messages reflect mixed motives. In Bugental's research, many of the mixed messages may reflect the fact that the mother wants obedience but does not expect to get it.

In these cases, where the misleading quality of the words is not deliberate, the listener seems able to pick up the discrepancy. But what happens when a person lies on purpose? Are there still nonverbal signs that give him away, as Freud argued? And if there are, does the perceiver have to be a Freud in order to detect these signs, or can ordinary people do it?

Surprisingly enough, there has been very little research on the cues people use in deciding whether or not someone is lying, or the accuracy of these decisions. The use of physiological measures to detect lies (Lykken 1974) is predicated on the assumption that the lie will leak out in the responses the person is powerless to control. As we have argued earlier, nonverbal channels also tend to be trusted because people assume that they are less subject to conscious control than the verbal message. Thus it would seem plausible that they would be used as evidence of deception. Coming at the issue from the opposite point of view, one might ask, "What makes a good liar?" The techniques of impression management have been the subject of extensive discussion by social scientists, most notably by Goffman, but there is as little experimental work on the creation of lies as there is on their detection.

Mehrabian (1971) found that when people attempted to deceive others they tended to give off more nonverbal signs of negative affect than when they told the truth. On the basis of these studies, however, it is impossible to specify *which* signs of negative affect go with lying, because signs that seemed important in one experiment were not diagnostic in others.

Ekman and Friesen have studied deception by examining people's attempts to conceal strong emotion. Subjects viewed two films and answered questions about them. In the truth condition they saw a nature film and were asked to describe their feelings honestly. In the deception condition they saw a gory film about amputations and burns and were asked to persuade an interviewer that they had seen another pleasant film. The authors (Ekman and Friesen 1969a, 1974) found that when observers saw only the liar's head and shoulders (and, of course, face) they could not tell whether she was lying, but that when they saw the body from the neck down, they could tell. Ekman and Friesen (1974) argued that the liars try successfully to assume a pleasant facial expression, but that nervousness "leaks out" in the movements of their hands and feet. In a further analysis of these subjects, Ekman, Friesen, and Scherer (1976) found that illustrative movements of the hands decreased during deception, while voice pitch became higher. Observers who could see the face judged the deceptive faces to be more *positive* than the honest faces, while observers who saw the body judged it to show more negative affect during deception. This supports Ekman and Friesen's notion that the face is the nonverbal channel most subject to conscious control in this situation, and indicates that the negative affect cues noted by Mehrabian are likely to have been nonfacial cues. Subjects who listened to tape recordings of the interview (filtered or not filtered for content) could not discriminate between the honest and the deceptive interviews. (Subjects in this reanalysis were not asked to guess whether the speaker was lying, only to rate her on a number of scales.)

It often happens in everyday life that we try to lie in order to conceal strong negative emotion as in Ekman and Friesen's research, but there are many other kinds of lies as well—deceptive situations in which the would-be sleuth does not have the leakage of strong emotion cues to guide him, and the liar doesn't have to worry about that particular kind of control. For example, when we are fifteen minutes late to meet someone, etiquette demands that we say *something*, and sometimes the real reason is sufficiently trivial, insulting, or embarrassing that we prefer to say something *else*. We are not feeling any particularly strong emotion, but we lie.

Research on the detection of deception in unemotional situations has only just begun. In a study by Krauss, Geller, and Olson (1976) a person asked another person questions about politics, religion, future plans, and personal values; the second person was instructed to lie about two of these topics. Subjects were fairly good at telling whether or not the other person was lying. Surprisingly, they were more likely to guess correctly when they could only hear the liar than when they could both see and hear him. Like Ekman, Friesen, and Scherer (1976), Krauss and his colleagues found that lies were accompanied by an increase in voice pitch. Observers tended to perceive deception when the speaker was nonfluent, nervous, unemphatic, and "not serious," and when she hesitated a long time before answering. In the face-to-face condition, Krauss, Geller, and Olson found that subjects were judged to be *less* nervous when lying (Ekman, Friesen, and Scherer 1976), but when they could only hear the speaker, they judged him to be more nervous when lying. Apparently visible cues—at least facial cues—are more easily controlled than vocal cues.

Other research, in which the subjects pretended that they were interviewing for a job (Kraut 1978), supports the finding that observers are moderately accurate in telling when someone is lying ($r = +.53$). Kraut (who did not measure voice pitch) found that truthful answers tended to be longer, to have fewer "ums" and "uhs," and to begin sooner after the end of the question than did false answers. Observers correctly picked up on the length of the answer and speech hesitation in making their judgments, which increased their accuracy. However, observers also felt that answers were more truthful when they were plausible and full of concrete details and when the speaker did not smile too much. Reliance on these cues did not improve accuracy, since they were not correlated with actual truthfulness. In looking over their subjects' judgments, Krauss, Geller, and Olson concluded that although people are pretty good at guessing when someone is lying, they don't really know how they do it: "Subjects are largely unaware of the cues they themselves use when attempting to detect deception. They both fail to use the cues they are likely to name and fail to name the cues they appear actually to use" (Krauss *et al.* 1976).

In some ways it is surprising that people can detect lies as well as they do. Confronting someone with the fact that he is bending the truth creates an awkward social situation, and, as Goffman (1959) argues, the "dupe" may often collaborate in the maintenance of the deception by keeping quiet about any suspicions. Thus it is difficult to learn the cues that go with lying because you often don't find out whether the suspicious statement was really true or false until long afterwards.

PERCEIVER GOALS AND COGNITIVE SETS AFFECT INTERPRETATIONS

The perceivers' emotions Given that many nonverbal behaviors tend to be relatively ambiguous, we might expect that their interpretation would be more than usually influenced by the perceiver's own mood, or goals, or cognitive set. Schiffenbauer (1974), for example, found that people who were emotionally aroused tended to judge slides of facial expressions as more intense and more in line with their own emotional state than people who were not aroused. In a face-to-face interaction, Ellsworth and Carlsmith (1973) found that subjects who were angry at the confederate were strongly affected by his gaze, but subjects who were not angry did not respond to it. That is, once the subjects were angry and emotionally involved in the situation, the visual behavior became an important influence on their behavior. Both of these studies provide preliminary, tentative evidence that emotional involvement may lead people to exaggerate the significance of nonverbal cues.

Perceiver expectations and goals In addition to one's own arousal, one's expectations may influence one's response to nonverbal cues. Certainly our perceptions of "abnormal," "informative" behavior depend on our expectations about what is "normal" behavior in the circumstances. There is very little work on expectations other than these basic cultural expectations. What there is tends to focus on behavior that *departs* from expectations, and indicates that such behavior is taken seriously. For example, in a very suggestive study Bond (1972) told subjects that they were to have a conversation with a woman who they believed was either a cold and distant person, or very warm and outgoing. The woman (actually nineteen different women, for the sake of generality) was given no particular instructions on how to behave, and did not know whether the subject thought she was warm or cold. Before interacting with the woman, the "warm set" subjects had very different impressions of her than the "cold set" subjects. After the interaction, although the two groups were still significantly influenced by their initial impressions, their ratings were much closer together. That is, the warm set subjects thought the woman was a little less warm than they had previously believed, while the cold set subjects thought she was considerably less cold than they had previously believed. Thus, subjects were quite sensitive to the *difference* between the woman's behavior and their own expectations.

Interestingly enough, the women behaved differently to warm set and cold set subjects. Since they didn't know what the subjects had been told about them, their behavior must have been influenced by differences in the subjects' behavior. They behaved *more warmly* to the cold set subjects than to the warm set subjects, as though they had guessed the subjects' initial impression, and were going out of their way to compensate. In many situations, however, it seems likely that when we expect someone to be warm and sociable we ourselves will behave in a more outgoing fashion, and in so doing, make our expectations come true: that is, the other person may be warm and sociable *in response* to our own encouraging behavior. Similarly, if we expect someone to be cold or unfriendly, we may approach her with reserve; when she responds in kind, we will take it as evidence that our expectations were correct, never considering the possibility that we made them correct. Snyder, Tanke, and Berscheid (1977) have obtained some evidence that perceivers do in fact influence others to behave according to the perceiver's stereotype (see p. 35).

Argyle and Kendon (1967) have suggested, following Jones and Thibaut (1958), that the perceiver's *goals* will also affect his or her selection and interpretation of nonverbal cues. Ellsworth, Friedman, Perlick, and Hoyt (1978) have shown that when a person wants to interact with somebody in order to obtain social comparison information, he will respond very positively to a relevant person who initiates and maintains eye contact. When a person wants to avoid social comparison, she will show the same warm response to a person who looks away. That this response is directly related to the person's immediate goals (that is, the person's need for social comparison) is shown by the subjects' response to a person who is completely irrelevant for social comparison purposes, and is therefore incapable of satisfying either goal: in this case the person's gaze has a relatively weak effect, which does not vary with the perceiver's goals.

A further influence of set on the perception of nonverbal behavior is simply the influence of the kind of question we are asking and the information we already have. Within any of the nonverbal channels, a cue may be taken as a meaningful sign for some kinds of inference, but not for others (Birdwhistell 1970; Argyle and Kendon 1967). For instance, if I ask a French woman how she feels about the new French diet cuisine, and if she briskly raises her shoulders, hands, and eyebrows while lowering the corners of her mouth, this behavior may tell me that she is French and that she is feeling that ineffable French emotion that goes with this kind of shrug (Wylie and Stafford 1977). That is, it will tell me about her cultural background and her reaction to my question. It may not, however, tell me anything about her personality. Of course, if I *know* she was born and raised in west Texas, I may use this same gesture to infer something about her personality. The meaningfulness of nonverbal cues depends on a great many factors, including the kind of question we are asking, the kind of inference we are trying to make, and the information we already have. Another example is the example of the close friend discussed above. When we feel we know someone well, we are not looking for new information about that person's personality, and thus we are not likely to use nonverbal cues as a source of information about personality.

Appropriate levels of intimacy People also have expectations and assumptions about the level of intimacy appropriate for an interaction, and one of their goals is to achieve or maintain this level. Argyle and Dean (1965) have developed a theory about the ways in which nonverbal cues are used to maintain the optimum level of intimacy between two people, a level they call the *equilibrium level.* Once a comfortable equilibrium level of intimacy has been reached, the nonverbal behaviors signaling intimacy tend to remain relatively constant. But if one person upsets this stability by moving closer, gazing more often, or talking about more intimate things, the other person will attempt a compensatory *decrease* in one or more of these behaviors in order to restore the interaction to its equilibrium level. Similarly, if the first person *reduces* one of these behaviors, the other person will increase one of them.

There is a good deal of evidence that such *compensation* occurs so that if one person moves closer or moves the conversation toward more intimate topics, the other gazes less (Argyle and Ingham 1972; Goldberg, Kiesler, and Collins 1969; Schultz and Barefoot 1974). On the other hand, there is also evidence that in some situations the opposite occurs: people *reciprocate* the intimate behavior by increasing the intimacy of their own behavior (Argyle and Cook 1976).

Patterson (1976) has proposed a theory to account for the diverse findings in this area. He argues, first of all, that when one person changes the intimacy of any channel, the other person will experience arousal. As we mentioned earlier, there is fairly good evidence indicating that direct gaze produces physiological arousal, and there is some evidence that moving closer does, too. According to Patterson, the person then interprets this arousal in terms of his cognitions about other aspects of the social situation, just as in Schachter and Singer's (1962) theory of emotion (cf. p. 92). If he decides the arousal is *negative* (that is, if he interprets a close approach as threatening), Argyle and Dean's equilibrium hypothesis will be confirmed, and he will *compensate.* That is, if Janet sits down one foot away from Miles, and Miles interprets his own ensuing arousal as nervousness, he will look away, turn away, or even run away. But if Miles interprets his arousal as positive, he will *reciprocate*—not compensate for—Janet's behavior by increasing the intimacy of his own behavior. For example, if Miles interprets his reaction to Janet's gaze as love, he will gaze back, move forward, embrace Janet, or do something else to encourage the new, higher intimacy level.

Argyle and Cook (1976) and Ellsworth (1975) have also suggested a central role for arousal, with particular reference to the gaze. There is now general consensus that the gaze and many other nonverbal cues have no intrinsic valence, but may be interpreted as positive or negative depending on the perceiver's goals and on other information from the social situation. In simplified terms, the argument is that the arousal produces the need to interpret, and the context and motives provide the specific content of the interpretation. The context may be as small as the accompanying facial expression or as large as the history of the relationship, the norms governing the social setting, or a cultural belief system, such as the belief in the evil eye.

These studies also point to the possibility of a closer relationship between studies of nonverbal behavior and studies of attribution biases. The same sorts of cognitive set effects found in studies of attribution may also operate in our interpretation of nonverbal cues. Horn (1977), for example, found a strong "self-esteem" bias when she asked subjects to rate a list of nonverbal behaviors. Subjects were asked to imagine themselves in a conversation with another person who showed one of the nonverbal behaviors, and then to answer two questions: (1) To what extent was the behavior caused by you or by other things? and (2) How positive or negative was the behavior? She found that the behaviors that were rated the most positively ("face lights up," "smiles," "looks attentively at you") were also rated as most likely to be caused by the subject herself, while the most negative behaviors ("leaves the room," "yawns," "avoids your glance") were more likely to be considered due to other things. Correlations between positivity and attribution to self were .49 and .63 in two separate studies.

On the other hand, there are other "sets" that might be expected to affect this bias. Argyle and Williams (1969) suggest, for example, that whether one feels like an observer or like a person who is being observed in a dyad affects one's goals and perceptions in the interaction. The observer watches the other's behavior in order to evaluate it; the person who feels observed is watching for feedback about how his or her performance is being evaluated. Thus, for both members the social performance of the *observed* member of the dyad is the focus of attention and evaluation in the interaction.

In this kind of evaluative interaction, then, the effects of observer/observed set may vary somewhat from what might be predicted by Jones and Nisbett's (1972) actor/observer distinction. Jones and Nisbett argue that for the actor, the situational factors are the central focus of attention, so that actors tend to attribute their own behavior to situational, rather than personality, factors. Observers, for whom the actor's behavior is the salient stimulus against a situational ground, tend to attribute the actor's behavior to stable personality dispositions. But in an evaluative situation, the evaluated actor may come to share the observer's focus of attention on himself. Horn (1977) found that the Argyle and Williams perspective was quite powerful in an evaluative situation, so that not only did the evaluator (observer) feel that the actor's behavior was caused by internal factors, but the actor (the person being evaluated) shared this bias. The people being evaluated felt responsibility not only for their own behavior, but for the evaluator's behavior as well. Thus, in a teacher-student, boss-worker, or therapist-patient interaction, the subordinate person may tend to underestimate the extent to which her behavior is influenced by her superior, and the superior may also tend to underestimate her own influence. Horn found that in more than two-thirds of all attributions made in her experiment, the person being evaluated was held responsible—both for her own behavior and for the evaluator's. If the person evaluating me yawns, it means that I'm boring (not that she's lazy or tired or rude); if I yawn, it means that I'm lazy, not that my evaluator is boring. This effect overwhelmed the self-esteem bias Horn had found in the ratings of lists of nonverbal cues. Similar results were found in a somewhat more realistic setting by Ludwig and Ellsworth (1974). The actor, in these settings, does not see the situation as responsible for his behavior, but his behavior as responsible for changes in the social situation. The observer, as predicted by Jones and Nisbett, agrees.

CONCLUSION

Thus, although there are some major differences between our perception of nonverbal "expressive" cues and our perceptions of more purposeful behaviors, there are also many similarities in the underlying processes. Our attention is seized and our interpretive faculties are engaged by behaviors that depart from our assumptions about normal behavior, and by behaviors that seem inconsistent with other behaviors or other aspects of the situation. Research on perceiver motives and cognitive sets is still rather sparse, but promises to uncover new relationships between the study of nonverbal cues and the more traditional areas of person perception. The research on lying and on the perception of the artistic representation of nonverbal cues is even newer. The nonverbal behaviors involved are unusual because they are intentional, and these two lines of research may ultimately uncover important information about the role of perceived intentionality in the attribution process.

Summary

Although the study of person perception and the study of nonverbal behavior have developed separately, it is clear that nonverbal cues have a strong influence on our interpretation of others' behavior and our assessments of their personalities. Like appearance cues, nonverbal behaviors can lead to immediate, unreasoned snap judgments, and the processes are probably identical in the two cases. But we also make more complicated attributions about motives and character on the basis of nonverbal cues. These are different from the attributions we make on the basis of other behavior because nonverbal cues are relatively ambiguous, since they are seen as indicative of inner feelings that we cannot or will not label precisely. Also, nonverbal cues are seen as unintentional *reactions* to stimuli. Thus, instead of inferring a disposition from an intention, we infer a disposition from a person-stimulus interaction.

On the other hand, attributions based on nonverbal cues are similar to those based on other behaviors in that (1) perception is an active process, so that the perceiver's purposes and expectations affect what is perceived, and (2) unusual and undesirable behaviors are more likely to provoke us to dispositional attributions than are normal socially desirable behaviors. Thus, in general, we tend to make reactive attributions to nonverbal behaviors and purposive attributions to other behaviors, but we do not think much about them or pursue them to a dispositional attribution in either case unless there is something unusual about the behavior.

impression formation

Attribution theories tell us how perceivers infer the causes of behavior, but they do not tell us very much about how perceivers go beyond these inferences from behavior. Surely, more is involved in person perception than decisions about whether behavior was internally or externally caused, and, if it was internally caused, what psychological dispositions constitute the causes. Consider, for example, what happens as you get to know someone even over a very brief period of time. You may observe behavior and make some inferences about what kind of person would perform those behaviors. You may, in short, perform some attribution work. Your interest in the other person may stop with this preliminary cognitive work, but you may also want to know more about the person. Perhaps she is interesting, or you have some business or personal reason for getting to know her better. Perhaps she seems fascinating because she seems to have unusual physical or personal characteristics, or perhaps she seems contradictory and complex. Or perhaps you are simply interested in people or are stuck in a situation with nothing better to do than to figure her out.

To be even more concrete, suppose you have been watching a woman at a party. A lot of other people are congregated around her and you discover that she has just had a novel published. You observe her long enough to draw some tentative conclusions about her. Some of these result from attribution work; she is smart, ambitious, but particularly hard-working—conclusions you are able to draw because few people write novels and because you discover that this is her second novel and fourth published book. Let's also face the possibility that you may be a bit inclined to see women succeeding because of hard work (see p. 76). However, you also manage to draw other conclusions without the benefit of an attributional analysis. You note that she is in her early 40s and reasonably attractive; her hair is a rather unnatural shade of yellow. Furthermore, she is wearing an expensive long dress. Your snap judgment is that artificial blondes who wear expensive dresses are on the frivolous side. You note that the woman is witty, and that she giggles a great deal; these inferences do not require attribution work, because those are

151

relatively objective descriptions of her behavior. Finally, you note she is consuming drinks at a rapid pace and that she has smoked several cigarettes. You summarize the behavior by saying she is nervous.

What have you decided? Our novelist is intelligent, ambitious, hard-working, frivolous, witty, "gigglely," and nervous. Now your work really begins. How, you might ask yourself, can a person be both hard-working and frivolous? Perhaps she is not frivolous after all; surely, not all blondes fit that category. Or perhaps she is trying to create a really good impression for someone so that her hairstyle does not so much indicate frivolousness as a concern to create a good impression. That would certainly fit with her nervousness. But why would she be nervous? She's a hit, the star of the party. Maybe she is insecure (all those giggles); nervous people and people who try to create a good impression frequently are nervous—or so you believe. Why is she insecure? Perhaps she is really shy; you think that intelligent people are generally shy, and her novels are *so* introspective. Or your inference work might go another direction. You might decide that she is really a frivolous creature who is not intelligent. On second thought, her novels are really quite superficial and she has good reason to feel insecure. She's afraid someone will discover that she is a fraud.

All this time you are drawing conclusions about our hypothetical novelist, conclusions that are based on your past experiences and biases. When you decide she is insecure, you have gone well beyond observing her behavior. You may, of course, check out your conclusions through subsequent attributional analysis; it is probably quite common for perceivers to make inferences and then to analyze whether they can explain behavior. Not only have you drawn conclusions about this hapless victim of all this concentrated attention, but you are concerned that your conclusions be consistent with one another. You are bothered that she can be both hard-working and frivolous. So you work at making these traits consistent by subordinating one of the traits (she is really not frivolous), or by seeing both traits as part of a larger pattern (insecure people are both hard-working and frivolous). You check each new inference against previous ones. Her insecurity, which involves shyness, is consistent with her intelligence. In short, you try to organize all the data you have into a consistent, coherent, stable impression.

In this chapter we consider the process of inferring psychological characteristics from behavior and other psychological characteristics and also how perceivers organize the various inferences into a consistent meaningful whole. Historically, this area of research has been called *impression formation*. In a classic article, Solomon Asch (1946) discussed these kinds of inference and organizational processes which are crucial in getting to know another person. The field of impression formation is perhaps a bit misnamed because the research on impression formation does not cover everything that happens as you get to know someone. Perhaps *impression organization* might be a better title. However, we will continue to use the term *impression formation* for this research, because so many of the research problems have deep roots in Asch's pioneering attempts to understand what happens when we do form impressions.

The Asch Paradigm

Asch suggested two general models of impression formation. A simple *additive* model predicts that the final impression is based on the sum of the impressions of the individual characteristics or traits possessed by the stimulus person. In forming an impression we treat each of the traits independently—not as related. Asch preferred a second model, which states that the traits are immediately organized to form a whole, or Gestalt. Thus, each trait affects each of the others, and the final impression is a dynamic one not easily predictable from the individual traits taken separately.

Asch performed a series of experiments to explore these alternative models. His method was simple and direct, and it has served as a paradigm for much of the later experimental work in this area. He gave subjects a list of traits that were said to characterize a particular person. He then had the subjects write a paragraph describing their impressions of the person, and then had them select from pairs of opposing traits the one they felt would best characterize the person. The words given to the subject at the beginning are the *stimulus* traits, and the words the subjects chose at the end are the *response* traits. In his first experiment Group *A* heard the stimulus person described as intelligent-skillful-industrious-*warm*-determined-practical-cautious. Group *B* heard the stimulus person described as intelligent-skillful-industrious-*cold*-determined-practical-cautious. The two lists of stimulus traits are identical except for the terms "warm" (*A*) and "cold" (*B*). It is clear from the pattern of response traits chosen that quite different impressions were formed by the two groups (see Table 7.1, columns *A* and *B*). Note that many traits, such as generous, were greatly affected by whether the stimulus person was described as being warm or cold. Other traits, such as reliable, were seen as being possessed equally by warm and cold stimulus persons.

Asch suggested that Group *A* and Group *B* formed very different kinds of impressions. Perhaps Group *A* subjects (the "warm group") saw the stimulus person as a talented person who feels secure enough to help others, while Group *B* subjects (the "cold group") saw the stimulus person as talented but egocentric and selfish. "Warm" and "cold" were particularly important traits, since Asch was also able to show that a stimulus list including neither warm nor cold elicited less polarized responses than one on which warm or cold was included (Table 7.1, column *E*). For example, 55 percent of the subjects inferred that an industrious, skillful, intelligent, determined, practical person was generous; when told that the person was also *warm*, 91 percent inferred generosity, and when told the person was *cold*, only 8 percent inferred gener-

TABLE 7.1
Representative Results
(From Asch 1946)

Stimulus list A	Stimulus list B	Stimulus list C	Stimulus list D	Stimulus list E
intelligent	intelligent	intelligent	intelligent	intelligent
skillful	skillful	skillful	skillful	skillful
industrious	industrious	industrious	industrious	industrious
warm	*cold*	*polite*	*blunt*	
determined	determined	determined	determined	determined
practical	practical	practical	practical	practical
cautious	cautious	cautious	cautious	cautious

Percentage of subjects indicating that trait is characteristic of person

	A (warm)	B (cold)	C (polite)	D (blunt)	E (no key trait)
generous	91	8	56	58	55
wise	65	25	30	50	49
happy	90	34	75	65	71
good-natured	94	17	87	56	69
reliable	94	99	95	100	96
important	88	99	94	96	88

osity. Clearly, the inclusion of *warm* or *cold* has acted to increase the uniformity of trait attribution. Given these data, Asch argued that warm and cold were *central traits;* they seemed to bear a large responsibility for organizing the impression his subjects had formed. Other traits did not serve to organize the impression as effectively and did not create polarization of the inferences drawn about the stimulus person. For example, when *polite* or *blunt* was inserted in the position previously occupied by warm or cold, the group exposed to the *polite* stimulus person formed inferences that were not radically different from those made by the group exposed to *blunt* (Table 7.1, columns *C* and *D*).

Asch further argued that whether a given trait was central or peripheral in the formation of an impression depended on its relationships to all other stimulus traits (its context). There are at least three testable derivations from that argument. The first, demonstrated above, is that some pairs of traits will produce stronger effects in a given group of stimulus traits than will other traits: the change of warm to cold in the stimulus list affected the impression more than the change of polite to blunt in the same list. Second, if the centrality of traits is indeed a function of other stimulus traits, then in some stimulus contexts warm-cold would not be central traits. Asch did find some evidence that warm and cold are less central when embedded in the list of obedient-weak-shallow-unambitious-vain. Subjects' responses indicated that the inclusion of warm or cold had little effect on their impressions.

A final implication of the stimulus-context argument is that the same results could not have been produced by the presentation of warm and cold alone. In one experiment Asch found that impressions formed from the warm-cold traits alone were slightly more uniform that those formed when they were embedded in a context: whereas 55 percent of the subjects saw as generous an intelligent-skillful-industrious-determined-practical-cautious person, 91 percent saw that person as generous if that person was also warm, but 100 percent saw as generous a person who was simply warm. Asch argued that these results supported his Gestalt approach, since the other stimulus traits must have "dampened" the effects of warm and cold.

Asch did several other experiments that yielded data consistent with his view that in many impressions there are central traits or pieces of information about the stimulus person that tend to dominate the impression, around which the other traits seem to be organized for their meaning. Certainly that position is close to most people's feelings about impression formation, and Asch's article contains a wealth of phenomenological description from his subjects that is consistent with his view.

Asch's article led to two important lines of research. The first concerns the relationships among stimulus and response traits, and it asks the question whether specification of such stimulus-response relationships will allow a researcher to predict what subjects will infer from a given list of stimulus traits. That research will be considered in the next section. The second line of research concentrates on the way the stimulus information is combined and processed, the way inconsistencies in the stimulus information are resolved. That approach is focused primarily on the relationships among the stimuli, and we will consider it in the section entitled *Processes of Impression Formation*.

Implicit Personality Theory

ASCH'S GESTALT POSITION

Asch believed that the stimulus traits produced a coherent impression which in turn led to further inferences about the stimulus person. Keep in mind that he had subjects write a description of the stimulus person, a description he believed approximated the impression. For example, one of Asch's subjects wrote the following description of the intelligent-skillful-industrious-cold-determined-practical-cautious person: "A very ambitious and talented person who would not let anyone or anything stand in the way of achieving his goal. Wants his own way, he is determined not to give in, no matter what happens" (Asch 1946, p. 263). If subjects were then asked to check which traits were characteristic of the stimulus person, they would probably check traits such as strong, important, reliable; they would avoid checking traits like generous, altruistic, and humorous. Asch believed that it was the intervening impression that made it possible for the subject to generate new information. It was then a two-step process: stimulus traits → impression → response inferences.

TRAIT IMPLICATIONS

There is an alternative possibility. Perhaps we generate inferences about another person directly from the information we have, without generating an intervening impression at all. If we know that Person *A* is cold, we may immediately infer that he is also unkind or aggressive. In their 1954 review of the literature on person perception, Bruner and Tagiuri suggested that more attention should be paid to the question of how we generate information about others from partial cues. Why is it that a warm person is seen as generous, and a happy-intelligent person is perceived to be honest? Bruner and Tagiuri proposed that such inferences were generated by a naive, *implicit theory of personality*. We all somehow have a sense of which characteristics "go with" which other characteristics.

Wishner (1960) studied the relationships among traits when he attempted to reinterpret the original Asch experiments. Wishner had undergraduate subjects rate their instructors on 53 of the Asch traits, and he simply determined from these data the correlations among all traits. Wishner reasoned that if warm and cold make a difference in the selection of response traits, then the dimension warm-cold must be correlated with the response traits. He was able to show that the correlations of warm-cold with response traits do predict how much those traits are affected by the inclusion of warm or cold in the stimulus list. For example, in the initial Asch experiment, the warm stimulus person was seen as more imaginative than the cold one. Wishner found a correlation of 0.48 between ratings of warmth and imaginativeness. On the other hand, warm and cold stimulus persons were seen as equally strong, and Wishner found no correlation ($r = .07$) between strength and warmth.

Wishner clearly showed that if we know the relationships among traits, we can predict response traits from stimulus traits. That is, we can predict what traits people will infer if we know what traits they were given. He has also provided us with a genuine definition of a central trait. Whereas Asch could only guess which would be central traits, Wishner showed that a trait is central to the extent that it correlates highly with the response traits. That means that the centrality of a trait is more a function of the given response traits than of the other stimulus traits as Asch had suggested. Remember that Asch believed the stimulus traits formed a Gestalt, and therefore the centrality of a particular stimulus trait would depend on what other stimulus traits were present. Wishner showed that whether or not "warm" was a central trait depended on what you *wanted* to know about the other person, on the question you were asking (the response trait). If you were trying to figure out whether someone was strong, it wouldn't help you very much to know that she was warm—"warm" would not be a central trait, because it isn't strongly related to "strong." But if you were trying to figure out whether she was generous, it would help to know if she was warm—for the response trait of generosity, "warm" is central.

We hasten to point out that although the centrality of stimulus traits can be predicted from the response traits, the predictions are not perfect. It is possible that relationships among stimulus traits also help to define centrality in some cases. It has also been shown that some traits seem to have particular power to imply other traits independently of stimulus context. These powerful traits are those that people perceive as being dispositional in the sense of being both internal and stable (Schneider 1978). Even so, however, Wishner clearly showed that the relationships between stimulus and response traits were important, if not all-important in defining centrality.

The most important feature of Wishner's analysis is that it suggests people have a clear idea of what traits are closely or not so closely related to other traits. Thus, we are able to infer whether a person is likely to be happy from prior knowledge about that person's warmth. This set of perceived trait relationships has to come to be known as *implicit personality theory*.

A SHORT EXCURSION INTO METHODOLOGY

Trait relations Much of the support for the idea of implicit personality theory comes from research using correlations among traits, factor analyses of such correlations, or multidimensional scaling of implicative relationships among traits. It would therefore be appropriate to discuss those methods briefly. A correlation indicates the extent of relationship between a paired set of observations. There are various ways of obtaining correlations among traits (see Schneider 1973). For example, we could determine the extent to which traits are seen to occur together across many different stimulus persons. In judging political figures, we might find that politicians who are seen as honest are usually seen as idealistic or imaginative, whereas those politicians who are perceived as dishonest are seen as pragmatic and unimaginative. We would then conclude that there is positive correlation between perceptions of honesty and idealism.

While this sort of technique is common, there are other possibilities. For example, in the Wishner study, correlations among traits were calculated across perceivers. If several people rate the same stimulus person(s), we may discover that whereas Joe sees the person as being both honest and kind, Mary sees her as being dishonest and unkind. These ratings would produce a positive correlation between honesty and kindness.[1]

Unfortunately there are major problems with correlational measures (c.f., Anderson 1977), but one need not be restricted to correlational methods in studying trait relationships. One could simply ask subjects directly how similar two traits are, or ask subjects to give their ideas about which traits imply which other traits. The advantage of this method is that perceived relationships are obtained directly, whereas with correlations the relationships are generated through standard statistical procedures. Todd and Rappoport (1964), however, report that correlational and implicative measures yield similar estimates of the perceived relationships among traits.

A third method used by Seymour Rosenberg (see Rosenberg and Sedlak 1972) gets trait relationships indirectly but through rather natural procedures. Subjects place traits into piles representing people. For example, one pile might represent Great-Uncle Harry, who is sly, unhappy, and bitter. When all subjects have created trait piles, a measure of trait disagreement is calculated. This measure, described fully by Rosenberg and Sedlak (1972), assumes that traits that appear often together or that appear often with the same third trait are perceived as similar or closer together than traits that do not have co-occurances. This measure also is moderately related to correlational measures (Riley and Bryson 1977).

The matrix of relations   Each of these methods generates a matrix of trait-by-trait relationships, and with several traits there will be many different relationships to consider. There would be considerable advantage to finding a

---

1.   For students who are unfamiliar with statistics and correlations, we include the following brief explanation. The degree of relationship between two variables is indicated by the absolute size of the correlation, with a perfect relationship indicated by 1.00 and no relationship indicated by .00. The sign of the correlation indicates whether the relationship is positive or negative. So perceived honesty and idealism might correlate .70, honesty and intelligence .20, and honesty and pragmatism − .50. In the first case, most honest politicians would be seen as idealistic; in the second case, there would be a slight tendency to see honest politicians as intelligent; and in the third case, there would be a moderate tendency to see honest politicians as *non*pragmatic. Thus, we could predict ratings of idealism fairly precisely from ratings of honesty, and we could predict ratings of pragmatism better than ratings of intelligence from honesty.

parsimonious representation of those relationships. For example, if we found that strong, tall, and aggressive were strongly related traits, we would have little trouble inferring a cluster of masculinity underlying that set of relationships. If, on the other hand, the traits varied in how positive they are, we might infer a dimension of general evaluation.

A hypothetical example involving correlations among six traits is given in Table 7.2. Keeping in mind that correlations vary from −1 to +1, note that the correlations are all positive, reflecting the fact that all the traits included are at least somewhat positively related. Note also that there are two distinct clusters of traits: warm, happy, sincere, and intelligent, skillful, determined. Relationships of traits within the clusters are higher than relationships between clusters. The two clusters might correspond to dimensions of social success and intellectual success, respectively.

Typically, when the trait relationships are expressed as correlations, factor analysis is used to determine underlying dimensions. When the trait relationships are expressed as similarities, implications, or co-occurances, the relationships are interpreted as distances, and the dimensions underlying the distances are determined by multidimensional scaling. Thus, if the traits cold and unhappy are seen to imply one another or are often used to describe the same people, it is assumed that this close relationship of the traits can be indicated by a close physical distance on a graph.

With both factor analysis and multidimensional scaling, these dimensions are usually labeled. The investigator looks at the traits that lie at the extremes of each dimension and provides a label to describe the ways in which they differ. For example, if traits such as warm, happy, and kind lie at one end of a dimension, and traits such as cold, impolite, and tactless lie at the other end, the dimension would seem to be one of social skills or social goodness. Rosenberg and Sedlak (1972) give examples of less subjective ways of labeling dimensions, but such discussion is beyond the scope of this book.

While we have emphasized dimensional representation of trait relationships, there are other important techniques for summarizing these data. One can also arrange traits in hierarchies such that several traits cluster as examples of some more general quality. Rosenberg and Sedlak (1972) and Jones, Sensenig, and Haley (1974) give examples of the use of these clustering approaches.

TABLE 7.2
Hypothetical Correlations among Traits

	Warm	Happy	Sincere	Intelligent	Skillful	Determined
Warm	—	.75	.80	.30	.25	.35
Happy		—	.60	.35	.20	.25
Sincere			—	.30	.20	.10
Intelligent				—	.80	.70
Skillful					—	.70
Determined						—

As one example of research involving multidimensional scaling methods we might consider an important study by Rosenberg *et al.* (1968). They had subjects place 60 traits into piles representing people, and then calculated the co-occurances or distances among the traits on the basis of how much any two traits tended to be placed together. They then used a multidimensional scaling procedure to find the underlying dimensions of the distances. The results are given in Fig. 7.1. You should note several things. First, some of the traits lie close together, and those were traits that subjects tended to see as related or close in the sense that they were used to describe the same person. Second, the trait distances all lie in two dimensions, and there are two main dimensions: intellectual and social; both dimensions have a good and a bad end. This means that while many traits—such as *important*—are good in both senses, and others—such as *unreliable*—are bad both intellectually and socially, there are some discrepancies. For example, *warm* is good in a social sense but bad in an intellectual sense, while *cold* is the opposite. However, you should note a third feature of this figure: the two dimensions are not at right angles to one another. This means that the two dimensions are related, that generally good

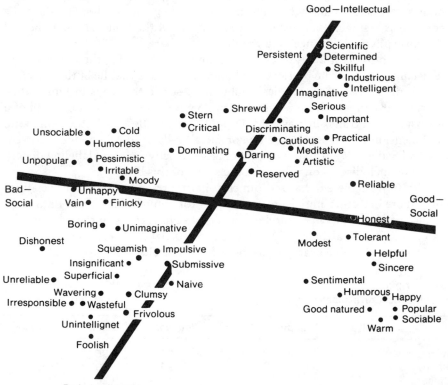

Fig. 7.1 Dimensions of traits. (From Rosenberg *et al.* 1968.)

traits on one dimension are good on the other. Later in this chapter we will return to the question of the basic dimensions of trait relationships.

Zanna and Hamilton (1972) have shown the relevance of these two dimensions in the Asch impression formation procedure. Zanna and Hamilton classified traits as either socially desirable (e.g., warm), socially undesirable (e.g., cold), intellectually desirable (e.g., imaginative), or intellectually undesirable (e.g., unimaginitive). They reasoned that when the socially relevant traits were varied in the stimulus list, there would be greater effects on the responses of other social than of intellectual traits. The opposite should be found for intellectual traits. This means that varying whether a stimulus person is warm or cold should have a greater effect on how happy and altruistic he is perceived than on how intelligent or skillful he is. The results of Zanna and Hamilton supported this reasoning, further showing that the centrality of a trait is partially dependent on the response traits.

ORIGINS AND STRUCTURE OF IMPLICIT PERSONALITY THEORY

Whether we conceive of implicit personality theories as a set of relationships among individual traits or as more general dimensional or hierarchical structures, we still have to account for the origins of these ideas. How does the individual come to have a theory of personality? This question is as broad as the question that asks how people come to have stable ways of interpreting experience. Although there are no specific answers, it is likely that implicit personality theories are learned all through the socialization process. Parents may point out the joint occurrence of traits in various individuals, or may often repeat such abstract phrases as "cleanliness is next to godliness." Many of the relationships between traits are probably inferred by the individual after she has repeatedly noted joint occurrences of characteristics in her encounters with other people; for example, she may have observed that churchgoers appear to be well-scrubbed. On the other hand, perceived trait relationships may be all in the mind of the perceiver.

The realism-idealism issue   There seems to be some agreement within a given culture on implicit personality theories. One could take either a realist or an idealist position in explaining within-culture similarity of implicit personality theories. The realist position is that perceived relationships among traits reflect actual covariation of traits in other people. The idealist position suggests that the subjects' ratings of the traits of actual other people reflect little about the traits the stimulus persons possess (Passini and Norman 1966; Mulaik 1964; D'Andrade 1965). Perhaps there is no correspondence between our theories of personality and the actual relationship of traits among individuals in the population.

It has long been recognized that perceived trait relationships do not inevitably mirror actual relationships. For example, Thorndike (1920) noted that personality ratings were often affected by a tendency to see positive characteristics as more related to other positive characteristics than they should be if experience were the only guide. Thorndike called this the *halo effect*. A recent demonstration has been provided by Nisbett and Wilson (1977b). Subjects saw an interview with a professor who was either warm or who was cold and hostile. Not surprisingly, they liked the former professor more, but they also rated the warm professor's physical appearance as being more pleasant. Because physical appearance is presumably not affected by warmth, we can safely say that subjects allowed their evaluative reactions to the professors to influence their ratings of physical appearance. As we will see, the evaluative aspect of traits does have general and pervasive effects on perceived relationships.

One of the more influential sets of studies that has been used to support the idea that implicit personality theories do not reflect experience was done by Norman. In one study (Norman 1963), he collected and analyzed a large set of peer ratings. A clear and rather stable structure emerged, and the number and kinds of dimensions of judgment were very similar for subjects who had lived together for three years in a fraternity and for those who had experienced less prolonged and intimate contact. Norman felt he had isolated some basic dimensions of personality. Passini and Norman (1966), however, raised the possibility that those results could be reflecting perceptual tendencies of the raters instead of real dimensions of the stimulus persons' personalities. They asked subjects to rate complete strangers, and the resulting dimensions were highly similar to those used by subjects in the earlier Norman (1963) study. Since the same dimensions of judgment seem to arise whether the perceivers know the stimulus person or not, it is reasonable to argue that the dimensions of perception are implicit in the perceiver. We argued in Chapter 1 that perceivers have large roles in organizing their perceptual worlds, and the Passini and Norman research seems to support that contention. In this connection you may also remember our Chapter 1 discussion of the children's camp study by Dornbusch *et al.* (1965), which showed that more category overlap occurs with a single perceiver describing two stimulus persons than with two perceivers describing a single stimulus person.

These results tend to support an idealism position, but other studies give support to a realist position. Lay and Jackson (1969) and Stricker, Jacobs, and Kogan (1974) have found a high correspondence between the dimensions underlying actual responses to a personality inventory and the dimensions that perceivers used in making personality ratings. There is at least some correspondence between our perceptions of trait relationships in others and the actual measured relationships between traits in others. However, those who wish to maintain the position that implicit personality theories are not based primarily on experience can argue that when subjects fill out personality questionnaires, even for self, they do so on the basis of their implicit personality theories. In that case, these results would indicate only that the original subjects and the perceivers share an implicit personality theory.

Furthermore, Mirels (1976) has shown that judgments of co-occurrence and actual co-occurrence are not closely related. For example, given that a person has answered *true* to the statement, "My work is carefully planned and organized before it is begun," how likely is the person to also answer *true* to the statement, "My papers are always neat?" If you thought the likelihood was high you are in good company, because the average probability estimate by subjects was 92 percent. The two statements look as if they should go together, but, in fact, only 44 percent of subjects who endorsed the first proposition actually endorsed the second. Generally, Mirels found a low correspondence between empirical co-occurrences and estimated ones. These results are not directly comparable to the Lay and Jackson and Stricker *et al.* results because the former looked at correspondence of dimensions while Mirels looked at item correspondences. However, it is fairly clear that it is not inevitable that actual and perceived relationships among traits and behavior will match.

In fact, many research studies have examined the ability of people to estimate relationships or correlations among stimuli and events, and the data suggest that estimates of such relationships are subject to considerable bias (Smedslund 1963; Jenkins and Ward 1965; Dewhirst and Berman 1978). One classic phenomenon that shows this clearly has been called *illusory correlation*. Chapman and Chapman (1967, 1969) found that people—including clinical psychologists—infer personality and psychopathetic characteristics from certain "signs" on projective tests. For example, most people seem to infer that males who draw feminine male pictures are homosexuals. Although there is no evidence of an actual relationship between homosexuality and picture quality, both clinicians and lay people use drawings to infer homosexuality because the relationship seems logical. Chapman (1967) has provided some additional evidence for illusory correlation. In this study, subjects saw several word pairs a varying number of times and were asked to estimate how often certain word pairs had occurred. Subjects remembered that certain words had appeared together much more often than they had during the actual presentation. Particularly uncommon, unusual, or distinctive stimuli were judged as going together more often than they empirically had, and words that had an associative connection (such as bacon-eggs or leaf-tree) were also seen as having been paired together too often.

Berman and Kenny (1976) have also explored the ability to estimate trait relationships. They exposed subjects to a number of stimulus persons, each defined by a pair of traits. Sometimes the trait pairs were traits that are generally seen as going together, while sometimes the traits were pairs that do not generally go together. Over the several stimulus persons, the actual covariation of traits was varied so that, for example, some subjects saw that *understanding* and *tolerant* did occur together, while others saw that the two traits did not occur together. Later, when subjects rated stimulus persons, traits that had been presented together empirically were seen as more highly related than those that had not gone together. So subjects were sensitive to their actual experiences. However, subjects also tended to perceive closer relationships between traits that "should" go together (such as *understanding* and *tolerant*) than traits that they had previously thought did not go together (such as *shy* and *domineering*). Subjects allowed their assumptions about trait relationships to affect the perceived associations.

One must be careful in applying this type of research to real-life situations because typically subjects have limited experience with actual trait covariation (Block 1977; see also Berman and Kenny 1977); for example, Berman and Kenny only provided subjects with two exposures to each stimulus person. There is some evidence that perceived trait relationships are stronger for unfamiliar than for familiar people (Koltov 1962), so that the illusory correlations might be reduced with further exposure. However, the Berman and Kenny research does suggest that there *can be* systematic biases in perceived trait relationships.

The realism-idealism controversy, like so many others in the area of person perception, generates more heat than light.[2] It is probable that people are sensitive to the the actual covariation of characteristics and behaviors, but there is also abundant evidence that they often assume stronger (and on occasion, weaker) relationships than their evidence warrants.

Semantic organization   The nature of trait dimensions themselves may introduce some bias in perceived trait relationships. You may have noticed that the dimensional structures we have considered are systems of interrelationships among *words*, the names of traits. Some investigators have argued that when you give people the task of making personality ratings of others, maybe they are not thinking much about real people at all, but simply producing judgments on the basis of which words — or trait names — seem to go together. Certainly some of the dimensions that emerge in subjects' ratings of people are very like the dimensions that emerge in research on the general connotative meanings of words. Almost all studies, for example, find at least one *evaluative* dimension: one of the first judgments people make about a person (or a thing or a word) is whether they like the person or not, whether he or she is generally good or bad (Levy and Dugan 1960; Mulaik 1964; D'Andrade 1965; Rosenberg *et al.* 1968). You will recall that Thorndike pointed to the same kind of phenomenon which he labeled *the halo effect*. In many trait studies other dimensions first discovered in studies of linguistic relationship, dimensions such as potency and activity (Osgood, Suci, and Tannenbaum 1957), are also found in ratings of personality traits (Rosenberg and Olshan 1970; Rosenberg *et al.* 1968). It has also been shown that relationships among traits that are rated after direct observation of behavior do not closely correspond to trait relationships when ratings are done from memory; instead, the remembered trait relationships look like abstract ratings of the relationships among the names of the traits (D'Andrade 1974).

---

2.   There has been a related controversy about the implications of this research for actual personality assessment with some (Shweder 1975, 1977; D'Andrade 1974) arguing that the seeming consistency of personality reflects implicit personality theory biases and others (Block *et al.* 1978; Reed and Jackson 1977) defending the traditional personality research emphasis on actual personality consistency. This issue goes beyond the scope of this book.

This has led many researchers to believe that perceived trait relationships largely reflect similarity in their connotative—particulary evaluative—meanings. In making judgments about traits, perhaps people consider mainly their connotative meaning. For example, in considering the relationship of the traits *bold* and *honest*, subjects might consider that both are positive traits and, therefore, judge them as similar on that basis. However, people may also take into account the denotative meanings of trait words. They may think about what kinds of people are honest and bold or what kinds of behaviors bold people and honest people would exhibit. Therefore, one might also judge *bold* and *honest* to be similar because the same people tend to have both or neither of these traits, or because the two traits imply many of the same behaviors (such as taking an unpopular stand on an issue). The question is whether connotative or denotative similarity is more important in generating perceived trait similarity.

Peabody (1967) studied this question in a clever way. First, he formed quartets of traits that differed in evaluative as well as descriptive (denotative) content. For example, *bold* and *rash* could both be used to describe the same behavior, but *bold* is generally a positive term while *rash* is negative. These terms share descriptive content, but they differ evaluatively. At the other extreme, *cautious* and *timid* could describe behaviors opposite from *bold-rash*, but *cautious* and *timid* differ in their evaluation. Thus, the quartets of traits may be divided as in Table 7.3. Then Peabody presented one of the terms asked subjects to say whether other terms would be implied by it. For example, given a *cautious* person, how likely would she be *bold*? *timid*? Peabody found that the inferences were stronger to descriptively similar but evaluatively dissimilar (*cautious-timid*) than to descriptively dissimilar but evaluatively similar traits (*cautious-bold*). These types of data plus other kinds of analyses led Peabody to suggest that descriptive content was more important than evaluative content. In many studies of trait inferences the two are confounded, as when subjects are asked to judge how likely a cautious person would be rash; when separated, though, the descriptive content seems more important.

TABLE 7.3
Denotative and Connotative Differences among Traits
(From Peabody 1967)

	Positive	Negative
Boldness	Bold	Rash
Timidity	Cautious	Timid

	Positive	Negative
Confidence	Confident	Conceited
Nonconfidence	Modest	Self-disparaging

While Peabody's procedures and data analyses have been criticized (see Rosenberg and Olshan 1970; Felipe 1970; DeBoeck 1978; Peabody 1970, 1978) for technical reasons, Peabody has clearly shown that semantic and particularly evaluative similarity has been somewhat overdramatized in trait inference studies. It is impossible to say generally how important each kind of similarity is for perceived trait relationships because similarity is likely to vary with the task, the method of measuring relationships (Riley and Bryson 1977), and other features of the situation.

Other bases of implicit personality theories   In recent years several psychologists have begun to investigate other bases of implicit personality theories. We have already discussed the possibilities that perceived trait relationships are based on exprienced co-occurances or on semantic similarities. Both of these approaches see trait relationships as rather passively generated.

Recently Cantor and Mischel (1977a, b) have argued that trait (and behavior) information may be organized in a more dynamic fashion. They have suggested that there are certain basic personality categories called prototypes that serve to organize impressions. A prototype such as extroversion may consist of several related traits (such as *outgoing*) and behaviors (likes to attend loud parties). While such traits and behaviors are seen as related, what seems to hold them together is that they are all part of a stereotype or prototype of extroversion.

Two major implications of this approach have been studied empirically. The first is that prototypes ought to aid in the memory of more specific information. For example, in one study (Cantor and Mischel 1977a) subjects were shown a number of traits characteristic of a person; some of these traits fit a prototype (such as energetic for the extroversion prototype), and others were irrelevant to the prototype (such as *neat*). Later subjects were asked whether they had seen the trait in the list. As expected, subjects were fairly clear that they had seen the items they had. However, they also felt they had seen traits that had not been presented, particularly when those traits fit the prototype. Other studies show that people are likely to remember they have seen instances of behavior which are consistent with material previously presented (e.g., Woll and Yopp 1978). In another study (Cantor and Mischel 1977b), subjects were given behaviors representing a person. Some of the stimulus persons were described by several behaviors, all related to a particular prototype, while other stimulus persons were inconsistent because both introverted and extroverted behaviors were presented. In later recall, subjects remembered more of the behaviors when the stimulus person had clearly fit the prototype than when he or she did not. Moreover, there was a tendency for written impressions to contain more information for the consistent than for the inconsistent stimulus person. This research by Cantor and Mischel strongly suggests that perceivers do not merely store concrete items of information about another but seem to store a more abstract, prototypic, representation. Traits are not merely verbal labels used by perceivers, but are parts of a highly integrated set of other traits and behaviors organized at several levels of abstractness.

In a second implication of the prototype idea, Schneider and Blankmeyer (1978) argued that traits and behaviors that were part of a particular prototype would be seen as being more closely related when the prototype was salient than when it was not. They found that when the stimulus person was described as being extroverted, extroverted traits and behaviors were seen to imply each other more than when the stimulus person was described as being introverted or when the stimulus person was not described with any prototype. Introverted traits were seen as more closely related when the person was described as being introverted.

Cantor and Mischel's model clearly suggests that there are important or relevant schemata that determine how we process information about others. However, traits such as extroversion are not the only kinds of relevant prototypes. Markus (1977) has advanced related ideas in the self-perception area. She has suggested that self-schemata are cognitive generalizations about the self that guide the processing of information about the self; and self-descriptions are relevant to the person only insofar as they fit into self-schemata. She asked subjects to rate themselves on independence and dependence, and classified those who rated themselves extremely and who felt that the scales were important as having a self-schema for either independence or dependence. She then asked subjects to rate whether certain traits were descriptive of them, and she found that subjects with the schema were much quicker in making judgments for traits that were related to the schema, whereas there were no important differences for those without self-schemata in these areas. Subjects were also asked to give behavioral examples for various traits. Again, those with a self-schema could more readily provide examples for traits relevant to the schema. Finally, subjects with strong self-schemata tended to reject the results of a fake personality test that was inconsistent with their self-views.

Rogers and his colleagues (Rogers 1974, 1978; Rogers, Kuiper, and Kirker 1977) have further elaborated the self as an important component in information processing. In the experiment by Rogers et al. (1977) subjects were asked to make a variety of decisions about traits. For example, they were asked whether the trait was printed in large or small letters, whether it rhymed with another word, or whether it meant the same as another word. They were also asked whether the word described them or not. Subjects were not warned that they would be asked to recall the words, but recall was best for traits when subjects had been asked whether those traits described them, and within this category recall was better for words that did rather than did not describe the subject. The research of Rogers et al. suggests that trait words that are relevant by virtue of self-reference have a certain privileged status in information processing, and we might further speculate that the self-schemata may be useful not only in understanding self, but in understanding others as well.

The idea of prototypes suggests that people may have dynamic, non-linguistic reasons for seeing traits as closely related. If one takes seriously the idea that implicit personality theories are actually theories about personality, then perhaps perceivers—like psychologists—have images of several levels of personality. In particular they may feel that some traits and characteristics are more central or basic than others; prototypes such as extroversion are, of course, one example.

Schneider (1978) has argued that traits vary in their centrality and power to explain behavior and other traits. For example, a trait such as *mature* seems somehow more important, more central, more involved in causing other traits than does a trait such as *restless*. Not only do such central or basic traits imply other traits more strongly than do noncentral traits (Schneider 1978, 1971; Gifford 1975), but they are more highly interrelated than are the more peripheral traits. The central traits also seemed to convey more information; subjects wrote longer descriptions of people who were defined by these central traits than of people defined by less basic qualities. Snodgrass (1977) has also shown that traits which are seen as casually related are particularly likely to have high perceived co-occurences, and Koltov (1962) has found that perceived relationships are especially high for important rather than for unimportant traits. Wegner and Buldain (1977) have shown that traits that are general in the sense of describing many people are more similar in meaning to their implications than are less general traits. All these studies point to the possibility that not only are the more central traits are more tightly integrated, but that they imply other traits more strongly than do the more peripheral traits.

Thus far relatively little attention has been directed to the dynamic (as opposed to the structural) properties of implicit personality theories, and there has been relatively little attention paid to the basis of trait relationships. Clearly experience with actual co-occurence plays some role, but it appears likely that the meaning of traits is also used as a basis for co-occurences. Furthermore, people seem to have assumptions about more dynamic, causal relationships among traits.

Stimulus person and set effects   Up to this point it has been convenient to assume that implicit personality theories are rather static and stable. However, perceived trait relationships are affected by a number of factors. For example, Hanno and Jones (1973) found that perceived relationships among traits were somewhat different when the traits were said to describe a family doctor and a national political figure. Schneider and Blankmeyer (1978) found that relationships were different for introverted and extroverted stimulus persons, and Koltov (1962) found higher trait correlations for unfamiliar than for familiar stimulus persons. The idea of prototypes that we have just discussed should alert us to the possibility that people may have somewhat different implicit personality theories for different classes of stimulus persons.

Cognitive sets surely also play a role in affecting perceived relationships. O'Neal (1971) argued that a need to be certain about another person's qualities ought to lead to higher perceived relationships. Assuming that people need to be more certain about people they will interact with than those they will not, O'Neal found that trait correlations were higher when subjects anticipated meeting the people they were rating.

Although we need more research in this area, the available evidence does suggest that implicit personality theories do vary somewhat according to stimulus person and cognitive sets. Another obvious factor that might affect these theories is the personality of the perceiver.

INDIVIDUAL DIFFERENCES

There are, in fact, several reports of individual differences in perceptions of trait relationships (Steiner 1954; Jones 1954; Benedetti and Hill 1960; Lay 1970). These differences are moderately related to other personality and gender differences among people. Several researchers have found differences in terms of the trait dimensions used (Pedersen 1965; Messick and Kogan 1966; Walters and Jackson 1966; Posavac 1971; Hamilton 1970), but neither the number nor type of dimensions used is strongly related to traditional personality variables. At present the attempt to discover personality correlates of implicit personality theories does not seem promising, but there may be other important individual differences.

Information salience   We have already emphasized (in Chapters 1 and 2) that people differ in what kinds of information they attend to as well in what kind of inferences they draw. One study by Wiggins, Wiggins, and Taber (1969) showed that people differ in what characteristics they assume are related to intelligence.

Judges were asked to rate the intelligence of a number of hypothetical students who varied systematically along several dimensions (such as grades, study habits, mother's education and so on). Their ratings were analyzed in a way that allowed the researchers to uncover eight types of judges. The judges differed in the way they made their ratings of intelligence—the way they utilized the various cues. For example, Group 1 relied most heavily on high school grades in making their judgments of intelligence, Group 2 relied most heavily on a test of English effectiveness, and Group 3 relied most heavily on grades, English effectiveness, responsibility, and study habits. In a sense, each group seemed to have a different theory of intelligence—one group saw it revealed in grades, another saw it revealed in aptitude tests. The authors were also able to show differences among the personalities of the different groups of judges. For example, Groups 1 and 2, who emphasized grades and aptitude, tended themselves to be quite intelligent and to be low in authoritarianism. Members of Group 3, who emphasized responsibility and study habits, were less intelligent and more authoritarian than members of Groups 1 and 2.

Other studies have looked at how the salience or relevance of dimensions affects perceptions of relationships. Sherman and Ross (1972) asked subjects to judge the similarity of political figures, and several dimensions of perceived similarity such as *Hawk-Dove* and acceptability as a Presidential candidate emerged. Several measures of the subject's liberalism predicted how salient the various dimensions were for the subjects. Wish, Deutsch, and Biener (1970) had subjects judge the similarity of nations. Generally the nations were seen to differ along four dimensions, but these dimensions were not equally important for all subjects. For example, subjects who were Doves on the Vietnam issue were inclined to stress an economic development dimension, whereas Hawks were inclined to stress whether the countries were politically aligned with the United States. Sherman (1973) also found that Hawks and Doves emphasized different dimensions in their political judgments. However, he also manipulated whether the subjects expected to cooperate or compete, and he found that Hawk-Dove differences were strongest when subjects expected to cooperate. Thus judgments are not only affected by stable values and attitudes, but by psychological sets as well.

Personal constructs If we believe that perceptions of other people are partially determined by perceiver variables, and that individual perceivers may have somewhat different theories about the way other people "really are," then we may be tempted to say that the perceivers' inferences about another reveal more about that perceiver than about the stimulus person.

Just such a position was taken in an influential book, *The Psychology of Personal Constructs*, published in 1955 by psychotherapist George Kelly. He argued that we can tell a great deal about a person by how that person categorizes others, or by knowing the constructs he uses to describe his interpersonal world. A *construct* is the way any two things are like each other and different from a third (for instance, A and B are kind, but C is cruel). Constructs, then, are like pairs of traits. People differ in the traits they generally use to describe people, but Kelly warns that just the fact that two people say that a given other is kind does not mean that they perceive him in the same way. Kindness may mean different things to two different people, and Kelly determines whether a discrepancy exists by finding out what the opposite of "kind" is for the two perceivers. Perceiver A says that X and Y are kind and that Z is "cruel," but B says that X and Y are kind and that Z is "hostile." A's construct is *kind-cruel*; B's is *kind-hostile*. Similarly, one person may use a construct *happy-sad*, whereas another uses *happy-dislikes me*. In practice, constructs are hard to pin down precisely, both because there may be distortion and lack of articulation of one or both ends of the construct and because our common linguistic heritage specifies certain "acceptable" opposites for traits. It may therefore require considerable clinical perceptiveness and insight to find out that a particular perceiver has a construct *happy-angry*, rather than the more traditional construct *happy-sad*.

Kelly's theory has generated a large number of theoretical analyses about the ways individuals perceive others (see Bannister and Fransella 1971; Landfield 1977), particularly in the area of psychopathology (Landfield 1971), and to many active attempts—especially by British psychologists—to develop methods of evaluating the theory (see Bannister and Mair 1968).

The Rosenberg approach Recently Seymour Rosenberg has used sophisticated mathematical techniques to study individual implicit personality theories.

In his most recent summary (Rosenberg 1977) he has acknowledged a debt to Kelly's work. First, consider a study of the implicit personality theory of a novelist, revealed through his description of characters, a study that also shows the generality of the implicit personality theory notion. Rosenberg and Jones (1972) used Theodore Dreiser's *A Gallery of Women* for their work. In this work, Dreiser used considerable character description, and the researchers calculated the extent to which different traits tended to appear together in descriptions of people. In effect, they assumed that Dreiser had placed his traits into piles, the procedure used to calculate co-occurrences of traits in other work (see p. 158). In a multidimensional scaling of the co-occurrences of traits in Dreiser's characters, a strong conformity dimension emerged, with traits such as *communist, radical, serious, sad,* and *free* defining one pole, and *successful, clever, society person, repressed,* and *careful* defining the conforming pole. Also, a *soft-hard* dimension appeared that was related also to distinctions between femaleness and maleness.

As Rosenberg and Jones point out, it is significant that sexual attraction to and involvement with women dominated Dreiser's life; also his famous novels in the early part of this century were seamy enough to bring him into rather constant conflict with conventional views of morality, and he relished the role of nonconformity. Note, however, that *sad* appeared in the nonconformity pole, indicating that Dreiser felt the nonconforming role was an unhappy one. Although it is plausible that a writer's own values would influence his character description, it is still interesting that these particular dimensions were so powerful in Dreiser's descriptions, since they would not be so powerful for most of us.

Rosenberg (1977) has begun intensive analyses of single perceivers. He has come to feel that giving subjects a preprogrammed list of traits may yield less satisfactory structures than letting subjects think up their own traits. He has subjects generate the names of at least 100 people they know and a list of traits and feelings elicited by each; subjects typically provide 100 or so traits and around 50 feelings, so that the typical subject might have 125 people and 150 traits and feelings. Then each trait or feeling is rated for applicability to each stimulus person.

Rosenberg uses both multidimensional scaling and clustering techniques, and he uses the two in tandem so that clusters rather than individual traits get represented in the multidimensional space. At the moment his techniques allow a researcher to spot various interesting and unique clusters (such as red hair, dumb, never-in-trouble) that may provide insights into individual personality, not to mention person perception processes. The techniques can even be used to study self-perception (Kingsley 1978; Jones *et al.* 1974). What general principles about person perception emerge from this research remain to be seen, but the study of concrete individuals is useful (think of the applications in psychotherapy processes), theoretically interesting, and, up to now, unjustly neglected in psychology.

STEREOTYPES

Implicit personality theories are, in the final analysis, stereotypes we hold about other people. A *stereotype* is a set of characteristics that is assumed to fit a category of people. We are all aware of stereotypes about blacks, Jews, college professors, and bearded students. There is little doubt that many — perhaps most — people in our society would agree that Jews are clannish, that professors are impractical, and that bearded students are radical. For example, a classic study (Katz and Braley 1933) showed that Princeton students had a clear consensus on which traits characterize various national and ethnic groups. College students also have stereotypes about one another (see discussion of Fink and Cantril in Chapter 1). In all fairness, those stereotypes may be much less strong now than they were in the 1930s, but some data indicate that stereotypes for national groups are nearly as strong now as they were in the original Katz and Braley experiment (Karlins, Coffman, and Walters 1969).

It may not have occurred to the reader that to say warm people are imaginitive (as did Asch's subjects) is a kind of stereotype that may involve the same sorts of processes as saying that English people are sportsmanlike (as did Katz and Braley's subjects). In each case the perceiver infers something about the stimulus person that is not given directly by the information known about him.

We argued in Chapter 1 that stereotypes and implicit personality theories are inevitable consequences of our needs as perceivers to make sense of the world. There simply is not enough time to treat every new situation in its full particularity, nor would we be able to store the full uniqueness of each event in our memories. We are incensed about stereotypes because they imply too much about another person, and because frequently they imply negative and wrong attributes. Not all stereotypes are negative, however. The English are intelligent, the Italians artistic, college students hardworking. These are hardly negative generalizations. We must also remember that at least some stereotypes have a basis in fact. A music lover who believes that Italians are musical may be correct if she means that she will be more likely to hear good opera in Milan than in Calcutta. She is, of course, wrong if she means that every Italian loves or understands opera better than every Indian, or prefers the late masterpieces of Verdi to the less masterful operas of Mascagni. Given the capacity of most people to process information, stereotypes are inevitable, although no one would defend them as an absolute good. We should recognize them for what they are: overgeneralizations.

We need not restrict stereotypes to groups of people, since it may make sense to discuss stereotypes of specific individuals. After all, if you have a good friend whom you have always seen as more athletic than intellectual, you may come to believe in that pattern of interests so strongly that you will be unable to take seriously his new interest in art history. The point is that we probably overgeneralize about the behavior of single-stimulus persons over time, and this tendency also results from our need to impose stability on the behavior of others.

While we have suggested that some stereotypes may have a basis in fact, overgeneralization from experience cannot be a full explanation of stereotypes. It does not account for obvious cases where stereotypes are not based on experience, for the fact that some people seem to form stereotypes about everyone and everything (the Archie Bunker type—that term itself being a stereotype, of course), and for the fact that most stereotypes are negative. There have been several theories of why stereotypes are formed (see Brigham 1971). Many theories emphasize motivational and personality variables; they see people as forming stereotypes to protect vulnerable images of themselves (see Allport 1954 for a classic discussion). However, in recent years there has been greater attention to cognitive explanations.

Needless to say, people have a variety of characteristics, and each of us can be categorized or classified in several ways. When a perceiver has to process a great deal of information about several people, there may be tendencies to simplify the process by storing information in terms of categories rather than in terms of individuals. Then you may not recall that Professor Jones was nice, but only that a college professor was nice. If people store information by group-category rather than by individual, they should tend to forget which individual in the group-category did what. Taylor *et al.* (1978) showed that when subjects tried to recall the particulars of a group discussion, they were more inclined to make mistakes *within* rather than *between* racial and gender groups. Subjects may correctly remember that a woman made a particular comment, but they may not be able to recall correctly which woman it was.

Rothbart *et al.* (1978) have suggested that if one remembers behavior by group rather than by individual, stereotyping will be likely. Suppose a professor has 10 students in a course and that 9 of them do 3 routinely pleasant, intelligent things per class meeting while the tenth is obnoxious in 23 different ways. If the professor classifies behavior by individual, he will tell a friend that he has 9 pleasant students and an obnoxious one; students are basically all right. However, if he classifies by group he will say that almost 50 percent (23 out of 50) of the student behaviors in the class are obnoxious, and that, therefore, students are obnoxious. Rothbart *et al.* did find that as perceivers were required to process more trait information they tended to categorize by group rather than by individual, and that under those circumstances the perception of the group was affected by the frequency of "bad" information, even when it occurred predominantly for a few deviant individuals.

This kind of bias is particularly likely when there are relatively few deviant individuals who are salient. Rothbart and his colleagues showed subjects descriptions of individuals behaving in various ways. Some of the descriptions were of criminal behavior, and subjects saw descriptions of either ten serious or ten mild crimes. Subjects who had seen examples of serious crimes remembered that there were more examples of crimes than did the subjects who were exposed to less serious crimes. Presumably extreme behavior is salient and thus remembered better than nonextreme behavior. (See Chapter 10 for a more extended discussion of this principle.)

Another explanation for the tendency to see certain traits as going with certain groups of people rests on the idea of illusory correlation. You will recall that Chapman (1967) found that stimuli which ought to go together are, in fact, perceived to go together. Rothbart (1977) and Hamilton (1977) have both reported that subjects' expectations about what traits go with what groups influenced their recall of how often various stimuli were presented with the groups. For example, Hamilton gave subjects several sentences in which people in various occupations were said to have certain traits, and subjects remembered too many pairings of occupations with stereotypic traits (for example, they were more likely to remember a librarian than a stewardess as being serious). In our previous discussion of perceptions of behavior (Chapter 2) and proto- types we noted similar kinds of effects, where expectations affect what we perceive and remember about another person.

Not only did Chapman report that stimuli which are expected to go together were actually seen as going together, but he also found that distinctive or unusual stimuli were seen as being highly related. Hamilton and Gifford (1976) have suggested that a similar process many underlie some racial stereotyping. They note that for many whites, black people may be relatively rarely encountered and hence distinctive stimuli; because of social norms, negative behaviors may be rarer than positive behaviors, and thus, negative behaviors may also be somewhat distinctive. If this is the case, the co- occurance of the two distinctive stimuli may be seen as too highly related.

Hamilton and Gifford presented subjects with stimulus pairs consisting of a stimulus person and a behavior. Two-thirds of the stimulus persons were described as belonging to Group *A*, while one-third belonged to Group *B*. Thus subjects encountered stimulus persons from Group *A* more than they did stimulus persons from Group *B*. Despite the fact that subjects saw the same proportion of positive and negative behaviors paired with Group *A* and Group *B* stimulus persons, they recalled a disproportionate number of negative behaviors as having been paired with Group *B* stimulus persons. Thus, negative behaviors were overascribed to the group with which subjects had least contact. While this experiment did not directly study racial stereotyping, it does suggest that such stereotyping could result from illusory correlation.

Not only does research on implicit personality theories have something fundamental to say about stereotyping, it also points to one of the most important person perception processes, namely, how we go beyond information given. Without the ability to do this, we should forever be stuck at a most concrete level of thinking about others. We should never be able to say more about another than that we had observed him performing certain behaviors. We must be able to generalize beyond behaviors and single traits; knowing only behaviors would lead to inefficient prediction about others. With this in mind we should note that implicit personality theories are not limited to trait relationships. We also assume relationships among behaviors, styles of dress, nonverbal cues and physical characteristics (Schneider 1973). In Chapters 2 and 6 we have already suggested that appearance and expressive cues are important in making snap judgments about others. This is very much a matter of implicit personality theory processes. People need to be able to generalize beyond concrete behaviors and physical cues. The fact that we can do this successfully is one of the glories of human information processing. The fact that we sometimes make mistakes and frequently overgeneralize is the penalty we pay for the glory.

Processes of Impression Formation

RESOLUTION OF CONTRADICTORY INFORMATION

Asch's work led to an interest not only in how inferences are drawn from partial information, but also in how perceivers combine different kinds of information to produce an overall impression. The emphasis here is on the stimuli and their organization. As you might expect, the problem of organization becomes most salient when the stimulus information is inconsistent, either evaluatively or logically. Given that intelligence is a good trait and that inconsiderateness is a bad trait, we might ask how an intelligent, inconsiderate person is perceived.

Asch felt that the study of how inconsistent information is resolved would reveal something about impression formation in general. The difficulty in dealing with inconsistent information was shown very clearly in the following demonstration: One group of students (Group A) was asked to form an impression of a person who is intelligent-industrious-impulsive. Group members made their usual selection of response traits. Then they were told to form an impression of a person who is critical-stubborn-envious. After they had made their ratings, they were told that the two lists actually described the same person. Under those circumstances, subjects had great difficulties reconciling their two impressions. Group B, which heard all six traits at once, had less difficulty forming a unified impression.

There are various ways that subjects can resolve inconsistencies. For our purposes, it is convenient to classify them as *relational tendency*, in which either the inconsistent information is changed in meaning or new traits are inferred to relate the inconsistencies, or *linear combination*, in which the impression is some additive combination of the properties of the stimuli. The relational tendency hypothesis suggests that traits are combined to produce a meaningful *Gestalt* and that this *Gestalt* arises from the unique meaning relationships among the traits. Among other things this suggests that a trait will have somewhat different connotations, depending on its context. So the trait *happy* may mean something different in the context *stupid-silly* than in the context *warm-relaxed*. The linear combination hypothesis, on the other hand, assumes that the traits do not change meaning and that the information contained in the traits is simply combined by adding or averaging the value of each trait.

Linear combination models   Linear combination models concern themselves with responses to trait information that can be captured on a single dimension, and they assume that the response along this dimension is made by adding or averaging relevant information from the various traits. Frequently the evaluative dimension is taken as fundamental, and in that case the evaluation of a person described by several traits is the sum or average of the evaluations of the separate traits. No provision is made for Asch's suggestion that the final impression involves the relationships among the traits.

The choice of an evaluative dimension is not arbitrary. Many researchers feel that the evaluative response to another person is fundamental and accounts for a substantial portion of the rating variance. Empirically, an evaluative dimension nearly always accounts for a large share of the rating variance of both objects and people (Osgood *et al.* 1957; Warr and Knapper 1968; Frijda 1969); halo effects are pervasive in ratings of others. You will recall the previous discussion of the importance of a general evaluative dimension in trait implications on page 164. It is also clear that the evaluative dimension has great relevance for our behavior toward a stimulus person. Typically, we would expect to interact in different ways and to different extents with liked versus disliked others.

It is important to emphasize that although the evaluative dimension is important, linear combination models are not restricted to evaluative information. Any dimension along which traits differ can form the content for a linear combination model. For example, traits that differ in potency can affect a general rating of potency (see Hamilton and Huffman 1971), and traits that lie at extremes on the intellectual desirability dimension (see p. 160) affect ratings of respect (Hamilton and Fallot 1974). Furthermore, there is surely more to a final impression than a general evaluative response. You may evaluate a kind, happy, sincere friend just as positively as a warm, intelligent, altruistic one, but their equivalent positiveness obviously does not capture all the differences in your impressions of them. However, the linear combination models we will be considering are less concerned with the total impression you have formed of your friends than with how you combine the information you have. It is convenient to use a general evaluative dimension because it is important and because traits differ so obviously in how positive they are.

The two simplest linear combination models are the *Summation* and the *Averaging* models. The Summation and Averaging models both have a simple additive basis, but they can, under some circumstances, imply different things. The Summation Model is based on the premise that responses are dictated by the total favorability of the stimuli. For example, I may value an expensive stereo and a new car equally positively, but my fantasy life suggests that next Christmas I would be happier getting both than only one. On the negative side I hate my car more when I have two flat tires rather than one.

On the other hand, the Averaging Model may be appropriate in certain circumstances. There are surely times when you would prefer to receive one or two really nice gifts (high average) than a great many less expensive ones, even though the sum cost of the less expensive items may be more than the sum cost of the really nice gifts.

The question is how this applies to judgments of traits. Let us suppose that subjects are presented with some or all of the following stimulus traits, with their evaluations (on a 10-point scale) in parentheses: moral (10), bold (6), happy (8) industrious (6). Group *A* subjects are given moral, happy, and industrious; Group *B* subjects are given moral, bold, happy, and industrious. The Summation Model predicts that Group *B* subjects will have the more favorable final evaluation because their total amount of positive information is greater, whereas the simple Averaging Model says that Group *A* subjects will see the stimulus person more favorably because the Group *A* traits produce a higher average evaluation (see Table 7.4). The difference between the two models is not trivial. In terms of presenting yourself to others, the Additive Model suggests that you keep trying to add positive information to what others already know about you, while the Averaging Model implies that if others have already formed a good impression you should resist trying to add weakly favorable information.

To test the differences between these two models, Anderson (1965) did a systematic study varying the number, quality, and mix of the stimuli. A subject got either two or four traits as stimuli, there were four levels of favorability of stimuli. (Generally negative stimuli were designated as L for low, moderately negative were M−, moderately positive were M+, and the most positive were designated H for high.) The two or four stimuli presented to a subject were either uniformly of one type or varied. The Averaging Model predicts that adding moderately positive stimuli (M+) to highly positive stimuli (H) will lower the final evaluation because the average of the set will decrease; the Summation Model predicts that the larger set will be more positively evaluated because of the greater quantity of positive information. Some data seem to support the Averaging Model; for example, evaluations of an HHM+M+ set are lower than those of an IIII set. However, an HHHH stimulus person is

TABLE 7.4
Averaging and Additive Models Compared

Group A			Group B		
S_1	moral	10	S_1	moral	10
S_2	happy	8	S_1	happy	8
S_3	industrious	6	S_3	industrious	6
			S_4	bold	6
ΣS_k	=	24	ΣS_k	=	30
$\dfrac{\Sigma S_k}{N}$	=	8.0	$\dfrac{\Sigma S_k}{N}$	=	7.50

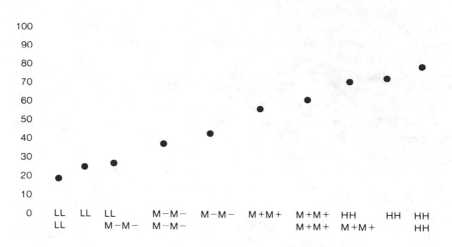

Fig. 7.2 Evaluations of trait sets varying in size and evaluation. (From Anderson 1965.)

evaluated more positively than an HH stimulus person—a result that does not fit a simple $(E = S_k/N)$ Averaging Model, since the average of four highly favorable stimuli is presumably the same as the average of the two (see Fig. 7.2).

The weighted Averaging Model The simple Averaging Model clearly does not account for all the results of this experiment. Does that mean that the Averaging Model is incorrect? Not necessarily. Perhaps the equation is too simple; in a more complex version Anderson has included two additional factors: trait weights (w) and an initial impression (S_0). The full equation is:

$$E = \frac{w_0 S_0 + \Sigma wS}{w_0 + \Sigma w}$$ 7.1

The equation explicitly assumes that traits vary not only in how positive they are (S) but also in how important they are or how heavily they are weighted (w). Actually weighted averages are fairly common. A final grade in a course may weight the grade on the final exam more heavily than that of the midterm or term paper. If you have a grade of 92 on a term paper weighted .25, a grade of 85 on a midterm weighted .35, and a grade of 91 on a final exam weighted .40, your final grade will be: [(.25)92 + (.35)85 + .40(91)]/(.25 + .35 + .40) = 89.15. Note that your grade is a weighted average of all your grades, and the equation used to determine the grade corresponds to the right-hand parts of the numerator and denominator of Equation 7.1. We will take up the importance of the left-hand portion of the equation shortly.

The important point about the weights is that they may vary from trait to trait. Although for the equation to make precise predictions we do not need to know what the weights "mean," we will likely feel more comfortable if we could assign some psychological meaning to the weights and perhaps if we could even increase or decrease the weights by changing psychological variables. In this regard we might suggest that weights for traits are increased because the trait information becomes more important, central, or credible as the person pays more attention to the traits. For example, it would be reasonable to suppose that intelligence and warmth would be weighted more heavily than toe length or eye color in most judgments we make about another, although it would be easy to think of contexts (such as evaluating a photographic model) where the latter two might be weighted more.

What is the meaning of S_0 (the initial impression) in Equation 7.1? it may be considered as a kind of general bias based on past experience which judges use in their ratings. You might, for example, have reason to believe you would like someone, so you would begin with a positive bias that more specific information could then raise or lower. If, on the other hand, you had no previous experience with the stimulus person, then S_0 might be fairly neutral.

How can this concept allow us to account for the set size affect, the fact that the HHHH person was judged more positively than the HH person? The model would predict a higher evaluation of the HHHH person than of the HH person in the following way: Assume that we have scaled stimuli from 0 (negative) to 100 (positive), with 50 being the neutral point. Further assume that an H stimulus has a scale value of 90, that each stimulus trait is weighted .6, and that the initial impression is neutral—namely, 50—and is weighted .4. For the HHHH and HH collections, the equation would produce higher evaluations for the HHHH set (see Table 7.5). In other words, when you start

TABLE 7.5
The Set Size Effect

$$F = \frac{w_0 S_0 + \Sigma wS}{w_0 + \Sigma w}$$

$$S = 90 \qquad w = .6$$
$$S_0 = 50 \qquad w_0 = .4$$

HHHH	HH
$E = \dfrac{50(.4) + (.6)(90) + (.6)(90) + (.6)(90) + (.6)(90)}{.4 + (.6) + (.6) + (.6) + (.6)}$	$E = \dfrac{50(.4) + (.6)(90) + (.6)(90)}{.4 + (.6) + (.6)}$
$= \dfrac{20 + 54 + 54 + 54 + 54}{2.8}$	$= \dfrac{20 + 54 + 54}{1.6}$
$= \dfrac{236}{2.8}$	$= \dfrac{128}{1.6}$
$= 84.29$	$= 80.00$

with an initial neutral impression of 50, each H trait of 90 raises the neutral average a bit, and so four H's would raise the average more than two H's would. The point of the initial impression, S_0, is that very extreme impressions are often hard to achieve for someone you have just met, because if you begin with a neutral bias it will dampen the effects of the stimuli.

Of course the initial impression need not be neutral, and one suspects that people differ in their initial assumptions about people; there are, in fact, reliable individual differences in these "baseline" or initial impressions. We all know some perceivers who assume that most people are nice and other perceivers who assume that most people are fools or knaves. Presumably the former have a more positive initial impression. Martin Kaplan has investigated individual differences in this kind of general outlook by asking subjects to check words they would use in describing others. If subjects check more positive than negative traits, they are assumed to have a disposition to judge others positively. As one might expect, positive disposition subjects form more positive impressions than do negative disposition subjects when they are run through the typical Anderson paradigm (Kaplan 1971a, 1973).

Other interesting predictions can be made from a close examination of Equation 7.1. One prediction is that the effects of the initial impresion should decrease as the number of stimulus traits increase, and, in fact, differences between positive and negative disposition subjects are lessened with larger sets of stimulus traits (Kaplan 1972). Also, if the weights of the new traits are somehow reduced, the weight of the initial impressions should also increase. Kaplan (1971a) varied trait weights by telling subjects that the traits were provided by either a high- or a low-valued source. As predicted, the differences between positive and negative disposition subjects were greatest when the stimulus traits were given a low weight because of assignment to a low-valued source. The evidence is consistent with the idea that without any information people have predispositions to evaluate others positively or negatively and that these predispositions are given less weight as the stimulus information is given more weight by virtue of credibility or amount.

PRIMACY-RECENCY

For evaluation of traits, the Averaging Model seems superior to the Summation Model, and we will continue to use the Averaging Model as our representative of linear combination models.[3] There are major differences between any Linear Combination Model and Asch's Gestalt position. One of the strongest conflicts comes in explaining primacy and recency effects. Asch had shown that when positive information about a stimulus person is presented before negative information is presented, the general impression is more positive than it is when the reverse order is used. A *primacy effect* occurs when information presented first is more influential in determining the final impres-

---

3. Strictly speaking, the general weighted Average Model is linear in terms of the scale values, but it is nonlinear in terms of the weight or importance parameters.

sion. An experiment by Luchins (1957) illustrates the general phenomenon. Luchins presented subjects with two one-paragraph descriptions of a stimulus person, Jim. One paragraph described Jim as friendly, outgoing, and extroverted (*E*), and the other described him as shy and introverted (*I*). Subjects rating the two paragraphs separately did indeed see Jim-*E* as more friendly than Jim-*I*. The question asked by Luchins was to what extent subjects who read both paragraphs would have their overall impressions affected by the as more friendly than would subjects who read them in an *I-E* order? Luchins, like Asch, found that the information read first had the more powerful impact: subjects who read the paragraphs in the *E-I* order did see Jim as more friendly than subjects who read them in the *I-E* order.

The Asch change-of-meaning hypothesis Asch favored a relational tendency explanation of these results. He argued that the first information sets up a directional tendency to which later information is assimilated.

> When the subject hears the first term, a broad, uncrystallized but directed impression is born. The next characteristic comes not as a separate item, but is related to the established direction. Quickly the view formed acquires a certain stability, so that later characteristics are fitted—if conditions permit—to the given direction (Asch 1946, pp. 271-72).

One could argue that new information is inferred that helps relate the inconsistencies. Suppose that you receive information first that a person is *kind* and then that he is *dishonest*. You might infer that the person is a modern Robin Hood who steals to help the sick and needy. In a sense, the person is basically seen as kind, and his dishonesty is somewhat subordinate. If the traits are presented in the opposite order, you might assume that the stimulus person is a con-man whose kindness is subordinate to his more basic dishonesty.

A related possibility (and the one seemingly favored by Asch) is that the terms actually change meaning in relation to one another. Surely the neuroticism of a great author or painter is of a quality different from the neuroticism of your neighbor. For the author or painter, having a messy room is creative eccentricity; for your neighbor it is sloppiness. It is, of course, hard to measure changes in meaning or, for that matter, the meanings of words themselves. This change-of-meaning hypothesis will be further considered on page 184.

The Averaging Model explanation When perceivers have a lot of information about a person, they might tend to ignore, forget, or pay less attention to some of the information; that information would presumably be weighted less in forming the impression. Within the weighted Averaging Model, primacy effects could be produced by lessened weights for the latter traits. Assume that we present positive (scale values 100) and then three negative (scale values 30) traits, and suppose that as subjects read the list they weight each succeeding trait somewhat less. The result might look like those in Table 7.6.

TABLE 7.6
Hypothetical Primacy-Recency Results

	Positive-Negative				Negative-Positive		
	S	w	Sw		S	w	Sw
A	100	6	600	F	30	6	180
B	100	6	500	E	30	5	150
C	100	4	400	D	30	4	120
D	30	3	90	C	100	3	300
E	30	2	60	B	100	2	200
F	30	1	30	A	100	1	100
Sum	390	21	1680	Sum	390	21	1050

$$\Sigma Sw / \Sigma w = 1680/21 = 80 \qquad \Sigma Sw / \Sigma w = 1050/21 = 50$$

Note that a much more positive impression is formed when the positive information comes first, because the initial information is weighted more heavily. Why would the first information have a higher weight? The *attention decrement hypothesis* is that subjects get tired and forget or pay less attention to the later stimuli. Another possibility is that the subjects assume that the later information is less credible or less important—that, in fact, it has been placed later in the list for exactly that reason. You may recall the discussion of the Jones *et al.* (1968) research on primacy effects for ability attribution (p. 77). Jones and Goethals (1972) argued that subjects assume that behavioral manifestations of stable entities such as abilities will be equally spaced over time. Jones and Goethals postulate that subjects remember more successes toward the end of the sequence than they should if the person has initially been successful. This assimilation of later events to earlier in memory may reflect decreased attention in the latter stages of the sequence.

The *discounting hypothesis* says that the later information is discounted *because* it is inconsistent with the former information. Assume that a subject has read three positive traits and now encounters the first negative trait. The subject may not be able to handle this inconsistency except by discounting or ignoring either the positive or the negative information. Since there is more positive than negative information, it would be most reasonable to discount the negative trait. By discounting the one negative trait, the subject gives it a lower weight, and the resultant HHHL impression will be more positive than it ought to be if the negative trait had received its full weight. If a second negative trait is now encountered, it too will be discounted, because the previous HHHL impression is higher than it "should be."

Attention decrement: The attention decrement hypothesis is easy to test. If primacy effects presumably result from lowered attention at the end of the list, primacy effects should be destroyed when the subjects pay equal attention to (and presumably weight equally) each trait. Anderson and Hubert (1963) performed such a test. Subjects read a list of adjectives; some subjects were told that they would have to recall the adjectives they read, while nothing about recall was stated to the other subjects. The usual primacy effect was found for the no-recall subjects, but there was no primacy effect (indeed, there was a slight recency effect) for the recall subjects. While these data are consistent with the attention decrement hypothesis, the results for memory of the adjectives were sufficiently complex that the primacy effect cannot be a simple function of memory for the words.

In a different kind of test, Stewart (1965) asked the subjects to form a new impression for each new piece of information, reasoning that this would equalize attention to all traits, and he obtained a recency effect. It has also been shown that writing an impression after each block of information produces recency effects (Luchins 1958; Rosenkrantz and Crockett 1965), possibly because having dealt with the first information, subjects concentrate more on the second.

Discounting: The discounting hypothesis has fared less well. The hypothesis suggests that when subjects are faced with inconsistent information, they actively discount the elements that are inconsistent with the preponderance of the information. Anderson and Jacobson (1965) showed that this is a plausible hypothesis. They *simultaneously* presented subjects with three traits, one of which was markedly more positive or negative than the other two. In some conditions subjects were explicitly told that one of the traits actually did not describe the person. As expected in these conditions where subjects were presumably encouraged to discount the "deviant" trait, the final evaluation was closer to the evaluation of the two other traits.

However, while this result shows that discounting can occur, it does not show that subjects discount the inconsistent adjectives when they are presented in *serial* order. Hendrick and Costantini (1970a) tested discounting with serial order. They reasoned that if a set of positive and negative traits could go together consistently in the same person (traits such as energetic, vigorous, resourceful, stubborn, dominating, egotistical), there would be no particular reason for discounting to occur. If discounting is a major reason for primacy effects, there should be less primacy for consistent than for inconsistent sets of traits. However, if anything, the results showed the reverse. In a second experiment, Hendrick and Costantini (1970b) had subjects guess the average of a series of numbers and a primacy effect was obtained (that is, the average weighted the first numbers more than the latter). Because there is no reason to assume inconsistency among numbers, this experiment also tended to rule out discounting because of inconsistency. It should be pointed out that although discounting because of inconsistency cannot explain this series of results, attention decrement can. Therefore, attention decrement seems a better explanation of primacy effects than does discounting. We have not, however, addressed the third hypothesis—change of meaning—first suggested by Asch.

CHANGE OF MEANING

The change-of-meaning hypothesis seems quite straightforward, but it has proved elusive to test adequately. Part of the problem is specifying what is meant by a change in meaning—a difficult task, since it is by no means clear what *meaning* means. Asch seemed to feel that words mean something different in different contexts, but he did not say clearly what the implications of that position are. Perhaps some examples might illustrate some of the possibilities. Sometimes a term can seemingly switch from positive to negative, depending on its context. While *father* is a generally positive term and *irresponsible* is generally a negative one, an *irresponsible father* is probably highly negative (Rokeach and Rothman 1965). How can averaging a positive and a negative trait produce an evaluation that is seemingly more negative than either? Or consider a generally positive term such as *happy*. Is the *happy* of "rich, successful, mature, generous, kind, happy" the same *happy* as the *happy* in "stupid, silly, unambitious, irresponsible, happy"? Or, finally consider terms that have two distinct meanings, such as *sensitive*. Are parents who are *sensitive* to the needs of their children sensitive in the same way as neurotics who are *sensitive* to criticism? Seemingly, each of these examples suggests that traits do change meaning as a function of context, but it is not clear what this change is, how it occurs, and how it should be measured.

Context effects   One kind of change in meaning has been extensively studied. If subjects are asked to rate how much they would like a particular trait alone and how much they would like it when placed in a particular context, the context often changes the evaluation of the trait as a kind of halo effect (Anderson 1966, 1971; Anderson and Lampel 1965; Wyer and Watson 1969). For example, the term *happy* would be evaluated more positively alone than in the context "happy, stupid, insensitive." These kinds of results are rather strong and can be easily explained with a variant of the general Averaging Model. In fact, Equation 7.2 has been used (Anderson 1971).

$$S' = wS + (1 - w)I \qquad\qquad 7.2$$

where S' is the judgment of the trait in context, S is its value alone, w is the weight of the trait, and I is the general evaluation for the entire impression

Without even plugging numbers into the equation, one can see that if the general impression (I) is positive, S' will have to be more positive than S, and that S' will be more negative than S if the general impression is negative. In fact, Equation 7.2 does a good job of predicting evaluative changes of traits in contexts, but it is unclear what one ought to make of this. Strictly speaking, all that one has shown is that the evaluation or affective value of a trait has changed and not that the trait has changed meaning in some broader sense. Of course, affective value is *part* of the meaning of a trait, but it surely does not constitute all the meaning, and it does not seem to capture fully what Asch was talking about when he first discussed change of meaning.

There have been several attempts to demonstrate change of meaning in the broader sense. Wyer and Watson (1969) suggested the rather straightforward but interesting idea that change of meaning ought to be most pronounced for traits that can take on a wide range of evaluative meanings. The idea is this: Some words have a relatively fixed meaning and cannot change meaning in different contexts, while others have a more variable meaning and should be ready to change according to the context they are in. Wyer and Watson had subjects rate traits on their general favorability and also get ratings of the maximum and minimum possible favorability of the trait. For example, a trait such as *loyal* is generally positive, but it could range from extremely positive to extremely negative, depending on how it is viewed (consider the differences between the loyalty of a battlefield hero to his men and the loyalty of one of Hitler's henchmen), whereas a trait like *sincere* would be generally positive however it is viewed. A trait that has a large difference between its judged favorability and the most extreme possible ratings should be able to change meaning more.

Wyer and Watson thus predicted greater context effects on these "more variable" traits. They found some support for their hypothesis, but only when variability was measured as the difference between the trait's favorability and the trait's lowest possible value. Kaplan (1971b) measured trait variability in terms of the variance of ratings of favorability by several subjects, and found that the highly variable traits were *not* more subject to context effects than the low variability traits, a result that does not support the Wyer and Watson hypothesis. However, when Wyer (1974a) used yet a different and better measure of trait variability, namely, the certainty of judgments of favorability, he found that variable traits do show a greater context effect.

Aside from the ambiguity in the results, there are two reasons for not pursuing this particular approach to the change-of-meaning hypothesis. First, while evaluative ratings are certainly an important part of meaning, they are not what we normally think of as meaning. A second and related reason is that the experiments have all tried to test the change-of-meaning hypothesis indirectly. They have all had this form: if meaning change takes place, then ratings will change more for variable (presumably in meaning) traits than for nonvariable traits. None of the experiments measured meaning change directly.

Other demonostrations of change of meaning One way of measuring meaning is to examine the associations of words. Ostrom has suggested that a word has several shades of meaning and the context would determine which kind of meaning is chosen. For example, *loyal* can refer to a kind of moral integrity as well as to unthinking, dog-like devotion. In the context "loyal, moral, honest, sincere," it is likely that the meaning of moral integrity would come to mind, whereas in the context "loyal, stupid, cold, immature," the dog-like devotion meaning would be chosen. One way of capturing this difference would be to look at implications or associations of the term *loyal* in both contexts. In the former context, associations such as integrity, true, and strong spring to mind, while in the latter context, conforming and mindless might seem more appropriate associations. Wyer (1974) examined associates to terms in different contexts and did find that the associations were generally more positive in a positive than in a negative context. However, this test is not a definitive test of meaning change, because the context itself might have affected the associations independently of the stimulus word. What was needed was a more precise test.

Hamilton and Zanna (1974) attempted to provide a more precise test in a clever way. They first replicated the familiar result that stimulus trait evaluations are affected by their context. However, they also measured meaning change for each trait by asking subjects to respond to a closely related dimension composed of synonyms. For example, for the trait *proud* they used the response dimension *confident-conceited*, and for the trait *undecided* they used the dimension *openminded–wishy-washy*. Note that both ends of the response dimension are synonyms of the stimulus trait, but that they differ in social desirability. If a proud person with other context positive traits is seen as more confident and if a proud person with other context negative traits is seen as more conceited, one might argue that *proud* has changed meaning, depending on context. As predicted, a positive context led to ratings more toward the socially desirable end of the response continuum, and a negative context moved the ratings toward the socially undesirable end.

While the Hamilton and Zanna experiment seems to constitute strong evidence for meaning change, there are still problems (Kaplan 1974). A principal problem is that the rating on the response dimension may be affected by changes in evaluative meaning. Rather than deciding directly that a person who is proud in a context of positive traits is confident (as Hamilton and Zanna's analysis suggests), the subjects may have decided that in a positive context, proud is more positive, and then they may have decided that such a positive person must also be more confident. Lending support to the latter analysis, Kaplan (1975) found that changes in rating depending on context were not only found for synonym dimensions, but also for completely unrelated dimensions.

Kaplan's data seem to suggest that subjects first adjust the evaluation of the trait in context, and that this change in evaluation affects ratings on other evaluative scales; this is, of course, what the Anderson model suggests. However, both Kaplan (1975) and Zanna and Hamilton (1977) have found that the context for a trait affects ratings on related scales more than on unrelated scales, a result generally in line with the Asch interpretation.[4]

Another phenomenon that supports the meaning-change idea is that some combinations of traits and roles produce evaluations not easily predictable

---

4.   However, even this result can also be predicted by Anderson's Integration Model. For example, if we assume that the response dimension *confident-conceited* is analogous to a general evaluative dimension, then the response can be predicted from the weighted confidence scale values of the traits. The fact that the context affects responses on related dimensions can be explained in terms of the context affecting trait weights.

from the evaluations of either separately. We have already mentioned the finding of Rokeach and Rothman (1965) that *irresponsible father* is judged more negatively than *father* or *irresponsible* alone. Higgins and Rholes (1976) have argued that in addition to evaluating traits and people or objects separately, people also evaluate the extent to which the trait fulfills their expectations for the person or object (or what the authors call the *role*). Thus, *slow* and *relaxed* are traits that fulfill the role *stroll*, whereas *frantic* does not. Higgins and Rholes predicted that evaluations of trait-role pairs would be more positive than either trait or role taken separately when the trait fulfills a positive role or a trait does not fulfill a negative role, and more negative when the trait does not fulfill a positive role or does fulfill a negative role. The data generally support this prediction. Thus, even though *slow* is a generally negative trait, and *stroll* a positive role, the combination is more positive than stroll is separately. On the other hand, a frantic stroll is evaluated more negatively than either term separately because strolls are not supposed to be frantic. For negative roles, a *beneficient* (good) *virus* (bad) is evaluated more positively than either of them are evaluated separately, whereas a *harmful virus* is more negative than either *harmful* or *virus*. While the Higgins and Rholes model is interesting in its own right, its primary value at this point is that it illustrates how traits and objects can have an evaluative connotation quite different from either taken separately. The simple averaging models of Anderson cannot predict this, and the data fit a change-of-meaning interpretation quite well.

Finally, Ostrum and Essex (1972) have examined the implicative associations to single traits and to pairs of traits. If the same associate was given to two traits, it was given 50 percent of the time to the two traits when paired, and if the associate was given to only one of the two traits, it appeared as an associate to the pair 17 percent of the time. However, a quite surprising result was that 60 percent of the associations to the pair were not given as associations to either trait singly. The latter result would seem to suggest that meaning may be created by combinations of traits as Asch had suggested. However, the Anderson model can explain these results with some additional assumptions about thresholds for associations (Anderson 1974a).

The change-of-meaning controversy is important, although the debate about interpreting results has been technical. At issue is whether the information we have about another changes depending on its context. We know that evaluative meaning is changed, but do the changes go beyond that? Part of the answer depends on what we mean by *meaning change*. Certainly, the evidence suggests that the formal Anderson model can explain most or all of the evaluation change results without resorting to more general meaning change. Ostrom (1977) has argued that neither theory is specific enough to generate predicted data the other theory cannot also explain. Another part of the problem is that psychologists and linguists have trouble defining the pscychological processes underlying meaning change and they have trouble measuring meaning change unambiguously.

GENERAL APPLICATIONS OF JUDGMENT MODELS

The general approach to human judgment that sees judgments as based on the values and weights of the component information has been called Integration Theory by Anderson. The general model has been used widely to predict judgments about guilt in defendants in trails (Kaplan and Kemmerick 1974; Ostrom *et al.* 1978), judgments of criminals based on the severity of their offenses (Leon, Oden, and Anderson 1973), bail setting by judges (Ebbesen and Konečni 1975), dating choices (Shanteau and Nagy 1976), and judgments of social class (Himmelfarb and Senn 1969), to give just a few examples.

There have even been some attempts to show basic similarities between Integration Theory and attribution models (Himmelfarb 1972; Himmelfarb and Anderson 1975; Lopes 1972). Such attempts rely heavily on the idea that considering situational and internal forces is, in principle, similar to giving them different weights in an Integration Model. Anderson (1976b) has a detailed survey of this work.

It is also important to recognize that there are many other models of human judgments used to predict how people make inferences about others. Gollob's (1974) model based on assumptions people make about what sorts of people do (or feel) certain sorts of things has received particular attention (Wyer 1975), as has a Bayesian statistical model (Ajzen and Fishbein 1975). Unfortunately, we do not have space for discussing this work, but Wyer (1974b) reviews these and other models.

INDIVIDUAL DIFFERENCES

So far, we have discussed general tendencies in resolving contradictory information. There may, however, also be individual differences in this process. One could imagine that people differ in their tolerance for contradiction so that some people might expect everyone to be either all good or all bad, while others may be willing to accept the fact that people may have both good and bad traits. Another possibile individual difference might be in the *ability to resolve* contradictory information; there might also be differences among people in *how* they resolve contradictions. Some people may be meaning-changers while others may be discounters. While there are bound to be individual differences in these tendencies, a more salient question is whether they are related to standard personality measures. One likely candidate is cognitive complexity.

Cognitive complexity   While there are significant disagreements among researchers as to the definition and measurement of cognitive complexity, nearly everyone agrees that the cognitively complex person has more categories and makes more distinctions in perceptions. One implication of this view is that cognitively simple people will be likely to rate others as extreme because they have fewer categories of judgment. In the extreme case, they may use only one dimension (good-bad) and may be able to place others into only one or the other of those two categories. The complex person has more dimensions and can presumably make finer discriminations along each dimension. Although our hypothetical extremely simple judge can label people only as good or bad, a more complex judge can say not only that a stimulus person is more or less good or bad, but also that the person is kind or unkind, happy or sad, and so on. Scott (1963) and Supnick (discussed in Crockett 1965) found that complex subjects were less likely than simple ones to see the world in dichotomized terms. Perhaps the cognitively complex subjects have a greater capacity to tolerate contradictory information about a single person (Crockett 1965). The cognitively complex person appears to be able to live with the fact that people can be contradictory—that, for example, an honest person on occasion can do an unkind thing or can be ingratiating.

How well do cognitively complex and simple subjects integrate contradictory information about others into their impressions? One line of research on this problem was conducted by Crockett (Mayo and Crockett 1964; Rosenkrantz and Crockett 1965). He has suggested that some recency effects described by Luchins (1958) might be accounted for primarily by the low-complexity subjects. Luchins had subjects form impressions after each of two contradictory blocks of information had been presented, and he found that under these conditions, the later information tended to predominate in the final impression. The argument is that cognitively complex people have a differentiation of traits, a subtlety of relationships among traits, and a tolerance for contradictory information not possessed by the cognitively simple subjects. It might be said that cognitively simple people have rigid, brittle structures that must give way under the force of competing information, and that complex people have more resilient structures. Thus, the complex people would be able to incorporate the disconfirming evidence into a modified structure, but the simple people would be more inclined to discount the first impression (which is destroyed by the second, contradictory information) and to build a new impression around the second information. Mayo and Crockett (1964) found that the cognitively simple subjects showed large recency effects. They reacted to favorable information with very favorable impressions and then, when presented later with negative information, became quite negative in their impressions. The cognitively complex subjects, on the other hand, became less extreme when they encountered the new information, and they achieved a final impression that was a balance of the two kinds of information. Leventhal and Singer (1964) also reported data which showed that cognitively simple judges changed more with disconfirming evidence, but Rosenkrantz and Crockett (1965) have reported such effects only for males (but not females).

Although the evidence is not completely clear, it is consistent with the proposition that cognitively simple subjects are inclined to form simple and evaluatively unambiguous impressions of other people. We hypothesize that they employ discounting as the mechanism for dealing with inconsistent information, but that cognitively complex subjects are more likely to use relational mechanisms and linear combinations.

Sets It may also have occurred to you that how contradictory information is resolved might be affected by what the perceiver is trying to do or what the perceiver wants to know about the other person. Jones and Thibaut (1958) have commented that a perceiver's set may determine how he or she processes information. For example, trying to understand and trying to evaluate might force quite different cognitive strategies on a perceiver. A clinical psychologist and a judge might be expected to deal quite differently with the same information about a person. Indeed, Crockett, Mahood, and Press (1975) have shown that subjects formed more differentiated and organized impressions when asked to understand rather than to evaluate a stimulus person; this effect was particularly pronounced for cognitively complex subjects. Another model that emphasizes the role of purpose in impression formation is Zajonc's (1960) theory of cognitive tuning, which argued that a person who expected to transmit a message to another would have a more rigid and polarized cognitive orientation toward the material, whereas a person who did not expect to have to transmit information should be prepared for any kind of material, and the cognitive structure would be more flexible.

Cohen (1961) applied that model to impression formation. Subjects were asked to form an impression of a person described by ten moderately or highly contradictory traits. Some subjects believed they would have to transmit their impressions to others, while other subjects believed they would receive another's message about his impression. As predicted, subjects in the transmission condition were inclined to suppress contradictory elements in their impressions and to polarize their evaluations of the stimulus person. Leventhal (1962) also found evidence consistent with Zajonc's theory.

Not only the goal of communication but also the goal of communicating certain kinds of information can affect impression formation. Higgins and Rholes (1978) presented subjects with written descriptions of a stimulus person. When subjects had to communicate their impression to another person who supposedly liked the stimulus person, the communicated impression was more positive than when they had to communicate the impression to someone who disliked the stimulus person. This is not surprising, but the effects were not limited to the communicated impressions. When subjects were asked to reproduce their impressions at a later time, the reproductions tended to become consistent with the impression they had communicated. That is, the act of communicating a positive impression tended to create a positive impression. More generally the study suggests that sets to organize material in a certain way tend to affect the way the material is remembered.

Summary

The area of impression formation deals with how people integrate and combine stimulus information about another person. In a highly influential study,

Asch presented subjects with lists of traits representing a stimulus person and then asked the subjects to write a description of the person and to select other traits they felt would also characterize the stimulus person. Asch felt that the choice of response traits was dictated by an impresion formed by considering relationships among the stimulus traits. However, subsequent research has shown that choice of response traits can be predicted in part from the stimulus traits and that it is not necessary to assume that the stimulus traits are organized into a unique impression.

This general result has led to the postulation of implicit personality theories that are considered to be perceiver assumptions about the relationships among traits. Research in this area has been largely directed to discovering dimensional and hierarchical organizations of these trait relationships and to whether perceived relationships are based on experience or are manufactured by assumptions about what traits ought to be related. In addition to experience, perceived relationships may be based on semantic similarity or on more general assumptions about personality organization.

A second issue raised by Asch was how people resolve contradictory information. This problem has been pursued in a research paradigm of how people combine information to produce a general judgment, especially an evaluation of the stimulus person. Anderson's Integration Theory proposes that perceivers average the evaluative values of each trait and that each trait is weighted according to its importance or according to how much attention is paid it. The model can be used to explain primacy effects, the finding that typically perceivers form a more positive evaluation if positive information is presented before negative information is presented.

Anderson's model explicitly assumes that perceivers do not take account of relationships among stimuli, but others have defended the proposition that the meaning of a trait may change depending on its stimulus context. At present it appears that the proponents of each position are able to explain the available research data, so there is no resolution of the meaning-change controversy.

Asch's pioneering idea that impressions are formed by considering relationships among the stimuli has not fared well in research over the past 30 years. In Chapter 11 we will reexamine Asch's position, and we will argue that perhaps different research paradigms might lead to a different set of conclusions.

The Value of Prediction

prediction of behavior

ATTENTION TO STIMULI

We have examined the coding of information, snap judgments, attribution, and impression formation as important component parts of the person perception process; we might not be faulted if we stopped here, because most person perception models stop here. And yet, we would do well to remember that person perception is an important element in the whole matrix of social behavior. The perception of others is not necessarily a final stage, but can be an intermediate step in the behavioral process. Presumably the practical importance of person perception lies in the effects of perceptions on social behavior. One major impetus for the study of person perception processes has been the general phenomenological assumption that our behavior is less a response to the objective social situation than to the perceived situation. Thus to understand social behavior we have to understand what the relevant actors see as the important features of the general situation (including, of course, other people). Person perception researchers have not been notably interested in the effects of snap judgments, attributions, and impressions on the perceiver's behavior, but there is ample common-sense and experimental data to suggest that people do respond to the perceived characteristics of others.

PERCEPTION AND PREDICTION

One of the common assumptions in the person perception, particularly the attribution, literature is that we try to understand other people because we wish to predict their behavior. The argument is that if I wish to obtain favorable outcomes from interacting with you, I need to know how you will behave so that I can coordinate my behavior with yours. Thibaut and Kelley (1959), Jones and Gerard (1967), and others have argued that such behavior coordination does require some implicit understanding of and explicit knowledge about the possible behavior of the other.

Evaluations of predictability Thus it might be argued that one of the major motives in trying to understand others is that we wish to predict their behavior. Certainly such understanding would be useful in prediction, and the ability to predict the behavior of others is an important element in a search for a stable, structured, meaningful world (Chapter 1). Furthermore, everyday experience suggests that while unpredictable people may be charming at times, they can also be frustrating. People who are untrustworthy, unpunctual, or generally undependable are ordinarily negatively evaluated.

An experiment by Kiesler (1973) shows that responses to norm violators depend on whether predictability is valued. When subjects valued predictability they tended to like the person who did the appropriate, expected behavior more than the norm violator, but when they were encouraged to value unpredictability, the norm violator was preferred.

Because unresponsiveness to norms and general unpredictability are major symptoms of mental illness, Gergen and Jones (1963) studied how people respond to unpredictability in normal and mentally ill people. Subjects tried to predict the response of another person, and, as expected, they evaluated much more favorably the person whose behavior they could predict than the person whose responses they could not predict. When the stimulus person was presented as being mentally ill, the effects of predictability depended on consequences to the subject. When the negative consequences of making a wrong prediction were high, the mentally ill person was evaluated much more negatively when unpredictable than when predictable. However, when the consequences were low, subjects did not respond differently to the mentally ill person as a function of his predictability. Perhaps we expect unpredictability from mental patients and thus do not react to it negatively as long as it presents few problems. However, aversive consequences may override this charitable reaction.

Do we perceive to predict?   It seems clear that we value our abilities to predict the behavior of others, and that we like the people we meet to be at least moderately predictable. However it does not follow that the *only* reason we wish to understand others is to predict their behavior. While we would not want to deny that understanding other people is sometimes useful in predicting their behavior, such understanding is not sought only for—or even primarily for—the utilitarian purpose of prediction. People are, after all, curious, and other people are, after all, fascinating stimuli. To say that people undertake attribution work to aid prediction does not give people enough credit for simple curiosity, and it makes about as much sense as saying that scientists want to study natural phenomena only to be able to predict them. Most scientists do research because they are curious; the ability to predict is a way of gauging understanding and is often a rather nice byproduct of the ability to understand. So we suspect that naive perceivers try first to understand, and only in special circumstances do they go through the various person perception processes from a need to predict.

A related reason for wanting to understand other people is the desire to adjust our behavior to theirs. For this it is not necessary to predict their future behavior, but it is necessary to understand what they are up to. If, for example, I hear someone make an ambiguous remark to me, I may wish to know whether to interpret this as a compliment or as criticism. I am not the least bit interested in predicting her next remark, but I am concerned as to how I should behave as a function of the present one.

It is also not crucial to know how a person whose feelings are hurt will respond; you may be content just to sooth them at the first sign of trouble. We have previously emphasized (pp. 34-35) that there are a variety of reciprocal influences between behavior and perception. Ordinarily we suspect one's own behavior is adjusted to "fit" the behavior of others and although for such adjustment it is not necessary that an explicit process of interpretation of the others' behavior go on, often enough it does.

DISPOSITIONS AND PREDICTION

Thus far we have argued that people may have many reasons for wanting to understand others, but that the desire to predict future behavior may be an important one, especially for relevant others. And certainly there are times when we explicitly need to predict the future behavior or performance of others. How do we make such predictions?

One of the fundamental assumptions of attribution models is that we need to understand the underlying causes of behavior in order to predict future behavior. Furthermore, such models have argued that the most relevant information is information about dispositional or personal causes. After all, situations vary, but dispositions stay stable and consistent from one situation to the next. Therefore, to the extent that we are interested in predicting a given person's behavior, it should be most helpful to know her or his consistent qualities. However, these assumptions need further examination. It is obvious that this assumption is not always correct, because we frequently make predictions about others based on past behavior, situation attributions, and unique stimulus-person interaction attributions.

Past behavior　Several experiments have pointed to the role of past behavior in making predictions about future behavior. For example, Mischel *et al.* (1974) have shown that when asked to predict a person's future behavior, subjects preferred information about the person's past behavior in a similar (but not in a dissimilar) situation to information about that person's dispositions. Schneider and Glickstein (1977) have shown that subjects make more confident predictions when they have information about past behavior in similar situations rather than about the actor's intentions. These studies both suggest that when making predictions about behavior, subjects find information about past behavior in a similar situation especially useful. Trait information is probably seen as more useful in predictions for dissimilar situations.

How do people make predictions without knowing about dispositions and intentions? One very simple strategy is to use a form of analogical reasoning. For example, Abelson (1976) has suggested that people simply assume that what has happened in the past will happen in the future if the situations are similar. That form of reasoning ought not to be hard to understand, because we all use it many times every day. I know that when I flip the light switch the light will go on. I do not know this because I understand anything at all about electricity or the nature of physical causality; rather I know that flipping the switch will cause the light to shine because I judge this switch to be similar to other switches and my flipping behavior to be similar to my past flipping behavior. Similar behavior in similar situations leads to similar results. Surely the same kind of reasoning goes on in behavior prediction. Prediction can, after all, be relatively mindless, and it need not involve sophisticated causal reasoning.

Logic of situation   Sometimes we also employ a *logic of situation* in making predictions. In the language of attributions models, we can use situational and situation-person interaction attributions to make predictions. Purely external attributions are important in prediction. Comedians, politicans, college pro fessors, and parents all program their own behavior on the assumption that certain sorts of stimuli they can present will affect the behavior of most others in particular ways. I know that a properly placed joke in my lecture will make my students laugh and will relieve boredom. We all know that harsh criticism will make others sad and angry, and that hostility makes others defensive. We all have wide knowledge about the kinds of environmental stimuli that produce particular reactions in others. Often this knowledge is based on attributions for reactive behavior.

Person-situation attributions   When the actor is someone we know well, we have explicit knowledge about the kinds of stimuli this person responds to; frequently this results from a stable person-situation attribution. To know that Joe is the sort of person who registers a hurt expression (or is simply hurt) by your criticism, to know that Mary looks happy when she is praised by a particular teacher, gives you as much ability to predict their behavior as if you knew they were generally sensitive to criticism or were approval-conscious. Such attributions are likely to be especially important for people we know well and in situations where the perceiver constitutes a part of the external situation for the actor. If I wish to impress my friend Woody, I need know nothing general about him. All I have to know is how he responds to particular kinds of comments that I might make. Indeed I may explicitly realize that he does not suffer fools gladly, but that he responds quite favorably to my own brand of foolishness. In short, when I wish to predict the behavior of a particular friend, I may be less concerned with her or his general dispositions than I am to how this person responds to me as a unique stimulus. You may recall the previous example (pp. 52-53) of a love relationship. Ordinarily as relationships between people become closer, more of their mutual behavior will be explained in unique person-stimulus interaction terms.

Although it may be gnerally useful to make dispositional or person-situation attributions when you wish to predict the behavior of a specific other person, particularly someone you know well, situational attributions are probably much more useful in predicting the behavior of a generalized other. Much of the time we interact with groups of people or with strangers for whom we have no specific knowledge. Ordinarily you can get along just fine in such situations by knowing that certain situational stimuli (perhaps your own behavior) will elicit certain reactions in most people most of the time. As we know people better, we suspect that stimulus-person interaction or dispositional attributions become more common.

Even so, it is important to recognize that you can behave quite effectively with a friend for long periods of time without doing any attribution work at all. Your knowledge of normative rules and the logic of situations will carry the day. Much of the time you respond to your friend like you do to any other person, and your behavior is governed by generalized expectancies and by the implicit knowledge that people in certain contexts behave in certain ways.

You may, of course, also carry some implicit knowledge to the interaction about your friend that is based on past attribution work. You simply "know" that you have to be super-careful with Jim because he gets his feelings hurt easily. However, it is very unlikely that you will do much explicit attribution work during the course of your conversation. You might do explicit attribution later when you reflect on your conversation, but you won't just now. Of course, there are times when you do a quite explicit and detailed attribution "workup" on Jim. This is especially likely if Jim does something unexpected, something for which your logic of situation does not make an adequate prediction. Or there may be times when you would like a very detailed analysis of Jim's possible behavior. Perhaps you are preparing to ask him a favor, and it is not sufficient to know merely that most people are nice in most situations. You want to know how nice this particular Jim will be in this particular situation.

In summary, there are a variety of ways we predict the behavior of others. We may use evidence of past behavior, and we may assume that the best prediction of future behavior is past behavior, or we may rely on a logic of situation. We may also use dispositional or person-situation attributions as aids in prediction. The latter are especially likely when the other person's behavior is unpredictable or when the perceiver needs quite detailed knowledge about the actual, concrete behavior of others. Finally, we note that although attribution work can be useful for making predictions, we also try to understand the behavior of others out of simple curiosity.

Models of Prediction

Generally, person perception researchers have been uninterested in the use of person perception outcomes to make predictions, although there is an interesting and growing research literature on the general psychology of prediction (see Peterson and Beach 1967; Goldberg 1968; Slovic and Lichtenstein 1971; and Fischhoff 1976 for reviews). From the standpoint of person perception, there are two basic approaches to prediction that one might take. The first would see prediction as a kind of judgment made about the stimulus person, and would then rely on various models of judgment such as Anderson's Averaging Model. A second approach would be to view prediction as a kind of reverse attribution going from general disposition back to behavior. In fact, there is no real reason to treat these approaches as being dramatically different because they do share basic similarities. However, we will preserve the distinctions implicit in the rest of this book and will consider the two as somewhat separate approaches.

THE JUDGMENT APPROACH

In the last chapter we discussed judgment models, most prominently Norman Anderson's. This model describes a final judgment as a weighted average of component information. To apply this model to prediction of behavior, we need only assume that the prediction is a judgment and that the perceiver has various kinds of information that are more or less important. For example, suppose you wished to predict whether a person would vote Democratic in the next Presidential election. You might have information about how liberal the person is and how he or she voted in the last election. If you think of such information as being scaled with liberalism and votes for Democrats as being high-scale values, the weights could be conceived as the validity of the information for the prediction. You might weigh information about past votes more heavily than information about liberalism because you feel the former is more predictive or diagnostic.

The point we wish to emphasize is that prediction judgments can be described in much the same way as evaluative judgments can. The information used for prediction could be evidence of past behavior, situational forces, or dispositional or trait data. The prediction itself could be about concrete behavior (Will Peggy lend me $100?), about generalized behavior (What will Joe's grade-point average be?), or even about generalized behavior by a collection of people (Will my guests drink more than three bottles of wine?). We would also like to emphasize that there are a variety of judgment models that are useful for prediction. One is not limited to a Weighted Average Model. In fact, there are other models based on social logic (Gollob 1974) and probability judgments, most notably Baysian models (see Ajzen and Fishbein 1975; Trope 1978; and Slovic and Lichtenstein 1971 for some useful discussions and applications); however many of these other models are complex, and for the sake of simplicity we will continue to concentrate on simpler linear models (Wyer 1974b discusses several models of social inference).

Linear models   While in principle the Weighted Average Model could be used to study predictions, the most common linear model used in such research is based on multiple regression techniques. The model of prediction is derived from correlations between the predictors and the criterion. As an example we might use success in college or graduate school as the criterion, and we might use information about past academic success, intelligence, creativity, and motivation as predictor variables.

Generally the subjects are presented with several "cases" that vary in several diagnostic cues. The subject might read the credentials of several candidates for admission to graduate school: Graduate Record Exam scores, recommendations from past professors, and the like. The subject would then make some sort of prediction (success in graduate school) or decision based on that prediction (whether to admit the student) about each. Table 8.1 gives some examples together with the predictions of several hypothetical judges. For each judge (or for all of the judges combined) one can determine which of the cues were weighted most strongly in the prediction. In practice these weights are determined by correlating the values of the cues with the decisions. In the example in Table 8.1, Judge A seems to favor students who had high college grade-point averages, and this is reflected in a high correlation between predicted success and past grade-point average. Note that she predicts a higher grade-point average for students with a past high grade-point average, and does not pay so much attention to Graduate Record Exam scores. Judge B, on the other hand, seems to weight Graduate Record Exam scores more highly,

TABLE 8.1
Hypothetical Cases of Prediction of Graduate School GPA from College GPA and GRE Scores for Four Judges

| | Predictors | | Predicted Graduate School GPA | | | |
| | | | Judges | | | |
	College GPA	GRE scores	A	B	C	D
Case 1	3.85	1600	3.75	3.90	3.90	3.80
Case 2	3.75	1550	3.60	3.50	3.85	3.65
Case 3	3.50	1400	3.50	3.25	3.40	3.05
Case 4	3.35	1350	3.25	3.00	3.00	2.75
Case 5	3.00	1585	3.00	3.75	3.50	3.90
Case 6	3.00	1400	2.95	3.20	3.25	3.00
Case 7	2.85	1375	2.75	3.10	3.00	2.90
Case 8	3.75	1400	3.55	3.25	3.80	3.80

Correlations with predicted GPA

Judges	College GPA	GRE
A	.99	.40
B	.36	.97
C	.78	.71
D	.49	.81

Prediction equation for A: Graduate $GPA_z = .96\ CGPA_z + .08\ GRE_z$
Prediction equation for B: Graduate $GPA_z = .04\ CGPA_z + .96\ GRE_z$

and for this judge the correlation between Graduate Record Exam scores and predicted success is .97. Multiple regression procedures allow the investigator to write an equation reflecting how much each judge has weighted each cue. The weights of the cues depend on how highly they correlate with the criterion. The prediction equations for Judges *A* and *B* are given in Table 8.1. The numbers refer to weights, and note how much more heavily *A* weights college grade-point average than does *B*.

Judgment models have been used to describe the predictions of people in a wide variety of settings, including graduate school performance (Dawes 1971; Wiggins and Kohen, 1971), stockbrokers' decisions about stocks (Slovic 1969), physicians' diagnostic decisions (Slovic *et al.* 1971), psychologists' diagnoses about mental illness (Wiggins and Hoffman 1968), and bail-setting by judges (Ebbesen and Konečni 1975). Some of these studies have been done with simulations of real-life data and college student judges, but may have been done with real decisions using both judges and information representative of everyday life.

Nonlinear models   Multiple regression linear models assume that the use of one cue is not affected by other cues; the cues are examined independently. However, the judges themselves often report that they use quite elaborate and nonlinear judgment strategies. For example, members of graduate school or college admissions committees often report that they judge each candidate as an individual. One judge might report that she likes to admit students with low grades if they have high Graduate Record Exam scores or outstanding letters of recommendation; she feels that good grades often stem from conformity and that bright, curious, and creative people often get bad grades. In effect, our judge is saying that she does not weight the cues in a linear fashion but instead tries to take account of their relationships to one another.

There are several possible nonlinear models. With nonlinear models the value of one kind of information changes depending on the value of other information. You may recall our discussion in the last chapter where Asch proposed that traits change meaning depending on context; he was proposing a nonlinear model of processing trait information.

One kind of non-linear model in prediction is exhibited by Judge *C*. She tends to weight highly previous grade-point average when it has been high, but when it has been low she is more inclined to weight Graduate Record Exam scores highly. She might reason that when the previous grade-point average has been in the *B* or *C* range it should be weighted moderately (after all, who can tell what may have caused a student to get *C*s?), but when a student has a past record of all *A*s, this should be weighted quite strongly on her assumption that high grade-point averages implying both ability and motivation are more predictive than are low grade-point averages.

Another way our perceiver's informal model could be nonlinear is if she explicitly took account of the patterns of the information. In the case of predicting grades Judge *D* might reason that grades and aptitude test scores should be weighted about equally unless there is a major discrepency between them. She might feel that a pattern of high aptitude scores with low grades indicates a late bloomer who will perform quite well in graduate school. In fact, she might even assume that the smart person with low college grades will out-perform the smart person with high grades because a person with high grades and low Graduate Record Exam scores is an overachiever who has already peaked and will not do well in graduate school. We hasten to remind you that she may be wrong, but we are trying to understand her model of prediction, correct or not. The point here is that her prediction involves an interaction or relationship between past grades and aptitude test scores. Sometimes these models are called configurational because they include configurations or special combinations of the prediction information.

There are a variety of other nonlinear models, some of which are described by Einhorn (1970). Nonlinear—especially configurational—models have seemed quite appealing because they seem to describe what most of us feel we do: look at the given information and manipulate it creatively in a very complex fashion. Often when we refer to intuition we mean that predictions are not simple functions of the information, that we have a special sense that allows us to manipulate the information in special (and often indescribable) ways.

Unfortunately it is hard to demonstrate configurational judgments with multiple regression techniques (see Anderson 1972 and Birnbaum 1973 for relevant criticism). In general, however, the evidence—flawed as it might be—does suggest that configurational judges are relatively rare, and that even when we do take account of various relationships among cues, simple linear models seem to explain most of the judgments. (See Slovic and Lichtenstein 1971 for a more extended discussion.)

PREDICTION AND ATTRIBUTION

We might compare the process of prediction with that of attribution. In attribution, perceivers see instances of behavior and generalize by forming an attribution that the actor is the kind of person who is disposed to perform a class of behaviors of which the observed instance(s) are examples. A person who performs one or more helpful acts is declared to be a person who is likely to perform many kinds of helpful acts. In prediction, the perceiver goes from a general disposition to a concrete act. The perceiver says in effect that this, and no other, act will be performed. If the latter seems intuitively like a more risky cognitive activity, it is.

To understand why this is the case, we need to examine the attribution and prediction processes a bit more closely. The two processes differ in at least two important ways. First, attributions deal with fixed events that have occurred, while prediction deals with events that have not occurred. Second, attributions require a canceling out of situational forces, whereas predictions require putting the situation back into the equation. To put the two differences together, it is fair to say that attributions occur when the perceiver sees that one or more events occur in the presence of situational forces, whereas future behavior will be caused by some unknown mix of dispositional and situational forces. It would be a foolish person who would assert that a helpful person will always help. Surely even the most helpful person is sometimes too busy to help or is putting helpful dispositions to other uses.

It is also important to recognize that people get called helpful not so much because they perform any one kind of helpful behavior, but because they perform a number of helpful behaviors. However, in prediction we are concetrating on a particular behavior. In fact, attitudes (which are one kind of disposition) predict specific behaviors poorly, although they predict the number of relevant behaviors performed quite well (see Ajzen and Fishbein 1977). Prediction of a specific behavior is risky business both psychologically and empirically. I may know you are likely to be helpful in several ways next week, but still feel little confidence that you will loan me $250.

In order to make good predictions about you loaning me money, I would have to know at least three things: (1) your disposition, (2) how you perceive the behavior, and (3) what the situational forces are. Let's assume that I know you are a helpful person. I still need to know whether you would perceive loaning me $250 as being helpful. Perhaps you are inclined to feel that loaning money is really a form of condenscension to me, and therefore that it is not ultimately helpful at all. Or perhaps you feel that you could help me by loaning me $250, but also feel that you would be even more helpful by giving the $250 to your favorite political candidate. So I will need to know whether you will construe your act as helpful and how helpful you would consider the loan to be relative to other acts. Third, I will need to know something about situational forces. Perhaps your helpfulness only manifests itself when behavior is unsolicited. Or perhaps you respond more to requests for your time than your money. Or you may be helpful to colleagues but not to friends. And you may not have $250.

In short, I need to know far more about you than your dispositions in order to make good predictions about your behavior. And we *all* know this. If I need $250, I might first mentally search through my list of friends for the most helpful person I know. I pick you as a particularly helpful person. Now I have a person (you) with the relevant disposition, but I need much more. I will ask myself a series of questions about your wealth, your responsiveness to requests for money, and the like. Still, you pass the test and you remain the softest touch for a loan. I will now try to structure my request to appeal to you and I will take far more into account than your helpful disposition. I will try to put you in a good mood, I will try to show you how needy I am, and I may even try to get you to suggest loaning me the money without my having to ask. The point is that I try to enhance the accuracy of my prediction by structuring the situation as well as your perception of it.

Another way of approaching the differences between attribution and prediction is in terms of a difference between induction (discovering the general from the particular) and deduction (going from the general to the particular). Abelson and his students (Abelson and Kanouse 1966; Gilson and Abelson 1965; McArthur 1972; and Kanouse 1972) have studied the differences, a problem that turns out to be quite complex. For example, perceivers seem more willing to generalize from an action than from a feeling. However, deductive inferences were more readily made for negative than for positive verbs.

Kanouse (1972) explains these effects in the following ways. First, verbs that readily lead to inductive inference have low implicit quantifiers. To say that "John solves equations" means that John solves some — but not necessarily many — equations, but to say "John hates equations" means that John hates nearly all equations. Thus, to know that John solves some equations leads to the inference that John solves equations because the statement is not a very general one; but to say that John hates a particular equation does not imply the much stronger statement that John hates equations, in the implicit sense of *all* equations. The positive-negative verb differences in "prediction" are explained somewhat differently. Positive reactions need more reasons than negative reactions. You need many reasons for liking a person or a movie but only one reason for hating the same. Consider examples provided by Kanouse. It makes perfect sense to say that you dislike a particular soup because it has many good qualities but too much salt. It does not make sense to say that the soup is rancid but good because it has so many other good qualities. Although there has been no precise test, it would seem likely on the basis of this reasoning that people should be more willing to predict avoidance or disliking behavior than their positive opposites.

Attributional approaches would also be inclined to stress the role of causal factors in predictions of future behavior. After all, all this attribution work is designed to discover causes of behavior, causes that are fairly stable and that should be effective in the future as well as in the past. Ajzen (1977) asked subjects to predict a student's grade-point average from information that was either highly or not highly correlated with grade-point averages. As he expected, the information that was highly correlated with grade-point averages was more used in making the predictions. However, Ajzen also varied whether the information was causally related to grade-point averages. Causal information (intelligence and number of hours studied) was used more than equally highly related, but noncausal information (income and distance from campus). This study would suggest that dispositional products of attribution work are particularly useful for predictions.

Whether or not there are major differences between attributional and judgment approaches to prediction remains to be seen. At the very least they do seem to point to somewhat different features of the prediction process. We should imagine that in the future there will be more explicit attention paid to prediction by people in the person perception area.

Summary

It is clear that the ability to predict the future behavior of another person is a useful benefit of the person perception process. However, it is just as clear that there are many reasons for going through the process other than the desire to predict. It is equally clear that predictions about the behavior of others are made without going through the complexities of a full person perception processing.

Person perception researchers have increasingly been concerned with how people predict the behaviors of others. One can conceive predictions as a judgment, similar to evaluation, and can use linear models to study the predictions of people. Or one can conceive of predictions as reversing the attribution paradigm. Instead of going from concrete behavior to abstract dispositions, prediction involves going from the abstract to the concrete. It seems likely that even more attention will be directed to prediction in the future.

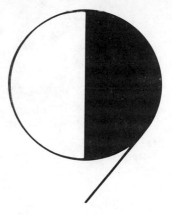

Introduction

accuracy in person perception

We perceive persons as unitary entities possessing certain physical and personality characteristics, thoughts, and feelings. The attributes of a person vary in several ways. Physical and personality characteristics are relatively enduring properties of the person; thoughts and feelings are more fleeting. Our ideas about other people also vary according to whether they stem from overt, easily observable characteristics of the person or from inferences on our part. Physical characteristics and strong emotional states are noticeable, intrusive characteristics of persons. Another's thoughts may be expresed, or we may infer them. Perhaps one of the most salient aspects of another is emotional expression. We typically assume that how a person "looks" reflects some inner emotional or feeling state.

Historically, research regarding the accuracy of our perceptions of the diverse characteristics of others has been divided into two topic areas: the perception of emotions and the perception of personality characteristics. The major difference between the areas has been the focus of the research. The goal of those interested in the perception of emotions was to identify the stimuli that elicit our perception that the other person is experiencing a certain emotion: when we experience the other as being happy, what are the facial features that serve as significant stimuli for such an experience? Does the mouth (a smile) or do the eyes play a role? This approach represented an extension of a traditional concern of students of perception to a new quality of experience. Having specified the aspects of physical stimuli that are correlated with the experiences of color, pitch, and pain, we wished to specify, in like manner, the stimuli that lead to the perception of specific emotions.

On the other hand, psychologists interested in our experiences of more enduring characteristics of others were concerned primarily with identifying differences in accuracy among perceivers and with characterizing the more accurate and less accurate perceivers. Since the issues raised in these two areas are somewhat different, we will make the same distinction. In the section immediately following, we will discuss the accuracy of judgments of overt behavior, principally of emotional expression: in the next section we will deal with the accuracy of more indirect inferences about personality traits.

Accuracy in Perceiving Emotion

THE MAJOR ISSUES

The emotion-expression link   The assumption that the movements of the face reveal important information about mood and character enjoys a long and honorable history. It is difficult to find a novel that does not use descriptions of facial expression to convey intentions, feelings, or attitudes, and in the language of film, a closeup of the face is a standard technique for conveying an emotional reaction. The very term *facial expression* is an indication of how fundamental this assumption is: a feeling wells up "inside" the person, and cannot be contained; it propels itself outwards until it appears on the face as a pattern that others may read to infer the inner state. But of course the fact that a belief is firmly embedded in the popular culture doesn't necessarily mean that the belief is true. There is no evidence, for example, that a frail man is more likely than a robust man to be homosexual or that artists have long slender fingers, yet those beliefs have also been embedded in the popular culture. Consensus is not enough to establish the truth of a proposition.

The popular agreement about the relation between facial expression and inner emotion has not extended to the scientific world: here consensus has been replaced by controversy. This controversy has involved two distinct questions. The first question can be divided into two related issues. First, (1a) Are certain facial configurations associated with particular inner states? For example, can we assume that a wrinkled nose *means* that the person is disgusted, or that a gaping mouth means that the person is dumbfounded? This question has usually been considered in conjunction with a closely related question; (1b) Are facial expressions of emotion *universal*? Even if it could be established that a wrinkled nose indicates disgust in Boston, might it not indicate delight in Bangkok?

In considering these questions, we can imagine three distinct points of view that mark points on a continuum. At one end, there is the universalist point of view: in all cultures there exist certain qualitatively distinct emotional states, and in all cultures these states are associated with the same distinctive facial configurations. Second, there is the cultural relativist position: within a particular cultural group, certain emotional states are associated with characteristic facial expressions, but the language of faces, like the language of words, is essentially arbitrary and culture-bound. According to this position we would not expect a wrinkled nose to indicate disgust in Bangkok any more than we would expect the English sentence "I am disgusted" to be understood by a Thai. Some proponents of this point of view would argue that even the emotional states themselves are culturally learned, so that the Thai might not even have a concept that corresponds to our idea of "disgust." Finally, there is a position we may call the randomist position: even within a culture there is no real correspondence between the experience of emotion and the appearance of the face.

All of these positions are concerned with whether or not the appearance of the face really corresponds to the emotional state. Even if we could prove the existence of such a correspondence, however, it is possible that the average person could not decipher the facial expression and arrive at a correct judgment of the underlying emotion. Thus the second major question that has been asked by investigators is:

The accuracy question   Are perceivers accurate in judging emotional states on the basis of facial expressions? One of the earliest major scientific treatments of these questions was Charles Darwin's *The Expression of the Emotions in Man and Animals*, published in 1872. Darwin believed that facial expressions were innate and therefore universal within a species. This belief followed from his evolutionary theory that the expressions derived from movements that had once been functional in emotional situations—so that, for example, the bared teeth of anger are a vestigal form of biting, while the facial expression of disgust is a token version of vomiting.

Compared with many later investigators, Darwin was wonderfully inventive, and approached his hypothesis by collecting information from many different sources. He observed his own children; he questioned the directors of insane asylums about the expressions of their patients—"whose passions are unbridled" (1896, 1872, p. 242), and therefore presumably more evident in facial expression; he studied animals; and he used photographs of a man whose facial muscles were electrically stimulated to produce different configurations (Duchenne 1862). Since he was a universalist, he felt that information about emotional expression in different cultures was particularly important: "whenever the same movements of the features or the body express the same emotions in several different races of man, we many infer with much probability that such expressions are true ones—that is, are innate or instinctive" (1896 [1872], p. 15).

Perhaps Darwin's most influential methodological invention was the technique known as the *judgment study* (Ekman, Friesen, and Ellsworth 1972), which was to become the most popular method by far in subsequent research. In a judgment study, the investigator shows pictures (usually photographs) of facial expressions to a number of observers, and asks them to name the feelings expressed by the people in the picture. Darwin concluded that on the whole people could judge the emotion accurately, yet there were also many sources of inaccurate judgments: some photographs were harder to judge than others, some emotions were harder to judge than others, and some judges were less successful than others.

Darwin located the source of the difficulty primarily in the judges. He pointed out that since expressions were often very fleeting, and therefore hard to see clearly, other factors might have a correspondingly strong influence on the perceiver's judgment. In the first place, he felt that the perceiver's own emotional state could bias his or her interpretation: "When we witness any deep emotion, our sympathy is so strongly excited that close observation is forgotten or rendered almost impossible" (1896 [1872], p. 12). In a recent experimental study, Schiffenbauer found that subjects who were emotionally aroused often reacted by labeling the facial expressions they saw in terms of their own arousal: thus subjects who felt disgusted were more likely to say that faces showed disgust or other negative emotions than subjects who were happy (Schiffenbauer 1974; see also Tomkins and McCarter 1964).

Second, Darwin felt that "when we expect to see any expression, we readily imagine its presence" (1896 [1872]; p. 13). As we noted in Chapter 1, perceptions of other people are profoundly influenced by the perceivers' active construction of reality, and this construction is typically in accord with previously existing expectations. A simple demonstration of this principle with regard to facial expression is to show a person a series of happy faces followed by a neutral face. The person will say that the neutral face looks slightly sad. But if the same neutral face is preceded by a series of sad faces, it will be seen as slightly happy. The previous context sets up an expectation, and the neutral picture seems relatively sad or happy by contrast. Of course, this is not the sort of effect that Darwin postulated, but it does illustrate his more general hypothesis that expectations influence perception. In recent years, researchers have become acutely aware of the effects of expectation on perception (Rosenthal 1969), and precautions designed to guard against these effects have become much more sophisticated since Darwin's time. Nowadays experimenters routinely use many different judges—rather than just one or a few—in order to protect themselves against the influence of idiosyncratic moods or ideas. Also, experimenters try to test people in situations where prior expectations are very unlikely.

But the fundamental question remains. Granted that people's judgments are biased by their own moods and expectations, are these influences simply nuisance factors that sometimes obscure an underlying ability to judge facial expressions accurately, or are people's judgments entirely a result of the biases? Darwin, of course, took the former position. Many subsequent researchers have disagreed.

The accuracy question has generated a certain amount of academic storm and strife over the years. In part, the intensity of this controversy results from the fact that certain answers to the accuracy question have implications for the very existence of a link—possible an innate link—between emotion and expression. If people *cannot* make accurate judgments, there are two possibilities: either (1) there really is a link between expression and emotional experience, but people don't know how to perceive it; or (2) facial expressions are really idiosyncratic or random, with no systematic relation to emotion. But if people *can* make accurate judgments, then facial expressions cannot be random, because no one can make accurate judgments of random events. A finding of accuracy implies a link between emotion and expression: this link may still be a learned, conventional, culture-specific rule, or it may be an innate and universal connection. It is because of these deeper issues that the question of accuracy has continued to occupy researchers' attention.

The early research   With the rise of the behaviorist point of view in psychology and the rise of the cultural relativist point of view in anthropology, Darwin's hypothesis of an innate link between emotion and facial expression fell into disrepute. Early research results from studies of accuracy were interpreted as supporting the new point of view because the percentage of "correct" identifications was often rather low and there was substantial disagreement among judges (Feleky 1914; Langfeld 1918; Ruckmick 1921).

However, these studies suffered from a variety of problems. First, terms that were nearly synonymous were often treated as separate categories, so that, for example, if one person called an expression "astonishment" and another person called it "amazement," it was scored as a disagreement. Even when a multiple-choice format was used, the range of emotions studied was often quite limited. For instance, Buzby (1924) concluded that people were inaccurate judges of emotion on the basis of a study that compared only the emotions of dismay, horror, disdain, disgust, and bewilderment. Allport (1924) and Woodworth (1938) felt that accuracy was being underestimated by these methods, and that some "errors" were less erroneous than others. A confusion of disdain with disgust, for example, might be considered less serious an error than a confusion of happiness with disgust. A number of workers also criticized the actual faces used as stimuli for judgment in these studies. Most of the early researchers used drawings, while a few used posed photographs, and it seemed possible that the observers' "inaccuracy" might be due to the fact that the pictures they were asked to judge were not very good representations of the emotions.

In the 1920s, however, two experiments were performed using unposed subjects in real, emotion-eliciting situations, and the results of these experiments were accepted for a long time as definitive evidence against the possibility of accurate judgments and against the existence of an innate connection between the face and emotion. The first of these was a study by Landis (1924), who took photographs of his subjects as they sat through a series of "emotional" situations—beginning with a recording of *Die Walküre*, progressing through "vulgar pictures of direct sex appeal," "feeling around" without looking in a bucket of water that contained either brains or live frogs, and finally feeling around in another bucket, this one wired to give an electric shock. In a second experiment Landis asked his subjects to saw off the head of a live rat with a knife. Landis (1929) concluded that the observers of the photographs were inaccurate. He also tried to decide for himself, by examining the photographs of his subjects, whether any particular configuration of muscles characterized the expression of all the subjects exposed to a given emotional situation (1924). He concluded that "in many cases the actual situation gives rise to a wide range of expressions, and that the correlation between any given facial expression and a standard situation would be low" (1924, p. 34). Unfortunately, most subsequent researchers (Bruner and Tagiuri 1954) have ignored this careful wording and have instead concluded that the connection between facial expression and *emotion* is low; it is just as possible, however, that "vulgar pictures of direct sex appeal," for example, do not elicit the same emotion in all people.

Landis also asked his subjects to explain what they had felt as they went through each emotional situation, and their answers tend to support the idea that the situations did not elicit the same emotions in all subjects. In many of the situations less than half of the subjects reported the same emotion, and often when they did agree they used phrases that did not really refer to emotions at all. For example, the most common "emotion" reported for listening to jazz was "rhythmical feeling." Another problem with the study is that subjects may have been embarrassed and unwilling to let Landis know what they really felt. When asked to look at pictures of people suffering from horrible skin diseases, for example, subjects most commonly reported that they felt "professional interest," and in many of the situations they reported "no feeling." It is likely that these reports were not entirely truthful, and subjects may have used their faces as well as their words to hide their true feelings. Landis reports that smiling was a common response to all his situations, but says he thinks it is unlikely that the subjects were enjoying themselves. It is much more likely that they were forcing a rigid smile in order to mask more negative emotions. There are many other problems with this study, most of which have been pointed out numerous times in the writings of others; for many years, however, the criticisms were forgotten and the apparently discouraging results were taken as conclusive evidence against the ability of perceivers to make accurate judgments, and against the very existence of an association between the face and emotion.

The other study that was widely cited as evidence against the ability of perceivers to make accurate judgments was published by Sherman in 1927. Sherman took movies of two babies, one of whom was three days old and the other of whom was six days old. He filmed these babies in four different situations: (1) when they had missed their scheduled feeding time by fifteen minutes (hunger); (2) when they were dropped two feet onto a bed (surprise); (3) when their heads and faces were held down on a table (anger); and (4) when they were pricked six times with a needle (pain). The judges did not see films of the eliciting stimulus, of course; they saw the babies' behavior right afterward. Using a free response measure, Sherman found fairly low agreement among judges, and concluded that they could not accurately judge the emotion.

As in the Landis study, we may wonder what the subjects (babies) really *were* feeling. In this study we haven't even self-reports to check on Sherman's conjectures of what the "correct" emotion was. Thus about half of the judges in one group referred to the baby who had been dropped as "angry" rather than "surprised." How do we know that these judges were inaccurate—especially since both babies cried in all four situations.

The second major problem is that any broad conclusion saying people cannot judge emotion accurately seems unwarranted on the basis of data that people disagree about the emotions expressed by two crying babies less than a week old. Even if there were an innate association of facial expression and emotion, we would not necessarily expect it to be fully developed at birth. Certainly there are characteristics that we *know* are genetically determined that are not apparent in week-old infants. Many species characteristics such as the capacity to walk, talk, and make love, and many individual characteristics with genetic involvement—such as the capacity to discriminate blue from purple, roll one's tongue, or compose acceptable music—are not manifest until much later in development.

THE MODERN POSITION

The context issue Despite these and numerous other flaws in the Landis and Sherman studies (see Ekman, Friesen, and Ellsworth 1972), their influence was pervasive. Disheartened by what appeared to be conclusive evidence of inaccuracy, investigators turned away to other problems. Assuming that people could not judge emotion from the face alone, researchers began to entertain the hypothesis that people use other cues—especially their knowledge of the situational context—to make inferences about what a person is feeling. In studying this hypothesis, the investigator usually asks the subjects to judge the facial expression alone; then these (or another set of judges) are given some sort of contextual information and asked to judge the combination of face and context. Types of "contextual information" have included suggested names for the emotion (Fernberger 1928), the whole photograph from which the stimulus face had been taken (Munn 1940; Vinacke 1949), past and future information in a filmed sequence (Goldberg 1951), and descriptions of the situation (Frijda 1958). On the basis of this kind of study it has generally been claimed (Frijda 1969; Tagiuri 1969) that situational, temporal, and behavioral context—as well as verbal suggestion—increase the agreement among judges, and likewise their accuracy (in terms of the investigator's predictions). It was also assumed that if an *incorrect* verbal suggestion were given, accuracy would decrease. Thus, in one of the earliest studies of this type Fernberger (1928) found that subjects would accept "erroneous" labels for drawings of emotional facial expressions most of the time. He proposed that his false labels provided a *set* in the same way that an actual context does, and thus suggested an interpretation for a facial expression that would by itself be much more ambiguous. He was among the first to articulate what was later to become the dominant point of view: "if a stimulus situation is indicated, the emotional state is judged in accordance with that situation rather than in accordance with the facial expression" (1928, p. 567).

By 1970, this opinion had changed drastically. In 1968 Frijda found that when the emotion expressed by the face was not what one would expect from a description of the situation, judges tended to rely on the facial expression rather than on the context. Mehrabian's work on the relative influence of facial, vocal, and verbal cues described in Chapter 6 found similar results for situations where these cues were inconsistent. In judging how positive a speaker felt, subjects trusted the face most, the voice next, and the words spoken least of all (Mehrabian and Wiener 1967; Mehrabian and Ferris 1967).

Even though the spoken word is rather a different kind of "context" from those used in the earlier studies, there is clearly a contradiction between Mehrabian's finding that facial expression is the most important determinant of emotion judgments and the earlier argument that facial expression provides little information in the absence of contextual cues. The earlier researchers tended to assume that faces were generally ambiguous and that contexts were generally clear, and their experimental stimuli were often biased in the direction of these assumptions. For example, in one study the "context" from which one face was taken showed that the woman in the picture was bent over a rosary, and one of the emotion choices was "reverence" (Vinacke 1949). However, as we argued in Chapter 6, it is also easy to imagine ambiguous situational contexts. For example, if the context consisted of a picture of a group of people talking on a street corner, or a verbal description such as "the woman is looking at an animal," people would probably find it ambiguous, and would not agree in naming the characteristic emotion.

If the experimenter combines an informative face with an ambiguous context, he will conclude that the face is more important in judging emotion than the context. But if he shows subjects an ambiguous face in a clear and informative context, he will find that the context is more important than the face.

Can people perceive emotion accurately?   Our resolution of the *face versus context* controversy depends upon the assumption that there *is* such a thing as a clear, informative face. That is, if people were asked to judge the face without any context, they could do so with a high degree of agreement and accuracy. Yet the findings of low agreement and low accuracy by Landis and Sherman and some of the other early researchers were exactly what led investigators to turn their attention to context. Here again, recent research by Ekman (Ekman, Sorenson, and Friesen 1969) and Carroll Izard (1971) has arrived at quite different results. Unlike their predecessors, these investigators devoted a great deal of attention to the *selection* of faces that they showed to their subjects. They restricted themselves to a number of simple, basic emotions: Ekman studied joy, sorrow, anger, fear, disgust, and surprise; Izard added interest and shame to this list. They then selected pictures that seemed to portray these emotions unambiguously, and showed them to groups of judges. For many of these pictures, American judges showed almost perfect accuracy (in terms of the poser's intention) and agreement. It now seems undisputable that there are certain basic emotional expressions, and even certain expressions of mixed emotions (Nummenmaa 1964) that can be judged with very high accuracy.

This does not mean that as we walk along the street we can look at each passerby and instantly arrive at a correct judgment of that person's feelings. The face does many things besides express emotion, and we know very little about other kinds of judgment one might make on the basis of the appearance of the face. If the person is not feeling a strong emotion, or even if she is trying not to permit us to see that emotion, we may not be able to draw any inferences on the basis of the face. This is one basic reason for the difference between the results of Ekman and Izard's research and those of the earlier researchers: the earlier researchers seem to have assumed that if the face was informative, it was *always* informative, and therefore they did not need to pay particularly close attention to their selection of faces for judgment. On the basis of these methods they would have been quite justified in concluding that the face is *not always* informative, but instead they went to the opposite extreme and concluded that the face is *never* informative. What Ekman and Izard have done is to show that the face *can be* informative about basic emotional feelings.

Ekman and Izard's investigations are important for another reason. They did not stop with the demonstration that American subjects could accurately interpret American facial expression of emotion, but went on to ask how people in other cultures judged the same pictures of American facial expressions. The work of Ekman, Sorenson, and Friesen (1969) is particularly important in this regard, since they obtained judgments from groups of people in New Guinea and Borneo who had almost no contact with Westerners. While agreement and accuracy were a little lower in these groups, they were still much greater than might be expected by chance. These cross-cultural studies constitute something of a breakthrough. It is now apparent that there are a number of fundamental facial expressions of emotions that can be recognized by people all over the world, and which mean the same thing. The facial expressions of happiness, anger, disgust, and interest are distinguished with very high agreement across cultures; fear, sorrow, shame, and surprise are also recognized at far above chance levels—except that in the New Guinea sample, subjects were not successful at distinguishing surprise from fear. One may speculate that the experience of pure surprise, unmixed with fear, is a cultural luxury that is not readily available in small villages isolated in the wilderness. Imagine, for example, that you are walking down the street and you hear a loud noise: you may be startled, and your face may register a classic surprise expression. But if it is a city street, and it is nighttime, it may be impossible to experience surprise without a component of fear. If a culture provides few situations in which surprise is likely to occur without some overtones of fear, it may be very hard for members of the culture to distinguish the two.

That people *can* judge faces accurately, as we have mentioned, indicates that there is a link between emotion and expression: if the two were not associated, people could not agree or identify expressions. That people in widely diverse cultures recognize the same faces as associated with the same emotions indicates that this link is not simply a language-like convention restricted to our own culture. On the basis of these results, the hypothesis that there is an innate link between emotion and expression becomes increasingly plausible. How else could the New Guinea native correctly label the faces of American natives? While it is possible that there are universal learning experiences, the possibility of an innate face-emotion link seems considerably more likely than it used to.

It is important to remember that these new results simply mean that there are certain facial expressions that "go with" certain emotional states, and that when a person is feeling such a state and not trying to hide it, other people will be able to recognize it. The new research does *not* imply that we can walk into a room full of people and recognize what everyone is feeling. First of all, as we pointed out earlier, people are not always feeling *any* strong emotion, and we have almost no evidence about other things besides emotion that might be read from the face. Second, different cultures have very different rules and taboos about the acceptability of giving free expression to an emotion. In middle-class America, for example, if you are invited to a party and you find it annoying or depressing, you are nonetheless expected to maintain an expression of at least interest and preferably of delighted hilarity. Insofar as these deceptive masks are successful, people in the course of daily life will be unsuccessful at reading the true emotions. If, however, the underlying feeling "leaks out" in subtle (or obvious) ways, then the mask of delight will look a little different from the natural expression of delight.

So far, we have been discussing accuracy in reading transient feeling states from the face, and we have concluded that when people are feeling certain emotions and are not making successful efforts to hide them, these emotions are manifest on the face and can be recognized by others. We can also ask whether people can read more permanent personality characteristics from the face, but here there is very little relevant research. If emotions are registered on the face, it is possible that after many years they leave traces. Thus if a person is quick to anger in a wide variety of situations, expressing anger almost as a habitual response, perhaps his face gradually changes so that even in repose it retains the habit of compressed lips and the lines of a frown. In this case, people might be justified in inferring from the person's face that he was a "hostile" person, since "hostile" means "habitually angry." At our present stage of knowledge, however, this is all speculation: we do not know for sure whether commonly-experienced emotions do leave traces, or whether these can be read by others. It has been said that after the age of thirty we are responsible for our faces, and maybe this is so. We simply don't know yet.

What can we conclude from the century of research on the ability to perceive emotions accurately? If perceivers are given a fair chance they can judge the emotions a person is experiencing quite accurately from looking at that person's face. The fair chance means that the perceivers must see good examples of facial expression, and they must be asked to judge emotion in terms of relatively few, basic emotions. Obviously some people express an emotion such as fear in peculiar ways at least some of the time, and perceivers may have trouble perceiving such peculiar expressions correctly. However, there are standard ways of displaying emotions, ways that transcend cultural boundaries, and perceivers are generally accurate in perceiving these expressions. It is also important that the perceivers not be asked to make minute discriminations among emotions such as awe and amazement, emotions that may not be distinct at either the physiological or the feeling level.

Basically, then, people are accurate when exposed to clear facial expressions and when they are asked to judge emotions that are distinct. When you stop to think about it, that conclusion has to be true. If people could never accurately perceive emotions, then people could never accurately communicate whatever emotions they happen to be feeling. Not only would that make for considerable interpersonal mischief, but actors would not be able to create any emotions on the stage. Surely everyday observations indicate that not only are we able to communicate emotions, but that other people are aware of our sadness, happiness, and anger. The available research does not suggest that we are always accurate in our perceptions of emotion, but we certainly *can* be.

The Ability to Judge Personality Traits Accurately

In addition to perceiving the emotional states of others, we are aware that others also possess enduring characteristics or personality traits that presumably are potent determinants of their behavior. Historically, the accuracy question in this area has been directed not so much toward our ability to assess accurately the personality traits of others as toward the identification of the kinds of perceivers who are particularly sensitive to the enduring characteristics of others. The pertinent studies were designed to determine the relative accuracy with which various judges could infer the personality characteristics of others, and to discover the attributes of good and poor judges of personality. Originally the existence of a general ability to judge accurately the attributes of others was assumed: later the validity of that assumption was questioned.

The motivation of those who conducted the early accuracy studies was very pragmatic: accurate judges may well occupy special positions in various social groups by virtue of their ability—or at least, it might be beneficial if they did. It might be functional for the groups involved if leaders were especially accurate perceivers of their followers, if teachers could make veridical assessments of students, if psychotherapists could see patients as they really are. Thus, on the assumption that some people are more sensitive than others, it would be useful to know the characteristics of those who are. One could then use the information to select potential group leaders, teachers, and psychotherapists.

What would we need to know before we could assert the existence of an ability to perceive accurately the personality characteristics of others? If we look to other types of ability—say intelligence or athletic skill—we find that abilities are stable capacities to perform a fairly wide range of related but dissimilar tasks and that, furthermore, people seem to differ in those capacities. An intelligent person can reason more abstractly, remember more things, and work math problems more effectively than someone less intelligent. Similarly, a good athlete has more endurance, is better coordinated, and can run faster than a poor one. Such capacities are about the same over short and long periods of time: tomorrow a good athlete will probably be better than a poor one in physical tasks, just as he is today.

The more general and stable the ability, the more invariant it will be over time and over a wide variety of environmental conditions. In the realm of person perception we can say that a person has the ability to perceive others accurately to the extent that he can accurately assess many different qualities in many different people. If he is good at perceiving only hostility but not friendliness, or if he is accurate in perceiving only very close friends, we will probably not feel justified in saying that he has a *general* ability to perceive others accurately. Thus, in asking whether some people have a general ability to perceive others accurately, we have committed ourselves to looking for individual differences in the ability to perceive many different aspects of many different people over time. Our working conceptualization assumes that perceptual accuracy in one situation is associated with accuracy in another.

THE EARLY RESEARCH

The early studies in this area, of which we will examine three, were conducted according to the reasoning outlined above. The researchers were looking for judges who could accurately predict different characteristics and behaviors of various persons: they also wished to describe the characteristics of the good and poor judges. In the first study (Vernon 1933), 48 male students took tests of intelligence, personality, and artistic tendency; they also made a good many ratings of themselves, of other men they knew well, and of strangers. Subjects rated their friends (who were also subjects in the experiment) on the dimensions on which all were tested; they rated strangers by matching examples of handwriting or artwork with photographs or character sketches of the strangers. Accuracy was determined by comparing subjects' judgments with the test performance of the person judged.

Vernon identified three types of judges: accurate raters of self whose self-ratings agreed with test results and with others' ratings of them; good raters of friends; and good raters of strangers. Accurate self-raters were said to have a good sense of humor, high abstract intelligence, and moderate artistic ability. Good raters of friends, on the other hand, were said to be more artistic, less social (slightly introverted), and less intelligent. Finally, good raters of strangers were intelligent, artistic, and not very social. Vernon's study hence provides little evidence that accuracy in judging others is a general trait.

A second study, which employed a somewhat different methodology, was conducted by Estes (1938). He compiled a number of two-minute motion pictures of 15 subjects who had been instructed to do the following: walk into the corner of the room and remove coat and tie; play a modified game of blackjack; hold a lighted match until it is burned out; build as elaborate a house of playing cards as possible; Indian wrestle. The actors in the film sequences had participated in a long-term study of personality, and many judgments of them had been made by trained clinicians. In general, the ratings of the clinicians provided the criterion for accuracy of judgment. In a series of experiments, Estes presented the motion pictures to various groups of judges, including college students, psychiatric social workers, painters, and psychologists. He asked the judges to rate the stimulus persons on personality dimensions or to select the appropriate personality description for each stimulus person from several possible ones. Estes found that he could differentiate good judges from poor judges; the former were better at judging all dimensions for all stimulus persons. Certain personality dimensions (such as inhibition-impulsion; apathy-intensity; ascendance-submission) were easier to judge accurately than were others (note, however, the high probability that behaviors relevant to the judgment of the "easy" dimensions were more likely to appear in the films). Some stimulus persons seemed to be more open than others; they tended to be judged more accurately on all dimensions and by all perceivers. Finally, accuracy was greater when judges were asked to make global judgments, to match personality descriptions with a person who appeared in a film clip, than when they were asked to rate the stimulus person on a series of precise dimensions.

Since the best judges were more accurate than the worst judges across all rating scales and all stimulus persons, Estes attempted to discover the characteristics possessed by the accurate judges. He found, for example, that judges who had strong artistic interests tended to have high accuracy scores. However, he could determine no significant relationships between the judges' accuracy scores and intelligence, neurotic tendency, or other personality characteristics.

The last study we will consider was conducted by Dymond (1949, 1950), who tried to develop a scale to measure empathic ability, or accuracy in judging others. She had students rate fellow members of the small groups into which a college class had been divided. She employed six traits: superior-inferior, friendly-unfriendly, leader-follower, shy–self-assured, sympathetic-unsympathetic, secure-insecure. Each subject was asked (1) to rate himself on each trait; (2) to rate another person on each trait; (3) to predict what rating the other would give himself; and (4) to predict what rating the other would give the subject. Two scores were obtained for each subject: the difference between his prediction of the other's self-rating (3) and the other's actual self-rating (1); the difference between his prediction of the other's rating of the subject (4) and the other's actual rating of the subject (2). Dymond reasoned that since both measurements involved the subject's abilities to "take the role of the other" (Mead 1934) and predict his responses, both must measure empathic ability; the two scores were then summed to provide a Deviation Score. The greater that score, the less accurate was the subject in making his predictions about the reactions of others. Dymond found individual differences among her subjects on the Deviation Score—in itself a trivial finding, since random processes would also generate such differences—but she also found that the differences were related to other personality variables—a finding that is far from trivial. For example, the more empathetic subjects tended to have higher performance IQ's on the Wechsler-Bellevue Adult Intelligence Scale and to give answers on the Rorschach Ink Blots that were interpreted as showing greater personal spontaneity.

The Vernon, Estes, and Dymond studies illustrate some of the ways research on accuracy of judging personality has been conducted. By 1955 Taft could review over 50 similar research studies. However, the Taft paper was not comforting to those engaged in accuracy research. In the first place, he found little evidence from the published research that supported the existence of a *general* ability to perceive others accurately. People who were accurate on some kinds of judgments and with some kinds of stimulus persons were not necessarily accurate on other judgments with other kinds of stimulus persons. In the second place, the personality correlates of general or specific accuracy abilities were either not strong or were inconsistent from study to study.

METHODOLOGICAL PROBLEMS

The Taft paper, then, suggested that either there was no general ability to perceive others accurately or accuracy had not been appropriately conceptualized and measured. About this time there were also a number of questions about the ways accuracy was measured. Consider some methodological problems with the three studies we have discussed. In all three studies, subjects were asked to rate stimulus persons on personality dimensions, but they could have been asked to make judgments about stimulus persons' socioeconomic background, mathematical ability, or impulsiveness. The researchers could also have asked for predictions about stimulus persons' behavior, past or future. In short, there is a range of variables that can serve as rating dimensions in the typical accuracy study, and the Estes study should alert us to the possibility that some kinds of dimensions may encourage accuracy more than others.

Second, there were differences among the studies in the kind and quantity of information the subject had about the stimulus person. Estes' subjects viewed short film clips of each stimulus person engaging in various kinds of expressive behavior, whereas Dymond had her subjects interact briefly with each stimulus person. We might argue that "true" accuracy requires inter-action, perhaps of relatively long duration. Conversely, it may be that accuracy is at its height with moderate information; too much information may be confusing. There is also the problem that when stimulus persons and judges interact, the different judges may elicit different kinds of behavior from the stimulus person. If one stimulus person behaves quite differently toward two judges as a function of the personalities of the judges, it might be said that the judges do not rate the same stimulus person.

The criterion problem   Another issue concerns the criterion for accuracy. If Joe rates Janice's hostility, we must have some measure of how hostile Janice is before we can determine Joe's accuracy. Vernon used test scores, Estes used the evaluations of trained clinicians, and Dymond employed the stimulus person's own self-rating. Several criteria (that is, clinical ratings, self-ratings, personality tests, peer-ratings, and behavior patterns) have been most frequently employed, although there are problems with each. There is no guarantee that therapists' ratings are accurate, and furthermore, since therapists often utilize a set of cues (such as responses to projective tests) that are not available to the average subject, one could argue that therapists' ratings are different in kind from subjects' ratings and are therefore inappropriate as a criterion. Likewise, Janice may have little insight and may as a result make poor self-ratings, or she may have friends who are biased judges of personality. Furthermore, people do not always show close agreement in their descriptions and ratings of the same person (Dornbusch *et al.* 1965; Bourne 1977). Standard tests and behavior measures can also pose problems (Mischel 1968), and indeed we could probably get only fair agreement that any given criterion for accuracy is an appropriate one.

This criterion problem involves more than difficulties with the measurement of personality. As Mischel (1968, 1973) and others have argued, personality traits do not manifest themselves in constant and identical ways. Janice's hostile behavior can take many forms, and there is always a question of whether specific behaviors (such as yelling at her mother after criticism) should be construed as hostile or not. So what we call hostility is a matter of definition — and personality tests, friends, or clinicians may define it differently than a given perceiver would. Furthermore, even if Janice is hostile, she surely is not equally hostile in every situation. She might be more hostile with her mother than with her psychology professor; so Janice's mother and her professor could both be accurate when they say she is hostile and is not hostile respectively. This criterion problem is a difficult one — not so much because of measurement problems, but because of difficulties in conceptualizing personality characteristics.

Fortunately, there are ways of getting around the criterion problem. Unambiguous behavioral criteria could be used. Archer and Akert (1977) have presented subjects with videotaped behavior and have asked subjects to make an objective interpretation of the action. For example, one sequence shows two women playing with a baby, and subjects are asked to identify which is the mother. Subjects were generally accurate in these sorts of judgments.

Reed and Jackson (1975, 1977) presented subjects with descriptions of several idealized personality types and then asked them to predict whether a person fitting that personality type would endorse items describing behavior. The criterion for accuracy was the actual endorsement frequencies by people who fit the idealized personality types. For this kind of task subjects in general are quite accurate, although some subjects were more accurate than others. This research does not suggest that people are accurate in predicting every behavior by every person in every situation; it does suggest that there are certain clear personality types that allow accurate prediction. Note that in some ways this is analogous to our conclusions about recognition of emotion. If the personality (or emotion) is clear and if care is taken to give perceivers a decent sample of possible responses, predictive or recognition accuracy is possible. In both cases the claim is not that people are inevitably accurate, but that they *can be* accurate under some circumstances.

The measurement of accuracy   As we have indicated, the criterion problem is an important one, but it can be overcome. There is another difficulty, however, that has probably been more salient and, at least in the short run, more damaging to the study of accuracy: the issue of how one measures accuracy. The most popular accuracy measure is based on differences between predicted and actual scale positions. People are seemingly accurate to the extent that their predictions match some criterion of the trait. However, the difference between predicted and actual scale values may reflect more than accuracy of the judge.

   Hastorf and Bender (1952) pointed out that part of an individual's empathy score might result from projection or from assuming similarity (Fiedler 1964). In later research (Bender and Hastorf 1953) judges were asked to predict the responses of four friends to a series of statements. Four deviation scores were computed: (1) *projection*, the difference between the judge's own response and his prediction (a judge who predicts scores for others similar to his own may be projecting his own characteristics to the other); (2) *similarity*, the difference between the judge's response and his friend's response; (3) *raw empathy*, the difference between the judge's prediction and the other's response; and (4) *refined empathy*, a score derived by subtracting the raw empathy score from the projection score. The authors suggested that the particular difficulty in interpreting these scores was that if the judge and the friend he was judging were actually similar in their responses to the items, the judge could gain accuracy credit on the raw empathy score by simply projecting. Consider, for example, a subject who has a score of 32 on the religious value scale, and assume that he rates person X, whose score is 37, and person Y, whose score is 45. If our subject is a projector and gives ratings of 31 and 33 for the two subjects (that is, if he gives ratings close to his own score), he will appear to be more accurate in judging X than in judging Y. If we generalize from this example, we can begin to see real problems. Now imagine two projectors, A (whose score is 32) and B (whose score is 21), and further suppose that the mean score for all stimulus persons is 37. A's average prediction, which will be close to his own score of 32, will be more "accurate" than B's average prediction, which will be close to his own score of 21. This seemingly greater accuracy is really an artifact of the circumstance that *A* has a score closer to the average of the stimulus persons than *B*. Bender and Hastorf (1953) suggested that in the future researchers might correct empathy scores for the effects of the bias produced by projection.

Later, Cronbach (1955) presented a more general criticism of measures of accuracy in person perception. He focused his critique on those studies in which a judge was asked to predict another's response to some scale, and accuracy was measured by taking the gross deviation of judges' predictions from the stimulus person's response. He argued that the accuracy score was made up of four components, which he labeled *elevation, differential elevation, stereotype accuracy*, and *differential accuracy*.

The first of Cronbach's components, *elevation*, refers to the tendency of the judges to use the same part of the rating scales that the stimulus persons use. Assume that *A*, *B*, *C*, and *D* all rate themselves relatively high on traits: for instance, the mean of all their responses might be 7. Judge *X*, who tends to use the lower part of all three scales, might have had a mean for all his predictions of 4, while *Y* and *Z* "correctly" used the higher part of the scale with means of 6 and 8, respectively. It is quite likely that the discrepancies between judge *X*'s predictions and the self-ratings of *A*, *B*, *C*, and *D* will be greater than the discrepancies of either *Y* or *Z* simply because *X* habitually uses a different part of the rating scale than the stimulus persons use. Generally the elevation component is treated as a nuisance, and it can easily be corrected by adding to or subtracting from a judge's predictions; in our example, we could "correct" judge *X*'s score by adding 3 points to all his predictions so that they average 7, just as the stimulus persons' responses do.

Differential elevation is concerned with the judge's ability to order differentially the mean self-ratings of all stimulus persons. Assume that across all traits *A*, *B*, *C*, and *D* have self-rating means of 6.0, 6.5, 7.5, and 8.0, respectively. Can the various judges correctly predict those mean responses if we ensure, by eliminating the elevation statistically, that all judges have mean predictions of 7.0, which is the grand mean for the four stimulus persons? Differential elevation is a measure of the extent to which the judge can rank the average self-ratings of a group of stimulus persons.

Third, we have *stereotype accuracy*, which is similar to differential elevation, but here the unit of analysis is traits rather than stimulus persons. The question is whether some judges produce a more accurate ranking of traits averaged across stimulus persons. Do some judges have a more accurate stereotype in the sense that they correctly perceive that *A*, *B*, *C*, and *D* have "more" of trait *M* than of trait *N*? That is, are these judges aware that some traits are more prevalent in the sample of persons rated than are other traits? Again, we would have to ensure that the judges use the same part of the scale, that is, that they do not differ in their elevation scores. It should be clear that a particular judge could consistently use the "wrong" part of the scale (high elevation score) and not be able to rank-order stimulus persons correctly (high differential elevation error), yet be quite accurate because he could correctly rank-order traits for the sample of stimulus persons.

Finally, Cronbach discusses *differential accuracy*, which is the ability to predict differences among stimulus persons for each trait. It amounts to that part of the total discrepancy score for our given judge's ratings that remains after the other components have been subtracted. This score is probably closest to what a sophisticated reader of the research literature in this area would regard as a "true" accuracy score because the various "response bias" components (elevation, differential elevation, and stereotype accuracy) have been eliminated.

In summary, *elevation* concerns a bias of the perceiver to use a different part of the scale from that used by the stimulus persons, *differential elevation* concerns the perceiver's ability to rank-order the stimulus persons' total scores, *stereotype accuracy* is the ability to rank-order traits, and *differential accuracy* is the ability to rank stimulus persons for *each* trait.

The immediate effect of Cronbach's article was to render invalid or uninterpretable most of the previous research in this area, since it was not possible to determine how "accurate" judges achieved their scores in the absence of the raw data on which the published reports are based. Cronbach's critique was not entirely negative, however. For example, it allowed a mathematically sophisticated and differentiated treatment of the projection problem raised by Hastorf and Bender. Projection could affect either the elevation or the stereotype accuracy scores and in that way produce seemingly greater accuracy or inaccuracy when gross deviation scores were used.

Two points should be made clear. The first is that Cronbach did not imply that it was meaningless to ask whether one person had greater ability to perceive others accurately. He did suggest that we should analyze how the more accurate person achieves his accuracy. Is it because he uses the scale correctly (low elevation score) or because he has high differential accuracy?

The second point is that Cronbach merely provided a mathematical foundation for such analysis. Mathematically there are several components to accuracy, but empirically some may be trivial or relatively unimportant. In actual studies if no judge "misused" the rating scale, elevation would contribute little to error. Similarly, differential elevation may have a limited role to play in specific studies because judges do not differ in their ability to rank-order people over all traits rated.

In the period since 1955, fewer studies on accuracy of person perception have been reported. To be able to ask and answer the proper questions in this area requires extreme care in collection and analysis of data. Research does continue, nonetheless, and it has largely concentrated on the extent to which the various components contribute to general accuracy and on the implications of various scoring procedures for the relative contributions.

Crow and Hammond (1957) investigated the accuracy issue, using a wide variety of stimulus persons and criteria. They calculated one form of the differential-accuracy score and found that the correlations among various kinds of ratings did not in general differ significantly from zero, a finding they interpret as suggesting that differential accuracy among judges is not general across rating tasks. They also showed that various stereotypic "response sets" are more stable over time for individual judges than are their differential accuracy scores. These findings strongly suggest that general accuracy of person perception is due more to stable response tendencies than to differential accuracy. Cline and Richards (1960) also investigated this problem, and their analysis indicates that the most powerful component of gross accuracy difference among judges was stereotype accuracy.

One might argue in the light of all the suggested qualifications and restrictions that the accuracy question has lost some of its intuitive charm. Certainly we have learned that the scientific investigation of common sense problems often results in reconceptualization and the realization that the initial question was not properly put. Initially it seemed that accuracy ought to be correlated with a variety of personality measures, but this proved to be a disappointing line of approach. Similarly, attempts to relate accuracy to interpersonal effectiveness largely failed. Interest has shifted from attempts to measure accuracy as a first step toward defining a trait of interpersonal skill to trying to understand person perception processes.

While accuracy has given way to process as the major focus of person perception research, interest in accuracy has not completely disappeared. Several people (Cline 1964; Reed and Jackson 1977) have shown that with careful attention to the nature of the traits to be rated, the kinds of information available, and precision in defining accuracy, not only can accuracy be measured, but people differ in how accurate they are. Another tradition sees empathy as a fundamental personality variable, and various scales have been developed to measure empathy (Hogan 1969). Finally, there is renewed interest in accuracy, not as the study of the adequacy of the final person perception product, but rather as the study of the adequacy of the process itself. This is commonly called *bias*, and we will consider bias in the next chapter.

Summary

The question of whether we can perceive the emotions and personality of others accurately is both obvious and historically important. Research into the ability to perceive emotions accurately was stimulated by a series of questions having less to do with person perception than with the universality and biological foundations of emotional expression. The early research generally found that people were not accurate in perceiving emotions, but this research was flawed in several ways. It is now clear that when perceivers are given relatively clear stimuli and relatively broad labels to apply, their level of accuracy is quite high. There is even considerable cross-cultural ability to recognize emotions accurately.

Research on accuracy of judging personality has had a reverse trend. Early research stimulated by a practical need to identify particularly accurate perceivers tended to find moderately stable individual differences in accuracy among perceivers. However, after considerable research it also became clear that such accuracy was not a promising individual difference, because accuracy depends heavily on the nature of the task and stimuli. Several people have also suggested that such research is fundamentally flawed because we do not have—nor can we have—measures of "true personality" to use as a criterion. Furthermore, there are serious (although far from fatal) flaws in the ways accuracy is measured. Because such research is more difficult to do than it seems, and is of dubious theoretical significance, interest in the area has waned in recent years.

The Nature of Bias

bias

The accuracy issue has all but faded from view in recent years, at least for personality judgments. There is not much present interest in questions about whether people are accurate or about what kinds of people are accurate. There is, in short, almost no concern with normative questions of accuracy. On the other hand, in recent years there has been renewed interest in how, why, and in what circumstances people are inaccurate.

In several of the past chapters, particularly Chapters 4 and 5, we have considered bias in some detail, but the perceptive reader may have noted that there are some major issues in how we define bias. After all, one person's truth is another's bias. If the idea of bias is to be more than a term used to identify disagreement of opinion, we must be able to tell when a person is biased and we must have some way of measuring the extent of the bias.

The term *bias* refers to a kind of prejudice or prejudgment, and need not necessarily imply error. Nonetheless, the term is often used as a synonym for error or a lack of accuracy. However, as we have already argued in the last chapter, accuracy is hard to measure because criteria for what people are like are so hard to come by. So in ordinary circumstances we will have trouble directly assessing the degree of bias by comparing perceptions with some version of reality. However, often we can still feel comfortable asserting that there is some bias, although we cannot specify how much. For example, the halo effect (see p. 161) was hypothesized as a kind of bias because ratings among personality variables seemed too highly correlated, although it was not clear by how much. Still, we should remind ourselves that it is dangerous to use such informal criteria because even experts disagree as to the "facts."

A second way of establishing bias is to examine whether judgments about others are affected by perceivers' needs, sets, and values; such variables ought not affect the judgments, if we assume that the perceiver responds only to the "real" qualities of the actor. Thus, if people who have recently failed are more inclined than those who have succeeded to see the success of others as due to luck, one can assert that at least one perceiver is biased by personal needs. But there are at least two major difficulties with this approach. The first is that bias is established generally by comparing subjects in one psychological state (such as defensiveness) with those in another. So in the example just given, we compare the judgments of perceivers who have just failed with those who have succeeded; because there is a difference, we are fairly sure that bias is present. But the question remains—where? Who is biased? While it seems natural enough to assume that the failure subjects are biased by their needs to protect bruised egos, logically it makes as much sense to say that the successful subjects may be biased toward magnamity by a warm glow of success or are unwilling to admit they could just be lucky. The problem is that there is rarely (if ever) a neutral baseline of no needs, no affect, no values—a neutral baseline against which to assess the effects of introducing particular needs. Even "control subjects" without the particular manipulated needs or values are not devoid of some motives and values. Thus, if people with two different psychological states differ, we may say that one or the other (or probably both) is biased, but we can rarely—if ever—say which is biased and by how much.

A second problem with this approach to bias is that it implicitly assumes that the perceiver's personality has no effect on the actor. Obviously, it is possible to create situations in the laboratory where this is true, but in the real world of interaction between perceiver and actor, a defensive perceiver may well create behavior in the actor that makes the initially defensive perceptions correct. Of course, bias still enters into the process, but the locus has shifted somewhat from the actual perception to the behavior. You may wish to reread our previous discussion of self-fulfilling prophecies (p. 34) for examples of how this process could happen.

A third way of assessing bias is to compare the perceptions of actual subjects with predictions of models of person perception processes. In this case, departures from predictions are taken to reflect nonrational processing of information. This view has been particularly prevalent in attribution research. However, the logic of this is a bit tricky.

Most attribution models are what Jones and McGillis (1976) term *rational baseline models*. In essence they say, "If people are processing information about others rationally or logically, this is how they should behave." On what grounds can these theories or models make that claim? The answer is that they have few—if any—such grounds. The Jones and Davis Correspondent Inference Theory may be an appealing theory and it may make sense to many people (including the present authors), but that is hardly justification for calling it either rational or logical. It would be extremely difficult—if not impossible—to derive the model from any external and clearly defined logical theory. It might be argued in defense that the model, while not strictly logically derived or rational, does embody a certain distillation of the wisdom of the ages. That may well be true, but it is not quite to the point. Rationality and logic are supposed to transcend beliefs about psychological matters by individuals, and it will hardly do to set up a Gallup Poll as our criterion for correct psychological wisdom. Obviously if a given perceiver's judgments do not match those predicted by a particular theory, we know that at least one is incorrect. But it is by no means clear which one is incorrect.

Other models, such as the Kelley Covariation Model, make a greater pretense of being derived from (or at least consistent with) generally accepted models of rational decision-making, in this case the logic of analysis of variance. Work by Kahneman and Tversky, which we will consider later in this chapter, essentially also uses a statistical model as a baseline of rationality. Leaving aside the possibility that statistical models are themselves only codifications of what people believe to be rational processes, what can we say when we discover that people's perceptions do not necessarily match the predictions made by the model? Are people thus biased? Not necessarily. In the first place, we can always argue that the particular model has been misapplied or mis-translated into the person perception area.

Another criticism of this kind of approach is that in some senses it is not quite fair to our everyday perceiver. If the perceiver does not process infor-mation the way the model says she should, one obvious reason might be that she doesn't know the rules of the model. She may be ignorant, but it hardly seems fair to call her biased for not using rules she does not understand correctly. To use an analogous example, if when presented with several addition problems, a three-year-old child gave random answers, we could safely conclude she cannot add (and is therefore ignorant), but it would hardly be fair to say she is biased.

There are, however, special cases when it is appropriate to speak of bias even from ignorance. If the three-year-old in the above example always responded to every addition problem with the answer "four," we could cer-tainly say that her answers were biased in the sense that they are prejudged. Whether from ignorance of the laws of addition or failure to apply what she knows, she is departing from the model of addition in a *systematic* way. She would also be biased if all her answers were three less or half as great as the true answer, although these would obviously be somewhat more sophisticated biases.

We have discussed several possible definitions of bias, and we think that each has major problems. For the purposes of this chapter, bias will be considered as any systematic, consistent, and predictable departure of person perception processes or outcomes from processes or outcomes prescribed by a particular model. We have discussed bias issues in such detail because person perception bias is obviously going to be a major research problem in the next few years, and thus far there has been liittle attention given to a careful definition of what bias means.

Kinds of Bias

MOTIVATIONAL BIAS

Ego-bias There are several potential biases in attribution that might occur because of the perceiver's needs. One example would be perceivers liking to take too much credit for success and too little for failure because of a desire to maintain self-esteem. We have termed that kind of tendency ego-bias. As we saw on pages 71-73, some studies have found evidence that in teaching situations subjects take more credit for their students' successes than failures. Other research reviewed on page 106 suggests that in competitive situations people are inclined to see their own wins as due to their ability and their own losses as due to external factors. Furthermore, the large literature on attributions for own success and failure in achievement situations shows consistent results: we attribute our successes to internal factors and our failures to external factors. On the surface this would seem to be strong evidence for the influence on attribution of ego needs.

Unfortunately, matters are not so simple. Many studies also find that the success of *others* are also attributed to internal factors and that their failures are also attributed to external factors. So the attribution results for self may be a special case of a general attributional process. Arguing against this interpretation are the many studies which find that attributing success more than failure to internal factors tends to be a stronger tendency for self than for other (see pp. 104-105). But again, matters are not as simple as they seem. For one thing, I may have more—or at least different—information about my own performance than about yours, and the different attributions may reflect information differences (see Miller and Ross 1975). For example, I may have consistency and distinctiveness information about my own performance that I do not have about yours.

However, there are now a number of studies that are more readily explained in terms of motivational bias than information differences (Bradley 1978). Particularly compelling are those studies which show that factors designed to increase ego-involvement or ego-biases do result in greater tendencies for self to accept responsibility for success and less tendency to accept responsibility for failure.

Additional support for the operation of motivational bias comes from the research literature on attribution of responsibility. People assign responsibility for accidents in a way that protects them from the implication that they could be blamed for similar accidents (see pp. 79-80). However, even here the tendency to hold others responsible for severe accidents might have a partial cognitive basis (see p. 80).

Projection Perhaps one of the most intensively studied forms of bias is projection. Classic Freudian theory suggests that people may defend against recognition of undesirable traits in themselves by assigning either the same or a complimentary trait to others. So a person who has unconscious hostility toward others may see others as being even more hostile, as if to say, "I may be hostile, but by comparison to others I am meek as a lamb." Alternatively our neurotic perceiver may see others as being evil or immoral so that her hostility can be justified as the reactions of a normal, moral person to the forces of evil. As careful reviews by Holmes (1968, 1978) make clear, there is little or no evidence of projection of traits the person is unaware of, but there is evidence that people project traits they consciously attribute to themselves. For example, in one demonstration Schiffenbauer (1974) showed that subjects often projected the emotions they were feeling onto pictures of facial expressions.

Bramel (1962) showed that people may project unfavorable traits onto others when these traits have been attributed to one's self. In this case male subjects were led to believe that they were aroused by homosexual pictures. High self-esteem subjects for whom this information was presumably dissonant attributed homosexuality to others, whereas low self-esteem subjects were somewhat less inclined to project this attribution. It might also be pointed out that people do not project unfavorable information on just any target. Secord, Backman, and Eachus (1964) found the greatest projection onto liked others, and Bramel (1963) and Edlow and Kiesler (1966) found greatest projection onto similar others.

Another form of projection has been called complementary projection and involves projecting traits onto others that would justify one's own reactions. If the world is hostile then my fear, greed, or unhappiness are justified. There are some demonstrations (Bramel, Bell, and Margulis 1965) of this form of projection, although the evidence is not as compelling as for projection of similar traits.

In general, at least for traits one is aware of, there is evidence that they may be attributed to other people. We remind you that perceivers may also use their own values to label or explain ambiguous behavior (see Chapter 2). Imagine observing a friend loan $100 to an out-of-work acquaintance. We could imagine a perceiver who values kindness seeing the act caused by altruism, while a perceiver who fears dependence and being taken advantage of might be more inclined to see the loan as resulting from weak-kneed compliance to social pressure.

Other motivational bias   There are other forms of motivational bias ego-bias. We may have a particular stake in seeing certain sorts of people as more or less responsible for the outcomes of their behavior. For example, the successes of women tend to be seen as due to external and/or unstable factors, whereas women are more likely to be seen as causing their failures. Also, people with negative characteristics are generally given greater punishments for crimes than are people with more positive characteristics. This tendency may be part of a more general bias to assign causality for behavior to maintain a kind of cognitive balance or feeling of equity or justice. Perhaps we have a need to see good people (like ourselves) as causing good acts and bad people (unlike ourselves) as causing bad acts. So we may be inclined to see more internal causality for good people doing good things and bad people doing bad things; and we may be more inclined to see more external causality for good people doing bad things and bad people doing good things.

The bulk of the evidence suggests that there are various motivational effects on person perception. Unfortunately, the research in this area has gotten bogged down in trying to defend the existence of motivational bias against those who claim that what seems to be motivational bias is cognitive bias in disguise. Psychologists from both camps have written as if there could only be one kind of bias. Everyday experience as well as the research literature confirms that motivational bias does exist, and research now needs to be directed to analysis of the conditions that foster or inhibit its display. How important such effects are probably depends on degree of ego-involvement, norms about modesty, and how concerned the perceiver is with being accurate.

We think that it is also likely that motivational and cognitive biases are related in a variety of ways. One possibility is that our motives, goals, and purposes not only help determine what is salient in a situation, but what we look for and how we process information. In the next section we will examine several different kinds of cognitive bias, and it seems reasonable to believe that the strengths of at least some of these biases may be affected by the perceiver's motivational state.

COGNITIVE BIAS

In recent years attribution researchers have directed considerable attention to cognitive bias. Such bias results even when perceivers are trying to be accurate and fair, and it shows up when perceptions depart systematically from predictions of various information-processing models. Note that it is not the fact that people's perceptions are discrepant from some version of what they ought to be, but rather the fact that these discrepancies are *systematic*, which leads to the idea of bias. Not mere error, but systematic, predictable error is the key. Such biases result from characteristic ways we have of simplifying and processing information.

Relationship bias There are two general cognitive biases that seem particularly important in person perception. First, there is the tendency to reduce informational complexity by seeing events, things, and characteristics as related. One manifestation of this desire to find order through relationship is the emphasis placed on cause. Heider argued that the perception of causality is an absolutely fundamental way of ordering events, and several lines of research on perceptions of causality, feelings of self-control, and attribution of responsibility (see Chapters 3 and 4) suggest that perceivers are all too ready to see a causal texture to their world. Wortman (1976) has reviewed research which suggests that people are quite willing to assume that someone must be responsible for accidents and natural disasters; even victims often feel responsible for accidents that have happened to them (Bulman and Wortman 1977). It is also common for relatives of terminally ill patients to feel responsible and guilty for the illness (Wortman 1976).

Gambling behavior is another rich source of data on perceptions of causal relations. Henslin (1967) has commented that gamblers often act as if they can control the roll of dice. In an experimental demonstration, Strickland, Lewicki, and Katz (1966) asked subjects to bet on the roll of dice either before the dice were rolled or after they had been rolled but before the subjects knew the outcome. Subjects placed larger bets (suggesting greater confidence) when they bet before the dice were rolled. People may feel that they can control even random events before they have occurred, but obviously, one cannot control the outcome of an event that has already happened.

Ellen Langer (1975; Langer and Roth 1975) has further investigated what she calls illusion of control. For example, people valued their football lottery tickets more when they had randomly chosen the ticket themselves rather than when someone else had randomly chosen it for them. Langer has suggested that illusions that we control chance events are enhanced when the task appears to involve some element of skill, such as actually choosing the ticket oneself. In another demonstration, subjects were asked to bet whether they or another person would randomly draw the higher card from a deck of cards. Subjects bet more, seemingly had more confidence that they exercised some control over the random outcome, when their competitor was poorly dressed and appeared ill-at-ease than when he appeared confident. Presumably, the subjects' own feelings of relative skill were enhanced in the former condition, which is why they were willing to bet more. Obviously, however, the dress and demeanor of another person cannot control what card either person picks from a deck, so that subjects acted as if they had more control than they actually did.

Throughout the book we have seen several examples of where people are unwilling to perceive random chance events as uncaused. Assumptions of causality are not only important ways we have of making sense of the world, but our readiness to perceive causality leads us to see the world as more structured than it is. Particularly in attribution research, this constitutes an important bias in our perceptions of others and their behavior.

A second kind of fundamental relationship is based on similarity. Perceivers seem to feel that similar events and characteristics go together. There are, of course, an infinite number of dimensions along which similarity can be assessed, but in person perception evaluative similarity seems particularly crucial. As we saw in Chapter 7, perceivers are likely to see positive characteristics as implying one another, and negative characteristics are also seen as going together. There are also suggestions that generally "good people" are held responsible for bad events than are "bad people" (see Chapter 4). Thus it seems that there are general tendencies to associate events, people, and characteristics on the basis of their evaluative similarity.

Sources of information-processing bias   Relationship biases exist throughout the person perception processes. However, in recent years two general problems have stimulated concern for other information-processing bias.

First, research into attribution processes has shown that actual attributions depart from predictions derived from models in certain ways. The most obvious is the tendency to perceive others' behavior as dispositionally caused and own behavior as due to situational forces (see Chapter 5). Lee Ross

(1977) has argued that this represents the *fundamental attribution error*, the tendency not to take external forces enough into account in explaining the behavior of others.

The other major push toward the study of cognitive bias came from research by various cognitive psychologists on the ability of people to process statistical data. Much of the time we make predictions or judgments about people or events based on variable and inconsistent data. Statistical theory was developed to help scientists make decisions about causes and to predict future events given data that are "messy," unclear, and filled with error. In our everyday lives we also have data that are far from ideal in making decisions. Can people function as good statisticians? The research of Kahneman and Tversky (1972, 1973; Tversky and Kahneman 1971, 1973, 1974) has been particularly influential not only in showing that people (including psychologists) are poor statisticians in everyday life, but also in demonstrating that people have systematic ways of dealing with data that lead to biased decisions and predictions.

The Tversky-Kahneman heuristics   These authors point to several informal and often implicit rules (called *heuristics*) that people use to make decisions. The *availability* heuristic (Tversky and Kahneman 1973) is the use of the ease of remembering or imagining events to make judgments about frequency. When you are required to estimate the probability of an event or the relative frequency of some category of objects, you may search your memory for instances. Suppose you are asked to judge the relative proportions of male or female college professors. Most students will be able to recall more males than females in the role for the simple reason that there are more male professors. Often availability of categories (in the sense of ease of thinking of examples) mirrors the actual frequency in the world. However, it may not always do so. Suppose you had recently seen a large group of female professors having lunch together. Now as you think of instances of professors you may imagine "too many" females because they are easier to recall, having been more recently seen. This might lead you to overestimate the relative number of female professors, because *female professor* has become a more available category.

Factors such as popularity, fame, recent experience, and perceptual salience may operate to make some categories more available than others. For example, Tversky and Kahneman (1973) gave subjects lists of famous men and women. Subsequently, subjects were asked the relative frequencies of men and women on the lists. Subjects overestimated the frequency of the sex that had the more famous members, presumably because their names were more available.

A second heuristic or informal decision rule is *representativeness* (Kahneman and Tversky 1972, 1973). Generally, people predict outcomes on the basis of salient features of events, and they ignore other important characteristics of their evidence including the validity and reliability of the data as well as baseline probabilities of the events occurring. In a sense perceivers assume that certain salient stimuli are representative of a larger domain and then make their predictions on the basis of salient—but not necessarily representative—events.

There are several features to this form of bias. One is that people seem to underutilize base-rate information in making predictions (Kahneman and Tversky 1973). Suppose you are asked to predict whether an introverted, intelligent person who reads classic novels is more likely to be an English professor or a housewife. Most of you would probably predict that the person is far more likely to be the English professor. Let's examine some possibilities. To make the most extreme case, suppose that *all* English professors fit the description and that only 10 percent of housewives do (and we emphasize that we have no idea of what the exact percentages would be). Since there are perhaps 15,000 English professors and 15,000,000 housewives, we could immediately calculate that 15,000 English professors and 1,500,000 housewives are introverted, intelligent people who read classic novels. This means, according to our imaginary figures, that such a person is 100 times more likely to be a housewife than an English professor, and yet it would be safe to say that most of you would be more likely to predict that such a person is an English professor than a housewife. This rather striking error results from a failure to consider the far greater number of housewives than English professors: to ignore or underutilize base-rate information.

Fischhoff (1976) has pointed to a different kind of representativeness bias. When an event has actually occurred, its perceived probability of occurrence is magnified. This is probably another case of the availability heuristic at work. When an event has actually occurred it probably becomes more available in memory and its perceived frequency is increased. Carroll (1978) and Ross, Lepper, Strack, and Steinmetz (1977) have shown that merely thinking about or trying to explain an event increases its perceived probability. The availability heuristic also would lead people to underestimate the probability of low-frequency events and to overestimate the frequency of high-probability events. The net result is that people are more frequently surprised than they should be. They will experience more low-frequency events and fewer high-frequency events than they think they should.

All these biases in representativeness act to a common end. Generally, people make nonconservative (that is, extreme) predictions. Hence, they will often be surprised by events and, given our strong biases to have satisfactory interpretations for events, they will be motivated to invent explanations for the failures of prediction. For example, a student who has made a high grade in one course may expect (unreasonably according to this analysis) a similarly high grade in a second course. When the second grade regresses back to the mean (is lower or closer to the mean), the student may be inclined to blame the teacher. In fact, however, one high performance might be rather accidental and would not necessarily be repeated.

People also have a tendency to make extreme predictions because they do not sufficiently take into account unreliability of data and limited validity of predictors. People often see predictors as much better than they are. There were many examples of this in our discussions of the halo effect and implicit personality theory. Correlations among behaviors, traits, and performance variables are generally assumed to be higher than they are in fact.

A study by Amabile (1975) looked at predictions of academic performance from verbal Scholastic Aptitude Test scores. At Stanford the verbal SAT correlates with freshman grade-point average about .20. However, subjects assumed that the correlation was about .60. The result of this incorrect assumption that Scholastic Aptitude Test scores predict grade-point average better than they do would be predictions that are too extreme; for example, people who had high Scholastic Aptitude Test scores would be predicted to do better than they do. People overestimate the validity of predictors.

Trope (1978) has pointed out that fallable memory also produces bias in prediction. Ordinarily in a prediction situation the person has to deal with data acquired over a period of time or with a large amount of data. In either case, not all of the relevant data are likely to be remembered correctly. Trope gave subjects grades for several students, and the subjects were asked to predict whether the students were admitted to graduate school. As expected, when the students had to remember grades for many students they did not do a good job. Ideally, the unreliability of memory ought to be taken into account in making predictions; unreliable data should not be weighted as heavily. However, subjects made just as extreme predictions from unreliable as from reliable data.

Salience effects   Throughout this book we have emphasized the fact that people are selective in what they pay attention to as well as how they code stimuli. For example, Higgins et al. (1977) have found that the salience of certain ways of categorizing behavior affects evaluation of that behavior. In this experiment subjects read a description of a person; many of the behavioral descriptions could be labeled in various ways. For example, "By the way he acted one could readily guess that Donald was well aware of his ability to do many things well" could be seen as evidence of either self-confidence or conceit. Needless to say, one way of coding the behavior is more socially desirable than the other. Before reading the description of Donald subjects were exposed to several words to create category salience. The words were either positive or negative, and they were either relevant to the story (such as self-confident) or nonapplicable (such as neat). Subjects exposed to the positive-applicable terms (such as self-confident) later characterized Donald in more positive terms than subjects exposed to the negative applicable terms. Non-applicable terms had almost no effect on how Donald was characterized. In this study subjects were not encouraged to code the behavior one way or another, but apparently exposure to a particular list of words made them more accessible categories for coding.

The salience of information also affects subsequent information processing. Information that stands out in some way (salient) becomes more available and hence enters more readily into associative relationships. For example, research on illusory correlation suggests that unusual information tends to be seen as occurring together more often than it does. Kanouse and Hanson (1972) have reviewed evidence suggesting that negative information is weighted more in decision-making than positive information; one explanation is that negative information is more usual and hence more salient.

You may also recall our discussion of salience explanations of the tendency to see behavior of others as too dispositional. Several people have argued that perceivers find the other person more salient than the environment, and that explanations in terms of causality "flow" toward more salient stimuli. We need not restrict this interesting hypothesis to an explanation for self-other differences in attribution. Perhaps salient stimuli in general draw more than their share of causal attention. This particular hypothesis has been tested several times (see Taylor and Fiske 1978 for a complete review.)

Taylor and Fiske (1975) found that in a conversation, observers tended to see the person they sat across from (and, therefore, presumably observed more) as being more causally active. McArthur and Post (1977) have shown that if one of several actors was made particularly salient, his or her behavior was seen as more dispositional than was the behavior of less salient actors. In their experiments salience was manipulated by having the "target" stimulus person be more brightly lit in a videotape, or be moving in a rocking chair. However, manipulations of salience through novelty (having the target stimulus person wear a different kind of shirt or be of a different gender than other stimulus persons) produced opposite results: perceptions that the novel person's behavior was controlled more by the situation.

McArthur and Post argue that novelty manipulations focus attention on the situation because something is novel only in the context of the entire situation. Paradoxically, novel people are sometimes perceived as especially influential. In a study by Taylor et al. (1978), groups of different racial or gender combination held a discussion. Perceivers rated a solo person (such as the only black in a group of whites) as particularly influential and talkative, and the solo person was often seen as having traits particularly stereotyped for his or her group. McArthur and Solomon (1978) staged an encounter where one person was extremely aggressive to the other. The aggressive behavior was seen as being more due to the victim, and the victim was rated as more extreme on personality dimensions (such as passive, friendly) when she was salient, by virtue of having striking red hair or wearing a leg brace.

The data from these studies are not perfectly consistent. Whereas the McArthur studies generally found that salience affected a general measure of situational versus dispositional attribution, Taylor and Fiske (1975) and Taylor et al. (1978) found no generalized attributional differences, but did find differences for more specific dispositions such as influence and talkativeness. However, if we can ignore these inconsistencies among dependent measures, the general results do point to effects of salience for attributions.

The effects of salience may also depend partially on set. Eisen and Mc-Arthur (1978) had subjects watch a videotape of a staged trial. Salience was manipulated by how much time the defendant was "on camera." In addition, some subjects were told that they were to arrive at a verdict and sentence if appropriate, while others were given a set to form impressions of the defendant and plaintiff. When the subjects were in the judgment set, the salience of the defendant led to their seeing him as more negative but did not affect their judgments of guilt or length of sentences. When the subjects were in an impression set, the salient defendant was given a shorter sentence and was seen in somewhat more positive terms. Eisen and McArthur argue that when perceivers need to be "rational," salience has limited effects, but when they are not trying to be rational, their judgments may come off the top of their heads and thus be more affected by salience.

A theory of self-awareness proposed by Duval and Wicklund (1972) suggests that focus of attention may also affect self-attributions. Duval and Wicklund (1973) found that when subjects worked on a task while looking in a mirror (thus, making self more salient) they showed increased self-causality. Arkin and Duval (1975) argued that having a video camera present would increase the tendencies of subjects to see self as salient, and the data do show that having a camera present increases dispositional and decreases situational attributions on the part of the actor. In a further demonstration Sherrod and Goodman (1978) argued that when women were in an achievement situation they should have a more salient self-image when they were observed by men rather than by women. As predicted, women made more dispositional self-attributions for both success and failure when they were observed by men than when they were observed by women.

The question naturally arises as to what the precise cognitive foundation of salience effects is. One possibility is that salient stimuli are better remembered, but while some studies find that people recall more about salient than nonsalient stimuli (McArthur and Post 1977), memory effects seem to be inconsistent or weak (Taylor and Fiske 1978).

Another possibility makes use of Tversky and Kahneman's availability heuristic. Taylor and Fiske (1978) have argued that attention to particular aspects of a given situation somehow makes codings or categories related to those aspects more available as a way of understanding the situation. When subjects are making judgments off the tops of their heads, availability affects judgment. The most direct test of that hypothesis was performed by Pryor and Kriss (1977). In the first part of this experiment, they manipulated the salience of persons and objects in sentences of the type used by McArthur (1972) in her test of Kelley's Covariation Model (see pp. 53-55). A person-salient sentence would read: "Joe liked the movie." An object-salient counterpart would be: "The movie was liked by Joe." Paragraphs were constructed using sentences of these types and also sentences with consistency, consensus, and distinctiveness information. Subjects saw paragraphs for 15 seconds and then were asked to indicate whether various probe words had appeared in the paragraph. Pryor and Kriss reasoned that when subjects could answer the question quickly, the concept related to the probe word was more available than when the answer required more time. As expected, they found that when the person came first in the sentence and was therefore presumably more salient, the person word was more available, in the sense of requiring a relatively short reaction time, than when the person came second.

In a second experiment, subjects took part in a typical McArthur attribution experiment where object- and person-salience was manipulated by the form of the sentence, and various combinations of consistency, consensus, and distinctiveness were also presented. Pryor and Kriss found that sentences of the form "Joe likes the movie" led to more person-oriented attributions, whereas "The movie is liked by Joe" pushed attributions to a more subject-oriented attribution. Because the form of the sentence also affected availability, Pryor and Kriss argue that availability mediates attribution results.

In Chapter 5 we argued that salience of person or situation can explain tendencies of perceivers to see own behavior as situationally caused and others' behavior as dispositionally caused. Work reviewed in this section suggests that salience also affects a variety of person perception processes. It influences coding of behavior, evaluations of people, and attributions for their behavior. There is a strong suggestion that salient stimuli lead to coding in terms of available categories and that the availability of the category can bias subsequent explanation processes.

Consensus bias　Attribution models differ in many ways, but they all place considerable emphasis on the proposition that the popularity of behavior gives us information about the power of situational forces. Yet, many studies seem to find that subjects tend to underutilize consensus information. For example, McArthur (1972) found that information about what others do accounts for a significant but practically trivial (3 percent) of variance in causal attributions. Other experiments (McArthur 1976; Gilson and Abelson 1965) have also found that people generalize more about objects than about people. Nisbett and Borgida (1975) presented subjects with information about how a group of subjects behaved in an experiment; such subjects did not use such information in predicting what a single subject would do. In a test more central to present concerns Nisbett and Borgida gave a description of a subject who had behaved extremely. Perceivers who were told (correctly) that most subjects had also performed the extreme behavior were no less likely to make dispositional attributions for the subject's behavior than perceivers not given this consensus information. Thus, consensus information was underutilized.

As Nisbett and Borgida point out, this tendency is similar to the tendency explored by Tversky and Kahneman to underutilize base-rate data. As we saw earlier in this chapter, people tend to concentrate on particular instances or on especially salient features of people and ignore the often more valid statistical data on what other similar people are like.

However, the behavior of a single individual is vivid and concrete while statistical summaries of the reaction of others are relatively abstract (Nisbett and Borgida 1975). Perceivers may concentrate on behavior, not statistics. To see (or read about) John laughing while lots of others either laughed or did not laugh forces attention to John and away from the collective others. To see John laughing and to also *see* Jean, Bill, Mary, and Sam laughing or not (rather than reading a statistical summary of their behavior) might focus attention more on the consensus.

Nisbett *et al.* (1976) report results on the effects of abstract and concrete information on people's actual choices. Students were asked to choose courses on the basis of data on other students' choices. One group saw mean evaluations of several courses based on ratings of several students. The other group heard a small panel of students rate the courses and make a few comments about the courses. The subjects' own choices were far more influenced by the small panel of students than by base-rate data based on many more students.

There may be other reasons for the relatively weak consensus effects. For one thing, consensus information may conflict with what people feel is true of the world. Ross (1977) has emphasized that people normally assume that their own reactions or behaviors are shared by others. This perceiver-generated *False Consensus Bias* may be more important to the perceiver than the real consensus information provided by statistical abstractions. This would further suggest that if the stimulus person's behavior differs from the behavior the perceiver thinks she would perform (and which she therefore thinks is quite common), other consensus information might be distrusted. Hansen and Donoghue (1977) showed that for environmental attributions statistical consensus information had a greater effect when the subjects thought that others agreed with them than when they did not. Lowe and Kassin (1977) found that manipulations of how reasonable (and therefore presumably how likely) behavior is affects attributions more than experimenter provided base-rates that might conflict with subjects' notions of liklihood.

Hansen and Lowe (1976) have argued that most studies that fail to find consensus effects use socially undesirable behavior that subjects may feel they (and most other people like them) might not perform. They did find consensus effects for neutral behaviors, and Zuckerman (1978b) found that consensus effects were stronger for positive than for negative behaviors. All these studies tend to support the idea that what people think is likely may be more important in their judgments than what the experimenter tries to convince them is likely. Of course, people's estimates of how likely behavior is may be seriously in error.

Others have argued that subjects may have other reasons to mistrust consensus information or to feel that it is unrepresentative. Wells and Harvey (1977) have pointed out that in the Nisbett and Borgida experiments nothing is said about the representativeness of the samples used to provide consensus information. Perceivers might feel free to conclude that the higher consensus was based on unrepresentative samples. When care is taken to assure subjects that the samples are representative, high consensus does result in greater situational and less person-attribution than does low consensus (Wells and Harvey 1977; Hansen and Donoghue 1977).

Perceivers may also be smarter than attribution models give them credit for. Consensus information is not causal and does not necessarily provide information about a single person's behavior. John may laugh because he finds the comedian funny, or because he is drunk, giddy, or deranged. Consensus information provides no information about these things. John could laugh because he is drunk while his sober friends laugh because the comedian is funny. We need to know whether John is like his friends or not. In a different context Goethals (1972) has shown that consensus information is utilized more when others are similar rather than dissimilar to the actor. But the essential point is that what John's friends do says nothing about John directly, although we surely would want to look at John more carefully if he behaves differently from others.

The data suggest both a reluctance to generalize over actors and a tendency to underutilize such information to make judgments. This would seem to imply a tendency to assume that because people are so different it is dangerous to infer something about one person from what others have done. Perhaps this reflects our beliefs that people are unique and not easily reduced to a statistical average. So while perceivers easily use information about how a single individual reacts to several entities (distinctiveness), they feel uncomfortable using information about how the generalized other has responded (consensus).

We have advanced several reasons why consensus information might be underutilized in at least some attribution situations. We hasten to point out that there are several demonstrations that perceivers do use such information (Wells and Harvey 1977; Hansen and Stonner 1978; Ruble and Feldman 1976). There has been some debate about the power of consensus information (Borgida 1978; Wells and Harvey 1978), but it seems clear that it is often— although not inevitably—underutilized. This point is important because consensus information is, in theory, an important means of distinguishing actor from entity attributions. Underweighing consensus information must bias attributions away from entities or situations and toward persons as causes of behavior.

The Fundamental Attribution Error Ross (1977) has claimed that there is a pervasive tendency to underestimate the extent to which behavior (especially that of other people) is affected by situational forces, a notion originally suggested by Heider (1958). This is, of course, a variant of the Jones and Nisbett (1972) hypothesis that we see our own behavior as relatively situationally caused and the behavior of others as dispositionally caused. Certainly, the Jones-Harris effect (the failure to weight external forces controlling expression of attitudes) and the tendency to hold people responsible for accidents also support the basic idea of the Fundamental Attribution Error. Recently, there have been other demonstrations. Ross, Amabile, and Steinmetz (1977) had a subject make up hard questions to ask a contestant in a general knowl-dege quiz. Even though the questioner used his or her own idiosyncratic knowledge to make up the questions, thus putting the contestant at a real dis-advantage, the questioner, the contestant, and an observer all felt the ques-tioner had superior knowledge than the contestant, thus ignoring the power of the questioner. In effect, the perceivers ignored the role of external forces, in this case the social power of the questioner to define the nature of the inter-action. This is somewhat analogous to the failure of subjects in the Jones and Harris (1967) experiment (see pp. 66-68) to take enough account of the power of the experimenter to decide what a subject should write.

There are several possible ways of explaining the Fundamental Attri-bution Error. We have already seen that subjects tend to ignore consensus information that tends to provide (in theory) information about situational causes. Of course, it could also be plausibly maintained that ignoring con-sensus information is a result of a general bias to prefer person-oriented to situation-oriented explanations for behavior.

A related explanation for the Fundamental Attribution Error is the general failure noted by Tversky and Kahneman to consider representativeness in samples. In effect, perceivers tend to assume that a single sample of behavior is representative of what the actor ordinarily does. Particularly when the be-havior of the actor is different than what the perceiver feels he or she would do (and attribution experiments do dote on unusual behavior), the False Con-sensus Bias may lead the perceiver to feel that others would act differently from the actor, further pushing attribution toward unique actor causes. Finally, we note that behavior makes categories relevant to that behavior particularly salient or available, and we have seen that category availability tends to bias explanation toward that category.

Attribution perseveration Subjects persist in self-attributions even after they have been explicitly told the attributions are erroneous. For example, in an experiment by Ross, Lepper, and Hubbard (1975), subjects were led to succeed or fail on an experimental task. Even though they were later explicitly told that the success or failure had been manipulated by the experimenter, suc-cessful subjects continued to feel that they had higher abilities than failure subjects. There are several possible reasons for this perseverance effect (see Heider 1944 and Ross 1977), but the most obvious is that once a dispositional attribution has been formed, consistent information is used to confirm the attribution while disconfirming evidence is assigned to unstable, environ-mental forces. Put another way, dispositional attributions are seen as primary and environmental forces are underweighted.

Another explanation for such effects has recently been studied by Ross, Lepper, Strack, and Steinmetz (1977). They argue that once a perceiver has gone to the trouble of explaining an event, the explanatory concepts continue to be highly available and to continue to imply the event. This in turn suggests that such perceivers should come to feel that the event in question is quite common or probable. You may recall that Fischhoff (1976) has shown that even relatively improbable events are viewed retrospectively as having been more probable than objective evidence warrants. Carroll (1978) has also found that merely thinking about an event makes it seem probable. In both cases category availability may be the explanation.

Ross *et al.* (1977) had subjects read case histories of people who had various psychological difficulties. Subjects were then asked to imagine that the person in question had either committed suicide or made contributions to the Peace Corps, and they were further asked to invent an explanation for this imagined event. Subsequently, they were asked to estimate the likelihood of these events actually occurring for these patients. As one would expect, subjects who had imagined and explained a suicide saw the suicide as more likely than those who had imagined the financial contribution to the Peace Corps, and those who had "explained" the financial contribution were more likely to feel that the event had actually happened. While the precise explanation of these effects needs further clarification, it is obvious that merely thinking about something affects subjective probabilities of the reality of that event. There are, of course, major social implications of that bias because therapists, teachers, prison wardens, social workers, and other people dedicated to behavior change are frequently found to imagine a number of courses of action or probable scenarios for their charges.

The Awareness Issue

The study of person perception began with a strong basis in phenomenology. Early theorists such as Allport, Asch, and Heider wanted not only to describe the processes of person perception, but to give accounts that were phenomenologically valid in the sense of being recognizable to perceivers as a more or less faithful rendition of what was in their heads as they tried to make sense of behavior.

However, as you have considered the various processes examined in this book, you may well feel that nothing in your head corresponds to anything the models say you do. For example, although subjects give evaluations of people that are a weighted average of component traits, very few people report any experience of averaging (or doing anything else to) the traits. Traits are judged as similar on linguistic grounds by people who feel they never consciously took meaning into account. Subjects discount and weight various kinds of information in attribution tasks without being able to report what they are doing. Throughout the book we have stressed snap judgments, those we make immediately and seemingly without conscious thought. We have also suggested that people are not always aware of the inferences they draw from expressive behavior. Furthermore, Taylor and Fiske (1978) have argued that salient stimuli particularly affect our judgments when we make them "off the top of our heads." Thus there are several examples of how judgments are made without any conscious awareness.

The issue of awareness becomes especially salient when we deal with bias. Throughout this chapter we have emphasized the great many ways people make systematic errors in their judgments. We reemphasize that our concern has not been with random errors or those that arise out of stupidity or ignorance. Bias is a set of predictable errors that occur even when bright, knowledgable people try hard to be rational. They occur both because people's needs and values interfere with their ability to process information, but even more fundamentally because there seem to be systematic errors built into the cognitive system. Yet, the dilemma is not only that people are unaware that they have committed errors, but they are unaware that these errors are systematic. They have no experience of being biased.

While it would certainly be nice if all our cognitive processes were available to consciousness and if models of those processes correspond to how people think they think, the validity of the models is in no way affected by whether people agree that the models seem valid. Models that attempt to describe how people think may or may not be attempts to describe phenomenologies, they may or may not have their roots in someone's own introspections about the working of his or her mind, but as scientific models their validity is assessed in the same way any model is tested: by empirical research. Of course, some psychologists would argue that there are other forms of validity than scientific-empirical, but so long as we organize our conceptions around scientific models, we use scientific criteria of validity. The validity (or more accurately, the utility) of a model or hypothesis is proportional to its ability to generate predictions that are confirmed by empirical data. The scientific validity does not depend on whether you or I feel the theory is an adequate description of our minds.

Recently, Nisbett and his colleagues have demonstrated quite forcefully that people are not aware of their own cognitive processes. Nisbett and Wilson (1977a) review evidence from a wide variety of social psychological studies which shows that not only do people frequently not know what cognitive processes have gone on, but that they also misreport their cognitions. All social psychology researchers have had the experience of asking subjects why they have responded the way they do. Even those whose data fit the predictions often come up with baroque explanations of the sort: "My grandmother always told me that if I had to do . . . "

Nisbett and Wilson report several demonstration experiments that can illustrate the difficulties. For example, people were asked to evaluate articles of clothing, and the data showed clearly that the article of clothing in the right-hand position was preferred. When asked whether position had influenced their choice, "virtually all subjects denied it, usually with a worried glance at the interviewer suggesting that they felt either that they had misunderstood the question or were dealing with a madman" (1977a, p. 244). In another experiment reported by Nisbett and Wilson (1977b), subjects saw an interview with a teacher who was either very warm or very cold and hostile. As expected, the warm teacher was evaluated more positively, but subjects also rated the physical appearance of the warm teacher as more pleasing. Not only does this represent a halo effect bias (because presumably warmth and physical appearance are relatively unrelated), but subjects consistently denied that the teacher's personality had affected any of their ratings.

These studies (and many others) demonstrate that people often cannot correctly report which stimuli have affected them. There are other demonstrations which show that subjects often report that stimuli which did not affect them really have. For example, subjects were asked to predict how much shock they would take in an experiment. Some subjects were reassured that the shock would do no permanent damage, while others were not given this reassurance. Despite the empirical fact that the reassured subjects did not actually predict they would take more shock than nonreassurance subjects, most of the subjects reported that the reassurance had affected their ratings.

We are not suggesting that people never know their own minds, but only that what people say they think and how they actually think can be two different things. One should not blindly trust people's reports of their cognitive processes because they are sometimes, perhaps frequently, in error. The fact that people cannot report what has actually gone on is a puzzling problem with broad philosophical as well as psychological implications. We propose to avoid those issues with the single statement that it is certainly possible to invent a theory (as the behaviorists did) in which introspections about cognitive processes are not necessarily reflections of "true" processes.

The more interesting and tractable issue—and one that is relevant to the concerns of this chapter—is where people get their ideas about what is in their heads. In some ways the most interesting phenomenon is not that people are ignorant or wrong, but that they so vehemently affirm their incorrect theories. These theories about what they have done may be wrong, but their true validity seems to have no impact on their perceived validity.

Nisbett and Wilson (1977a) suggest that much of the time people apply culturally or experientially derived rules for explaining their behavior. The subject "knows" that personality traits are not supposed to influence judgments of physical attractiveness and that certain stimuli are supposed to make a difference in behaviors. In a sense the person falls victim to the representativeness heuristic. Because a given reason (such as reassurance) seems representative of reasons for taking shock, it is judged as a major active reason. In another sense, explanations that have been frequently evoked in the past or that seem particularly plausible in light of a culturally determined common-sense psychology may be especially available as explanations for future events.

Some interesting implications of this kind of model have been tested by Nisbett and Bellows (1977). Verbal reports ought to be accurate when there are rules for making a judgment and feedback about the consequences of following the rules. Reports should be inaccurate when the influences on judgments are not a part of the common-sense psychology. In their experiment subjects were asked to make several judgments about an applicant for a job. In addition to filler information, other information about the applicant was either present or not. After subjects had made their judgments, they were also asked how much the various factors had influenced them, and observers were asked how much the various factors might be expected to influence judgment.

When the subjects judged intelligence they relied primarily on the applicant's academic credentials. Furthermore, they correctly reported that this factor had influenced them, and observers also felt that it would have an influence. There is apparently major cultural consensus on predictors of intelligence and so subjects' verbal reports are accurate. However, when asked to rate liking, subjects were greatly affected by whether the interviewer had spilled coffee during the interview but not by her academic credentials. However, both subjects and observers reported that academic credentials were more important (see Fig. 10.1). Again, while there may be general rules relating academic success to liking, there are probably not such rules for coffee-spilling. In general, the results suggest that whereas subjects and observers agree on some factors they take into account, for many judgments neither is able to predict very well what factors are weighted most heavily.

The issue of awareness needs further explanation. However, even these preliminary results suggest that we are not always aware of why we have behaved as we have. This creates special problems for bias control. It suggests that people will not only be unaware of cognitive biases because they will feel they have paid attention to and responded to stimuli the way they are supposed to, but also that they will likely deny that they were biased because they have no real awareness of it. It seems reasonable—but perhaps naive— that the first step in the control of bias is its recognition.

Interest in the cognitive sources of bias is likely to continue. Our conceptions of human rationality are at stake. It is one thing to assume a perceiver whose fundamental rationality is clouded over by emotion, but it is quite another to conceive of a perceiver who tries to cope with information but who cannot because of cognitive limitations. As Dawes (1976) has put it, ". . . we insist in the face of contradictory evidence that we can do more than we can do, and we tend to ascribe conflicts that can be explained on cognitive terms to motivational variables. Why? Again the answer can be found in our cognitive limitations" (p. 10). Our pride in human rationality perhaps is in reality hubris. It is one of the most important tasks facing human information processing to assess the limitations of the human mind, and so research in bias in person perception will likely continue.

Summary

Bias is considered any systematic consistent and predictable departure of person perception processes or outcomes prescribed by a particular model. Motivational bias occurs when the perceiver's needs intrude on the attribution process. The most obvious forms of motivational bias occur when we perceive others in an ego-defensive or self-esteem protective way and when we project

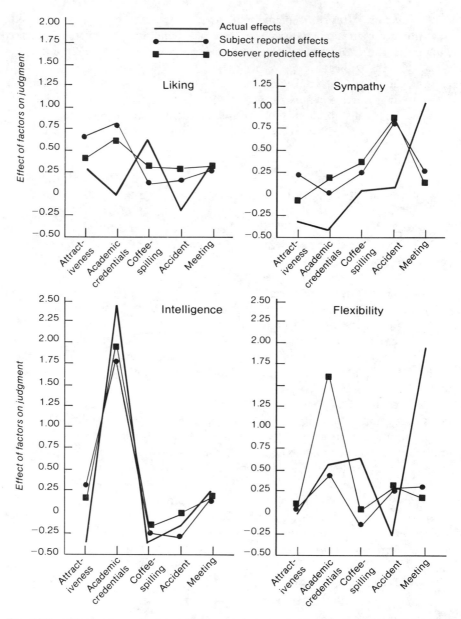

Fig. 10.1 Effects of manipulated factors on judgments, reports by subjects about the effects of the factors, and predictions by observers about the effects of the factors. (From Nisbett and Bellows 1977.)

unfavorable traits on to others when these traits have been attributed to ourselves.

Cognitive bias can occur even when the perceiver is trying very hard to be objective and fair. These biases appear to be systematic and result from characteristic ways we have of simplifying and processing information. Some examples are the tendency to simplify events by seeing them as related either by cause or by similarity. Other forms of cognitive bias derive from salience effects, the tendency not to take external forces into account (*the Fundamental Attribution Error*), errors in estimating the frequency or probability of events, salience effects, and false consensus. It is almost certain that both forms of bias do occur, so there is little point in arguing about the existence of one form of bias or the other. The real question would seem to be when and under what conditions the two forms of bias are most important.

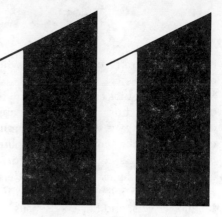

A Review of Process

AN OVERVIEW

The reader of this book may well have been bothered by the lack of a unitary conception of the person perception process. If the field of person perception were an untacked wilderness, without a history of research explorations, probably no rational surveyor would define the major territories and problems according to our chapter headings. These headings do not reflect a set of sensible, logical categories; instead they reflect the paths that have been followed by isolated explorers, who often had little knowledge of the outlines of the whole field or of the explorations of other investigators working nearby. Each of the chapters represents, in fact, a rather discrete body of research with its own history, theoretical concerns, and methodologies; for example, it is not uncommon for people working on attribution processes to know (or care) little about research on impression formation or on nonverbal behavior.

In this concluding chapter, we will concentrate on some general issues and some significant limitations on the ways person perception processes have been conceptualized. Our tone will be critical but optimistic. When possible, we will point to promising new ways of looking at person perception. This concluding chapter will attempt to summarize the various person perception processes and will view the various processes in a kind of temporal order.

The perceiver begins with an appearance-behavior-context pattern. The first—and in some ways most fundamental—process occurs as the perceiver selects out some aspects of the total stimulus pattern for special attention. The first step in making sense of raw stimuli is attention to specific features of the total array. Second, the perceiver must further reduce the complexity of the full stimulus array by categorizing, labeling, or coding the stimuli. Attentional and coding processes have been little studied by person perception researchers;

perhaps because the processes seem so natural, nonreflective, and immediate, they are taken for granted.

The end result of this initial stage of processing is that the perceiver has created a set of cues for further inference work. The perceiver has selected some features of the total appearance-behavior-context array, and has broken up a spatial and temporal continuity into categories. At this point, the perceiver may make any of a number of direct inferences or snap judgments about the stimulus person without any elaborate cognitive work. In addition, the perceiver may raise any of a number of questions about the causes of the stimulus person's behavior. If the behavior has had a purposive quality to it, the perceiver may try to understand what intentions seemed to "cause" the behavior. If, on the other hand, the behavior appears to be a reaction, the perceiver may scan the environment in search of the stimulus that caused the reaction. In either case, the perceiver may go on to interpret the behavior as a manifestation of various dispositions, reasons, and disposition-situation inter-actions. In short, the person makes inferences about the actor's psychological characteristics.

Beyond these initial inferences about psychological characteristics, the perceiver may wish to come to an even fuller understanding of the actor's personality by organizing and integrating all the information collected so far. The perceiver also may wish to make some composite judgment about the actor, say of overall trustworthiness or suitability for a job. Finally, the perceiver may wish to make some prediction about the stimulus person's future behavior. The complete sequence is portrayed in Table 1.2 (p. 16).

This sequence is a formalized schema of the set of possible processes, and is both too complicated and too simple to serve as a model of "typical" instances of person perception. First of all, the perceiver need not complete the entire process, and probably rarely does so. Perceivers may hardly notice the stimulus person, and even when they do they may not be interested enough to proceed with any additional cognitive activity. I may note that a person is laughing and infer that he is happy without caring about why or worrying about what he is likely to do next. A snap judgment may be sufficient, and even if causal attributions are made, the perceiver may not go further to form a complete impression. More elaborate processing may generally be reserved for stimulus persons who are especially important or relevant to our concerns. In this regard, Berscheid *et al.* (1976) found that subjects not only pay special attention to people who are potential dates, but that they also make relatively extreme and confident attributions about them. This would seem to indicate that more cognitive work may go into understanding more relevant others.

Second, the sequence may be entered at any point with already-constructed stimuli. For example, I may trust a political commentator's assessment that a politician is ambitious and make further inferences and predictions; I need not have drawn the inference about ambition from observing the behavior itself.

Third, for the sake of easy exposition, we assume that the processes follow one another in some temporal order, but this assumption is neither necessary nor true in every case. In fact, one theme of the chapter is that any and all of the processes of person perception can go on simultaneously and that often the perceiver is very active in moving back and forth among the various stages to check conclusions.

Finally, there is no necessary implication in all of this that the perceiver reaches accurate conclusions about the stimulus person. The perceiver may not notice relevant stimuli, may code behavior or context in various inadequate ways, may draw incorrect conclusions about the stimulus person's intentions, dispositions, or the stimuli to which the stimulus person was responding. Some of these inaccuracies result from the necessity to impose order on a rich stimulus array and the fact that our human capacities for processing information are both limited and biased. Some of the inaccuracies result from the needs and values of the perceiver, and such distortions are likely to enter at almost any stage. Under any circumstances, perceivers often end up with a more unified and coherent picture of other people than is justified. That seems to be a price we pay for our abilities to impose meaning on the world.

THE INITIAL PROCESSING: ATTENTION AND CODING

Most of what is known about the processing of stimuli for person perception was covered in Chapters 1, 2, and 6. When the perceiver observes behavior (whether it is action or unintended behavior), appearance, and context, the perceptual experience is immediately ordered; we do not perceive disembodied behavior, clothes without an actor, or a context without its substance. We see a person with a particular expression and appearance doing things in a particular context. Only with some effort can the perceiver separate out these various elements. However, it does not follow because of the "given-ness" of these perceptions that questions about how the concepts are related, ordered, and made meaningful are easy to answer. The processes of making sense of the raw materials of person perception are probably extremely important, but generally they have been ignored by most researchers and theorists in the area. Most person perception research begins with stimuli such as trait lists, obvious behaviors, and behavior descriptions that are already processed and that may not be representative of the products of natural coding activity. Before getting into some of the possible problems this presents, let us first review what we know about processing what we have called the raw materials.

Attention   In Chapter 2, we considered the initial responses of the perceiver to physical appearance, behavior, and context, and in Chapter 6 we further discussed expressive behavior. In each case, it is important to note that the perceiver engages in some cognitive activity involving initial classification and selection (see Chapter 1). People, behavior, and contexts are extremely complex stimuli. We can no more see everything about these stimuli than we can about a painting, a view of the high Sierra, or New York's Madison Avenue at 5 p.m. at first glance. We notice some things about a person—behavior and context—but not others. I may notice that someone I have just met has long hair and glasses, but not that she is wearing sandals or a wedding ring. I see her smoking a cigarette and note that she does not maintain eye contact, but I do not much heed her mouth as she talks and I do not observe her drumming her fingers. In short, I am selective in what I see.

We also pointed out that some of the attentional processes that dictate what I see are due to the *salience* of certain stimuli. Certainly, bizarre or unexpected stimuli will be particularly noticed. Departures from the perceiver's expectations are extremely important, not only in capturing attention but in shaping subsequent perceptions and inferences. Not only do we notice unexpected things, but we are likely to wonder what has caused them. There may also be differences among perceivers in what they find salient. People tend to notice stimuli related to things they really care about. Some people may notice a person's hairstyle, others may notice her figure. Some might see her smoking, while others might focus more on the way she drinks her coffee. One's own experiences, prejudices, and personality dictate, in part, what one observes about another person and his or her behavior as well as the context for that behavior.

In addition to these stable individual differences, the perceiver's present purposes also dictate attention. A man "on the make" at a party may notice whether a female is wearing a wedding ring. Football coaches presumably notice different features of young males on the football field than they would about people at a church service. Teachers are reported to be more attentive to the laughter of students after they have told a joke than while standing in line at the cafeteria. There may be other sources of stimulus salience, but we assume that the strangeness or unexpectedness of the stimulus, stable personality differences, and perceiver sets greatly affect our attention to particular cues in the environment.

Coding and categorization   Selective attention is not the only way that raw stimuli are made tractable. Appearance, behavior, and contexts must be coded and categorized. In Chapters 2 and 6 we discussed the coding of behavior. People divide continuous behavior into units of various sizes, and physical appearance and contexts may also be viewed more or less microscopically. Furthermore, behavior, appearance, and context must be labeled or categorized. The perceiver has to decide what to call the stimuli. Is the actor being competitive or aggressive? Is her appearance chic or merely trendy? Is the situation relaxing or dull? We do not suggest that perceivers must give an explicit verbal label to every behavior or context, but we do claim that the perceiver always performs some classification activity, if nothing more than deciding that behavior, appearance, and contexts appear normal. And we would expect that the labeling becomes quite explicit when the behavior, appearance, or context appears strange or unexpected.

Most research on person perception skips these early stages of attention and labeling by giving the subjects already-coded and labeled stimuli. In the real world, perceivers usually see real people behaving in a particular context, and we have argued that some initial cognitive work is necessary to get the stimuli "ready" for further inference work. In particular, there will be inferences about characteristics of the person based on the behavior, appearance, or context, and these characteristics will lead to inferences about other characteristics. It is these "second generation" inference processes that have been of most interest to person perception researchers. Entering the sequence in the middle, they must assume that certain processes have gone on before, and that the stimuli they give to their subjects resemble the natural outcomes of those processes. The attribution researcher may assume that behavior is coded, and that context is resolved into situational forces. The impression formation researcher may assume that the perceiver sees the stimulus person as a set of attributes.

We think it is likely that even when perceivers begin with raw behavior, they often do reduce the mass of possible information to the kind of highly coded stimuli assumed to be the raw materials for further attribution and impression formation. Nonetheless, by using prefabricated stimuli, experimenters automatically make it impossible to learn anything about certain questions. First, and most obvious, we can't find out whether the basic assumptions are right. What happens when behavior codings and situational forces are not as clear as they are in the typical attribution experiment? What happens if the perceiver never infers a set of traits? Does this mean that there can be no further attributions or global impressions? We suspect not, but we will not find out so long as our experimental stimuli are already processed.

Second, we cannot find out much about the *relationships* among the various stages. Surely, behavior coding affects attribution just as an attribution affects subsequent coding. Behavior coded as discontented will probably lead to a different attribution than will the same behavior coded as worried. Appearance and context codings and salience are also affected by attribution and impression formation. Seeing a behavior as discontented may focus attention to certain stimuli (such as the boring man who is talking too much), whereas seeing the behavior as worried may focus attention to other features of the person. For example, chewed-off fingernails may become salient as futher evidence of anxiety or worry, and the warmth of the room may become less salient as a possible cause for the discontented behavior. Our major point is not that coding affects attribution more than the reverse, but rather that often they mutually support one another.

This leads to the third problem: when researchers start in the middle of the person perception process, they may fail to capture the active information-seeking, hypothesis-testing aspects of person perception processes. For example, in the real world perceivers try on various inferences for size and then check them out by observing new behavior. A hypothesis that a person is anxious or unhappy may be tested by observations of new behavior or by consideration of its consistency with other known characteristics: "Yes, bitten fingernails confirm my suspicion that he is anxious, and that also fits with his immaturity." While there have been some studies of information-seeking in person perception (Frieze 1976; Berscheid *et al.* 1976; Garland *et al.* 1975), none of the studies has been able to capture the sequential hypothesis-testing nature of the process. In attribution studies subjects are typically presented with rather small amounts of clear information—information that might not be so salient in the real world. Impression formation studies begin with traits that might not be so nicely formulated in real life. Indeed, the processes of impression formation may well involve changing confidence of trait attributions as the traits are fitted together in some fashion.

A somewhat different drawback of the overwhelming number of research studies is that the perceiver is asked to judge a total stranger. What you notice about a stranger may be different from what you notice about a person about whom you already think you know something. Behavior, appearance, and situation codings are likely to be different for strangers and friends. In the real world, attribution and impression formation work takes place with a much richer set of assumptions and expectations which affect the way we process information.

INFERENCES ABOUT PSYCHOLOGICAL CHARACTERISTICS

Inference sets and goals Before continuing through the various stages, we would like to remind the reader of a set of factors that operate throughout the sequence: the perceiver's expectations and goals. At every stage of the person perception process, from attention to long-range prediction, part of what happens is dependent on what the perceiver thinks he knows already.

There are several general purposes a perceiver could have, and these purposes affect not only the nature of the cognitive process, but the salience of stimuli (Jones and Thibaut 1958). One kind of purpose is simply a desire to know how the actor will behave in the near future, say, whether the actor will accept an invitation or offer to help the perceiver. If there seems to be nothing special about the case, simple analogical reasoning may be appropriate, and there may be no need for complex attributional inferences. The perceiver may reason: If I know how Joe (or people like Joe) behaved in this context (or similar contexts), I can predict Joe's behavior. Such reasoning may bring to mind particular behavioral or contextual codings: "Joe accepted my last invitation, so he is likely to accept this one" or "Most people can't refuse to help after I have just done them a favor." In his discussion of scripts, Abelson (1976) notes that we generally have prototypes of situations and behaviors that allow us to reason by analogy. In general, such inference processes do not involve special knowledge about particular stimulus persons, but when the perceiver wants to make simple, short-range predictions about the behavior of another, this type of script-reasoning or reasoning by analogy may get the job done quite effectively. Long-range prediction or prediction of important unfamiliar events, of course, may require a more elaborate attributional analysis.

A second kind of purpose is a desire to explain or understand the actor's behavior. Why did Jane say such a nasty thing? As Heider and subsequent attribution theories have suggested, answering such a question may involve saying something about the causes of Jane's behavior. However, as we will argue shortly, the process of understanding and explaining may also involve discovering noncausal reasons for behavior. For example, while it might seem odd to say that Jane's immaturity *caused* her to say something nasty, we would certainly count immaturity as a kind of explanation for the behavior.

A third kind of purpose is a desire to arrive at a general evaluation or judgment. Do I respect nasty Jane or cooperative Joe? Would I be willing to admit either or both to medical school or to hire either one? Although we often arrive at a global feeling of like or dislike on the basis of a snap judgment, more considered judgments involve weighing various cues and combining them into a composite determination. Perceivers who have this purpose are likely to have ideas about what cues are relevant for prediction and to seek information about these cues. Normally, these cues are based on other inferences about traits, abilities, and motivations, but in principle, behavior, appearance, and contextual cues could be used to make such judgments. However, because composite judgments are usually based on higher-level inference products, we will defer discussion of them until later in the chapter.

There are basically two kinds of processes perceivers seem to use to make inferences about psychological characteristics. The first is the "direct inference" or snap judgment (see Chapter 2), and the second involves a family of more complex influences of a causal or quasi-causal nature.

Snap judgments As the research on appearance, nonverbal behavior, and implicit personality theory suggests, people are remarkably willing to infer one characteristic from another. One trait implies another, expressive behaviors imply affective states, behaviors can imply other behaviors, and traits and emotional states can also imply behaviors. Even contextual cues can imply personality characteristics and other variables.

What are the bases of such inferences? We could imagine a rather dull perceiver who has simply learned correlations or co-occurrences among variables. Our perceiver has, through experience, learned that bearded men and long-haired women generally say politically liberal things, that people who smile report that they are happy, and that people who inhabit book-lined studies are described as introverted. Even if based partially on experience, direct influences are often biased. It is always hard to know what the true relationships among physical features and personality characteristics are, but perceivers do seem to overestimate the extent of these relationships.

Another likely possibility is that such snap judgments are based on cultural stereotypes. Children and adults in this and other societies are constantly taught by parents, mass media, and other cultural agents how to interpret expressive features—what certain gestures and behaviors "mean"— and are given more or less articulated theories about how personality works and what kinds of characteristics go together.

Snap judgments may also have a foundation in more reflective processes. For example, I may have developed an elaborate theory of personality which suggests that when young men rebel against society, they develop radical political views and also grow beards. Thus my previously developed theory may lead me to make a snap judgment about the political beliefs of people with beards, because I see both as manifestations of the same underlying motivation. However, we must emphasize that even if such a theory were once thought over carefully (but not necessarily correctly), at the moment when the perceiver meets a bearded man the inference is direct, immediate, and nonreflective. It is, after all, a snap judgment.

Direct inferences from behavior, appearance, and contexts are extremely common, and perhaps because they seem so obvious, their cognitive basis has been little studied. Snap judgments are probably most likely when the cues seem not to be under the intentional control of the actor. In Chapters 2 and 6 we emphasized the role of snap judgments in drawing inferences from appearances, expressive behaviors, and contexts, However, as we saw in Chapters 7, 8, and 10, the same sort of nonreflective processes are apparent throughout the sequence of person perception processes. They form the basis of stereotypes, implicit personality theories, and some kinds of prediction. Person perception researchers have tended to emphasize more reflective processes of drawing inferences, and we sometimes forget that much of our cognitive activity is essentially nonreflective.

Causal inferences The inference porocesses most studied by person perception researchers are, of course, attribution processes. All attribution theories assume that perceivers want to explain at least some people some of the time. It is further assumed that the particular kind of explanation that is sought is causal; perceivers want to know what caused the stimulus person's behavior. Following Heider, it is assumed that the causes of behavior reside either in the person or in the environment. Most attribution theorists assume that person (or internal) causation is particularly important since it allows *prediction* of future behavior. The reasoning seems to be that internal, personal causes are relatively stable and naturally "follow" the actor around from situation to situation. Thus, so long as a type of behavior is seen to be caused by stable dispositions, it should occur in many different situations.

However, as we saw in Chapter 8, this reasoning is probably not completely correct. Dispositional or internal attributions are not always necessary or even desirable in making predictions about others. Frequently we make predictions on the basis of analogical reasoning or snap judgments, and it is not even clear that perceivers usually look for dispositional information when they want to make predictions.

"You say you're sorry. You act sorry. And you look sorry. But you're not sorry."

Drawing by Geo. Price; © 1977 The New Yorker Magazine, Inc.

Also locating the cause of the behavior in the person *or* in the environment may not be an appropriate or useful strategy. In the first place, internal and external attributions are not always treated by perceivers as being the opposite of one another (see Taylor and Koivumaki 1976 and Ross *et al.* 1974 for two relevant examples). Beyond that, internal and external attributions are not logically distinct.

Consider a pair of examples. Julie studies for the exam because she wants to. Bill studies for the exam because he has to. These two sentences illustrate the everyday language of internal and external causality, but taken as bare statements, they are not particularly informative. It is unlikely that Julie would study for the exam if it were three weeks away so her behavior is a partial response to external forces. On the other hand, while Bill does not *want* to study he certainly *intends* to, because studying is not one of the things one does inadvertently or reactively. So both Bill's and Julie's behaviors are a result of a mixture of internal and external forces.

This leads to a more fundamental point. As Kruglanski (1975) has pointed out, attribution involves more than the assignment of causality. People seek *reasons* in addition to *causes* for behavior. The term *cause* has a most ambiguous relationship to human behavior (see Davidson 1963; Danto 1965).

Ordinarily we see one event as causing another when the second rather immediately and apparently inevitably follows the other. In this sense, it makes some sense to use the notion of cause for reactive behaviors. Your scream of terror can be said to be caused by the appearance of the intruder. Ellen's laughter at the cleverness of the magician's trick may also be said to be caused to the extent that the laughter is an involuntary or at least unintentional reaction to the trick. The laughter clearly results from an interaction between internal and external events, but it appears to be caused, because Ellen appears to have had no choice but to laugh.

Purposive behavior does not seem to be caused in quite the same way. To say that an internal or external stimulus causes one to do some purposive act seems to stretch things a bit. Is not the essence of purposive behavior the appearance of free will? Thus, suppose that Ned decides to laugh at Hal's magic tricks in an effort to be polite. It is a bit odd to say that Hal's tricks caused Ned's laughter in this case, particularly given that Ned could just as easily have decided not to laugh; Ned may have formed his "internal" intention to laugh before the tricks even started, and his laughter may be relatively independent of the quality of the tricks.

Kruglanski (1975) has suggested that for purposive behaviors the internal-external distinction is not the fundamental one; assuming that all purposive behaviors are at least partly internal in that they are intended, the perceiver tries to distinguish between actions intended as ends in themselves (*endogenous motivation*) and actions intended as a means to some other end or goal (*exogenous motivation*). Thus, eating a meal is ordinarily thought to be an end in itself; we eat because we want to, just because it is pleasant in and of itself. However, some actions are perceived as means to other goals. Helping another person could be an end in itself, but often it is a means to making one look good or winning a promotion. Similarly, one could study because it is fun (endogenous) or because one wants to get a good grade (exogenous). Kruglanski suggests that ordinarily pleasure accompanies endogenous motivation, whereas exogenously determined activity is not pleasurable in itself.

There has been considerable debate (Calder 1977a, b; Zuckerman 1977 a, b; Kruglanski 1977) about whether the endogenous-exogenous distinction can replace the more classic internal-external one. The newer distinction does seem to solve some difficulties with the older one, and it does make phenomenological sense. However, it is likely that the means-end relationship is not a simple dichotomy but rather a continuum. No simple dichotomy is likely to be sufficient to account for the ways in which people attempt to explain other people's behavior. Still, Kruglanski's distinction is important in that it indicates that there is a lot more to explaining behavior than simply assigning an internal or external cause. There are other more complicated and perhaps more important forms of explanation.

Behavior explanation When you want an explanation for someone's behavior, you typically ask a "why" question. "Why did Joe yell at his professor?" There is a closely related "why" question: "Why did Joe hurt the professor's feelings?" The first qustion asks for an explanation of behavior while the second seeks an explanation for the consequences of that behavior. While why-behavior and why-consequences questions are similar in some ways, they often require somewhat different answers.

Our main concern for the moment is with questions of the form: Why did person A do behavior X? We must first know whether the behavior X is reactive behavior or action. Sometimes when the behavior is reactive behavior, that is, something such as a cough or falling down, an explanation in terms of physical causes seems appropriate. Joan coughed because her throat had a tickle, and she fell down because she slipped. For such reactive behavior nothing need be implied about Joan's thoughts, intentions, or psychological processes. However, as we suggested in Chapter 6, reactive behaviors often have interesting psychological explanations. Emotional expressions are one prime example. In this case we may note that a person has reacted to a particular stimulus in a particular way and wonder why. Why did John laugh when Jim fell down? Why was Dick angered by Lee? In other words, we might want to know what kind of person the actor could be to react in a particular (and often peculiar) way. We seek to identify personal characteristics of the actor which predispose certain reactions to certain stimuli.

Purposive behavior seems to require explanation in terms of reasons. We wish to know what reasons someone has for some action. Consider the example we used in Chapter 3 of a student who yells at his professor. Joe's yelling might be caused by the professor's yelling or laughing at him, in which case we would be oriented toward a reactive attribution. Or Joe may have wanted to yell at the professor in order to insult him or get him to change a grade. In the cases where he intended some particular consequences, we may further seek reasons for the intentions. Why did Joe want to get his grade changed? What were Joe's reasons? What was going on in Joe's mind when he decided to yell to get the grade changed? We might come to the conclusion that Joe wanted to get the grade changed to get a high enough grade to please his parents. In this case we might go further and ask what kind of a person has this goal. Is Joe dependent? Approval-seeking? Immature?

Thus, from the perceiver's point of view, a number of conclusions have been reached: (1) Joe intended to yell, (2) he intended to yell to get a grade changed, (3) he intended to get the grade changed to a higher grade, (4) he wanted the higher grade because he wanted to please his parents, and (5) he wanted to please his parents because he is emotionally and financially dependent on them. Note that this kind of analysis does not depend on an analysis of internal and external forces, but rather on the idea that ends provide reasons for means.

We ask you to note one more feature of this analysis. There is no single reason for Joe's yelling. *What we count as an acceptable reason depends heavily on what we want to know.* If our question is: Was Joe merely reacting with anger or was there a method to his madness, the first reason in the list will do. If our question is: Why did Joe want a higher grade, the fourth reason in the list is satisfactory. The questions we ask are usually determined by what seems problematic about the case. Ordinarily students want their grades changed to something higher, so the third reason seems a bit silly; nonetheless it is a perfectly good answer to a generally useless question—useless because it questions what we normally take for granted: that people desire positive outcomes of behavior.

How naive perceivers explain behavior, whether reactive or purposive, is a complex issue, and perhaps we can shed some light on it by considering several possible reasons for behavior.

1 *Ability*

   a Joe yelled at the professor because his vocal cords were in good working order.

   b Mary solved the equation rapidly because she is smart.

2 *Intentions*

   a Joe yelled at the professor because he intended to.

   b Joan spilled her drink all over her date because she intended to.

3 *Desires or Wants*

   a Joe yelled at the professor because he wanted to make him angry.

   b Joe went to the concert because he wanted to please his date.

4 *Motives*

   a Joe yelled at the professor because he wanted to assert his independence.

   b Mary worked hard because she wanted to get a raise.

5 *Goals*

   a Joe yelled at the professor because he wanted his grade changed.

   b Mary worked hard because she wanted to become company president.

6 *Needs*

   a Joe yelled at the professor because he needed to assert himself.

   b Charles smiled at the people because he needed approval.

7 *Emotions*

   a Joe yelled at the professor because he was angry.

   b Sally ran because she was afraid.

8 *Affective States and Moods*

   a Joe yelled at the professor because he didn't like his grade.

   b Mary smiled because she was in a good mood.

9 *Reaction to Stimulus*

   a Joe yelled at the professor because the professor embarrassed him.

   b Mark jumped because the noise was loud.

10 *Traits*

   a Joe yelled at the professor because he is immature.

   b Mary worked hard because she is ambitious.

11 *Stimulus-Person Interactions*

   a Joe yelled at the professor because he hates this particular professor.

   b Carrie likes to be with Sue because she likes her sense of humor.

12 *Attitudes*

   a Joe yelled at the professor because he dislikes authority figures.

   b Mary went to the concert with Jim because she likes him.

13 *Habit*

   a Joe yelled at the professor because he always talks loud.

   b Jim went to lunch at noon because he always goes then.

14 *Past Experience*

   a Joe yelled at the professor because he has found that yelling gets results.

   b Mary worked hard because her parents always stressed hard work.

Although this is perhaps not an exhaustive list, it ought to be sufficient to give you some idea of the variety of permissible explanations. You will also note several other immediately obvious aspects of this listing. First, some of the statements make more sense than others; statements 1a and 2a, for example, seem pedantic at best. However, there are circumstances where these answers not only make sense but are illuminating. Joe may have recently had laryngitis, which makes his vocal equipment worthy of present comment. As for 2a, it is conceivable that Joe lives in a society where people usually yell and the observer wants to make it clear that John was not merely responding to culturally ingrained habits. In statements 1b and 2b intentions and abilities do make complete sense as explanations for behavior.

As we will see, one reason that some of these explanations seem a bit peculiar despite the fact that they are perfectly logical is that they make use of "obvious" features of the situation and the actor to give reasons for unproblematic behavior. We *presuppose* that people have certain abilities, that certain kinds of behavior are normally unintended or intended, and we do not ordinarily use presuppositions as explanation. *Explanations are only interesting and valued if they add information to what we already know.* This will be somewhat clearer when we discuss ability and motivational explanation.

It is important to note that although each of these explanations can be used as reasons for behavior under some circumstances, as explanations they do not all have the same kind of logic. For the sake of simplicity, we may classify the explanations given above into four basic groups: *ability*, *purposive* (intentions, desires and wants, motives, goals, needs), *psychic states* (emotions, affective states, reaction to stimulus), and *dispositions* (traits, stimulus-person interactions, attitudes, habit, past experience). Each of these groups refers to a somewhat different kind of explanation.

Ability: Reference to ability is a part of the explanatory apparatus primarily for achievement situations. Our guess is that abilities are invoked when a person's achievement is unusually good or poor, or when the person has performed in some unusual way, or has made use of some ability not ordinarily used. For most everyday behaviors, ability is taken for granted. As Feinberg (1965) has pointed out in a most provocative article, what we take as the effective cause in a given situation often depends heavily on our own purposes and expectations. We are prone to assign causal efficacy to what is unusual or to what we can control and deal with remedially. Why did Joe yell at his professor? Surely, Joe's anger, his ability to yell, and the presence of the professor all count as necessary conditions for the yelling. However, we are likely to see the cause as due to Joe's anger because presumably in the situation where this all takes place, abilities to yell and professors are more common than students' anger. Also to mention features such as the presence of the professor adds nothing to our knowledge about Joe, nor does it explain why he is yelling and Susan is not.

Abilities are necessary for any behavior, but because of their ubiquitous nature and their general resistance to change they are not invoked often as explanations. Abilities are treated as obvious and often uninteresting *necessary* causes (except in achievement situations), but typically not as important *sufficient* causes. Before abilities can be translated into behavior, there must be some effective motivational forces; perceivers can see ability as more or less important, but never as a completely sufficient cause.

When a person *fails* to perform in the expected way, however, *lack* of ability may often be a sufficient and informative explanation. When someone performs a behavior, we automatically infer the ability, and thus information about the presence of the ability adds nothing to our presuppositions. But when someone does not perform a behavior, lack of ability is only one of several possible reasons, and so information about ability does add to our understanding. Even in the case of Joe and the professor, information about ability sheds some light on the situation: "Joe yelled because he is unable to control himself." This is not a complete explanation, but it is better than "Joe yelled because he is able to yell."

Purposive: Usually purposive or motivational explanations for human action make direct use of intentions. However, as we have noted, intentions can refer both to behavior itself and to desired consequences of that behavior. Ordinarily, of course, we assume that people intend their actions so that purposive or motivational explanations of behavior (but not of consequences) are usually trite. However, there are important exceptions. We may use such explanations to mark the differences between accidental behavior and action. Thus, when we say that Mary had a goal of spilling her drink or that Joe wanted to yell at his professor, we typically are making a point of saying that things which usually happen accidentally or in the heat of passion were done with foresight in this case. However, purposive reasons usually refer to the desired *consequences* of behavior. Joe wanted to (desired, was motivated to, had the goal of, needed to) insult his professor and Mary wanted to embarrass her date. Of course, a person can be incorrect in assuming that his or her behavior will achieve the desired consequence. Joe's professor may be frightened and not insulted. Purposive explanation involves a logic of situational presuppositions: One has to assume not only that Joe wanted to insult his professor, but that he assumed his professor would be insulted by his yelling. This, in turn, requires some assumptions about Joe's knowledge about the psychology of people, professors, or this particular professor. We have to assume that he understands that yelling at professors makes them angry and insulted; this, in turn, assumes that Joe understands normative rules. If we assume he does not, we may take refuge in ability or knowledge explanations. "Poor Joe has never learned that he insults people with his loud behavior." But a purposive explanation requires assumptions about Joe's knowledge of a variety of normative and situational factors; such explanations assume that Joe follows certain rules (see Peters 1958 and Harré and Secord 1972 for an elaboration of this point). Ordinarily, we may rely on common-sense assumptions about what people in general (and particularly Joe) are like, and we almost certainly will not articulate all these assumptions to ourselves. Nevertheless they serve as a kind of background for purposive explanation.

Purposive behavior presents a complex problem for the perceiver for at least one additional reason. All action has multiple consequences, and presumably only some of these are intended. When Joe yells at his professor he may make his professor angry or afraid, he may get his grade changed, he may impress his friends with his assertiveness, he may make himself feel better or guilty. We not only need to infer something about Joe's knowledge and assumptions to know which of these consequences Joe anticipated, but even among those which Joe (or any reasonable person) should have anticipated we have to decide which were intended. Of course, Joe is not limited to one and only one relevant intention; he may have wanted both to change his professor's attitudes and impress his friends. Questions about which of many consequences of action were intended are particularly salient in legal contexts, and for attribution of responsibility more generally. However, decisions about relevant intentions ought to be a salient issue for all attribution research; because attribution research has been so taken with the question of whether behavior was internally or externally caused, insufficient attention has been paid to decisions about which of many intentions may have "caused" the behavior.

However, even if the perceiver decides that one (or more) intentions produced the action, the perceiver's work is not necessarily done. In purposive behavior goals are organized in means-ends relations. Joe wants (intends) to change the professor's attitude, and that goal may be a means to getting the grade changed which may be a means to some further goal, say a high grade-point average. To account fully for Joe's behavior we need to know something about a whole sequence of means and ends. We seek reasons for intentions, reasons for reasons.

Thus explanations in terms of a single intention (whether for action or consequences) are not complete. The logic of such explanations requires that the perceiver understand something about the situation. Further depending on his or her purposes, the perceiver may go beyond immediately intended consequences to ask why these particular intentions were operating at this particular time. Why did Joe want to insult his professor? Intentions are intermediate—but ordinarily not final—reasons for behavior.

Psychic states: Explanations in terms of emotions and affective states present other complexities. Behavior performed under the press of strong emotion is usually not action, but reactive behavior. When we say, "Joe yelled because he was angry," we may mean he had not intended to yell, that there was no ulterior motive for his behavior. In this case, yelling happened to him; it was not something he did intentionally.

However, emotion explanations as well as psychic states (depression, nervousness) and reactive explanations may also function as motivational reasons. If we say that Joe yelled in anger, because the professor yelled at him, or because he was distressed, we may mean that he did what normal people do when they experience certain states or encounter certain situations. We may mean to imply that Joe's yelling was intentional; poor Joe was so angry that he "decided" to give the professor a taste of his own medicine and insult him back or that he felt a powerful but unarticulated need to lash out. In short, Joe is behaving just like a normal angry person, and anger can give rise to intentions.

Whether or not a psychic state explanation is meant to refer to intentions, one may still consider what sort of person experiences certain psychic states in response to certain stimuli. If the stimulus is clear—that is, if we are sure that it's the professor who is really responsible for Joe's behavior, and not the woman who jilted him right before class—we can go on to ask, "What sort of person gets angry at a professor?" What must Joe be like if he starts yelling when someone insults him? Often the answers to these questions are perfectly obvious, so the questions never get asked explicitly. Nonetheless, we may seek a reason for psychic states in terms of disposition.

Dispositions: Traits, habit, disposition, and attitude explanations all seem to refer the reasons for a person's behavior to his or her enduring qualities. There is nothing permanent or stable about purposes or psychic states, but presumably traits, habits, and attitudes are important constructs precisely because they imply stability. Traits are best thought of as summaries of past behavior. A person who reacts angrily in a wide variety of situations and a greater than normal number of times will be called aggressive.

People sometimes loosely (and incorrectly) think of traits as causing behavior. It is fairly easy to understand how this common error arises. When we say that Joe yelled at the professor because he is aggressive, we do not so much mean that aggressiveness *per se* causes the yelling as that some intention associated with aggressiveness does. Aggressive people are those who generally (or at least more often than average) intend to behave in an aggressive or perhaps angry manner. To put the matter somewhat differently, aggressive people are people who frequently are motivated to hurt or yell at others.

However, not all traits fit even this loose model of causality. Schneider (1971, 1978) and Gifford (1975) have shown that traits vary in how dispositional they are. Some traits, such as *intelligent* or *mature*, refer to relatively enduring qualities of the person in the sense that they are perceived to be stable over time and situation, and they also seem central for personality in the sense of "causing" behavior. On the other hand, traits such as *restless* or *happy* seem less stable and central or causal. In Chapter 7 we also discussed the idea that central traits and certain general traits used as prototypes play a particularly important role in inferences about other aspects of personality, an idea to which we return later in this chapter.

Another problem with the trait-as-cause idea is that not all traits are so easily reduced to a language of motivation and intention. As Peters (1958) has pointed out, a great many traits refer less to concrete goals and intentions than to styles of behavior. Immature people and dumb or silly people do not do anything in particular; rather, they do a great many things in a particular way. Therefore, when we say that Joe yelled because he is immature, we certainly do not mean to imply that Joe desired or intended immaturity or that the professor made him feel immature. In fact, we are hard pressed to name an intention associated with immaturity. Another related example is tactlessness. To say that Tom laughed at Joan's mistake because he is tactless is not to claim that Tom wanted to be tactless or indeed that he had any goal in mind at all. Many negative traits which imply the lack of certain capacities do not have implications for intentionality. "John bites his nails because he is nervous." Are we asserting that John intends to bite his nails? Not likely. Thus, not all traits are simple summaries of intentions; some simply refer to reactions or negative capacities.

Both negative capacities and habits have important functions in explanation of behavior. Negative capacities are the trait analogue to lack of ability; they are frequently used to explain non-normative behavior. Thus, immaturity or tactlessness are sensible reasons for Joe's yelling because they point to certain ways in which Joe differs from most people. Most people do not yell at professors, much as they might like to, because they feel that their purposes would be ill-served by such action. Both tactlessness and immaturity suggest that Joe has a crucial short-circuit in his ability to program his behavior effectively—that is, to achieve his purposes.

Traits may also be used to explain consistent kinds of reactions or even to explain the absence of normal reactions. Calm people react to external stimuli in certain ways and by implication in a somewhat unusual way. Calm people are undisrupted by stimuli that would bother most of us. Terms like polite may refer to inhibition of normal reactive behaviors. A polite person does not shout despite a stimulus that engenders anger.

We think it important to reemphasize that although traits and other dispositions may be the end product of an attributional process, traits can be and frequently are inferred in other ways. In Chapter 2 we emphasized the role of snap judgments based on appearance and context as one ready source for trait judgments. Both women who are seen in rundown bars and men with beards will have traits ascribed to them. We have also emphasized at various points in the book that certain behaviors are treated as symptomatic or diagnostic for certain personality characteristics. People who laugh loudly and shout at parties will be seen as extroverted; people who pray before· meals will be perceived as religious. Not only actions but reactive behaviors can serve as the basis for traits. A person who immediately bursts into tears at the sight of an injury may be seen as compassionate or weak. Note that in each case a snap judgment is made. The perceiver does not need to see several instances of behavior or weigh situational forces. The judgment is immediate and non-reflective. It is our guess that the majority of trait inferences that are made in everyday life are formed in this way.

We have discussed traits at some length, and much of what we have said applies also to the related attitude and past experience explanations. We have tried to emphasize that all these types of explanation usually refer to stable kinds of intentions, but there are clear cases where they may be used to explain non-normative or unusual behavior by implicit appeal to a failure to exercise certain intentions. We think it important to emphasize that although disposition is one important kind of explanation, it is not the only one.

There is a further reason for considering traits as a special category in person perception. Since traits have been used in most of the research on impression formation, it is justifiable to raise the whole question of how important traits actually are in the perceptions and interpretations of behavior. One way to examine this question is to ask how often traits are used in descriptions of others. Presumably, if traits are important they should appear relatively often in such descriptions.

Consider as an example one such description written by a student in one of the author's classes:

> Jim is an English major and that tells you a lot about him. He tries hard to be literary; he reads the *New York Review* and tries to believe all the "in-opinions"—or at least he tries to make everyone think he believes them. Most people think he's a bit of a fraud, but I think this is just his way of trying on ideas for size. He talks a lot about individuality and the need for more feeling and less rationality. He hates science and he practically has a fit when I mention psychology. It's a wonder we get along as well as we do. I suppose you could say that Jim is not particularly tolerant of others' views, but he sure does want others to take him seriously. He rubs a lot of

people the wrong way, but I find him interesting. He's actually read a great deal of modern fiction and he is the campus expert on poetry. He's smart and he makes good grades without working hard. It's funny though. He can be arrogant as hell about literature and art—he just won't tolerate the idea that other students can know as much as he does—but he really is interested in lots of things and until he feels he knows a topic he is quite open-minded. His professors seem to like him; they are always asking him to their homes, so I'd guess he doesn't seem arrogant to them. He really is basically a nice guy. He helped me a lot with an English course I took last semester and he didn't come on strong at all. I bet he will make a great professor although he thinks he might like to try to write poetry for a living. Part of his basic romantic nature. He's also not a snob. He gets along well with nearly everyone if they don't try to challenge his ideas about literature and current events. He also has a wry sense of humor, and I really enjoy spending an evening with him just *bs*ing. One more interesting thing about him. He's a good jock. He plays on the basketball and baseball teams and although he professes not to take it seriously, he is a tough but fair competitor. He displays a lot of rah-rah enthusiasm and was elected captain of the baseball team. I would consider Jim to be my best friend, but I don't think that feeling is reciprocated. He doesn't really open up to me; he presents an intellectual facade, although I know him well enough to see beyond that. I know he likes me, but he's not the sort of person to have a best friend.

This description, which is fairly representative of several collected, has several interesting features. First, most of the description of Jim involves his attitudes (toward literature and science, toward a career, toward sports), his accomplishments, and the relationships he has with others, particularly the narrator. Second, there are few out-and-out traits used. Jim is (1) a fraud, (2) arrogant, (3) romantic, (4) humorous, (5) helpful, (6) enthusiastic, (7) intolerant, (8) smart. However, most of these traits are either seen as surface characteristics — such as fraud—or are characteristics of Jim in only some situations—such as arrogance and intolerance. One does not have the feeling that Jim is a list of traits, but rather that he has a number of characteristics that fit together in a meaningful way. This was, of course, Asch's basic point about impressions.

Studies of person descriptions have also found surprisingly few traits. For example, Normand (1973) coded descriptions of people her subjects knew well and did not know well for both pure descriptions and letters of recommendation. She found an average of about 9 traits cited in descriptions that averaged about 120 words in length. However, in the same descriptions there were about 3 descriptions of behavior, 10 descriptions of the person's relationships to others, and 2 mentions of the person's interests and beliefs. In the Normand study traits were widely used, but they did not dominate the descriptions. Furthermore, traits were used more in describing people the perceivers knew well.

Fiske and Cox (1977) coded several descriptions and found that properties (which included traits as well as attitudes) accounted for only about one-fourth of the total ideas, with appearance descriptions being the most common. These researchers also found that properties were used more in describing friends than in describing relative strangers.

In another study Peevers and Secord (1973) examined the development of person constructs over age. They found that trait-type descriptions increased markedly from an average of almost zero in kindergarten children to about 11 per description for college students. However, even among college students traits were used less than items such as appearance, behaviors, age interests, beliefs, and the like. While the Peevers and Secord study did include some material in these categories that might be considered to be traits, one still has to be impressed with the fact that traits do not dominate descriptions of others.

Another approach to the study of the importance of traits is to find out what kinds of information perceivers seek about others. Ostrom (1975) has reported that in forming impressions subjects seek traits about 26 percent of the time, while other categories such as appearance, behaviors, attitudes, and family characteristics constitute the other 74 percent of the requests. In a more elaborate study, Mischel *et al.* (1974) asked subjects to predict the behavior of a person. They found that subjects preferred information about past behaviors in a similar situation to trait information for prediction.

A variety of other studies have examined how informative traits are in other kinds of person cognition tasks. For example, Rodin (1972, 1975) has shown that traits do not always convey much information. In one study (Rodin 1972) a group of people who knew one another well described one another in a variety of ways. Then subjects were required to guess the people described by particular traits or instances of behavior. Not only did the behavioral instances lead to greater accuracy than the traits, but the traits led to accuracy barely better than chance. In another study (Rodin 1975) subjects assigned traits to behaviors, but were not particularly accurate in picking the behaviors that went with the traits. These studies do not bear directly on the importance of traits in our perception of others, since people may continue to use traits in spite of (or because of) their uninformativeness. On the other hand, it would seem rather strange if this were the case.

Throughout this entire section on attribution processes we have argued that there are many levels of explanation for human behavior, and that what works as an explanation depends heavily on what the perceiver wants to know. Sometimes all we need is information about whether the actor intended particular consequences of behavior or not, and sometimes we wish only to identify the stimulus to which an actor is reacting. We may also infer psychic states, traits, or habits as explanations for behavior. However, it does not appear that traits always function as complete explanations. Not only are they not used as often as researchers assume them to be, but they are not always especially informative. Some traits seem to have purely descriptive functions, whereas others seem to have a more dynamic, causal, dispositional quality. To have a complete understanding of explanation, however, we need to know more about how person information is related and stored.

INFERENCES FROM PSYCHOLOGICAL CHARACTERISTICS

When the emphasis switches from causal analysis to finding reasons for behavior, the way is opened to a dynamic explanation for behavior. By this we mean that in trying to understand behavior, you will come to perceive a number of interrelated characteristics interacting in subtle ways to produce the behavior. Much of this analysis belongs to the study of impression information.

Asch revisited We need to remind ourselves of what Asch set out to demonstrate in his pioneering paper on impression formation. He wanted to show that people take whatever information they are given and combine it into a meaningful, organized total impression. Asch used traits as convenient stimuli and responses, but he was not fundamentally concerned with this type of information. However, as we indicated in Chapter 7, Asch's failure to provide a precise explanation for his results led researchers to seek explanations for these results in terms of trait relationships and combinations of trait information. Subsequent research has shown that at least some of the trait implication data could be explained without assuming that subjects form an organized impression. Furthermore, the evaluative tone of the impression could be captured by using general models of human judgment. In the meantime, Asch's more general concerns with how impressions are organized got left behind.

This illustrates a fundamental point. The stimuli of person perception are rich, and perceivers can do a variety of different kinds of cognitive work to produce a variety of different responses. People can infer other characteristics, and they can combine information to produce a final judgment. However, they can also do other things, and you will never find out what they can do unless you ask them. We have continually emphasized that what perceivers do is in part dictated by their purposes. If they intend to infer or judge, they will do exactly that. But if you ask them to organize, they will also do that.

Once a perceiver knows something about another person (Jane is helpful), he may lose interest in her. On the other hand, the perceiver may wish to know more about Jane and may try to infer some of her other characteristics. The research literature on implicit personality theory suggests that in making such inferences people can draw on elaborate networks of perceived relationships among traits and other psychological characteristics. Past experiences with co-occurrences of characteristics and semantic similarities of trait terms constitute two important sources for these perceived relationships.

However, for the moment, we remind the reader of one of the key assumptions we have made about person perception processes. They are not always merely passive, machine-like generation of inferences. Inferences of one trait to another are often checked against available behavior evidence, and perceivers operate with a rich set of assumptions about the workings of human personality. Most perceivers do not operate merely at one level of perceived personality. Traits do indeed imply one another, but the actual relationships are likely to be more complex than a set of implications. For example, consider the following kinds of statements: (1) "Joe acts happy even though he's depressed," (2) "Jane is hostile because she fears rejection," (3) "Sarah's need for approval causes her to be nice to high-status people." In each case, the person's traits are seen as "caused" by other, "deeper" qualities. There are levels to the perceiver's personality theories, and, of course, an articulate perceiver might be even more complex — "Joe acts happy even though he's depressed because he doesn't want anyone to feel sorry for him." At the level of an organized impression, qualities (such as traits) are not merely passively or linguistically related. Often they are related more dynamically. At the beginning of Chapter 7, we provided an example of how perceivers can confront complex stimuli. Our hypothetical perceiver tried to organize the information and tested various hypotheses and organizational strategies against the available data. The description of Jim on pages 263-264 provides a real example of the end result of such activity. In this chapter we have argued that the perceiver relates various characteristics of the actor by finding reasons for behavior and by developing a dynamic set of relationships among characteristics at various levels of personality.

Unfortunately, these processes are rather hard to pin down in any exact way. They can be studied through the analysis of written impressions. Recent analyses of written impressions (Crockett 1977; Schneider 1977; Lively and Bromly 1973; Peevers and Secord 1973; Fiske and Cox 1977) have shown that there is a rich fund of information in such material, but thus far there are few general models or theories to guide the search for interesting and productive research questions in the analysis of written impressions.

Schemata One recent development that promises to be important in understanding the ways perceivers process information is the growing interest in cognitive schemata. Psychologists have emphasized the proposition that people categorize stimulus input according to abstract and general representations. A person sees an object and compares it to abstract representations of several objects: chair, tables, sofa, etc., and "recognizes" it as a chair because it comes closest to matching the prototype for the chair. Such schemata aid, perhaps determine, our ability to recognize objects. They also aid in memory and recall. It is well known that verbal material is remembered best when it fits into some preexisting cognitive structure. Furthermore, schemata allow us to infer additional characteristics of objects and people. Generally, schemata are crucial components in our abilities to organize information we have about other people, and in the past few years the relevance of schemata for person perception processes has been widely discussed (Cantor 1977; Ostrom and Lingle 1977; Abelson 1976; Secord 1977; Crockett 1977).

There are at least three major implications of these schema and prototype models that also aid our understanding of explanation processes. First, the pattern recognition model of Cantor and Mischel (1977a, 1977b) provides an alternative to attributional models of trait inference. In Chapter 2 we emphasized that often we decide what people are like by making snap judgments based on information we feel is particularly diagnostic. Cantor and Mischel have suggested that for certain personality characteristics such as extroversion there are a range of other traits and behaviors which are imperfect but partially valid cues for inferring that trait. Just as we use a set of unrelated but not perfectly valid criteria to decide that an object is a chair or a person a female, so we may have a set of diagnostic cues or behavioral symptoms for certain personality traits. Everyday experience suggests that you do not have to make an attributional analysis every time you want to know what someone is like. Often you may simply say something like: "This person who seems to be enjoying himself at this loud party, who is drinking a great deal, and who is talking to lots of people is just like most of the extroverts I know."

Abelson (1976; Schank and Abelson 1975) has reminded us that we also have schemata of situations and behavior that aid inference processes. Behavior tends to be coded according to stored representations of event sequences, which are called *scripts*. Scripts vary in their generality from the very concrete—"The time I didn't study for the exam"—to the highly abstract—"Procrastination." Often even concrete scripts can come to represent a variety of other situations as when the perceiver says, "It's like the time I didn't study for the exam." Clearly, this use of examples from the past to represent present or even future situations is an important element in decision-making; consider, for example, how often politicans use "Munich" as a relevant script (or prototype) for international conflict.

Second, such models give us a way to understand how we code information about others, remember their past behavior and other characteristics, and process new behavioral information about them. We probably do not store concrete information about people; rather we store information in an abstract fashion and later "remember" by using partial cues and constructing probable inferences about what was done. If you ask me whether I told a lot of jokes at a party a year ago, I may not have access to information about which jokes I told to whom. Rather I might remember that the party was enjoyable, some of the people present usually like my jokes, and reason that therefore I must have told many jokes. If I know you to be an extrovert and remember the party as enjoyable, I may also "recall" that you told several jokes.

Third, and perhaps most relevant to our present emphasis on impression formation as an organizational activity, schemata help to organize the information we have about others. Recall Asch's major point that stimulus information is organized into a coherent impression around central traits. Whether or not a trait was central, whether it would provide this organizing function, was thought to be due to its relationship to the rest of the stimulus information. It may occur to you that central traits are very much like schemata. Just as *warm* serves to generate a written impression of a warm person to the extent that warm is related to the other stimulus traits, so *extro-version* tends to organize impressions of people who have extroverted characteristics (Cantor and Mischel 1977a). We emphasize that although Asch's notion of central traits may have limited validity in understanding particular trait inferences, there has been little or no research on the ability of central traits to explain organizational activity.

We also reemphasize that people do not always seek to form organized impressions of another. However, to the extent that they do seek organization having something to organize the impression around is probably extremely useful. As you try to make sense of the information you have about another you look for the central features, the main themes. Your choice of the central information is probably dictated in part by whatever prototypes or scripts seem most relevant. If the information makes you think the person is extroverted you will then draw on your assumptions about extroverted people in "fleshing out" the impression.

It is important to recognize that whereas general prototypes about characteristics such as extroversion are common and shared widely within a culture, prototypes can be much more specific. For example, many professors have prototypes about students who do not hand papers in on time. Prototypes may also be organized around occupations (Cantor 1977; Ostrom and Lingle 1977). If you are asked to form an impression about an introverted young mathematics professor, the task is probably quite easy.

Obviously, schemata also have something in common with stereotypes. Whereas traditional stereotype research has seen stereotypes as characteristics atributed to a group by prejudiced people (Brigham 1971), more recent research has emphasized cognitive bases of stereotypes. In the present context we remind you that it is just as easy to see race as a central trait or as a prototype as it is extroversion. Race may be thought of as a way of organizing trait, behavior, and situation information, and this implies that such information can be perceived as diagnostic for racial stereotypes just as party behavior is for extroversion.

We think it likely that constructs such as prototypes, schemata, and scripts will help us to a better understanding of how perceivers process, organize, and store information, and all these models presuppose an active information processor as perceiver, one with a rich theory about the personality dynamics of self and other, one that allows the use of both abstract and concrete information.

Judgment processes A final stage in the person perception process may involve a composite judgment or prediction about future behavior. Judgments about likeability or suitability for a particular job probably can be made without complex inferences about psychological characteristics, but because much of this research was stimulated by Asch's impression formation paper, traits and other psychological characteristics have generally been employed in research on judgments. The research of Norman Anderson on Integration Theory can stand as one example of this kind of research, and, as you may recall, Anderson has concentrated on judgments of liking. However, as we indicated in Chapter 7, other dependent measures may also be used. There is a rich literature in judgment processes involving a variety of dependent measures with considerable real-life validity (see Chapters 7 and 8).

Despite the diversity of stimuli and dependent measures, these studies largely agree in their conclusions. First, people do not use all the information available to them; further, they tend to weigh some information more heavily than other information. Second, they tend to combine the information in a very simple way. Ordinarily, they merely add or average the information, and they do not seem to take account of relationships among the stimuli.

However, these models may have some limitations. Let's concentrate for a moment on the work of Norman Anderson, because his work has stimulated a fair amount of controversy—or, at least, argument. Asch's original work was phenomenologically valid because he gave a description of how we integrate information, a description that seems close to what most of us think we do, but the model was imprecise and unclear in its implications. Anderson has provided us with a series of models that are precise but that do not seem to describe how we think. Thus, Asch and Anderson stand at two poles of a familiar dimension in psychological thought: phenomenological versus predictive validity. One group of theories claim that models that do do not allow precise prediction and derivation of hypotheses are scientifically suspect, while the other group says that scientific models are worthless if they do not describe how people actually think.

It is important to recognize that Anderson has provided a family of equations that *describes* the relationships between verbal stimuli and responses. There is little doubt that the model as defined by the various equations makes excellent predictions in the impression formation realm, given certain limiting conditions which we will discuss shortly. However, his equations do not necessarily describe the actual *process* of information integration. It would be preferable on aesthetic grounds, if nothing else, if people did average trait evaluations in the ways that the various equations suggest, but the predictive utility of the model in no way depends on whether you or I feel that we do consider each trait's evaluation and explicitly average them. We *can* perform such an activity and the model does predict evaluative responses nicely.

One of the problems with such models is that although they are potentially general information integration models, their validity in person perception has been assessed only along narrow lines. In particular, research has often been limited to a unidimensional evaluative response dimension using trait words as stimuli. The research has generally not asked whether traits are important or relevant stimuli, or whether dimensions other than an evaluative one are also important. It is quite possible that an evaluative dimension is not the place to look for meaning change, for example, yet almost all research on the problem of meaning change has accepted this dimension as fundamental. In effect, then, we are suggesting that judgment models may be less wrong than limited.

Anderson has shown the way to greatly improved methods and data analysis. His model has helped to focus attention on several important issues and on several important cognitive processes.

INFERENCES TO BEHAVIOR: PREDICTION

As we indicated in Chapter 8, insufficient attention has been paid to how people make predictions about the future behavior of others. It is clearly not true that in order to make predictions, the perceiver has to go through all, or even most, of the stages of the person perception process. Sometimes, for example, analogical reasoning will do just fine, and clearly people use knowledge of generalized behavior in given situations to predict the behavior of concrete individuals. It is also likely that the processing of information is not driven exclusively or even often by a desire to predict.

However, people sometimes need to predict. These predictions can be considered as a specific kind of judgment, in which case various judgment models can be applied. One can also construe prediction as a kind of reverse attribution. It is not entirely clear that these two models are fundamentally different.

Clearly more research needs to be addressed to the reasons for prediction, and how people predict relatively concrete behaviors. We also need more research on the effects of such predictions on the behavior of the perceiver. There is some evidence (pp. 238-239) that perceivers take too little account of the effect of their behavior on the behavior of the stimulus person. Even more interesting is the likelihood that perceivers may adjust their behavior as a result of their impressions, and thereby influence the stimulus person to behave in ways that confirm the initial perceptions (see pp. 34-35). Such processes would have important real-life implications.

Abelson, R. P. 1976. Script processing attitude, formation, and decision making. In J. S. Carroll and J. W. Payne (eds.), *Cognition and social behavior*. Hillsdale, N.J.: Lawrence Erlbaum.

references

Abelson, R. P., and D. E. Kanouse. 1966. Subjective acceptance of verbal generalizations. In S. Feldman (ed.), *Cognitive consistency*. New York: Academic Press.

Addington, D. W. 1968. The relationship of selected vocal characteristics to personality perception. *Speech Monographs* 35: 492-503.

Ajzen, I. 1971. Attribution of dispositions to an actor: Effects of perceived decision freedom and behavioral utilities. *Journal of Personality and Social Psychology* 18: 144-56.

————. 1977. Intuitive theories of events and the effects of base-rate information on prediction. *Journal of Personality and Social Psychology* 35: 303-14.

Ajzen, I., and M. Fishbein. 1975. A Bayesian analysis of attribution processes. *Psychological Bulletin* 82: 261-77.

————. 1977. Attitude-behavior relations: A theoretical analysis and review of empirical research. *Psychological Bulletin* 84: 888-918.

Allport, F. H. 1924. *Social psychology*. Boston: Houghton Mifflin, Riverside Press.

Allport, G. W. 1954. *The nature of prejudice*. Cambridge, Mass.: Addison-Wesley.

Allport, G. W., and P. Vernon. 1933. *Studies in expressive behavior*. New York: Macmillan.

Amabile, T. M. 1975. Investigations in the psychology of prediction. Unpublished manuscript, Stanford University.

Amabile, T. M., W. De Jong, and M. R. Lepper. 1976. Effects of externally imposed deadlines on subsequent intrinsic motivation. *Journal of Personality and Social Psychology* 34: 92-98.

Anderson, N. H. 1965. Adding versus averaging as a stimulus combination rule in impression formation. *Journal of Experimental Psychology* 70: 394-400.

————. 1966. Component ratings in impression formation. *Psychonomic Science* 6: 279-80.

————. 1971. Two more tests against change of meaning in adjective combinations. *Journal of Verbal Learning and Verbal Behavior* 10: 75-85.

————. 1972. Looking for configurality in clinical judgment. *Psychological Bulletin* 78: 93-102.

————. 1974a. The problem of change of meaning. CHIP Report No. 42: Center for Human Information Processing, University of California, San Diego.

272

————. 1974b. Cognitive algebra: Integration theory applied to social attribution. In L. Berkowitz (ed.), *Advances in experimental social psychology* (Vol. 7). New York: Academic Press.

————. 1977. Some problems in using analyses of variance in balance theory. *Journal of Personality and Social Psychology* 35: 140-58.

Anderson, N. H., and C. A. Butzin. 1974. Performance = motivation × ability: An integration-theoretical analysis. *Journal of Personality and Social Psychology* 30: 598-604.

Anderson, N. H., and S. Hubert. 1963. Effects of concomitant verbal recall on order effects in personality impression formation. *Journal of Verbal Learning and Verbal Behavior* 2: 379-91.

Anderson, N. H., and A. Jacobson. 1965. Effect of stimulus inconsistency and discounting instructions in personality impression formation. *Journal of Personality and Social Psychology* 2: 531-39.

Anderson, N. H., and A. K. Lampel. 1965. Effect of context on ratings of personality traits. *Psychonomic Science* 3: 433-34.

Anderson, R., S. T. Manoogian, and J. S. Reznick. 1976. The undermining and enhancing of intrinsic motivation in preschool children. *Journal of Personality and Social Psychology* 34: 915-22.

Archer, D., and R. M. Akert. 1977. Words and everything else: Verbal and nonverbal cues in social interpretation. *Journal of Personality and Social Psychology* 35: 443-49.

Argyle, M., F. Alkema, and R. Gilmour. 1971. The communication of friendly and hostile attitudes by verbal and nonverbal signals. Unpublished manuscript, Institute of Experimental Psychology, Oxford University.

Argyle, M., and M. Cook. 1976. *Gaze and mutual gaze.* Cambridge: Cambridge University Press.

Argyle, M., and J. Dean. 1965. Eye contact, distance, and affiliation. *Sociometry* 28: 289-304.

Argyle, M., and R. Ingham. 1972. Gaze, mutual gaze, and proximity. *Semiotica* 6: 32-49.

Argyle, M., and A. Kendon. 1967. The experimental analysis of social performance. In L. Berkowitz (ed.), *Advances in experimental social psychology* (Vol. 3). New York: Academic Press, pp. 55-98.

Argyle, M., L. Lefebvre, and M. Cook. 1974. The meaning of five patterns of gaze. *European Journal of Social Psychology* 4: 125-36.

Argyle, M., V. Salter, H. Nicholson, M. Williams, and P. Burgess. 1970. The communication of inferior and superior attitudes by verbal and nonverbal signals. *British Journal of Social and Clinical Psychology* 9: 222-31.

Argyle, M., and M. Williams. 1969. Observer or observed? A reversible perspective in person perception. *Sociometry* 32: 396-412.

Arkin, R. M., and S. Duval. 1975. Focus of attention and causal attributions of actors and observers. *Journal of Experimental Social Psychology* 11: 427-38.

Armsby, R. E. 1971. A re-examination of the development of moral judgments in children. *Child Development* 42: 1241-48.

Aronson, E., and J. M. Carlsmith. 1963. Effect of the severity of threat on the devaluation of forbidden behavior. *Journal of Abnormal and Social Psychology* 66: 584-88.

Asch, S. E. 1946. Forming impressions of personality. *Journal of Abnormal and Social Psychology* 41: 258-90.

Austin, J. L. 1956-7. A plea for excuses. *Proceedings of the Aristotelian Society* 57: 1-30.

Ax, A. F. 1953. The physiological differentiation between fear and anger in humans. *Psychosomatic Medicine* 15: 433-42.

Baldwin, C. P., and A. L. Baldwin. 1970. Children's judgments of kindness. *Child Development* 41: 29-47.

Bandler, R. J., Jr., G. R. Madaras, and D. J. Bem. 1968. Self-observation as a source of pain perception. *Journal of Personality and Social Psychology* 9: 205-9.

Bannister, D., and F. Fransella. 1971. *Inquiring man.* Harmondsworth, Middlesex: Penguin.

Bannister, D., and J. M. M. Mair. 1968. *The evaluation of personal constructs.* London: Academic Press.

Barefoot, J. C., and R. B. Straub. 1971. Opportunity for information search and the effect of false heart-rate feedback. *Journal of Personality and Social Psychology* 17: 154-57.

Barker, R. G., and H. F. Wright. 1955. *Midwest and its children.* New York: Harper & Row.

Bateson, G., D. D. Jackson, J. Haley, and J. Weakland. 1956. Toward a theory of schizophrenia. *Behavioral Science* 1: 251-64.

Batson, C. D. 1975. Attribution as a mediator of bias in helping. *Journal of Personality and Social Psychology* 32: 455-66.

Bavelas, A., A. H. Hastorf, A. E. Gross, and W. R. Kite. 1965. Experiments on the alteration of group structure. *Journal of Experimental Social Psychology* 1: 55-70.

Bear, G., G. Cairns, and L. S. Goodman. In press. The stare as a stimulus to social interaction between strangers. *Journal of Experimental Social Psychology.*

Beck, S. B., C. I. Ward-Hull, and P. M. McLear. 1976. Variables related to women's somatic preferences of the male and female body. *Journal of Personality and Social Psychology* 34: 1200-1210.

Becker, H. 1963. *Outsiders: Studies in the sociology of deviance.* New York: Free Press.

Beckman, L. 1970. Effects of students' performance on teachers' and observers' attributions of causality. *Journal of Educational Psychology* 61: 76-82.

————. 1973. Teachers' and observers' perceptions of causality for a child's performance. *Journal of Educational Psychology* 65: 198-204.

Bem, D. J. 1965. An experimental analysis of self-persuasion. *Journal of Experimental Social Psychology* 1: 199-218.

————. 1967. Self-perception: An alternative interpretation of cognitive dissonance phenomena. *Psychological Review* 74: 183-200.

————. 1972. Self-perception theory. In L. Berkowitz (ed.), *Advances in experimental social psychology* (Vol. 6). New York: Academic Press.

Bem, D. J., and A. Allen. 1974. On predicting some of the people some of the time: The search for cross-situational consistencies in behavior. *Psychological Review* 81: 506-20.

Bender, I. E., and A. H. Hastorf. 1953. On measuring generalized empathic ability (social sensitivity). *Journal of Abnormal and Social Psychology* 48: 503-6.

Benedetti, D. T., and J. G. Hill. 1960. A determiner of the centrality of a trait in impression formation. *Journal of Abnormal and Social Psychology* 60: 278-79.

Berglas, S., and E. E. Jones. 1978. Drug choice as a self-handicapping strategy in response to noncontingent success. *Journal of Personality and Social Psychology* 36: 405-17.

Berman, J. S., and D. A. Kenny. 1976. Correlational bias in observer ratings. *Journal of Personality and Social Psychology* 34: 263-73.

———. 1977. Correlational bias: Not gone and not to be forgotten. *Journal of Personality and Social Psychology* 35: 882-87.

Berscheid, E., W. Graziano, T. Monson, and M. Dermer. 1976. Outcome dependency: Attention, attribution, and attraction. *Journal of Personality and Social Psychology* 34: 978-89.

Berscheid, E., and E. H. Walster. 1978. *Interpersonal attraction* (2nd ed.). Reading, Mass.: Addison-Wesley.

Birdwhistell, R. L. 1970. *Kinesics and context.* Philadelphia: University of Pennsylvania Press.

Birnbaum, M. H. 1973. The devil rides again: Correlation as an index of fit. *Psychological Bulletin* 79: 239-42.

Block, J. 1977. Correlational bias in observer ratings: Another perspective on the Berman and Kenny study. *Journal of Personality and Social Psychology* 35: 873-80.

Block, J., D. S. Weiss, and A. Thorne. 1978. How relevant is a semantic similarity interpretation of personality ratings? Unpublished paper, University of California at Berkeley.

Bond, M. H. 1972. Effects of impression set on subsequent behavior. *Journal of Personality and Social Psychology* 24: 301-5.

Borgida, E. 1978. Scientific deduction-evidence is not necessarily informative: A reply to Wells and Harvey. *Journal of Personality and Social Psychology* 36: 477-82.

Bourne, E. 1977. Can we describe an individual's personality? Agreement on stereotype versus individual attributes. *Journal of Personality and Social Psychology* 35: 863-72.

Bradley, G. W. 1978. Self-serving biases in the attribution process: A reexamination of the fact or fiction question. *Journal of Personality and Social Psychology* 36: 56-71.

Bradshaw, J. L. 1969. The information conveyed by varying the dimensions of features in human outline faces. *Perception and Psychophysics* 6: 5-9.

Bramel, D. A. 1962. A dissonance theory approach to defensive projection. *Journal of Abnormal and Social Psychology* 69: 121-29.

———. 1963. Selection of a target for defensive projection. *Journal of Abnormal and Social Psychology* 66: 318-24.

Bramel, D., J. E. Bell, and S. T. Margulis. 1965. Attributing danger as a means of explaining one's own fear. *Journal of Experimental Social Psychology* 1: 267-81.

Brandt, L. W., and E. P. Brandt. 1972. Second-hand personication: A new model for "person perception" research. *The Canadian Psychologist* 13: 217-38.

Brewer, M. B. 1977. An information-processing approach to attribution of responsibility. *Journal of Experimental Social Psychology* 13: 58-69.

Brickman, P., K. Ryan, and C. B. Wortman. 1975. Causal chains: Attribution responsibility as a function of immediate and prior causes. *Journal of Personality and Social Psychology* 32: 1060-67.

Brigham, J. C. 1971. Ethnic stereotypes. *Psychological Bulletin* 76: 15-38.

Broverman, I. K., D. M. Broverman, F. E. Clarkson, P. S. Rosenkrantz, and S. R. Vogel. 1970. Sex-role stereotypes and clinical judgments of mental health. *Journal of Consulting and Clinical Psychology* 34: 1-7.

Brown, D., G. Klemp, and H. Leventhal. 1975. Are evaluations inferred directly from overt actions? *Journal of Experimental Social Psychology* 11: 112-26.

Brown, R. 1976. In memorial tribute to Eric Lenneberg. *Cognition* 4: 125-53.

Brown, R., and R. J. Herrnstein. 1975. *Psychology.* Boston: Little, Brown.

Bruner, J. S., and R. Tagiuri. 1954. Person perception. In G. Lindzey (ed.), *Handbook of social psychology* (Vol. 2). Reading, Mass.: Addison-Wesley.

Brunswik, E. 1956. *Perception and the representative design of psychological experiments* (2nd ed.). Berkeley and Los Angeles: University of California Press.

Buchanan, J. P., and S. K. Thompson. 1973. A quantitative methodology to examine the development of moral judgment. *Child Development* 44: 186-89.

Buck, R., R. E. Miller, and W. F. Caul. 1974. Sex, personality, and physiological variables in the communication of affect via facial expression. *Journal of Personality and Social Psychology* 30: 587-96.

Buck, R. S., V. J. Savin, R. E. Miller, and W. F. Caul. 1972. Communication of affect through facial expression in humans. *Journal of Personality and Social Psychology* 23: 362-71.

Buckhout, R. 1976. Guilt by fabrication: Psychology and the eyewitness. In M. H. Siegel and H. P. Zeigler (eds.), *Psychological research: The inside story*. New York: Harper & Row.

Bugental, D. E., J. W. Kaswan, and L. R. Love. 1970. Perception of contradictory meanings conveyed by verbal and nonverbal channels. *Journal of Personality and Social Psychology* 16: 647-55.

Bugental, D. E., and L. R. Love. 1975. Nonassertive expression of parental approval and disapproval and its relationship to child disturbance. *Child Development* 46: 747-52.

Bugental, D. E., L. R. Love, and J. W. Kaswan. 1972. Videotaped family interaction: Differences reflecting presence and type of child disturbance. *Journal of Abnormal Psychology* 79: 347-60.

Bugental, D. E., L. R. Love, J. W. Kaswan, and C. April. 1971. Verbal-nonverbal conflict in parental messages to normal and disturbed children. *Journal of Abnormal Psychology* 77: 6-10.

Bulman, R. J., and C. B. Wortman. 1977. Attributions of blame and coping in the "real world": Severe accident victims react to their lot. *Journal of Personality and Social Psychology* 32: 351-63.

Buzby, D. E. 1924. The interpretation of facial expression. *American Journal of Psychology* 35: 602-4.

Calder, B. J. 1977a. Endogenous-exogenous versus internal-external attributions: Implications for the development of attribution theory. *Personality and Social Psychology Bulletin* 3: 400-406.

———. 1977b. Attribution theory: Phenomenology or science. *Personality and Social Psychology Bulletin* 3: 612-15.

Calder, B. J., and B. M. Staw. 1975. Interaction of intrinsic and extrinsic motivation: Some methodological notes. *Journal of Personality and Social Psychology* 31: 76-80.

Calvert-Boyanowsky, J., and H. Leventhal. 1975. The role of information in attenuating behavioral responses to stress: A reinterpretation of the misattribution phenomenon. *Journal of Personality and Social Psychology* 32: 214-21.

Cantor, J. R., D. Zillmann, and J. Bryant. 1975. Enhancement of experienced sexual arousal in response to erotic stimuli through misattribution of unrelated residual excitation. *Journal of Personality and Social Psychology* 32: 69-75.

Cantor, N. 1977. Prototypicality and personality. Unpublished manuscript, Stanford University.

Cantor, N., and W. Mischel. 1977a. Traits as prototypes: Effects on recognition memory. *Journal of Personality and Social Psychology* 35: 38-48.

————. 1977b. From personality impression to social inference: The role of pre-existing knowledge in structuring information processing. Unpublished manuscript, Stanford University.

Carroll, J. S. 1978. The effect of imagining an event on expectations for the event: An interpretation in terms of the availability heuristic. *Journal of Experimental Social Psychology* 14: 88-96.

Chaikin, A. L., and J. M. Darley. 1973. Victim or perpetrator?: Defensive attribution of responsibility and the need for order and justice. *Journal of Personality and Social Psychology* 25: 268-75.

Chandler, M. J., S. Greenspan, and C. Barenboim. 1973. Videotaped and verbally presented moral dilemmas: The medium is the message. *Child Development* 44: 315-20.

Chapman, L. J. 1967. Illusory correlation in observational report. *Journal of Verbal Learning and Verbal Behavior* 6: 151-55.

Chapman, L. J., and J. P. Chapman. 1967. Genesis of popular but erroneous psychodiagnostic observation. *Journal of Abnormal Psychology* 72: 193-204.

————. 1969. Illusory correlation as an obstacle to the use of valid psychodiagnostic signs. *Journal of Abnormal Psychology* 74: 271-80.

Cline, M. G. 1956. The influence of social context on the perception of faces. *Journal of Personality* 2: 142-58.

Cline, V. B. 1964. Interpersonal perception. In B. A. Maher (ed.), *Progress in experimental personality research* (Vol. 1). New York: Academic Press.

Cline, V. B., and J. M. Richards, Jr. 1960. Accuracy of interpersonal perception—a general trait? *Journal of Abnormal and Social Psychology* 60: 1-7.

Clore, G. L., N. H. Wiggins, and S. Itkin. 1975. Gain and loss in attraction: Attributions from nonverbal behavior. *Journal of Personality and Social Psychology* 31: 706-12.

Cohen, A. R. 1961. Cognitive tuning as a factor affecting impression formation. *Journal of Personality* 29: 235-45.

Cohen, S., M. Rothbart, and S. Phillips. 1976. Locus of control and the generality of learned helplessness in humans. *Journal of Personality and Social Psychology* 34: 1049-56.

Condry, J. 1977. Enemies of exploration: Self-initiated versus other-initiated learning. *Journal of Personality and Social Psychology* 35: 459-77.

Cook, M., and J. M. C. Smith. 1975. The role of gaze in impression formation. *British Journal of Social and Clinical Psychology* 14: 19-25.

Corah, N. L., and J. Boffa. 1970. Perceived control, self-observation and response to aversive stimulation. *Journal of Personality and Social Psychology* 16: 1-4.

Cordray, D. S., and J. I. Shaw. 1978. An empirical test of the covariation analysis on causal attribution. *Journal of Experimental Social Psychology* 14: 280-90.

Costanzo, P. R., J. D. Coie, J. F. Grumet, and D. Farnell. 1973. A re-examination of the effects of intent and consequence on children's moral judgment. *Child Development* 44: 154-61.

Crockett, W. H. 1965. Cognitive complexity and impression formation. In B. A. Maher (ed.), *Progress in experimental personality research* (Vol. 2). New York: Academic Press.

————. 1977. Impressions and attributions: Nature, organization, and implications for action. Paper presented in a symposium, "New directions in the analysis of impression formation," American Psychological Association Convention.

Crockett, W. H., S. Mahood, and A. N. Press. 1975. Impressions of a speaker as a function of set to understand or to evaluate, of cognitive complexity, and of prior attitudes. *Journal of Personality* 43: 168-78.

Cronbach, L. J. 1955. Processes affecting scores on "understanding of others" and "assumed similarity." *Psychological Bulletin* 52: 177-93.

Crow, W. J., and K. R. Hammond. 1957. The generality of accuracy and response in interpersonal perception. *Journal of Abnormal and Social Psychology* 54: 384-90.

D'Andrade, R. G. 1965. Trait psychology and componential analysis. *American Anthropologist* 67: 215-28.

———. 1974. Memory and the assessment of behavior. In H. Blalock (ed.), *Measurement in the social sciences.* Chicago: Aldine-Atherton.

Danto, A. C. 1965. Basic actions. *American Philosophical Quarterly* 2: 141-48.

Darwin, C. 1896. *The expression of the emotions in man and animals.* New York: D. Appleton and Company. (First published 1872.)

Davidson, A. R., and I. D. Steiner. 1971. Reinforcement schedule and attributed freedom. *Journal of Personality and Social Psychology* 19: 357-66.

Davidson, D. 1963. Actions, reasons and causes. *Journal of Philosophy* 60: 685-700.

Davison, G. C., and S. Valins. 1969. Maintenance of self-attributed and drug-attributed behavior change. *Journal of Personality and Social Psychology* 11: 25-33.

Davitz, J. R., and L. J. Davitz. 1959. The communication of feelings by content-free speech. *Journal of Communication* 9: 6-13.

Dawes, R. M. 1971. A case study of graduate admissions: Application of three principles of human decision making. *American Psychologist* 26: 180-88.

———. 1976. Shallow psychology. In J. S. Carroll and J. W. Payne (eds.), *Cognition and social behavior.* Hillsdale, N.J.: Lawrence Erlbaum.

Deaux, K. 1976a. Sex: A perspective on the attribution process. In J. H. Harvey, W. J. Ickes, and R. F. Kidd (eds.), *New directions in attribution research* (Vol. 1). Hillsdale, N.J.: Lawrence Erlbaum.

———. 1976b. *The behavior of men and women.* Monterey, Calif.: Brooks/Cole.

Deaux, K., and T. Emswiller. 1974. Explanation of successful performance on sex-linked tasks: What is skill for the male is luck for the female. *Journal of Personality and Social Psychology* 29: 80-85.

DeBoeck, P. 1978. On the evaluative factor in the trait scale of Peabody's study of trait inferences. *Journal of Personality and Social Psychology* 36: 619-21.

deCharms, R. 1968. *Personal causation.* New York: Academic Press.

Deci, E. L. 1971. Effects of externally mediated rewards on intrinsic motivation. *Journal of Personality and Social Psychology* 18: 105-15.

———. 1972. Intrinsic motivation, extrinsic motivation and inequity. *Journal of Personality and Social Psychology* 22: 113-20.

———. 1975. *Intrinsic motivation.* New York: Plenum Press.

Deci, E. L., W. F. Cascio, and J. Krussell. 1975. Cognitive evaluation theory and some comments on the Calder and Shaw critique. *Journal of Personality and Social Psychology* 31: 81-85.

De Jong, W. 1977. The stigma of obesity: The consequences of naive assumptions concerning the causes of physical deviance. Unpublished doctoral dissertation, Stanford University.

Dewhirst, J. R., and J. S. Berman. 1978. Social judgments of spurious and causal relations between attributes and outcomes. *Journal of Experimental Social Psychology* 14: 313-25.

Dibiase, W., and L. Hjelle. 1968. Body-image stereotypes and body-type preferences among male college students. *Perceptual and Motor Skills* 27: 1143-46.

Dickman, H. R. 1963. The perception of behavioral units. In R. G. Barker (ed.), *The stream of behavior*. New York: Appleton-Century-Crofts.

Dienstbier, R. A. 1972. The role of anxiety and arousal attribution in cheating. *Journal of Experimental Social Psychology* 8: 168-79.

Dienstbier, R. A., D. Hillman, J. Lehnhoff, J. Hillman, and M. C. Valkenaar. 1975. An emotion-attribution approach to moral behavior: Interfacing cognitive and avoidance theories of moral development. *Psychological Review* 82: 299-315.

Dienstbier, R. A., and P. O. Munter. 1971. Cheating as a function of the labeling of natural arousal. *Journal of Personality and Social Psychology* 17: 208-13.

Dion, K. K., E. Berscheid, and E. Walster. 1972. What is beautiful is good. *Journal of Personality and Social Psychology* 24: 285 90.

Dittman, A. T., M. B. Parloff, and D. S. Boomer. 1965. Facial and bodily expression: A study of receptivity of emotional cues. *Psychiatry* 28: 239-44.

DiVitto, B., and L. Z. McArthur. 1978. Developmental differences in the use of distinctiveness, consensus, and consistency information for making causal attributions. *Developmental Psychology* 14: 474-82.

Dornbusch, S. M., A. H. Hastorf, S. A. Richardson, R. E. Muzzy, and R. S. Vreeland. 1965. The perceiver and perceived: Their relative influence on categories of interpersonal perception. *Journal of Personality and Social Psychology* 1: 434-40.

Duchenne, G. B. 1862. *Mecanisme de la physionomie humaine* Paris: Balliere.

Duffy, E. 1962. *Activation and behavior*. New York: Wiley.

Duncan, B. L. 1976. Differential social perception and attribution of inter-group violence: Testing the lower limits of stereotyping of blacks. *Journal of Personality and Social Psychology* 34: 590 98.

Duncan, S. D., and D. W. Fiske. *Face-to-face interaction: Research, methods, and theory*. Hillsdale, N.J.: Lawrence Erlbaum.

Duncan, S. D., and G. Niederehe. 1974. On signalling that it's your turn to speak. *Journal of Experimental Social Psychology* 10: 234-47.

Duval, S., and R. A. Wicklund. 1972. *A theory of objective self-awareness*. New York: Academic Press.

―――. 1973. Effects of objective self-awareness on attribution of causality. *Journal of Experimental Social Psychology* 9: 17-31.

Dweck, C. S. 1975. The role of expectations and attributions in the alleviation of learned helplessness. *Journal of Personality and Social Psychology* 31: 674-85.

Dymond, R. F. 1949. A scale for the measurement of emphathic ability. *Journal of Consulting Psychology* 13: 127-33.

―――. 1950. Personality and empathy. *Journal of Consulting Psychology* 14: 343-50.

Ebbesen, E. B., C. E. Cohen, and J. L. Lane. 1975. Encoding and construction processes in person perception. Paper presented at the American Psychological Association Convention.

Ebbesen, E. B., and V. J. Konečni. 1975. Decision making and information integration in the courts: The setting of bail. *Journal of Personality and Social Psychology* 32: 805-21.

Edlow, D. W., and C. A. Kiesler. 1966. Ease of denial and defensive projection. *Journal of Experimental Social Psychology* 2: 56-69.

Efron, D. 1941. *Gesture and environment.* New York: King's Crown.

Einhorn, H. J. 1970. The use of nonlinear, noncompensatory models in decision making. *Psychological Bulletin* 73: 221-30.

Eisen, S. V. 1977. Actor-observer differences in information inference and causal attribution. Unpublished manuscript, Brandeis University.

Eisen, S. V., and L. Z. McArthur. 1978. Evaluation and sentencing of a defendant as a function of the defendant's salience and the observer's set. Unpublished manuscript, Brandeis University.

Eisinger, R., and J. Mills. 1968. Perception of the sincerity and competence of a communicator as a function of the extremity of his position. *Journal of Experimental Social Psychology* 4: 224-32.

Ekman, P. 1972. Universals and cultural differences in facial expressions of emotion. In J. Cole (ed.), *Nebraska symposium on motivation.* Lincoln: University of Nebraska Press.

———. 1976. Movements with precise meanings. *Journal of Communication* 26: 14-26.

Ekman, P., and W. V. Friesen. 1969a. Nonverbal leakage and cues to deception. *Psychiatry* 32: 88-105.

———. 1969b. The repertoire of nonverbal behavior: Categories, origins, usage, and coding. *Semiotica* 1: 49-98.

———. 1971. Constants across cultures in the face and emotion. *Journal of Personality and Social Psychology* 17: 124-29.

———. 1974. Detecting deception from body or face. *Journal of Personality and Social Psychology* 29: 288-98.

Ekman, P., W. V. Friesen, and P. Ellsworth. 1972. *Emotion in the human face.* New York: Pergamon Press.

Ekman, P., W. V. Friesen, and K. R. Scherer. 1976. Body movement and voice pitch in deceptive interaction. *Semiotica* 16: 23-27.

Ekman, P., E. R. Sorenson, and W. V. Friesen. 1969. Pan-cultural elements in facial displays of emotions. *Science* 164 (3875): 86-88.

Ellsworth, P. C. 1975. Direct gaze as a social stimulus: The example of aggression. In P. Pliner, T. Alloway, and L. Krames (eds.), *Nonverbal communication of aggression.* New York: Plenum Press, pp. 53-75.

———. In press. The meaningful look. *Semiotica.*

Ellsworth, P. C., and J. M. Carlsmith. 1968. Effects of eye contact and verbal content on affective response to a dyadic interaction. *Journal of Personality and Social Psychology* 10: 15-20.

———. 1973. Eye contact and gaze aversion in an aggressive encounter. *Journal of Personality and Social Psychology* 28: 280-92.

Ellsworth, P. C., J. M. Carlsmith, and A. Henson. 1972. The stare as a stimulus to flight in human subjects: A series of field experiments. *Journal of Personality and Social Psychology* 21: 302-11.

Ellsworth, P. C., H. Friedman, D. Perlick, and M. F. Hoyt. 1978. Some effects of gaze on subjects motivated to seek or to avoid social comparison. *Journal of Experimental Social Psychology* 14: 69-87.

Ellsworth, P. C., and E. J. Langer. 1976. Staring and approach: An interpretation of the stare as a nonspecific activator. *Journal of Personality and Social Psychology* 33: 117-22.

Ellsworth, P. C., and L. M. Ludwig. 1972. Visual behavior in social interaction. *Journal of Communication* 22: 375-403.

Ellsworth, P. C., and L. Ross. 1976. Intimacy in response to direct gaze. *Journal of Experimental Social Psychology* 11: 592-613.

Enzle, M. E., R. D. Hansen, and C. A. Lowe. 1975. Causal attribution in the mixed-motive game: Effects of facilitory and inhibitory environmental forces. *Journal of Personality and Social Psychology* 31: 50-54.

Estes, S. G. 1938. Judging personality from expressive behavior. *Journal of Abnormal and Social Psychology* 33: 217-36.

Evans, G. W., and R. B. Howard. 1973. Personal space. *Psychological Bulletin* 80: 334-44.

Exline, R. V. 1972. Visual interaction: The glances of power and preference. In J. Cole (ed.), *Nebraska symposium on motivation*. Lincoln: University of Nebraska Press.

Fast, J. 1970. *Body language*. New York: M. Evans.

Feather, N. T. 1969. Attribution of responsibility and valence of success and failure in relation to initial confidence and task performance. *Journal of Personality and Social Psychology* 13: 129-44.

————. 1975. Positive and negative reactions to male and female success and failure in relation to the perceived status and sex-typed appropriateness of occupation. *Journal of Personality and Social Psychology* 31: 536-48.

Feather, N. T., and J. G. Simon. 1971a. Attribution of responsibility and valence of outcome in relation to initial confidence and success and failure of self and other. *Journal of Personality and Social Psychology* 18: 173-88.

————. 1971b. Causal attributions for success and failure in relation to expectation of success based upon selective or manipulative control. *Journal of Personality* 39: 527-41.

————. 1975. Reactions to male and female success and failure in sex-linked occupations: Impressions of personality, causal attributions, and perceived likelihood of different consequences. *Journal of Personality and Social Psychology* 31: 20-31.

Feild, H. S. 1978. Attitudes toward rape: A comparative analysis of police, rapists, crisis counselors, and citizens. *Journal of Personality and Social Psychology* 36: 156-79.

Feinberg, J. 1965. Action and responsibility. In M. Black (ed.), *Philosophy in America*. London: Allen and Unwin.

Feleky, A. M. 1914. The expression of the emotions. *Psychological Review* 21: 33-41.

Feldman-Summers, S., and S. B. Kiesler. 1974. Those who are number two try harder: The effect of sex on attribution of causality. *Journal of Personality and Social Psychology* 30: 846-55.

Felipe, A. I. 1970. Evaluative versus descriptive consistency in trait inferences. *Journal of Personality and Social Psychology* 16: 627-38.

Fernberger, S. W. 1928. False suggestion and the Piderit model. *American Journal of Psychology* 40: 562-68.

Festinger, L. 1957. *A theory of cognitive dissonances*. Evanston, Ill.: Row, Peterson.

Festinger, L., and J. M. Carlsmith. 1959. Cognitive consequences of forced compliance. *Journal of Abnormal and Social Psychology* 58: 203-11.

Fiedler, F. W. 1964. A contingency model of leadership effectiveness. In L. Berkowitz (ed.), *Advances in experimental social psychology* (Vol. 1). New York: Academic Press.

Fink, K., and H. Cantril. 1937. The collegiate stereotype as frame of reference. *Journal of Abnormal and Social Psychology* 32: 352-56.

Fischhoff, B. 1975. Hindsight $\neq$ foresight: The effects of outcome knowledge on judgment under uncertainty. *Journal of Experimental Psychology: Human Perception and Performance* 1: 288-99.

———. 1976. Attribution theory and judgment under uncertainty. In J. H. Harvey, W. J. Ickes, and R. F. Kidd (eds.), *New directions in attribution research* (Vol. 1). Hillsdale, N.J.: Lawrence Erlbaum.

Fishbein, M., and I. Ajzen. 1973. Attribution of responsibility: A theoretical note. *Journal of Experimental Social Psychology* 9: 148-53.

Fiske, S. T., and M. F. Cox. 1977. Describing others: Person impressions as person concepts. Unpublished manuscript, Harvard University.

Fitch, G. 1970. Effects of self-esteem, perceived performance, and choice on causal attributions. *Journal of Personality and Social Psychology* 16: 311-15.

Fontaine, G. 1975. Causal attribution in simulated versus real situations: When are people logical, when are they not? *Journal of Personality and Social Psychology* 32: 1021-29.

Forgas, J. P. 1978. Social episodes and social structure in an academic setting: The social environment of an intact group. *Journal of Experimental Social Psychology* 14: 434-48.

Forster, E. M. 1951. "Not looking at pictures" (1939). In *Two cheers for democracy*. London: Edward Arnold.

Frederiksen, N. 1972. Toward a taxonomy of situations. *American Psychologist* 27: 114-23.

Freedman, J., and S. Fraser. 1966. Compliance without pressure: The foot in the door technique. *Journal of Personality and Social Psychology* 4: 195-202.

Freud, S. 1959. Fragment of an analysis of a case of hysteria (1905). *Collected papers* (Vol. 3). New York: Basic Books.

Friendly, M. L., and S. Glucksberg. 1970. On the description of subcultural lexions: A multidimensional approach. *Journal of Personality and Social Psychology* 14: 55-65.

Frieze, I. H. 1976. The role of information processing in making causal attributions for success and failure. In J. S. Carroll and J. W. Payne (eds.), *Cognition and social behavior*. Hillsdale, N.J.: Lawrence Erlbaum.

Frieze, I., and B. Weiner. 1971. Cue utilization and attributional judgments for success and failure. *Journal of Personality* 39: 591-605.

Frijda, N. H. 1958. Facial expression and situational cues. *Journal of Abnormal and Social Psychology* 57: 149-54.

———. 1969. Recognition of emotion. In L. Berkowitz (ed.), *Advances in experimental social psychology* (Vol. 4). New York: Academic Press.

From, F. 1971. *Perception of other people*. New York: Columbia University Press.

Funkenstein, D. H. 1955. The physiology of fear and anger. *Scientific American* 192: 14.

Gale, A., B. Lucas, R. Nissim, and B. Harpham. 1972. Some EEG correlates of face-to-face contact. *British Journal of Social and Clinical Psychology* 11: 326-32.

Garland, H., A. Hardy, and L. Stephenson. 1975. Information search as affected by attribution type and response category. *Personality and Social Psychology Bulletin* 1: 612-15.

Gergen, K. J., and E. E. Jones. 1963. Mental illness, predictability, and affective consequences as stimulus factors in person perception. *Journal of Abnormal and Social Psychology* 67: 95-105.

Gibbins, K. 1969. Communication aspects of women's clothes and their relation to fashionability. *British Journal of Social and Clinical Psychology* 8: 301-12.

Gifford, R. K. 1975. Information properties of descriptive words. *Journal of Personality and Social Psychology* 31: 727-34.

Gilmor, T. M., and H. L. Minton. 1974. Internal versus external attribution of task performance as a function of locus of control, initial confidence and success-failure outcome. *Journal of Personality* 42: 159-74.

Gilson, C., and R. Abelson. 1965. The subjective use of inductive evidence. *Journal of Personality and Social Psychology* 2: 301-11.

Girodo, M. 1973. Film-induced arousal, information search, and the attribution process. *Journal of Personality and Social Psychology* 25: 357-60.

Goethals, G. R. 1972. Consensus and modality in the attribution process: The role of similarity and information. *Journal of Personality and Social Psychology* 21: 84-92.

Goffman, E. 1955. On face work: An analysis of ritual elements in social interaction. *Psychiatry* 18: 213-31.

———. 1959. *The presentation of self in everyday life*. Garden City, N.Y.: Doubleday, Anchor Books.

———. 1961. *Asylums*. Chicago: Aldine.

———. 1963. *Behavior in public places*. Glencoe, Ill.: Free Press.

———. 1976. Gender advertisements. *Studies in the Anthropology of Visual Communication* 3: 69-154.

Goldberg, G. N., C. A. Kiesler, and B. E. Collins. 1969. Visual behavior and face-to-face distance during interaction. *Sociometry* 32: 43-53.

Goldberg, H. D. 1951. The role of "cutting" in the perception of motion pictures. *Journal of Applied Psychology* 35: 70-71.

Goldberg, L. R. 1968. Simple models or simple processes? Some research on clinical judgments. *American Psychologist* 23: 483-96.

———. 1978. Differential attribution of trait-descriptive terms to oneself as compared to well-liked, neutral, and disliked others: A psychometric analysis. *Journal of Personality and Social Psychology* 36: 1012-28.

Goldin, J. 1975. Type of anticipated interaction and the effects of physical attractiveness and attitude similarity on interpersonal attraction. Unpublished manuscript, Yale University.

Gollob, H. F. 1974. The subject-verb-object approach to social cognition. *Psychological Review* 81: 286-321.

Gouldner, A. W. 1960. The norm of reciprocity: A preliminary statement. *American Sociological Review* 25: 161-78.

Greene, D., B. Sternberg, and M. R. Lepper. 1976. Overjustification in a token economy. *Journal of Personality and Social Psychology* 34: 1219-34.

Greenwald, A. G. 1975. On the inconclusiveness of "crucial" cognitive tests of dissonance versus self-perception theories. *Journal of Experimental Social Psychology* 11: 490-99.

Gross, E. 1967. The sexual structure of occupations over time. Paper presented at meetings of the American Sociological Association, San Francisco.

Gurwitz, S. B., and K. A. Dodge. 1977. Effects of confirmations and disconfirmations on stereotype-based attributions. *Journal of Personality and Social Psychology* 35: 495-500.

Gurwitz, S. B., and L. Panciera. 1975. Attributions of freedom by actors and observers. *Journal of Personality and Social Psychology* 32: 531-39.

Gurwitz, S. B., and B. Topol. 1978. Determinants of confirming and disconfirming responses to negative social labels. *Journal of Experimental Social Psychology* 14: 31-42.

Haggard, E. A., and K. S. Isaacs. 1966. Micro-momentary facial expressions as indicators of ego mechanisms in psychotherapy. In L. A. Gottschalk and A. H. Auerbach (eds.), *Methods of research in psychotherapy.* New York: Appleton-Century-Crofts.

Hall, E. T. 1966. *The hidden dimension.* Garden City, N.Y.: Doubleday.

Hamid, P. N. 1968. Style of dress as a perceptual cue in impression formation. *Perceptual and Motor Skills* 26: 904-6.

Hamilton, D. L. 1970. The structure of personality judgments: Comments on Kuusinen's paper and further evidence. *Scandinavian Journal of Psychology* 11: 261-65.

————. 1977. Illusory correlation as a basis for social stereotypes. Paper presented at a symposium, "Cognitive biases in stereotyping," American Psychological Association Convention.

Hamilton, D. L., and R. D. Fallot. 1974. Information salience as a weighting factor in impression formation. *Journal of Personality and Social Psychology* 30: 444-48.

Hamilton, D. L., and R. K. Gifford. 1976. Illusory correlation in interpersonal perception: A cognitive basis of stereotype judgments. *Journal of Experimental Social Psychology* 12: 392-407.

Hamilton, D. L., and L. J. Huffman. 1971. Generality of impression formation processes for evaluative and nonevaluative judgments. *Journal of Personality and Social Psychology* 20: 200-207.

Hamilton, D. L., and M. P. Zanna. 1974. Context effects in impression formation: Changes in connotative meaning. *Journal of Personality and Social Psychology* 29: 649-54.

Hamilton, V. L. 1978. Obedience and responsibility: A jury simulation. *Journal of Personality and Social Psychology* 36: 126-46.

Hanno, M. S., and L. E. Jones. 1973. Effects of a change in reference person on the multidimensional structure and evaluation of trait adjectives. *Journal of Personality and Social Psychology* 28: 368-75.

Hansen, R. D., and J. M. Donoghue. 1977. The power of consensus: Information derived from one's own and others' behavior. *Journal of Personality and Social Psychology* 35: 294-302.

Hansen, R. D., and C. A. Lowe. 1976. Distinctiveness and consensus: The influence of behavioral information on actors' and observers' attributions. *Journal of Personality and Social Psychology* 34: 425-33.

Hansen, R. D., and D. M. Stonner. 1978. Attributes and attributions: Inferring stimulus properties, actors' dispositions, and causes. *Journal of Personality and Social Psychology* 36: 657-67.

Hanusa, B. H., and R. Schulz. 1977. Attributional mediators of learned helplessness. *Journal of Personality and Social Psychology* 35: 602-11.

Harré, R., and P. Secord. 1972. *The explanation of social behavior.* Oxford: Blackwell.

Harris, B. 1977. Developmental differences in the attribution of responsibility. *Developmental Psychology* 13: 257-65.

Harris, V. A., and E. S. Katkin. 1975. Primary and secondary emotional behavior: An analysis of the role of autonomic feedback on affect, arousal and attribution. *Psychological Bulletin* 82: 904-16.

Hart, H. L. A. 1949. The ascription of responsibility and rights. *Proceedings of the Aristotelian Society* 49: 171-94.

Harvey, J. H., R. M. Arkin, J. M. Gleason, and S. Johnston. 1975. Effect of expected and observed outcome of an action on the differential causal attributions of actor and observer. *Journal of Personality* 43: 62-77.

Harvey, J. H., B. Harris, and R. D. Barnes. 1975. Actor-observer differences in the perceptions of responsibility and freedom. *Journal of Personality and Social Psychology* 32: 22-28.

Harvey, J. H., and J. M. Jellison. 1974. Determinants of perceived choice, number of options and perceived time in making a selection. *Memory and Cognition* 2: 539-44.

Harvey, J. H., and S. Johnston. 1973. Determinants of the perception of choice. *Journal of Experimental Social Psychology* 9: 164-79.

Hastorf, A. H., and I. E. Bender. 1952. A caution respecting the measurement of emphathic ability. *Journal of Abnormal and Social Psychology* 47: 574-76.

Hastorf, A. H., and H. Cantril. 1954. They saw a game: A case study. *Journal of Abnormal and Social Psychology* 49: 129-34.

Hastorf, A. H., W. R. Kite, A. E. Gross, and L. J. Wolfe. 1965. The perception and evaluation of behavior change. *Sociometry* 48: 400-410.

Heider, F. 1944. Social perception and phenomenal causality. *Psychological Review* 51: 358-74.

———. 1958. *The psychology of interpersonal relations.* New York: Wiley.

Heider, F., and M. Simmel. 1944. An experimental study of apparent behavior. *American Journal of Psychology* 57: 243-59.

Hendrick, C., and A. F. Costantini. 1970a. Effects of varying trait inconsistency and response requirements on the primacy effect in impression formation. *Journal of Personality and Social Psychology* 15: 158-64.

———. 1970b. Number averaging: A primacy effect. *Psychonomic Science* 19: 121-22.

Henley, N. M. 1974. Power, sex, and nonverbal communication: The politics of touch. In P. Brown (ed.), *Radical psychology.* New York: Harper & Row.

Henslin, J. M. 1967. Craps and magic. *American Journal of Sociology* 73: 316-30.

Hess, E. H. 1965. Attitude and pupil size. *Scientific American* 212: 46-54.

Higgins, E. T., and W. S. Rholes. 1976. Impression formation and role fulfillment: A "holistic reference" hypothesis. *Journal of Experimental Social Psychology* 12: 422-35.

———. 1978. "Saying is believing": Effects of message modification on memory and liking for the person described. *Journal of Experimental Social Psychology* 14: 363-78.

Higgins, E. T., W. S. Rholes, and C. R. Jones. 1977. Category accessibility and impression formation. *Journal of Experimental Social Psychology* 13: 141-54.

Himmelfarb, S. 1972. Integration and attribution theories in personality impression formation. *Journal of Personality and Social Psychology* 23: 309-13.

Himmelfarb, S., and N. H. Anderson. 1975. Integration theory applied to opinion attribution. *Journal of Personality and Social Psychology* 31: 1064-72.

Himmelfarb, J., and D. J. Senn. 1969. Forming impressions of social class: Two tests of an averaging model. *Journal of Personality and Social Psychology* 12: 38-51.

Hiroto, D. S., and M. E. P. Seligman. 1975. Generality of learned helplessness in man. *Journal of Personality and Social Psychology* 31: 311-27.

Hirschman, R. 1975. Cross-modal effects of anticipating bogus heart rate feedback in a negative emotional context. *Journal of Personality and Social Psychology* 31: 13-19.

Hogan, R. 1969. Development of an empathy scale. *Journal of Clinical and Consulting Psychology* 33: 307-16.

Holmes, D. S. 1968. Dimensions of projection. *Psychological Bulletin* 69: 248-68.

———. 1978. Projection as a defense mechanism. *Psychological Bulletin* 85: 677-88.

Horn, N. C. 1977. Attribution biases in evaluative situations. Unpublished doctoral dissertation, Yale University.

Hunt, R. G., and T. K. Lin. 1967. Accuracy of judgments of personal attributes from speech. *Journal of Personality and Social Psychology* 6: 450-53.

Izard, C. E. 1971. *The face of emotion*. New York: Appleton-Century-Crofts.

James, W. 1950. *The principles of psychology* (Vol. 2). New York: Dover (first published 1890).

———. 1884. What is an emotion? *Mind* 9: 188-205.

Jellison, J. M., and J. H. Harvey. 1973. Determinants of perceived choice and the relationship between perceived choice and perceived competence. *Journal of Personality and Social Psychology* 28: 376-82.

Jenkins, H. M., and W. C. Ward. 1965. Judgment of contingency between responses and outcomes. *Psychological Monographs* 79 (1, Whole no. 594).

Johnson, T. J., R. Feigenbaum, and M. Weibey. 1964. Some determinants and consequences of the teacher's perception of causality. *Journal of Educational Psychology* 55: 237-46.

Jones, C., and E. Aronson. 1973. Attribution of fault to a rape victim as a function of respectability of the victim. *Journal of Personality and Social Psychology* 26: 415-19.

Jones, E. E. 1954. Authoritarianism as a determinant of first-impression formation. *Journal of Personality* 23: 107-27.

———. 1964. *Ingratiation: A social psychological analysis*. New York: Appleton-Century-Crofts.

———. 1976. How do people perceive the causes of behavior? *American Scientist* 64: 300-305.

Jones, E. E., and S. Berglas. 1978. Control of attributions about the self through self-handicapping strategies: The appeal of alcohol and the role of underachievement. *Personality and Social Psychology Bulletin* 4: 200-206.

Jones, E. E., and K. E. Davis. 1965. From acts to dispositions: The attribution process in person perception. In L. Berkowitz (ed.), *Advances in experimental social psychology* (Vol. 2). New York: Academic Press.

Jones, E. E., K. E. Davis, and K. J. Gergen. 1961. Role playing variations and their informational value for person perception. *Journal of Abnormal and Social Psychology* 63: 302-10.

Jones, E. E., and R. deCharms. 1957. Changes in social perception as a function of the personal relevance of behavior. *Sociometry* 20: 75-85.

Jones, E. E., and H. B. Gerard. 1967. *Foundations of social psychology*. New York: Wiley.

Jones, E. E., and G. R. Goethals. 1972. Order effects in impression formation: Attribution context and the nature of the entity. In E. E. Jones *et al.* (eds.), *Attribution: Perceiving the causes of behavior.* Morristown, N.J.: General Learning Press.

Jones, E. E., G. R. Goethals, G. E. Kennington, and L. J. Severance. 1972. Primacy and assimilation in the attribution process: The stable entity proposition. *Journal of Personality* 40: 250-74.

Jones, E. E., and V. A. Harris. 1967. The attribution of attitudes. *Journal of Experimental Social Psychology* 3: 1-24.

Jones, E. E., and D. McGillis. 1976. Correspondent inferences and the attribution cube: A comparative reappraisal. In J. H. Harvey, W. J. Ickes, and R. F. Kidd (eds.), *New directions in attribution research* (Vol. 1). Hillsdale, N.J.: Lawrence Erlbaum.

Jones, E. E., and R. E. Nisbett. 1972. The actor and observer: Divergent perceptions of the causes of behavior. In E. E. Jones *et al.* (eds.), *Attribution: Perceiving the causes of behavior.* Morristown, N.J.: General Learning Press.

Jones, E. E., L. Rock, K. G. Shaver, G. R. Goethals, and L. M. Ward. 1968. Pattern of performance and ability attribution: An unexpected primacy effect. *Journal of Personality and Social Psychology* 10: 317-41.

Jones, E. E., and J. W. Thibaut. 1958. Interaction goals as bases of inference in interpersonal perception. In R. Tagiuri and L. Petrullo (eds.), *Person perception and interpersonal behavior.* Stanford, Calif.: Stanford University Press, pp. 151-78.

Jones, E. E., S. Worchel, G. R. Goethals, and J. F. Grumet. 1971. Prior expectancy and behavioral extremity as determinants of attitude attribution. *Journal of Experimental Social Psychology* 7: 59-80.

Jones, R. A., J. Sensenig, and J. V. Haley. 1974. Self-descriptions: Configurations of content and order effects. *Journal of Personality and Social Psychology* 30: 36-45.

Jourard, S. M., and R. Friedman. 1970. Experimenter-subject "distance" and self-disclosure. *Journal of Personality and Social Psychology* 15: 278-82.

Kahneman, D., and A. Tversky. 1972. Subjective probability: A judgment of representativeness. *Cognitive Psychology* 3: 430-54.

———. 1973. On the psychology of prediction. *Psychological Review* 80: 237-51.

Kane, T. R., J. M. Joseph, and J. T. Tedeschi. 1976. Person perception and the Berkowitz paradigm for the study of aggression. *Journal of Personality and Social Psychology* 33: 663-73.

Kanouse, D. E. 1972. Language, labeling, and attribution. In E. E. Jones *et al.* (eds.), *Attribution: Perceiving the causes of behavior.* Morristown, N.J.: General Learning Press.

Kanouse, D. E., and L. R. Hanson. 1972. Negativity in evaluations. In E. E. Jones *et al.* (eds.), *Attribution: Perceiving the causes of behavior.* Morristown, N.J.: General Learning Press.

Kaplan, M. F. 1971a. Dispositional effects and weight of information in impression formation. *Journal of Personality and Social Psychology* 18: 279-84.

———. 1971b. Context effects in impression formation: The weighted average versus the meaning-change formulation. *Journal of Personality and Social Psychology* 19: 92-99.

———. 1972. The modifying effect of stimulus information on the consistency of individual differences in impression formation. *Journal of Experimental Research in Personality* 6: 213-19.

————. 1973. Stimulus inconsistency and response dispositions in forming judgments of other persons. *Journal of Personality and Social Psychology* 25: 58-64.

————. 1974. Context-induced shifts in personality trait evaluation: A comment on the evaluative halo effect and the meaning change interpretations. *Psychological Bulletin* 81: 891-95.

————. 1975. Evaluative judgments are based on evaluative information: Evidence against meaning change in evaluative context effects. *Memory and Cognition* 3: 375-80.

Kaplan, M. F., and G. D. Kemmerick. 1974. Juror judgment as information integration: Combining evidential and nonevidential information. *Journal of Personality and Social Psychology* 30: 493-99.

Karaz, V., and D. Perlman. 1975. Attribution at the wire: Consistency and outcome finish strong. *Journal of Experimental Social Psychology* 11: 470-77.

Karlins, M., T. L. Coffman, and G. Walters. 1969. On the fading of social stereotypes: Studies in three generations of college students. *Journal of Personality and Social Psychology* 13: 1-16.

Karniol, R. 1978. Children's use of intention cues in evaluating behavior. *Psychological Bulletin* 85: 76-85.

Karniol, R., and M. Ross. 1976. The development of causal attribution in social perception. *Journal of Personality and Social Psychology* 34: 455-64.

Kasl, S. V., and G. F. Mahl. 1965. The relationship of disturbances and hesitations in spontaneous speech to anxiety. *Journal of Personality and Social Psychology* 1: 425-33.

Katz, D., and K. W. Braley. 1933. Racial stereotypes of one hundred college students. *Journal of Abnormal and Social Psychology* 28: 280-90.

Kelley, H. H. 1950. The warm-cold variable in first impressions of persons. *Journal of Personality* 18: 431-39.

————. 1967. Attribution theory in social psychology. In *Nebraska symposium on motivation*. Lincoln: University of Nebraska Press, pp. 192-238.

————. 1972a. Causal schemata and the attribution process. In E. E. Jones *et al.* (eds.), *Attribution: Perceiving the causes of behavior*. Morristown, N.J.: General Learning Press.

————. 1972b. Attribution in social interaction. In E. E. Jones *et al.* (eds.), *Attribution: Perceiving the causes of behavior*. Morristown, N.J.: General Learning Press.

————. 1973. The process of causal attribution. *American Psychologist* 28: 107-28.

Kellogg, R., and R. S. Baron. 1975. Attribution theory, insomnia, and the reverse placebo effect: A reversal of Storms and Nisbett's findings. *Journal of Personality and Social Psychology* 32: 231-36.

Kelly, G. A. 1955. *The psychology of personal constructs*. New York: Norton.

Kiesler, C. A., and S. B. Kiesler. 1969. *Conformity*. Reading, Mass.: Addison-Wesley.

Kiesler, C. A., and M. S. Pallak. 1976. Arousal properties of dissonance manipulations. *Psychological Bulletin* 83: 1014-25.

Kiesler, S. B. 1973. Preference for predictability or unpredictability as a mediator of reactions to norm violations. *Journal of Personality and Social Psychology* 27: 354-59.

King, M. 1971. The development of some intention concepts in young children. *Child Development* 42: 1145-52.

Kingsley, S. J. 1978. Implicit self theory. Unpublished doctoral dissertation, Rutgers University.

Kite, W. R. 1964. Attributions of causality as a function of the use of reward and punishment. Unpublished doctoral dissertation, Stanford University.

Kleck, R. E., and W. Nuessle. 1968. Congruence between the indicative and communicative functions of eye-contact in interpersonal relations. *British Journal of Social and Clinical Psychology* 7: 241-46.

Klein, D. C., E. Fencil-Morse, and M. E. P. Seligman. 1976. Learned helplessness, depression, and the attribution of failure. *Journal of Personality and Social Psychology* 33: 508-16.

Kleinke, C. L. 1974. Effects of gaze and touch on compliance to requests in field settings: The tribulations and rewards of the female experimenter. Unpublished manuscript.

———. 1975. *First impressions*. Englewood Cliffs, N.J.: Prentice-Hall.

Kleinke, C. L., and P. D. Pohlen. 1971. Affective and emotional responses as a function of other person's gaze and co-operativeness in a two-person game. *Journal of Personality and Social Psychology* 17: 308-13.

Kleinke, C. L., R. A. Staneski, and S. L. Pipp. 1975. Effects of gaze, distance, and attractiveness on males' first impressions of females. *Representative Research in Social Psychology* 6: 7-12.

Koller, P. S., and R. M. Kaplan. 1978. A two-process theory of learned helplessness. *Journal of Personality and Social Psychology* 36: 1177-83.

Koltuv, B. 1962. Some characteristics of intrajudge trait intercorrelations. *Psychological Monograph* 76 (33, Whole No. 552).

Korten, F. F. 1974. The influence of culture and sex on the perception of persons. *International Journal of Psychology* 9: 31-44.

Kramer, E. 1963. Judgment of personal characteristics and emotions from nonverbal properties. *Psychological Bulletin* 60: 408-20.

Krauss, R., V. Geller, and C. Olson. 1976. Modalities and cues in the detection of deception. Paper presented at the American Psychological Association Convention.

Kraut, R. E. 1973. Effects of social labeling on giving to charity. *Journal of Experimental Social Psychology* 9: 551-62.

———. 1978. Verbal and nonverbal cues in the perception of lying. *Journal of Personality and Social Psychology* 36: 380-91.

Krovetz, M. L. 1974. Explaining success or failure as a function of one's locus of control. *Journal of Personality* 42: 175-89.

Kruglanski, A. W. 1970. Attributing trustworthiness in supervisor-worker relations. *Journal of Experimental Social Psychology* 6: 214-32.

———. 1975. The endogenous-exogenous partition on attribution theory. *Psychological Review* 82: 387-406.

———. 1977. The place of naive contents in a theory of attributions: Reflections on Calder's and Zuckerman's critiques of the endogenous-exogenous partition. *Personality and Social Psychology Bulletin* 3: 592-605.

Kruglanski, A. W., and M. Cohen. 1973. Attributed freedom and personal causation. *Journal of Personality and Social Psychology* 26: 245-50.

Kruglanski, A. W., I. Friedman, and G. Zeevi. 1971. The effects of extrinsic incentives on some qualitative aspects of task performance. *Journal of Personality* 39: 606-17.

Kruglanski, A. W., A. Ritter, A. Amitai, B. S. Margolin, L. Shabtai, and D. Zaksh. 1975. Can money enhance intrinsic motivation? A test of the content-consequence hypothesis. *Journal of Personality and Social Psychology* 31: 744-50.

Kuiper, N. A. 1978. Depression and causal attributions in success and failure. *Journal of Personality and Social Psychology* 36: 236-46.

Kukla, A. 1972. Attribution determinants of achievement-related behavior. *Journal of*

Personality and Social Psychology 21: 166-74.

Kun, A., and B. Weiner. 1973. Necessary versus sufficient causal schemata for success and failure. *Journal of Research in Personality* 7: 197-207.

Lacey, J. 1950. Individual differences in somatic response patterns. *Journal of Comparative and Physiological Psychology* 43: 338-50.

Laird, J. D. 1974. Self-attribution of emotion: The effects of expressive behavior on the quality of emotional experience. *Journal of Personality and Social Psychology* 29: 475-86.

Landfield, A. W. 1971. *Personal construct systems in psychotherapy.* Chicago: Rand McNally.

Landfield, A. W. (ed.). 1977. *Nebraska symposium on motivation, 1976.* Lincoln: University of Nebraska Press.

Landis, C. 1924. Studies of emotional reactions: II. General behavior and facial expression. *Journal of Comparative Psychology* 4: 447-509.

―――. 1929. The interpretation of facial expresion in emotion. *Journal of General Psychology* 2: 59-72.

Landy, D., and E. Aronson. 1969. The influence of the character of the criminal and his victim on the decisions of simulated jurors. *Journal of Experimental Social Psychology* 5: 141-52.

Langer, E. J. 1975. The illusion of control. *Journal of Personality and Social Psychology* 32: 311-28.

Langer, E. J., and J. Roth. 1975. Heads I win, tails it's chance: The illusion of control as a function of the sequence of outcomes in a purely chance task. *Journal of Personality and Social Psychology* 32: 951-55.

Langfeld, H. S. 1918. The judgment of emotions from facial expressions. *Journal of Abnormal and Social Psychology* 13: 172-84.

Lanzetta, J. T., J. Cartwright-Smith, and R. W. Kleck. 1976. Effects of nonverbal dissimulation on emotional experience and autonomic arousal. *Journal of Personality and Social Psychology* 33: 354-70.

Lanzetta, J. T., and T. E. Hannah. 1969. Reinforcing behavior of "naive" trainers. *Journal of Personality and Social Psychology* 11: 245-52.

Lanzetta, J. T., and R. E. Kleck. 1970. Encoding and decoding of nonverbal affect in humans. *Journal of Personality and Social Psychology* 16: 12-19.

Lassen, C. L. 1973. Effect of proximity on anxiety and communication in the initial psychiatric interview. *Journal of Abnormal Psychology* 81: 226-32.

Latta, R. M. 1976. Differential tests of two cognitive theories of performance: Weiner versus Kukla. *Journal of Personality and Social Psychology* 34: 295-304.

Lawson, E. 1971. Haircolor, personality and the observer. *Psychological Reports* 28: 311-22.

Lay, C. H. 1970. Trait-inferential relationships and judgments about the personalities of others. *Canadian Journal of Behavior Science* 2: 1-17.

Lay, C. H., B. F. Birron, and D. N. Jackson. 1973. Base rates and informational value in impression formation. *Journal of Personality and Social Psychology* 28: 390-95.

Lay, C. H., and D. N. Jackson. 1969. Analysis of the generality of trait-inferential relationships. *Journal of Personality and Social Psychology* 12: 12-21.

LeCompte, W. F., and H. M. Rosenfeld. 1971. Effects of minimal eye contact in the instruction period on impressions of the experimenter. *Journal of Experimental Social Psychology* 7: 211-20.

Leeper, R. 1935. A study of a neglected portion of the field of learning—the development of sensory organization. *Journal of Genetic Psychology* 46: 41-75.

Lefcourt, H. M., E. Hogg, S. Struthers, and C. Holmes. 1975. Causal attributions as a function of locus of control, initial confidence, and performance outcomes. *Journal of Personality and Social Psychology* 32: 391-97.

Leon, M., G. C. Oden, and N. H. Anderson. 1973. Functional measurement of social values. *Journal of Personality and Social Psychology* 27: 301-10.

Lepper, M. R. 1973. Dissonance, self-perception and honesty in children. *Journal of Personality and Social Psychology* 25: 65-74.

Lepper, M. R., and D. Greene. 1976. On understanding "overjustification": A reply to Reiss and Sushinsky. *Journal of Personality and Social Psychology* 33: 25-35.

Lepper, M. R., D. Greene, and R. E. Nisbett. 1973. Undermining children's intrinsic interest with extrinsic reward. *Journal of Personality and Social Psychology* 28: 129-37.

Lerner, M. J. 1965. Evaluation of performance as a function of performer's reward and attractiveness. *Journal of Personality and Social Psychology* 1: 355-61.

Leventhal, H. 1962. The effects of set and discrepancy on impression change. *Journal of Personality* 30: 1-15.

Leventhal, H., and D. L. Singer. 1964. Cognitive complexity, impression formation and impression change. *Journal of Personality* 32: 210-26.

Levine, F. J., and J. L. Tapp. 1973. The psychology of criminal identification: The gap from Wade to Kirby. *Research Contributions of the American Bar Foundation* 4. Reprinted from *University of Pennsylvania Law Review* 121 (1973): 1079-1131.

Levy, L. H., and R. D. Dugan. 1960. A constant error approach to the study of dimensions of social perception. *Journal of Abnormal and Social Psychology* 61: 21-25.

Lindsley, D. B. 1951. Emotion. In S. S. Stevens (ed.), *Handbook of experimental psychology.* New York: Wiley.

Lippa, R. 1977. The effect of expressive control on expressive consistency and on the relation between expressive behavior and personality. Unpublished doctoral dissertation, Stanford University.

Livesley, W. J., and D. B. Bromley. 1973. *Person perception in childhood and adolescence.* London: John Wiley & Sons.

Loftis, J., and L. Ross. 1974. Effects of misattribution of arousal upon the acquisition and extinction of a conditioned emotional response. *Journal of Personality and Social Psychology* 30: 673-82.

Lopes, L. L. 1972. A unified integration model for norm expectancy and behavioral extremity as determinant of attitude attribution. *Journal of Experimental Social Psychology* 8: 156-60.

Lowe, C. A., and S. M. Kassin. 1977. On the use of consensus: Prediction, attribution, and evaluation. *Personality and Social Psychology Bulletin* 3: 616-19.

Luchins, A. S. 1957. Primacy-recency in impression formation. In C. Hovland (ed.), *The order of presentation in persuasion.* New Haven, Conn.: Yale University Press.

————. 1958. Definitiveness of impression and primacy-receny in communications. *Journal of Social Pscyhology* 48: 275-90.

Ludwig, L. M., and P. C. Ellsworth. 1974. Some effects of observation set on the interpretation of nonverbal cues. Unpublished manuscript, Yale University.

Luginbuhl, J. E. R., D. H. Crowe, and J. P. Kahan. 1975. Causal attributions for success and failure. *Journal of Personality and Social Psychology* 31: 86-93.

Lykken, D. T. 1974. Psychology and the lie detector industry. *American Psychologist* 29: 725-39.

McArthur, L. Z. 1972. The how and what of why: Some determinants and consequence of causal attribution. *Journal of Personality and Social Psychology* 22: 171-93.

―――. 1976. The lesser influence of consensus than distinctiveness information on causal attributions: A test of the person-thing hypothesis. *Journal of Personality and Social Psychology* 33: 733-42.

McArthur, L. Z., and D. L. Post. 1977. Figural emphasis and person perception. *Journal of Experimental Social Psychology* 13: 520-36.

McArthur, L. Z., and L. K. Solomon. 1978. Perceptions of an aggressive encounter as a function of the victim's salience and the observer's arousal. Unpublished manuscript, Brandeis University.

McBride, G., M. G. King, and J. W. James. 1965. Social proximity effects on GSR in human adults. *Journal of Psychology* 61: 153-57.

McKeachie, W. J. 1952. Lipstick as a determiner of first impressions of personality: An experiment for the general psychology course. *Journal of Social Psychology* 36: 241-44.

McKee, J. P., and A. C. Sherriffs. 1957. The differential evaluation of males and females. *Journal of Personality* 25: 256-71.

McKillip, J., and E. J. Posavac. 1975. Judgments of responsibility for an accident. *Journal of Personality* 43: 248-65.

Magnusson, D. 1971. An analysis of situational dimensions. *Perceptual and Motor Skills* 32: 851-67.

Magnusson, D., and B. Ekehammar. 1973. An analysis of situational dimensions: A replication. *Multivariate Behavior Research* 8: 331-39.

Markus, H. 1977. Self-schemata and processing information about the self. *Journal of Personality and Social Psychology* 35: 63-78.

Mayo, C. W., and W. H. Crockett. 1964. Cognitive complexity and primacy-recency effects in impression formation. *Journal of Abnormal and Social Psychology* 68: 335-88.

Mead, G. H. 1934. *Mind, self, and society.* Chicago: University of Chicago Press.

Mehrabian, A. 1967. Orientation behaviors and nonverbal attitude communication. *Journal of Communication* 17: 324-32.

―――. 1968. Inference of attitudes from the posture, orientation, and distance of a communicator. *Journal of Consulting and Clinical Psychology* 32: 296-308.

―――. 1969. Significance of posture and position in the communication of attitude and status relationships. *Psychological Bulletin* 71: 359-72.

―――. 1971. Nonverbal betrayal of feeling. *Journal of Experimental Research in Personality* 5: 64-73.

―――. 1972. *Nonverbal communication.* Chicago: Aldine-Atherton.

Mehrabian, A., and S. R. Ferris. 1967. Inference of attitudes from nonverbal communication in two channels. *Journal of Consulting Psychology* 31: 248-52.

Mehrabian, A., and J. T. Friar. 1969. Encoding of attitude by a seated communicator via posture and position cues. *Journal of Consulting and Clinical Psychology* 33: 330-36.

Mehrabian, A., and M. Wiener. 1967. Decoding of inconsistent communication. *Journal of Personality and Social Psychology* 6: 108-14.

Mesibov, G. B. 1974. Attributions of responsibility: A cognitive interpretation. Unpublished doctoral dissertation, Brandeis University.

Messick, D. M., and G. Reeder. 1972. Perceived motivation, role variations and the attribution of personal characteristics. *Journal of Experimental Social Psychology* 8: 482-91.

Messick, S., and N. Kogan. 1966. Personality consistencies in judgment: Dimension of role constructs. *Multivariate Behavioral Research* 1: 165-75.

Michotte, A. 1963. *Perception of causality*. New York: Basic Books.

Miller, A. G. 1970. Role of physical attractiveness in impression formation. *Psychonomic Science* 19: 241-43.

———. 1976. Constraint and target effects on the attribution of attitudes. *Journal of Experimental Social Psychology* 12: 325-39.

Miller, A. G., B. Gillen, C. Schenker, and S. Radlove. 1974. The prediction and perception of obedience to authority. *Journal of Personality* 42: 23-42.

Miller, A. G., N. Mayerson, M. Pogue, and P. Whitehouse. 1977. Perceivers' explanations of the attribution of attitude. *Personality and Social Psychology Bulletin* 3: 111-14.

Miller, D. T. 1976. Ego involvement and attributions for success and failure. *Journal of Personality and Social Psychology* 34: 901-6.

Miller, D. T., and S. A. Norman. 1975. Actor-observer differences in perceptions of effective control. *Journal of Personality and Social Psychology* 31: 503-15.

Miller, D. T., S. A. Norman, and E. Wright. 1978. Distortion in person perception as a consequence of the need for effective control. *Journal of Personality and Social Psychology* 36: 598-607.

Miller, D. T., and M. Ross. 1975. Self-serving biases in the attribution of causality: Fact or fiction? *Psychological Bulletin* 82: 213-25.

Miller, R. L., P. Brickman, and D. Bolen. 1975. Attribution versus persuasion as a means for modifying behavior. *Journal of Personality and Social Psychology* 31: 430-41.

Mills, J., and J. M. Jellison. 1967. Effect of opinion change of how desirable the communication is to the audience the communicator addressed. *Journal of Personality and Social Psychology* 6: 98-101.

Mirels, H. L. 1976. Implicit personality theory and inferential illusions. *Journal of Personality* 44: 467-87.

Mischel, W. 1968. *Personality and assessment*. New York: Wiley.

———. 1973. Toward a cognitive social learning reconceptualization of personality. *Psychological Review* 80: 252-83.

Mischel, W., K. M. Jeffery, and C. J. Patterson. 1974. The layman's use of trait and behavioral information to predict behavior. *Journal of Research in Personality* 8: 231-42.

Monson, T. C., and M. Snyder. 1977. Actors, observers, and the attribution process: Toward a reconceptualization. *Journal of Experimental Social Psychology* 13: 89-111.

Moos, R. 1976. *The human context: Environmental determinants of behavior*. New York: Wiley.

Morris, D. 1977. *Manwatching: A field guide to human behavior*. New York: Abrams.

Mulaik, S. A. 1964. Are personality factors raters' conceptual factors? *Journal of Consulting Psychology* 28: 506-11.

Munn, N. L. 1940. The effect of knowledge of the situation upon judgment of emotion from facial expressions. *Journal of Abnormal and Social Psychology* 35: 324-38.

Mussen, P. H., and R. G. Barker. 1944. Attitudes towards cripples. *Journal of Abnormal and Social Psychology* 39: 351-55.

Newtson, D. 1973. Attribution and the unit of perception of ongoing behavior. *Journal of Personality and Social Psychology* 28: 28-38.

――――. 1974. Dispositional inference from effects of actions: Effects chosen and effects foregone. *Journal of Experimental Social Psychology* 10: 489-96.

Newtson, D., and G. Engquist. 1976. The perceptual organization of ongoing behavior. *Journal of Experimental Social Psychology* 12: 436-50.

Newtson, D.; G. Engquist, and J. Bois. 1977. The objective basis of behavior units. *Journal of Personality and Social Psychology* 35: 847-62.

Newtson, D., R. Rindner, R. Miller, and K. LaCross. 1978. Effects of availability of feature changes on behavior segmentation. *Journal of Experimental Social Psychology* 14: 379-88.

Nicholls, J. G. 1975. Causal attributions and other achievement related cognitions: Effects of task outcome, attainment value and sex. *Journal of Personality and Social Psychology* 31: 379-89.

Nichols, K. A., and B. G. Champness. 1971. Eye gaze and the GSR. *Journal of Experimental Social Psychology* 7: 623-26.

Nisbett, R. E., and N. Bellows. 1977. Verbal reports about causal influences on social judgments: Private access versus public theories. *Journal of Personality and Social Psychology* 35: 613-24.

Nisbett, R. E., and E. Borgida. 1975. Attribution and the psychology of prediction. *Journal of Personality and Social Psychology* 32: 932-43.

Nisbett, R. E., E. Borgida, R. Crandall, and H. Reed. 1976. Popular induction: Information is not necessarily informative. In J. S. Carroll and J. W. Payne (eds.), *Cognition and social behavior*. Hillsdale, N.J.: Lawrence Erlbaum.

Nisbett, R. E., C. Caputo, P. Legant, and J. Marecek. 1973. Behavior as seen by the actor and as seen by the observer. *Journal of Personality and Social Psychology* 27: 154-64.

Nisbett, R. E., and S. Schachter. 1966. Cognitive manipulation of pain. *Journal of Experimental Social Psychology* 2: 227-36.

Nisbett, R. E., and S. Valins. 1972. Perceiving the causes of one's own behavior. In E. E. Jones *et al.* (eds.), *Attribution: Perceiving the causes of behavior*. Morristown, N.J.: General Learning Press.

Nisbett, R. E., and T. D. Wilson. 1977a. Telling more than we can know: Verbal reports on mental processes. *Psychological Review* 84: 231-59.

――――. 1977b. The halo effect: Evidence for unconscious alteration of judgments. *Journal of Personality and Social Psychology* 35: 250-56.

Norman, W. T. 1963. Toward an adequate taxonomy of personality attributes: Replicated factor structure in peer nomination personality ratings. *Journal of Abnormal and Social Psychology* 66: 574-83.

Normand, P. S. 1973. The influence of the perceiver, the perceived person, and the situation on the structure of free description. Senior honors thesis, Brandeis University.

Nummenmaa, T. 1964. The language of the face. *Jyvaskyla studies in education, psychology, and social research*. Jyvaskyla, Finland: Jyvaskylan Yliopistoyhdistys.

O'Neal, E. 1971. Influence of future choice, importance and arousal upon the halo effect. *Journal of Personality and Social Psychology* 19: 334-40.

Orvis, B. R., J. D. Cunningham, and H. H. Kelley. 1975. A closer examination of causal inference: The roles of consensus, distinctiveness and consistency information. *Journal of Personality and Social Psychology* 32: 605-16.

Osgood, C., G. J. Suci, and P. H. Tannenbaum. 1957. *The measurement of meaning.* Urbana, Ill.: University of Illinois Press.

Ostrom, T. M. 1975. Cognitive representation of impressions. Paper presented at the American Psychological Association Convention.

―――. 1977. Between-theory and within-theory conflict in explaining context effects on impression formation. *Journal of Experimental Social Psychology* 13: 492-503.

Ostrom, T. M., and D. W. Essex. 1972. Meaning shift in impression formation. Paper presented at the meeting of the Psychonomic Society.

Ostrom, T. M., and J. H. Lingle. 1977. Thematic constructions in person impressions. Paper presented in a symposium "New directions in the analysis of impression formation," American Psychological Association Convention.

Ostrom, T. M., C. Werner, and M. J. Saks. 1978. An integration theory analysis of jurors' presumptions of guilt or innocence. *Journal of Personality and Social Psychology* 36: 436-50.

Passini, F. T., and W. T. Norman. 1966. A universal conception of personality structure? *Journal of Personality and Social Psychology* 4: 44-49.

Patterson, M. L. 1976. An arousal model of interpersonal intimacy. *Psychological Review* 83: 235-45.

Patterson, M. L., and L. B. Sechrest. 1970. Interpersonal distance and impression forma tion. *Journal of Personality* 38: 161-66.

Peabody, D. 1967. Trait inferences: Evaluative and descriptive aspects. *Journal of Personality and Social Psychology, Monograph* 7, No. 4 (Part 2, Whole No. 644): 1-18.

―――. 1970. Evaluative and descriptive aspects in personality perception. A re-appraisal. *Journal of Personality and Social Psychology* 16: 639 46.

―――. 1978. In search of an evaluative factor: Comments on DeBoeck. *Journal of Personality and Social Psychology* 36: 622-27.

Pederson, D. M. 1965. The measurement of individual differences in perceived personality-trait relationships and their relation to certain determinants. *Journal of Social Psychology* 65: 233-58.

Peevers, B. H., and P. F. Secord. 1973. Developmental changes in attribution of descriptive concepts to persons. *Journal of Personality and Social Psychology* 27: 120-28.

Peters, R. S. 1958. *The concept of motivation.* London: Routledge and Kegan Paul.

Peterson, C. R., and L. R. Beach. 1967. Man as intuitive statistician. *Psychological Bulletin* 68: 29-46.

Pheterson, G. I., S. B. Kiesler, and P. A. Goldberg. 1971. Evaluation of the performance of women as a function of their sex, achievement, and personal history. *Journal of Personality and Social Psychology* 19: 114-18.

Piaget, J. 1930. *The child's conception of physical causality.* New York: Harcourt, Brace.

Polefka, J. T. 1965. The perception and evaluation of responses to social influence. Unpublished doctoral dissertation, Stanford University.

Posavac, E. J. 1971. Dimensions of trait preferences and personality type. *Journal of Personality and Social Psychology* 19: 274-81.

Price, R. H. 1974. The taxonomic classification of behavior and situations and the problem of behavior-environment congruence. *Human Relations* 27: 567-85.

Price, R. H., and D. L. Bouffard. 1974. Behavioral appropriateness and situational constraint as dimensions of social behavior. *Journal of Personality and Social Psychology* 30: 579-86.

Pryor, J. B., and M. Kriss. 1977. The cognitive dynamics of salience in the attribution process. *Journal of Personality and Social Psychology* 35: 49-55.

Reece, M. M., and R. N. Whitman. 1962. Expressive movements, warmth, and verbal reinforcement. *Journal of Abnormal and Social Psychology* 64: 234-36.

Reed, P. L., and D. N. Jackson. 1975. Clinical judgment of psychopathology: A model for inferential accuracy. *Journal of Abnormal Psychology* 84: 475-82.

———. 1977. Personality measurement and inferential accuracy. Research Bulletin No. 419, Department of Psychology, The University of Western Ontario.

Reeder, G. D., D. M. Messick, and E. Van Avermaet. 1977. Dimensional asymmetricality in attributional inference. *Journal of Experimental Social Psychology* 13: 46-57.

Regan, D. T., and J. Totten. 1975. Empathy and attribution: Turning observers into actors. *Journal of Personality and Social Psychology* 32: 850-56.

Reiss, S., and L. W. Sushinsky. 1975. Overjustification, competing responses, and the acquisition of intrinsic interest. *Journal of Personality and Social Psychology* 31: 1116-25.

———. 1976. The competing response hypothesis of decreased play effects: A reply to Lepper and Greene. *Journal of Personality and Social Psychology* 33: 233-44.

Richardson, S. A., A. H. Hastorf, N. Goodmen, and S. M. Dornbusch. 1961. Cultural uniformity in reaction to physical disabilities. *American Sociological Review* 26: 24-47.

Riley, M. S., and J. B. Bryson. 1977. A semantic basis for evaluative trait judgment. *Personality and Social Psychology Bulletin* 3: 95-98.

Rodin, J. 1976. Menstruation, reattribution, and competence. *Journal of Personality and Social Psychology* 33: 345-53.

Rodin, M. J. 1972. Informativeness of trait descriptions. *Journal of Personality and Social Psychology* 21: 341-44.

———. 1975. The trait coding of behavior. *Bulletin of the Psychonomic Society* 6: 638-40.

Rogers, P. C., K. R. Scherer, and R. Rosenthal. 1971. Content-filtering human speech. *Behavior Research Methods and Instrumentation* 3: 16-18.

Rogers, R. W., and C. W. Deckner. 1975. Effects of fear appeals and physiological arousal upon emotion, attitudes, and cigarette smoking. *Journal of Personality and Social Psychology* 32: 222-30.

Rogers, T. B. 1974. An analysis of two central stages underlying responding to personality items: The self-referent decision and response selection. *Journal of Research in Personality* 8: 128-38.

———. 1978 (in press). Self-reference in memory: Recognition of personality items. *Journal of Research in Personality.*

Rogers, T. B., N. A. Kuiper, and W. S. Kirker. 1977. Self-reference and the encoding of personal information. *Journal of Personality and Social Psychology* 35: 677-88.

Rokeach, M., and G. Rothman. 1965. The principle of belief congruence and the congruity principle as models of cognitive interaction. *Psychological Review* 72: 128-42.

Roll, S., and J. S. Verinis. 1971. Stereotypes of scalp and facial hair as measured by the semantic differential. *Psychological Reports* 28: 975-80.

Rosenberg, S. 1977. New approaches to the analysis of personal constructs in person perception. In A. W. Landfield (ed.), *Nebraska symposium on motivation, 1976*. Lincoln: University of Nebraska Press.

Rosenberg, S., and R. Jones. 1972. A method for investigating and representing a person's implicit theory of personality: Theodore Dreiser's view of people. *Journal of Personality and Social Psychology* 22: 372-86.

Rosenberg, S., C. Nelson, and P. S. Vivekananthan. 1968. A multidimensional approach to the structure of personality impressions. *Journal of Personality and Social Psychology* 9: 283-94.

Rosenberg, S., and K. Olshan. 1970. Evaluative and descriptive aspects in personality perception. *Journal of Personality and Social Psychology* 16: 619-26.

Rosenberg, S., and A. Sedlak. 1972. Structural representations of implicit personality theory. In L. Berkowitz (ed.), *Advances in experimental social psychology* (Vol. 6). New York: Academic Press.

Rosenkrantz, P. S., and W. Crockett. 1965. Some factors influencing the assimilation of disparate information in impression formation. *Journal of Personality and Social Psychology* 2: 397-402.

Rosenthal, R. 1969. Interpersonal expectations: Effects of the experimenter's hypothesis. In R. Rosenthal and R. Rosnow (eds.), *Artifact in behavioral research*. New York: Academic Press, pp. 181-277.

Rosenthal, R., and L. Jacobson. 1968. *Pygmalion in the classroom*. New York: Holt, Rinehart and Winston.

Ross, L. 1977. The intuitive psychologist and his shortcomings: Distortions in the attribution process. In L. Berkowitz (ed.), *Advances in experimental social psychology* (Vol. 10). New York: Academic Press.

Ross, L. D., T. M. Amabile, and J. L. Steinmetz. 1977. Social roles, social control, and biases in social-perception processes. *Journal of Personality and Social Psychology* 35: 485-94.

Ross, L., G. Bierbrauer, and S. Polly. 1974. Attribution of educational outcomes by professional and nonprofessional instructors. *Journal of Experimental Social Psychology* 29: 609-18.

Ross, L., D. Greene, and P. House. 1977. The "false consensus effect": An egocentric bias in social perception and attribution processes. *Journal of Experimental Social Psychology* 13: 279-301.

Ross, L., M. R. Lepper, and M. Hubbard. 1975. Perseverance in self-perception and social perception: Biased attributional processes in the debriefing paradigm. *Journal of Personality and Social Psychology* 32: 880-92.

Ross, L., M. R. Lepper, F. Strack, and J. Steinmetz. 1977. Social explanation and social expectation: Effects of real and hypothetical explanations on subjective likelihood. *Journal of Personality and Social Psychology* 35: 817-29.

Ross, L., J. Rodin, and P. G. Zimbardo. 1969. Toward an attribution therapy: The reduction of fear through induced cognitive-emotional misattribution. *Journal of Personality and Social Psychology* 12: 279-88.

Ross, M. 1975. Salience of reward and intrinsic motivation. *Journal of Personality and Social Psychology* 32: 245-54.

Roth, S., and R. R. Bootzin. 1974. The effects of experimentally induced expectancies of external control: An investigation of learned helplessness. *Journal of Personality and Social Psychology* 29: 253-64.

Rothbart, M. 1977. Judgmental heuristics in stereotype formation and maintenance. Paper presented at symposium "Cognitive biases in stereotyping," American Psychological Associaton Convention.

Rothbart, M., S. Fulero, C. Jensen, J. Howard, and B. Birrell. 1978. From individual to group impressions: Availability heuristics in stereotype formation. *Journal of Experimental Social Psychology* 14: 237-55.

Rubin, Z. 1970. Measurement of romantic love. *Journal of Personality and Social Psychology* 16: 265-73.

Ruble, D. N., and N. S. Feldman. 1976. Order of consensus, distinctiveness, and consistency information and causal attribution. *Journal of Personality and Social Psychology* 34: 930-37.

Ruckmick, C. A. 1921. A preliminary study of the emotions. *Psychological Monographs* 30, No. 3 (Whole No. 136): 30-35.

Sarason, I. G., R. E. Smith, and E. Diener. 1975. Personality research: Components of variance attributable to the person and the situation. *Journal of Personality and Social Psychology* 32: 199-204.

Schachter, S. 1964. The interaction of cognitive and physiological components of emotional state. In L. Berkowitz (ed.), *Advances in experimental social psychology* (Vol. 1). New York: Academic Press, pp. 49-80.

Schachter, S., and B. Latané. 1964. Crime, cognition, and the autonomic nervous systems. In *Nebraska symposium on motivation* (Vol. 12). Lincoln: University of Nebraska Press, pp. 221-75.

Schachter, S., and J. E. Singer. 1962. Cognitive, social and physiological determinants of emotional state. *Psychological Review* 69: 379-99.

Schank, R. C., and R. P. Abelson. 1975. Scripts, plans, and knowledge. Paper presented at the Fourth International Conference on Artificial Intelligence, Tbilisi.

Scheff, T. J. 1966. *Being mentally ill: A sociological theory.* Chicago: Aldine.

Scherer, K. 1974. Acoustic concomitants of emotional dimensions: Judging affect from synthesized tone sequences. In S. Weitz (ed.), *Nonverbal communication.* London: Oxford University Press.

Schiffenbauer, A. 1974. Effect of observer's emotional state on judgments of the emotional state of others. *Journal of Personality and Social Psychology* 30: 31-35.

Schneider, D. J. 1971. Extra-linguistic aspects of trait implications. Paper presented at a symposium entitled "Recent approaches to studying implicit personality theories," American Psychological Association Convention.

————. 1973. Implicit personality theory: A review. *Psychological Bulletin* 79: 294-309.

————. 1976. *Social psychology.* Reading, Mass.: Addison-Wesley.

————. 1977. Situational and stimulus factors in free descriptions of people. Paper presented in a symposium, "New directions in the analysis of impression formation," American Psychological Association Convention.

————. 1978. Traits as dispositions: Some phenomenological evidence. Unpublished manuscript, University of Texas at San Antonio.

Schneider, D. J., and B. Blankmeyer. 1978. The effects of prototype salience on trait inferences. Unpublished manuscript, University of Texas at San Antonio.

Schneider, D. J., and M. Glickstein. 1977. The road to hell is paved with good intentions:

The role of intentions and past behavior in inferences about future behavior. Unpublished manuscript, University of Texas at San Antonio.

Schneider, D. J., A. H. Hastorf, and G. Mesibov. 1978. The effects of stimulus person, situation, and trait type on attribution. Unpublished manuscript, University of Texas at San Antonio.

Schneider, D. J., and R. S. Miller. 1975. The effects of enthusiasm and quality of arguments on attitude attribution. *Journal of Personality* 43: 693-708.

Schopler, J., and B. Layton. 1972. Determinants of the self-attribution of having influenced another person. *Journal of Personality and Social Psychology* 22: 326-32.

Schultz, R., and J. Barefoot. 1974. Nonverbal responses and affiliative conflict theory. *British Journal of Social and Clinical Psychology* 13: 237-43.

Scott, W. A. 1963. Cognitive complexity and cognitive balance. *Sociometry* 26: 66-74.

Secord, P. F. 1977. Scripts, schemata, and typifications in attribution and impression formation. Paper presented in a symposium "New directions in the analysis of impression formation," American Psychological Association Convention.

Secord, P. F., C. W. Backman, and H. T. Eachus. 1964. Effects of imbalance in the self-concept on the perception of persons. *Journal of Abnormal and Social Psychology* 68: 442-46.

Secord, P. F., W. Bevan, and B. Katz. 1956. Perceptual accentuation and the Negro stereotype. *Journal of Abnormal and Social Psychology* 53: 78-83.

Secord, P. F., W. F. Dukes, and W. Bevan. 1954. Personalities in face: I. An experiment in social perceiving. *Genetic Psychology Monographs* 49: 231-79.

Selby, J. W., L. G. Calhoun, and T. A. Brock. 1977. Sex differences in the social perception of rape victims. *Personality and Social Psychology Bulletin* 3: 412-15.

Seligman, M. 1975. *Helplessness.* San Francisco: W. H. Freeman.

Shanteau, J., and G. Nagy. 1976. Decisions made about other people: A human judgment analysis of dating choice. In J. Carroll and J. Payne (eds.), *Cognition and social judgment.* Hillsdale, N.J.: Lawrence Erlbaum.

Shaver, K. G. 1970a. Redress and conscientiousness in the attribution of responsibility for accidents. *Journal of Experimental Social Psychology* 6: 100-110.

―――. 1970b. Defensive attribution: Effects of severity and relevance on the responsibilities assigned for an accident. *Journal of Personality and Social Psychology* 14: 101-13.

Shaw, J. I., and P. Skolnick. 1971. Attribution of responsibility for a happy accident. *Journal of Personality and Social Psychology* 18: 380-83.

Shaw, M. E., and J. L. Sulzer. 1964. An empirical test of Heider's levels in attribution of responsibility. *Journal of Abnormal and Social Psychology* 69: 39-46.

Sheldon, W. H. 1940. *The varieties of human physique: An introduction to constitutional psychology.* New York: Harper & Row.

Sherman, M. 1927. The differentiation of emotional responses in infants: I. Judgments of emotional responses from motion picture views and from actual observation. *Journal of Comparative Psychology* 7: 265-84.

Sherman, R. C. 1973. Dimensional salience in the perception of nations as a function of attitudes toward war and anticipated social interaction. *Journal of Personality and Social Psychology* 27: 65-73.

Sherman, R. C., and L. B. Ross. 1972. Liberalism-conservatism and dimensional salience in the perception of political figures. *Journal of Personality and Social Psychology* 23: 120-27.

Sherrod, D. R., and R. Downs. 1974. Environmental determinants of altruism: The effects of stimulus overload and perceived control on helping. *Journal of Experimental Social Psychology* 10: 468-79.

Sherrod, D., and J. Farber. 1975. The effect of previous actor/observer role experience on attribution of responsibility for failure. *Journal of Personality* 43: 231-47.

Sherrod, D., and C. L. Goodman. 1978. Effects of sex-of-observer on female actors' causal attributions for success and failure. *Personality and Social Psychology Bulletin* 4: 277-80.

Shuham, A. I. 1967. The double-bind hypothesis a decade later. *Psychological Bulletin* 68: 409-16.

Shultz, T. R., and R. Mendelson. 1975. The use of covariation as a principle of causal analysis. *Child Development* 46: 394-98.

Shweder, R. A. 1975. How relevant is an individual difference theory of personality? *Journal of Personality* 43: 455-84.

―――. 1977. Illusory correlation and the MMPI controversy: Reply to some of the allusions and illusions in Block's and Edward's commentaries. *Journal of Consulting and Clinical Psychology* 45: 936-40.

Siegler, R. S., and R. M. Liebert. 1974. Effects of contiguity, regularity, and age on children's causal inferences. *Developmental Psychology* 10: 574-79.

Sigall, H., and N. Ostrove. 1975. Beautiful but dangerous: Effect of offender attractiveness and nature of the crime on juridic judgment. *Journal of Personality and Social Psychology* 31: 410-14.

Sleet, D. A. 1969. Physique and social image. *Perceptual and Motor Skills* 28: 295-99.

Slovic, P. 1969. Analyzing the expert judge: A descriptive study of a stock broker's decision processes. *Journal of Applied Psychology* 53: 255-63.

Slovic, P., and S. Lichtenstein. 1971. Comparison of Bayesian and regression approaches to the study of human information processing in judgment. *Organizational Behavior and Human Performance* 6: 649-744.

Slovic, P., L. G. Rorer, and P. J. Hoffman. 1971. Analyzing the use of diagnostic signs. *Investigative Radiology* 6: 18-26.

Smedslund, J. 1963. The concept of correlation in adults. *Scandinavian Journal of Psychology* 4: 165-73.

Smith, M. C. 1975. Children's use of the multiple sufficient cause schema in social perception. *Journal of Personality and Social Psychology* 32: 737-47.

Snodgrass, S. R. 1977. Confounding of causal attribution and trait consistency in research on determinants of trait inference patterns. *Personality and Social Psychology Bulletin* 3: 628-31.

Snyder, Mark. 1974. Self-monitoring of expressive behavior. *Journal of Personality and Social Psychology* 30: 526-37.

―――. 1976. Attribution and behavior: Social perception and social causation. In J. H. Harvey, W. J. Ickes, and R. F. Kidd (eds.), *New directions in attribution research* (Vol. 1). Hillsdale, N.J.: Lawrence Erlbaum.

Snyder, Mark, and M. R. Cunningham. 1975. To comply or not comply: Testing the self-perception explanation of the "foot-in-the-door" phenomenon. *Journal of Personality and Social Psychology* 31: 64-67.

Snyder, Mark, and T. C. Monson. 1975. Persons, situations, and the control of social behavior. *Journal of Personality and Social Psychology* 32: 637-44.

Snyder, Mark, and W. B. Swann. 1976. When actions reflect attitudes: The politics of impression management. *Journal of Personality and Social Psychology* 34: 1034-42.

————. 1978. Behavioral confirmation in social interaction: From social perception to social reality. *Journal of Experimental Social Psychology* 14: 148-62.

Snyder, Mark, and E. D. Tanke. 1976. Behavior and attitude: Some people are more consistent than others. *Journal of Personality* 44: 501-17.

Snyder, Mark, E. D. Tanke, and E. Berscheid. 1977. Social perception and interpersonal behavior: On the self-fulfilling nature of social stereotypes. *Journal of Personality and Social Psychology* 35: 656-66.

Snyder, Mark, and S. W. Uranowitz. 1978. Reconstructing the past: Some cognitive consequences of person perception. *Journal of Personality and Social Psychology* 36: 941-50.

Snyder, Melvin, and E. E. Jones. 1974. Attitude attribution when behavior is constrained. *Journal of Experimental Social Psychology* 10: 585-600.

Snyder, Melvin L., W. G. Stephan, and D. Rosenfield. 1976. Egotism and attributions. *Journal of Personality and Social Psychology* 33: 435-41.

Sommer, R. 1969. *Personal space.* Englewood Cliffs, N.J.: Prentice-Hall.

Spiegel, J. P., and P. Machotka. 1974. *Messages of the body.* New York: Free Press.

Steele, C. M. 1975. Name-calling and compliance. *Journal of Personality and Social Psychology* 31: 361-69.

Steiner, I. D. 1954. Ethnocentrism and tolerance of trait "inconsistency." *Journal of Abnormal and Social Psychology* 49: 349-54.

————. 1970. Perceived freedom. In L. Berkowitz (ed.), *Advances in experimental social psychology* (Vol. 5). New York: Academic Press.

Steiner, I., M. Rotermund, and R. Talaber. 1974. Attribution of choice to a decision maker. *Journal of Personality and Social Psychology* 30: 553-62.

Stephan, W. G. 1975. Actors vs. observers: Attributions to behavior with positive or negative outcomes and empathy for the other role. *Journal of Experimental Social Psychology* 11: 205-14.

Stephan, W. G., D. Rosenfield, and C. Stephan. 1976. Egotism in males and females. *Journal of Personality and Social Psychology* 34: 1161-67.

Stevens, L., and E. E. Jones. 1976. Defensive attribution and the Kelley cube. *Journal of Personality and Social Psychology* 34: 809-20.

Stewart, R. 1965. Effect of continuous responding on the order effect in personality impression formation. *Journal of Personality and Social Psychology* 1: 161-65.

Storms, M. D. 1973. Videotape and the attribution process: Reversing actors' and observers' points of view. *Journal of Personality and Social Psychology* 27: 165-75.

Storms, M. D., and R. E. Nisbett. 1970. Insomnia and the attribution process. *Journal of Personality and Social Psychology* 16: 319-28.

Strachey, L. 1933. *Eminent Victorians.* New York: Modern Library.

Streufert, S., and S. C. Streufert. 1969. Effects of conceptual structure, failure, and success on attribution of causality and interpersonal attitudes. *Journal of Personality and Social Psychology* 11: 138-47.

Stricker, L. J., P. I. Jacobs, and N. Kogan. 1974. Trait interrelations in implicit personality theories and questionnaire data. *Journal of Personality and Social Psychology* 30: 198-207.

Strickland, L. H. 1958. Surveillance and trust. *Journal of Personality* 26: 200-215.

Strickland, L. H., R. J. Lewicki, and A. M. Katz. 1966. Temporal orientation and perceived control as determinants of risk-taking. *Journal of Experimental Social Psychology* 2: 143-51.

Strongman, K. T., and B. G. Champness. 1968. Dominance hierarchies and conflict in eye contact. *Acta Psychologica* 28: 376-86.

Taft, R. 1955. The ability to judge people. *Psychological Bulletin* 52: 1-23.

Tagiuri, R. 1969. Person perception. In G. Lindzey and E. Aronson (eds.), *The handbook of social psychology* (2nd ed., Vol. 3). Reading, Mass.: Addison-Wesley.

Taylor, S. E. 1975. On inferring one's attitudes from one's behavior: Some determining conditions. *Journal of Personality and Social Psychology* 31: 126-31.

Taylor, S. E., and S. T. Fiske. 1975. Point of view and perception of causality. *Journal of Personality and Social Psychology* 32: 439-45.

————. 1978. Salience, attention, and attribution: Top of the head phenomena. In L. Berkowitz (ed.), *Advances in experimental social psychology* (Vol. 11). New York: Academic Press.

Taylor, S. E., S. T. Fiske, N. L. Etcoff, and A. J. Ruderman. 1978. The categorical and contextual bases of person memory and stereotyping. *Journal of Personality and Social Psychology* 36: 778-93.

Taylor, S. E., and J. H. Koivumaki. 1976. The perception of self and others: Acquaintanceship, affect, and actor-observer differences. *Journal of Personality and Social Psychology* 33: 403-8.

Taynor, J., and K. Deaux. 1973. When women are more deserving than men: Equity, attribution, and perceived sex differences. *Journal of Personality and Social Psychology* 28: 360-67.

Tennen, H., and S. J. Eller. 1977. Attributional components of learned helplessness and facilitation. *Journal of Personality and Social Psychology* 35: 265-71.

Thayer, S. 1969. The effect of interpersonal looking duration on dominance judgments. *Journal of Social Psychology* 79: 285-86.

Thibaut, J. W., and H. H. Kelley. 1959. *The social psychology of groups.* New York: Wiley.

Thibaut, J. W., and H. W. Riecken. 1955. Some determinants and consequences of the perception of social causality. *Journal of Personality* 24: 113-33.

Thorndike, E. L. 1920. A constant error in psychological ratings. *Journal of Applied Psychology* 4: 25-29.

Thornton, G. R. 1944. The effect of wearing glasses upon judgments of personality traits of persons seen briefly. *Journal of Applied Psychology* 28: 203-7.

Todd, F. J., and L. Rappoport. 1964. A cognitive structure approach to person perception: A comparison of two models. *Journal of Abnormal and Social Psychology* 68: 469-78.

Tomkins, S. S., and R. McCarter. 1964. What and where are the primary affects? Some evidence for a theory. *Perceptual and Motor Skills* 18: 119-58.

Touhey, J. C. 1974. Effects of additional women professionals on ratings of occupational prestige and desirability. *Journal of Personality and Social Psychology* 29: 86-89.

Tourangeau, R., and P. C. Ellsworth. 1978. The role of facial response in the experience of emotion. Unpublished manuscript, Yale University.

Trope, Y. 1978. Inferences of personal characteristics on the basis of information retrieved from one's memory. *Journal of Personality and Social Psychology* 36: 93-106.

Trope, Y., and E. Burnstein. 1977. A disposition-behavior congruity model of perceived freedom. *Journal of Experimental Social Psychology* 13: 357-68.

Tversky, A., and D. Kahneman. 1971. Belief in the law of small numbers. *Psychological Bulletin* 76: 105-10.

————. 1973. Availability: A heuristic for judging frequency and probability. *Cognitive Psychology* 5: 207-32.

————. 1974. Judgement under uncertainty: Heuristics and biases. *Science* 185: 1124-31.

Uranowitz, S. W. 1975. Helping and self-attributions: A field experiment. *Journal of Personality and Social Psychology* 31: 852-54.

Valins, S. 1966. Cognitive effects of false heart-rate feedback. *Journal of Personality and Social Psychology* 4: 400-408.

Valins, S., and R. E. Nisbett. 1972. Attribution processes in the development and treatment of emotional disorder. In E. E. Jones *et al.* (eds.), *Attribution: Perceiving the causes of behavior.* Morristown, N.J.: General Learning Press.

Valins, S., and A. A. Ray. 1967. Effects of cognitive desensitization of avoidance behavior. *Journal of Personality and Social Psychology* 7: 345-50.

Verinis, J. S., and S. Roll. 1970. Primary and secondary male characteristics: The hairiness and large penis stereotypes. *Psychological Reports* 26: 123-26

Vernon, P. E. 1933. Some characteristics of the good judge of personality. *Journal of Social Psychology* 4: 42-58.

Vinacke, W. E. 1949. The judgement of facial expressions by three national-racial groups in Hawaii. I. Caucasian faces. *Journal of Personality* 17: 407-29.

Walster, E. 1966. The assignment of responsibility for an accident. *Journal of Personality and Social Psychology* 5: 508-16.

————. 1967. "Second-guessing" important events. *Human Relations* 20: 239-50.

Walters, H. A., and D. N. Jackson. 1966. Group and individual regularities in trait inference: A multidimensional scaling analysis. *Multivariate Behavioral Research* 1: 145-63.

Warr, P. B., and C. Knapper. 1968. *The perception of people and events.* New York: Wiley.

Watson, O. M. 1970. *Proxemic behavior: A cross-cultural study.* The Hague: Mouton.

Wegner, D. M., and R. W. Buldain. 1977. Attribute generality and the inference process in impression formation. *Personality and Social Psychology Bulletin* 3: 91-94.

Wegner, D. M., and K. Finstuen. 1977. Observers' focus of attention in the simulation of self-perception. *Journal of Personality and Social Psychology* 35: 56-62.

Weiner, B., I. Frieze, A. Kukla, L. Reed, S. Rest, and R. M. Rosenbaum. 1972. Perceiving the causes of success and failure. In E. E. Jones *et al.* (eds.), *Attribution: Perceiving the causes of behavior.* Morristown, N.J.: General Learning Press.

Weiner, B., H. Heckhausen, W. U. Meyer, and R. E. Cook. 1972. Causal ascriptions and achievement behavior: A conceptual analysis of effort and reanalysis of locus of control. *Journal of Personality and Social Psychology* 21: 239-48.

Weiner, B., and A. Kukla. 1970. An attributional analysis of achievement motivation. *Journal of Personality and Social Psychology* 15: 1-20.

Weiner, B., and J. Sierad. 1975. Misattribution for failure and enhancement of achievement strivings. *Journal of Personality and Social Psychology* 31: 415-21.

Wells, G. L., and J. H. Harvey. 1977. Do people use consensus information in making causal attributions? *Journal of Personality and Social Psychology* 35: 279-93.

————. 1978. Naive attributors' attributions and predictions: What is informative and when is an effect an effect? *Journal of Personality and Social Psychology* 36: 483-90.

Wells, G. L., R. E. Petty, S. G. Harkins, D. Kagehiro, and J. H. Harvey. 1977. Anticipated discussion of interpretation eliminates actor-observer differences in the attribution of causality. *Sociometry* 40: 247-53.

Wells, W. D., and B. Siegel. 1961. Stereotyped somatypes. *Psychological Reports* 8: 77-78.

West, S. G., S. P. Gunn, and P. Chernicky. 1975. Ubiquitous Watergate: An attributional analysis. *Journal of Personality and Social Psychology* 32: 55-65.

Wiener, M., S. Devoe, S. Rubinow, and J. Geller. 1972. Nonverbal behavior and nonverbal communication. *Psychological Review* 79: 185-214.

Wiggins, J., N. Wiggins, and J. C. Conger. 1968. Correlates of heterosexual somatic preference. *Journal of Personality and Social Psychology* 10: 82-90.

Wiggins, N., and P. J. Hoffman. 1968. Three models of clinical judgment. *Journal of Abnormal Psychology* 73: 70-77.

Wiggins, N., P. J. Hoffman, and T. Taber. 1969. Types of judges and cue utilization in judgments of intelligence. *Journal of Personality and Social Psychology* 12: 52-59.

Wiggins, N., and E. S. Kohen. 1971. Man vs. model of man revisited: The forecasting of graduate school success. *Journal of Personality and Social Psychology* 19: 100-106.

Wilder, D. A. 1978. Effect of predictability on units of perception and attribution. *Personality and Social Psychology Bulletin* 4: 281-84.

Wish, M., M. Deutsch, and L. Biener. 1970. Differences in conceptual structures of nations: An exploratory study. *Journal of Personality and Social Psychology* 16: 361-73.

Wishner, J. 1960. Reanalysis of "Impressions of personality." *Psychological Review* 67: 96-112.

Woll, S., and H. Yopp. 1978. The role of context and inference in the comprehension of social actions. *Journal of Experimental Social Psychology* 14: 351-62.

Wolosin, R., S. J. Sherman, and C. R. Mynatt. 1972. Perceived social influence on a conformity situation. *Journal of Personality and Social Psychology* 23: 184-91.

Woodworth, R. S. 1938. *Experimental psychology.* New York: Holt.

Word, C. O., M. P. Zanna, and J. Cooper. 1974. The nonverbal mediation of self-fulfilling prophecies on interracial interaction. *Journal of Experimental Social Psychology* 10: 109-20.

Wortman, C. B. 1976. Causal attributions and personal control. In J. H. Harvey, W. J. Ickes, and R. F. Kidd (eds.), *New directions in attribution research* (Vol. 1). Hillsdale, N.J.: Lawrence Erlbaum.

Wortman, C. B., and J. W. Brehm. 1975. Responses to uncontrollable outcomes: An integration of reactance theory and the learned helplessness model. In L. Berkowitz (ed.), *Advances in experimental social psychology* (Vol. 8). New York: Academic Press.

Wortman, C. B., P. R. Costanzo, and T. R. Witt. 1973. Effect of anticipated performance on the attributions of causality to self and others. *Journal of Personality and Social Psychology* 27: 372-81.

Wortman, C. B., L. Panciera, L. Shusterman, and J. Hibscher. 1976. Attribution of causality and reactions to uncontrollable outcomes. *Journal of Experimental Social Psychology* 12: 301-16.

Wyer, R. S. 1974a. Changes in meaning and halo effects in personality impression formation. *Journal of Personality and Social Psychology* 29: 829-35.

————. 1974b. *Cognitive organization and change: An information processing approach.* Hillsdale, N.J.: Lawrence Erlbaum.

Wyer, R. S., Jr. 1975. Some informational determinants of one's own liking for a person and beliefs that the other will like this person. *Journal of Personality and Social Psychology* 31: 1041-53.

Wyer, R. S., and S. F. Watson. 1969. Context effects in impression formation. *Journal of Personality and Social Psychology* 12: 22-33.

Wylie, L., and R. Stafford. 1977. *Beaux gestes*. Cambridge, Mass.: Dutton, The Undergraduate Press.

Younger, J. C., B. M. Earn, and A. J. Arrowood. 1978. Happy accidents: Defensive attribution or rational calculus? *Personality and Social Psychology Bulletin* 4: 52-55.

Zadney, J., and H. B. Gerard. 1974. Attributed intentions and informational selectivity. *Journal of Experimental Social Psychology* 10: 34-52.

Zajonc, R. 1960. The process of cognitive tuning in communication. *Journal of Abnormal and Social Psychology* 61: 159-67.

Zanna, M. P., and J. Cooper. 1974. Dissonance and the pill: An attributional approach to studying the arousal properties of dissonance. *Journal of Personality and Social Pscyhology* 29: 703-8.

Zanna, M., and D. L. Hamilton. 1972. Attribute dimension and patterns of trait inferences. *Psychonomic Science* 27: 353-54.

―――. 1977. Further evidence for meaning change in impression formation. *Journal of Experimental Social Psychology* 13: 224-38.

Zanna, M. P., P. L. Sheras, J. Cooper, and C. Shaw. 1975. Pygmalion and Galatea: The interactive effect of teacher and student expectancies. *Journal of Experimental Social Psychology* 11: 279-87.

Zillmann, D., R. C. Johnson, and K. D. Day. 1974. Attribution of apparent arousal and proficiency of recovery from sympathetic activation affecting excitation transfer to aggressive behavior. *Journal of Experimental Social Psychology* 10: 503-15.

Zimbardo, P. G., E. B. Ebbesen, and C. Maslach. 1977. *Influencing attitudes and changing behavior*. Reading, Mass.: Addison-Wesley.

Zuckerman, M. 1977a. On the endogenous-exogenous partition in attribution theory. *Personality and Social Psychology Bulletin* 3: 387-91.

―――. 1977b. The endogenous-exogenous distinction: A model of attribution or a theory of cognitive motivation. *Personality and Social Psychology Bulletin* 3: 606-11.

―――. 1978a. Actions and occurrences in Kelley's cube. *Journal of Personality and Social Psychology* 36: 647-56.

―――. 1978b. Use of consensus information in prediction of behavior. *Journal of Experimental Social Psychology* 14: 163-71.

author index

subject index

Ability attributions, 46, 73-76, 104-105, 107, 257, 259. *See also* Success-failure attributions

Action, 17, 42

Accuracy, 18
emotion perception, 205-14
measurement, 219-22
nonverbal behavior perception, 126, 143-45
personality perception, 214-22
See also Bias

Active perception. *See* Perception

Additive model, 153

Affective states, attribution of, 257

Ambiguity, of cues, 97-98, 130-34

Appearance cues, 15, 20, 22-24, 35, 246, 249-53
in free description, 264-65

Arousal, 93, 96, 100, 103, 147-48

Artifacts, as cues, 20, 24-25

Attention, selective, 5, 97-98, 134, 137, 246-49

Attention decrement hypothesis, 182-83

Attitudes, attributions of, 64-68, 258

Attractiveness, 24, 35

Attribution, 17-18, 253-55
defined, 42
and prediction, 194-97, 200-202
preservation, 239-40
and salience, 235-36
and schemata, 267-68
theories, 41-63

Augmentation, 57, 59-60, 65

Availability heuristic, 231-32, 235, 240

Averaging model, 176-80, 270

Awareness, 22, 134-35, 240-44

Base-rate information, 232, 236. *See also* Consensus information

Baysian models, 188, 197

Behavior
description and coding, 26-27, 28-33, 233
as dynamic, 9-10
effects of self-attribution on, 96-98
effects on self-attribution, 94, 99-100
habit, 32, 258, 262
interpretation, 25-26
past and prediction, 194-95, 258
purposive, 9, 17, 32, 42, 265, 259-61
reactive, 9, 17, 31-32, 254
style, 32, 67-68, 123
units, 17, 27-28
See also Expressive behavior; Nonverbal behavior

Behavior change and attribution, 69-72

Bias
attribution, 71-72
attribution preservation, 239-40
causality, 229-30
cognitive vs. motivational, 109-14, 173, 228-29
consensus, 55, 236-39
defensive attribution, 79-80
definition, 224-26
ego, 72, 104-106, 226-27
evaluative, 230
expectation, 4
false consensus, 111, 138, 237
fundamental attribution error, 231, 238-39
information processing, 110-13
judging emotion, 207
and needs, 224-25
in prediction, 232-33
and rationality, 225, 244
relationship, 229-30

317